Theoretical Bases of Indo-European Linguistics

This book presents, for the first time in English, a complete critical survey of the theory and methodology of Indo-European linguistics, from its origins two centuries ago to the present. The standard handbooks on the topic are both out-of-date and are not available in English. Accordingly the theoretical approaches of the leading authorities in the field have remained largely unknown, and it is generally assumed that linguistic theory, particularly in syntax, was not discovered until this generation. Lehmann makes this material accessible by providing an outline of the theories underlying these handbooks and presenting the current status of Indo-European linguistics. He examines the latest advances, notably by Soviet scholars in the area of typology, which have improved not only our understanding of Proto-Indo-European speakers and their background, but have important implications for further studies in the field. He also provides a succinct account of the phonology, morphology and syntax of pre- and Proto-Indo-European. This unique analysis shows the development of various problems and approaches in historical perspective as well as applying and exploring current linguistic findings and theory in this area.

It will be invaluable to specialists in Proto-Indo-European and the early dialects as well as for archaeologists seeking clues to the early location of the Indo-Europeans.

Winfred P. Lehmann is Louann and Larry Temple Professor Emeritus in the Humanities and Director of the Linguistics Research Center at the University of Texas at Austin. He has written extensively on historical and Indo-European linguistics and his books include *Historical Linguistics*, *Proto-Indo-European Syntax* and *A Gothic Etymological Dictionary*.

Theoretical Bases of Indo-European Linguistics

Winfred P. Lehmann

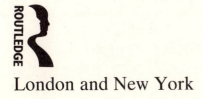

London and New York

First published in 1993 by
Routledge
11 New Fetter Lane, London EC4P 4EE

Simultaneously published in the USA and Canada
by Routledge
29 West 35th Street, New York, NY 10001

Reprinted 1995

First published in paperback 1996

© 1993 Winfred P. Lehmann

Typeset in 10/12 pt Times Linotronic 300
by Florencetype Limited, Kewstoke, Avon
Printed in Great Britain by
T. J. Press Ltd, Padstow, Cornwall

British Library Cataloguing in Publication Data
Lehmann, Winfred P.
   Theoretical Bases of Indo-European
   Linguistics
   I. Title
   410

Library of Congress Cataloguing in Publication Data
Lehmann, Winfred Philipp,
    Theoretical bases of Indo-European linguistics / Winfred P.
   Lehmanm.
      p.   cm.
   Includes bibliographical references and index.
   1. Indo-European languages – Research – History. 2. Proto-Indo-
European language.   I. Title.
   P561.L44 1992
   410–dc20   92-6898

ISBN 0-415-08201-3 (hbk)
ISBN 0-415-13850-7 (pbk)

Contents

Preface

Theoretical Bases of Indo-European Linguistics grew out of a series of lectures prepared for the Indo-European Institute held at the University of Texas during the summer of 1990 for university instructors. It became apparent from the background of the participants that, although they were familiar with one or more of the older languages, usually Latin, handbooks in a language other than English would be difficult to use for other purposes than finding examples. It has also been clear in the increasing number of works by archaeologists that many of the theoretical positions in the handbooks and monographs had remained inaccessible. For example, notable scholars have assumed that the early relationships among the dialects were viewed under the family-tree model. Further, linguists in general have neglected the important contributions of their predecessors under erroneous assumptions that they were not based on well-considered theory and were in general superseded. Accordingly, a totally different work seemed essential, one that would examine the status of the field with an eye to its theoretical bases.

The design of this work was determined by these findings. Theoretical positions are discussed with their implications, as presented in the handbooks. These may be consulted for their lists of forms, which have not been repeated here because of their accessibility and in order to keep this work within reasonable bounds. For even if the language in which such handbooks are written may be unknown to users, the forms themselves can readily be noted. It is hoped then that this work will lead those concerned with Indo-European studies to the large amount of publication that is available in Indo-European linguistics, with annual additions.

It is especially important to consult the comprehensive works that have been produced in attempts to summarize the achievements of earlier research. Those of primary importance today are: Brugmann's *Grundriss* (1897–1916), including Delbrück's three volumes of syntax, from the first edition (1893, 1897, 1900); Hirt's *Indogermanische Grammatik* (1921–37); and Gamkrelidze and Ivanov's *Indo-European and the Indo-Europeans* (1984), of which the English translation by Johanna Nichols will be especially useful when it appears. Of shorter works Brugmann's *Kurze vergleichende Grammatik* (1904a), Meillet's *Introduction* (1937) and Szemerényi's *Einführung* (1970 [1989]) are most useful. Fuller bibliographical information on these as well as on important works dealing with specific topics are listed in the References section.

All of these can be consulted for data. What has been lacking is a presentation of the theory and procedures maintained in arriving at the conclusions reached in these handbooks. An understanding of that theory, and the implications it has had, enables users to interpret the material in terms of subsequent advances, such as that gained by new information and subsequent hypotheses, such as the laryngeal theory. The theory maintained at any time affects dictionaries as well, such as those of Walde and Pokorny (1927–32), revised by Pokorny (1959), and of Buck (1949). Like the grammars, the form and contents of these represent the views of their period, which then can be upgraded.

The study of Indo-European linguistics may be divided into three periods. The first, from Bopp's monograph of 1816 roughly to Brugmann's manifesto (1878) and the contemporaneous discovery of the law of palatals, achieved control of the primary data; yet most works from the time are now superseded. The second, from 1868 to the 1927 article of Kurylowicz identifying Saussure's coefficients with elements recorded in Hittite, represents the classical period, when many of the fundamental handbooks were prepared. These are still of value, but may be characterized in Brugmann's term as "purely systematic," and accordingly in need of reinterpretation by users, especially with reference to the laryngeal theory and its implications for morphology. In the current period linguists deal with the texts in the early dialects, and with reconstructed Proto-Indo-European, as with actual languages, examined with reference to the societies in which they were used, as illustrated by the handbook of Gamkrelidze and Ivanov. The approach involves treatment of earlier stages of the proto-language as well as its division into dialects upon loss of intercommunication between its speakers.

The three periods may also be characterized for differences in theoretical views and procedures. The first period relied primarily on the comparative method, applying it to resolve problems in phonology and morphology as increasing amounts of the data were mastered. In the second period attention was given to determining phonological and morphological systems of the early dialects and the proto-language, aided by conclusions based on the method of internal reconstruction; while phonetics was now well developed, the phonemic approach was only gradually understood. The third period applies the well-established methods, in addition examining the results with reference to the findings of typological investigations. Moreover, study of syntax is now carried out with comparable rigor to that of phonology and morphology in the classical period.

In the effort to depict the increasing mastery of the field, the presentation here repeatedly refers to key approaches and problems. This procedure also illustrates how advances are achieved, probably in other sciences as well as linguistics. The initial advances at the beginning of the nineteenth century resulted from the recognition, prompted especially by theory developed in comparative anatomy, that languages must be regarded as systems and examined to determine their innermost structure, in the term of Schlegel. The resulting course of action is evident in Jacob Grimm's formulation of his rules relating the obstruents of Germanic with those of other dialects, and in the resulting impact of his formulation. While the structure of sets like the voiceless stops may not have been determined as fully as at the end of the century and later, Grimm and his followers did not deal with tokens but rather with underlying types, that is, with innermost form. Throughout the century the position was applied in treatment of phonology and morphology, but only in the current generation to the treatment of syntax. Yet for understanding of the course of action, the achievement of control in determining the relationships of the Germanic obstruents in their various environments was crucial.

Another important advance resulted from understanding the law of palatals. The advance is also instructive in illustrating how crucial problems almost produce their own solution eventually, which then clarifies a large number of previously unclear phenomena. When a number of linguists recognized in the 1870s that Indo-Iranian must at one time have included /e/ in its phonological structure, the way was open for understanding the vocalic alternations resulting from ablaut as well as the early verbal system, and in addition the relationships between the dialects. At the same time, the importance of regarding the accent system became apparent, as well as its effect on the system of segmental phonemes and of morphological sets.

While such key advances clarify a large number of problems, it is also remarkable how long it may take for their achievement. Hittite materials had been available for more than a decade before Kurylowicz pointed out in 1927 the correspondence between the Hittite sounds represented by ⟨h⟩ and Saussure's coefficients. After he made the correlation, it was widely obvious, and thereupon applied to clarify many problems in morphology as well as phonology.

Similarly, the recognition that Pre-Indo-European was an active language has clarified lexical, morphological and syntactic problems. The history of this advance is also intriguing, and well worth a detailed study. Applied thoroughly by Gamkrelidze and Ivanov in 1984, it had been foreshadowed in publications such as Uhlenbeck's from the turn of the century, and like the typological theory on which it is based gradually elaborated. Like the three other developments sketched here, it illustrates how genuine advances in understanding, rather than reformulations represented as revolutions, originate in treatment of data and not by theories sketched with reference to logical or mathematical formulations.

When such advances are made, they open the way to many further studies, as indicated above with reference to the law of palatals and

Verner's law. I have not mentioned yet the discovery of correlations among syntactic characteristics of OV and VO languages. The implications of this discovery have not yet been examined in many of the Indo-European languages. In each of them, for example, studies should be made of the development of complementation patterns, to mention only one of the important syntactic structures. Such studies would be highly welcome in the Indo-Iranian languages, which first shifted from OV towards VO structure, as is clear from study of Vedic Sanskrit and Classical Sanskrit. Then to varied extent they shifted again towards OV structure, probably through influence from the Dravidian languages, as is clear in the history of Sinhalese. Comparable studies would be important in each of the dialects, also of retentions of active structure in their early periods. Through thorough study of the relatively well-attested Indo-European languages we will become better informed of the "growth and structure" of individual languages (to use Jespersen's term) as the societies that use them change.

The societies themselves in their development will become better known as techniques of archaeologists are refined. Such advances as identifying relationships among remains of individuals through mitochondrial DNA will not solve the archaeologists' primary problem of relating their findings to societies known through texts; but such identification should clarify the mode of extension of peoples, and accordingly societies, that have become prominent and influential in part through the literary and other texts they have produced.

The theoretical bases underlying linguistics have been determined largely through study of Indo-European languages, in part because of their accessibility, in part because of their use in societies that have advanced the field during the past two centuries. Refinement of these bases, and their extension, will result from study of features that have not been examined as extensively as has phonology and morphology. Attention to problems disclosed here will then contribute to linguistics in general as well as to the Indo-European field. It will also lead to the solution of other problems, such as the origin of the Indo-European peoples and the way to their prominence.

The material presented here owes much to the institute at which it was first presented, as well as to its director, Edgar Polomé and other members of the staff. For its production, both during the institute and in subsequent revisions, I am grateful for the facilities of the Linguistics Research Center as managed by Maryrose Hightower-Coyle. In its final formulation it benefited from the recommendations of two readers, one of whom, Ladislav Zgusta, identified himself and suggested the addition of the notes on early and virtually forgotten publications. I am also grateful for the opportunity provided by the International Research and Exchanges Board (IREX) program to make first-hand acquaintance with scholars of the Soviet Academy of Sciences and their American counterparts who contributed to our growing understanding of typological structures. Their work, as well as the presentation here, may illustrate that much has been achieved in Indo-European studies but also that many opportunities remain for further clarification.

W. P. Lehmann

Abbreviations

abl.	ablative
acc.	accusative
adv.	adverb
conj.	conjunction
dat.	dative
gen.	genitive
Goth.	Gothic
imper.	imperative
ind.	indicative
Lith.	Lithuanian
mid.	middle
Myc.	Mycenaean (Greek)
nom.	nominative
OCS	Old Church Slavic
OHG	Old High German
OIr.	Old Irish
ON	Old Norse
PIE	Proto-Indo-European
pl.	plural
pres.	present
prn	pronoun
ptc.	particle
sg.	singular
Skt	Sanskrit
subj.	subjunctive

1 Aims

1.1 CONCERN WITH INDO-EUROPEAN LANGUAGE AND CULTURE AT THE BEGINNING OF THE NINETEENTH CENTURY

Indo-European linguistics arose as a new field at the end of the eighteenth century for a variety of reasons. Increased interest in Asia, especially India, had led to investigation of its literature, its law and religions among cultural concerns. The Asiatic Society of Bengal, at whose meetings its founder, Sir William Jones (1746–94),[1] delivered his influential lectures, was established in the aim of pursuing those investigations. At the same time the Romantic movement, especially in Germany, devoted considerable attention to the study of earlier periods, at least in part on the grounds that knowledge of simpler eras would assist an understanding of the culture of their own time. And gifted individuals, such as Franz Bopp (1791–1867), had great interest in learning the ancient language of India, to the extent of acquiring it from the manuscripts themselves, with little help from handbooks or teachers. Such motives led to one of the most fruitful intellectual pursuits of the nineteenth century – the investigation of the numerous languages of the Indo-European language family and determination of their background, ultimately also of the language of a preliterate period now referred to as Proto-Indo-European.

From the beginning of Indo-European studies, interest was not confined to the languages alone, but was extended also to the culture of their speakers, notably its literature. One of the most important instigators of those studies, Friedrich Schlegel (1772–1829), was a leading member of the older German Romantic school. After study of Sanskrit texts in Paris, he wrote a highly influential treatise "on the language and wisdom of the Indians" (1808).[2] The book expressed lofty aims, one of which was knowledge of the 'innermost structure' of language. It was also instrumental in prompting Franz Bopp to go to Paris, where he acquired the background that led to his treatise, which is credited as the starting point of Indo-European linguistics as well as comparative linguistics (1816).[3] In

Sources for this chapter: Bopp (1816, 1820); Lehmann (1967), for selections by Jones, Grimm, Brugmann, among others; Pedersen (1931); Szemerényi (1970 [1989]).

1

accordance with the two topics of Schlegel's title, Bopp's book includes translations of selected Sanskrit literary documents as well as an analysis of the Sanskrit verb in comparison with Greek, Latin and Germanic. The translations may have been useful at the time in providing access to the literature; but the lasting value of the book resulted from its masterly presentation of the Sanskrit verbal system. Bopp's structural portrayal of that system, later amplified in successive editions of his comparative grammar, earned him the title father of Indo-European comparative linguistics.

Bopp's title for the English version of his treatise (1820), *Analytical Comparison of the Sanskrit, Greek, Latin and Teutonic Languages, Shewing the Original Identity of their Grammatical Structure*, demonstrates his increasing confidence in portraying the linguistic interrelationships and their bases. After a series of lectures and publications on specific topics, he went on to publish his 'comparative grammar' (1833–52), which was devoted largely to morphology. During this period and subsequently he extended his control over additional languages. The third edition appeared posthumously in three volumes, with a comprehensive set of indices (1868–71). This version treats seven of the branches, as its title indicates: *Comparative grammar of Sanskrit, Zend (Avestan), Armenian, Greek, Latin, Lithuanian, Old Slavic, Gothic and Germanic.*

As Bopp's eventual concentration may suggest, the early aim of dealing with Indo-European language and culture was far too broad to be controlled by one scholar, especially during the period when additional languages needed to be mastered and analysed for their relationship to those already included in the grammatical discussion. The principal aim of Indo-Europeanists throughout the nineteenth century then came to be far narrower than that of the founders of the field. It was directed largely at the languages. Descriptions of the individual languages, and comparative studies with statements on interrelationships among them, as well as on their groupings, were not only the chief aims of Indo-European studies, but also the primary contributions of the century.

1.2 REASONS FOR THE NARROWER AIMS

In order to understand the reduction of breadth of concern it is useful to recall the situation in the study of language at the end of the eighteenth century. Scholars were, of course, thoroughly at home in the classical languages. Moreover, they had comprehensive grammars, especially of Latin; and the grammars of the modern languages were based on these. The way was then open for applying the new information from Sanskrit to clarify the interrelationships in the grammatical systems, though the procedures had to be worked out. Developing the methodology, and applying it to the increasing amount of information, made up a major effort of the Indo-Europeanists.

In addition, since the time of Leibniz there had been broad interest in determining the basic characteristics of all languages for which data could be assembled, that is, the universals underlying the diverse languages. Selected patterns were determined and compiled for every known language. Among publications of such patterns, the most notable is Adelung's *Mithridates*,[4] named after the king of Pontus, c. 132–63 BC, who was reputed to have mastered a large number of languages. A prime interest in compiling such data was the goal of achieving a universal grammar. This goal also led to philosophical treatises on language, and to the kind of dictionary that has survived in Roget's *Thesaurus*. Current editions of it still classify the lexicon under six major semantic classes that might be taken as universals (see 4.3.5). Such study was carried out with no attention to historical relationships, nor understanding of genealogical relationships. The statements published on genealogical relationships were naive, many of them deriving all languages from Hebrew.

Nor was there concern with the sound systems. Besides his compilation of languages and analyses for their characteristics, Adelung (1732–1806) produced a widely used grammar of German, and a large German dictionary. Based as these were on the procedures used for Latin, they concentrated their attention on grammar and usage rather than pronunciation. When used in speech, the classical languages were pronounced like the spoken language of the country in which they were learned; until recently Latin was pronounced like English in England, like German in Germany, and like Italian in Italy. Mastery of the correct forms and of word usage constituted the chief aim of language teaching.

Accordingly, in addition to lack of concern with historical relationships, there was virtually no understanding of phonetics. Elements of the sound system were referred to as "letters," to be sure as "letters with power [*potestas*]" when it seemed useful to point to spoken forms. But linguistics was virtually limited to concern with morphology in its role to teach languages, and in its theoretical pursuits of universals in meaning and grammar. When Sir William Jones made his notable pronouncement in 1786 on relationships between Sanskrit and the well-known classical languages, there was almost no experience in two fundamental prerequisites of comparative linguistics: understanding of sound systems and of historical relationships. Coming to terms with such requirements occupied a great deal of the attention in the study of language through the first half of the nineteenth century.

The efforts to gain control over these central procedures are clear in Bopp's publications. Although the third edition of his grammar is almost completely concerned with morphology, the grammar was increasingly devoted to statements on historical relationships. And unlike his first works, Bopp now dealt with the sounds; after producing a treatise on "vocalism" (1836), he devoted approximately 200 pages of the first volume of the grammar of 1868–71 to the writing and sound systems. Another 350 pages treat morphology – roots and nouns. Half of the second volume deals with adjectives and pronouns; the remainder as well as the first part of the third is devoted to verbs, before treatment of word formation. The fundamental handbook of Indo-European linguistics until about 1870 was limited in this way essentially to morphology. It is scarcely surprising that references to it today characterize it as only of historical interest.

Yet treatment of sound systems had also come to be pursued, and more precise information was gradually being assembled. At the time Bopp was working on his grammar, August Friedrich Pott (1802–87)[5] was publishing a work called "Etymological investigations in the sphere of the Indo-Germanic languages" (1833–6). This work relied heavily on phonetic analysis for its grammatical observations; in addition it contained a comparative account of verbal roots, in this way leading to an etymological dictionary for Indo-European. The expanded version of 1859–76 occupied ten volumes. Through phonological study and attention to derivational morphology, the lexical stock of the language family was being mastered. Pott's work supplemented the grammar of Bopp with a dictionary; his work, like Bopp's, was revised in accordance with increasing information and accuracy.

Attempts to account for the exceptions to Jacob Grimm's set of rules relating the obstruents of Germanic to those of Sanskrit, Greek and Latin (1819/1822–37) also led to better understanding of individual sounds and their treatment in various environments. This understanding was greatly amplified from other sources – physicians who were interested in problems of the deaf. One of these, Ernst W. von Brücke (1819–92), produced a descriptive treatise on the sounds of language: *Grundzüge der Physiologie und Systematik der Sprachlaute* (1856 [1876]). Through such publications the classification of sounds by classical grammarians, as into the broad sets called Tenues, Mediae and Aspiratae, was replaced by identification based on articulatory characteristics.

Brücke was also important as one of the scientists who introduced the methods of chemistry and physics into medical and biological study. His influence in linguistics may have added to the practice of analysing and classifying languages, as well as sets of sounds and forms, much like the objects of study in these sciences. Even earlier, linguists had profited from the methods of comparative anatomy that had led them to apply similar procedures to the classification of languages, as our terminology still indicates. By identification of selected characteristics, languages were assigned to "families" much as Carl von Linnaeus (1707–78) had set up genera for plants. But the linguistic terminology was less formal than the botanical. Languages with similar characteristics are said to be related; in keeping with the feminine gender of German *die Sprache*, subsequent stages of a language are referred to as "daughter" languages. The term "Indo-Germanic family" was introduced in 1810, subsequently to be replaced by Indo-European. A framework to classify languages by selected characteristics, somewhat like the classification of Linnaeus, was in this way established and is maintained to this day. Moreover, sets within individual languages or groups of languages are analysed for their common features, whether with diachronic or synchronic aims.

In short, the sixty years between the date of Schlegel's publication and Bopp's death had led to more specific aims in Indo-European studies than those pursued by Schlegel, but also to greater precision in pursuing those aims and in stating the findings. The results provided Indo-Europeanists, especially the younger members, with increasing confidence. That attitude led to restatement of the phonology, the grammar, and the lexicon, with ever greater restriction of aims; extensive monographs were now published that dealt with specific sets of forms, such as the perfect (Osthoff 1884). Profiting by this achievement, the generation after Bopp's death set out to treat the original language much like languages spoken today, applying methods that they considered as reliable as those of the physical sciences.

1.3 THE NEOGRAMMARIANS

In this situation of increasing mastery of the essential procedures of diachronic linguistics accompanied by upgraded production of the central handbooks, a number of capable and dedicated young scholars appeared, centered around the University of Leipzig. There they had the advantage of excellent training directed by a distinguished classicist, Georg Curtius (1820–85). And even before Bopp's death a highly systematic linguist, August Schleicher (1821–68) had published "A compendium of the comparative grammar of the Indo-Germanic languages" (1861) that introduced important innovations over the treatment by Bopp and his contemporaries.[6] Moreover, the dominant intellectual current now was not a Romantic search for origins, but a concern for the processes of development, most notably expressed in the evolutionary ideas of Charles Darwin (1809–82). Somewhat scornful of their elders, as bright young students often are, these linguists were labeled by their teachers as neogrammarians. Intelligent enough, like the early Christians, to adopt a pejorative label, they inaugurated probably the most important group of linguists that has appeared in the study of language.

Like any such group, their tenets and major figures have received various interpretations from subsequent scholars (see Jankowski 1972). What is clear is their insistence on rigor. Moreover, they sought to deal with language much as their colleagues in the natural sciences dealt with their selected topics. In their day the faculty of philosophy had not only developed much more widely than had the other three traditional faculties – law, medicine, theology – but it also came to be fragmented. Its major components were labeled "the natural sciences," which treat those areas where universally valid laws apply, and "the historical sciences," where generalizations apply differently in different periods and differing societies; today the second is generally further divided into the social sciences and, in the USA, the liberal arts or human sciences. An awareness of the structure of academic concerns and structure at that time is important because later the term "historical" has been interpreted by current views as diachronic. Equation of nineteenth-century "historical" with terms such as "social" or "behavioral" and "human" would be more accurate if these are taken to apply to all the areas not dealt with in the "physical" and "biological" sciences, which themselves cannot be equated directly with the early classification "natural sciences."

The major figures among the neogrammarians display varying temperaments and approaches. Among the more eminent, August Leskien (1840–1916) was the most insistent on attention to rigor as well as the oldest. More restrained, Karl Brugmann (1849–1919) laid down the fundamental principles of the group in an admirable essay, going on to brilliant observations and to producing its most distinguished work in his "Comparative grammar of the Indo-Germanic languages" (1897–1916, 2nd edn).[7] By contrast with Brugmann's concentration on phonology and morphology, his early colleague, Berthold Delbrück (1842–1922), carried out basic studies in Indic, Germanic and Indo-European syntax that are still highly important; fortunately for linguistics, he was defeated in his political ambitions, so that he continued a distinguished career as a cultured academician in Jena some distance away from the hectic center of the group. His biography produced by Eduard Hermann provides an excellent account of scholarship in what Hermann accurately labels "Germany's great era." Hermann Osthoff (1847–1909) was another collaborator of Brugmann, also highly productive, but less accurate in his judgements, somewhat like Jerzy Kurylowicz at a later time. The youngest of the group, Eduard Sievers (1850–1927), was probably the most brilliant, hitting on "Verner's law" before its credited discoverer, and generous enough never himself to mention the letter in which he had stated his finding (see Streitberg *et al.* 1927–36: 287–8); fortunately, he has enough remarkable contributions to his name, such as concluding that the Old English *Genesis* was an adaptation of an Old Saxon poem before that poem came to be known through discovery of a manuscript in the Vatican. Others might still be mentioned; but these five make up the nucleus that established Leipzig as the center for linguistic studies through the second decade of the twentieth century. Virtually all contemporary students in the Indo-European languages spent some time there, many completing their doctoral degrees under the direction of one of these eminent scholars.

Yet two more figures need to be mentioned, each located elsewhere. Hermann Paul (1846–1921) in Munich wrote the acknowledged theoretical handbook of the group in his "Principles of language history," first published in 1880 and, after translations into other languages, formulated in final form by the author in its fifth edition of 1920, subsequently reprinted under the unfortunate label of further "editions."[8] Its title as well is unfortunate, leading linguists today to assume that it is a handbook on diachronic linguistics; to be sure it treats language as changing, rather than as a socially abstract *langue* or as an "ideal language of an ideal speaker in an ideal society." But unlike these conceptions of language in subsequent theoretical works, Paul's *Prinzipien* does not downplay concern with language in use; nor does it make the sharp distinction between synchronic and diachronic linguistics that has often brought unfortunate consequences to the field. Like the other leading neogrammarians, Paul produced substantial works on language, notably his grammar of German, but also a Middle High German grammar in the frequently republished texts of the series based on the pattern of Wilhelm Braune's (1850–1926) Gothic grammar. The production of such works, in addition to theoretical writings that inevitably become outdated, is a major reason for the continued esteem in which the neogrammarians are held. Moreover, as we may note briefly, their chief tenets are irreproachable and have set the standards of linguistic study from the time they were formulated.

Yet first we may note the most highly acclaimed student of the many who came to Leipzig, Ferdinand de Saussure (1857–1913). The treatise that he published while in Leipzig on the system of vowels in Proto-Indo-European not only cites the leading scholars there – Curtius, Leskien, Brugmann, Osthoff as well as Sievers and Delbrück – but also carries out their ideas of rigor to the ultimate. As is well known, the young Saussure in his monograph proposed a virtually mathematical scheme for Indo-European roots; thereupon, through brilliant analysis of patterning, he hypothesized consonants that were nowhere attested (1879).[9] Following his period of study in Leipzig and Berlin, Saussure accepted a position in Paris, where he provided the inspiration that made it under Antoine Meillet (1866–1936) the center of linguistic study after the decline of Leipzig. Moving from Paris to his native Geneva, Saussure capped his earlier triumph by lectures whose publication is generally credited as shifting the goals of linguistics from those of his neogrammarian teachers (1916). Yet much of the shift involved repudiation of concerns narrower than those of Brugmann's "neogrammarian manifesto," while Brugmann and the others were almost completely occupied with production of the handbooks that represent the advances in a field.

1.3.1 The neogrammarian "manifesto"

The so-called manifesto was published as preface to a series established by Osthoff and Brugmann (1878: iii–xx). Although not so noted, it was written by Brugmann. A selection of its tenets is given here, with reference to the English translation (Lehmann 1967: 198–209). Since, while brief, it is crisply formulated, excerpts cannot make up for reading the entire essay. In view of the current preoccupation with "theory," contemporary linguists may be amused, and one may hope also instructed, by Brugmann's inveighing against the "hypotheses-beclouded atmosphere of the workshop" in which linguistic study was carried out during his day. In his view, too much emphasis had been put on investigation of language rather than on the human speaker. Moreover, he emphasized study of contemporary language, referring as model to Winteler's treatise on his own Swiss German dialect (1876). In an introduction to principles it may not be out of place to recall that it was Winteler's household in which the young Einstein was lodged after his less than glorious performance in schooling; at least in conversation, Roman Jakobson suggested that Einstein may have received some stimulation for his further ideas from the incipient phonemic approach of Winteler.

Besides directing attention to spoken language, Brugmann set as one of the goals of linguistic study the "attainment of a deeper understanding of the mental activity of human beings in general and of the individual Indo-European peoples" (Lehmann 1967: 208). That is to say, for Brugmann at this time actual contemporary speech, not abstract or classical patterns, is to be investigated to achieve an understanding of language. And since language has a twofold aspect – mental as well as physical – such study increases our understanding of its speakers. Moreover, in his view linguistic study contributes to an understanding of society and groups within it.

Brugmann's goals then are as admirable as any stated by subsequent students of language. Further, the procedures he promotes include psychological investigation as well as examination of speech mechanisms. Yet the neogrammarian movement is widely perceived to have maintained a positivistic approach towards written languages of the past or, even worse, towards reconstructed languages. In attempting to understand this perception, and to account for unfortunate developments among later members of the movement, we may review its "two most important principles" as stated by Brugmann.

By the first principle "every sound change . . . takes place according to laws that admit no exception" (1967: 204). Brugmann goes on to specify the situation in which the principle applies, that is, among the members of one linguistic community and in the same linguistic environment. But a shorter version – "sound-laws have no exceptions" or the like – is frequently cited, giving the impression that Brugmann's first principle proposed laws like those in the natural sciences. While choice of the term "law" may have been unfortunate, in view of later applications, Brugmann's qualifications in his use of the term clearly provide adequate safeguards against a false interpretation.

By the second principle, new forms may arise by association, that is through morphological or syntactic or semantic patterning, for example, *cows*, the replacement of *kine*. Brugmann was especially concerned to have this process recognized as operating in earlier periods as well as today; in this way many of the extreme reconstructions, such as forms made up of a succession of laryngeals, might be avoided today. If the phrase "form association" or the like, rather than the term "analogy," had been adopted, the process might not have encountered such varied interpretation and so many objections. Yet, whatever the label, it is obvious that phonological change takes place by specific sounds and subsequently modifications may be brought about in sets.

While the two important principles of the neogrammarians are irreproachable, and while he recommended attention to contemporary languages, there is no denying that Brugmann and his colleagues devoted themselves almost entirely to the study of languages of the past. Even works like Paul's German grammar treat the language in its historical development. But it should also be clear from Brugmann's statement of principles that the aims of the neogrammarians as he stated them are almost ideal for pursuing study in the humanities. One arrives at generalizations by examining data within specific limits; but one also admits that influence is exerted on individual items to which such generalizations may apply by the other elements within a set.

1.3.2 Solution of the "exceptions" to Grimm's rules

Successes in the solution of problems contributed great energy as well as confidence to the neogrammarians, and at the same time deepened their understanding of language. The most notable examples of such success may be the series of explanations of the so-called exceptions to Jacob Grimm's rules.

The lack of change of *p*, *t*, *k* in words like *spew*, cf. Latin *spuō* or German *Nacht*, cf. Latin *noctem*, was ascribed to its environment after fricatives, as here *s-* and *-ch-*. Besides solving this problem, the observation directed the attention of linguists to sequences of elements in language in addition to treatment of individual items. Made in the fourth decade of the century by several linguists, among them Rudolf von Raumer (1815–76), the solution prompted him and other linguists at the time to concern themselves further with phonetics (see Streitberg *et al.* 1927–36: 281–3).

The supposed exception by which Germanic unaspirated stops correspond to aspirated stops in Sanskrit and Greek, as in *bind*, cf. Sanskrit *bandh-* rather than **bhandh-*, was clarified by Hermann Grassmann (1809–77) in an influential article published in 1863. Grassmann pointed out that the "irregularity" is to be ascribed to these languages rather than to Germanic. Besides providing a solution to the problem, his observation made the further contribution that linguists now saw the need to take into account entire words, not merely individual sounds and neighboring elements. Further, it had the important consequence of demonstrating that Sanskrit might not always maintain the oldest forms. About this same time Schleicher introduced reconstructed forms like **bhandh-* for the original language. As a result, rather than citing Sanskrit forms in discussion of the parent language, Indo-Europeanists now made use of reconstructed forms (indicated with an asterisk * and accordingly also called starred forms) in accounts of the language family and its origins.

An even more influential article, possibly the most influential that ever was published in linguistics, is Verner's of 1875 that clarified the appearance of Germanic voiced rather than voiceless fricatives corresponding to voiceless stops in the other dialects, as in Gothic *fadar*, cf. Latin *pater*. As Verner showed in 1877, this correspondence is found when the accent of such forms in Sanskrit or Greek, and accordingly in the proto-language, did not stand before the sound. His observation had many consequences. As one, linguists now concerned themselves with accents, or suprasegmentals, rather than only with segmental elements. As another, it indicated that Germanic at one time had a movable pitch accent like Vedic Sanskrit, and that consequently such an accent would have to be assumed for the original language. Further, it led to massive concern with early verse; the basic principles of Germanic alliterative verse were now determined, and journals of the time are filled with analyses of verse form in it and other language groups.

But probably most important for theoretical concerns, Verner's observation suggested that if one understood completely the environment of elements, all phenomena in language might be explained. Stated more generally, that conclusion may be equated with the first principle of the neogrammarians. That is to say, when the environments of sounds are completely known, any change that takes place does so throughout specifiable environments. Following on the solution of all of the exceptions to Grimm's rules, the neogrammarian principle simply summarized the conditions for the events. Leskien stated the principle in its strongest form the year after Verner's formulation (1876); the manifesto two years later was only slightly less assertive. Assurance concerning the validity of the principle led linguists to endure the tedium of examining the minutest phenomena and describing them thoroughly, with further expectations of explaining any change.

In the same year that the manifesto was published, a number of linguists independently solved the problem of Sanskrit *ca* beside Greek *te*, Latin *que*, Gothic *-uh*, and similar alignments in other sets. The palatal *c* in Sanskrit beside the labio-velar in Latin had been highly puzzling. And previously *a* had been assumed as the most common vowel in the original language on the basis of the further assumption of the greater antiquity of Sanskrit. But with their achievements in phonetics, it now became clear that the Latin form was most like that of the parent language, and that Sanskrit too must earlier have had an *e* before which the velar was palatalized. This observation, often called "the law of palatals," was highly important for reconstructing the original language. But its significance in illuminating the widespread advance in understanding of language is of greatest interest here. Confidence in that understanding narrowed further the aims of linguists, but also brought about the clarification of the early languages and of the parent language, which will be the major topic of the chief part of this book.

Virtually all work in language now was carried out in accordance with the principles of the neogrammarians; some linguists objected to excessive reliance on the principles, though they too assumed regularity in patterns of change. As a first step, all the data of a language were determined, including accent phenomena. Thereupon the data were carefully described, not only by their forms as Bopp had done, but also for their sounds. Finally, explanations were proposed. These three steps have been restated again and again. Practices have varied in description, and the goal of explanation has been interpreted variously. For the neogrammarians themselves explanation was sought through determination of earlier forms; the procedures involved limitations, since reconstruction invariably results in loss of information. Others have sought explanation through psychological principles, with inevitable disappointment; as Bloomfield concluded, such an aim proposes to explain one set of unknowns through another.

Investigation of further languages has provided linguists with wider perspective than the neogrammarians had achieved with their concerns devoted almost entirely to the Indo-European languages; but the general procedures in linguistics were set by the fourth quarter of the century. Those procedures now simply needed to be applied when dealing with individual languages and groups of languages.

1.4 IMPROVED PROCEDURES IN THE CLASSIFICATION OF LANGUAGES

The findings resulting from application of the neogrammarian principles prompted linguists to take up new aims. Among these was the goal of determining by historical criteria the relationships between the languages in a family, and the bases for similarities and differences among them.

The early Indo-Europeanists set out to determine the characteristics of the various languages, distinguishing individual dialects like Germanic in contrast with Latin and Greek; they also identified the eastern dialects, though not until the time of the neogrammarians was Armenian recognized as a distinct dialect, not a member of the Iranian subgroup. Similarly, characteristic vocabulary for dialects and subgroups was determined. As we have noted, Pott published his first studies on Indo-European etymology in 1833. Yet even as dedicated a comparativist as Schleicher classified the languages of Europe by typological characteristics as late as 1850. The repeated editions of Fick presented characteristic vocabulary of the various Indo-European branches; but no accurate determination of possible larger groups among them was achieved until the basic sound systems were better known. Until that time the major groups were identified geographically, those of Asia and those of Europe.

To portray the relationship between the dialects, Schleicher used the metaphor of the family, assuming that an original language had developed like successive generations in a family. He drew up a family tree that was intended to represent the successive branches of such a language family. The tree made use of shared characteristics to determine the branches, arraying, for example, Germanic with Baltic and Slavic. But Schleicher's grouping was still largely geographic, aligning, for example, Albanian with Greek.

A generation later, through examination of the sound systems, Peter von Bradtke proposed a classification of the Indo-European dialects into two major subgroups, providing designations for them that have been maintained until recently (1890; cf. Szemerényi 1970 [1989]: 61). He based his classification on the treatment of palatal tectals. These show up as sibilants in the eastern groups then known, Baltic, Slavic, Albanian, Armenian and Indo-Iranian, as velars in the western, Greek, Italic, Germanic, Celtic. Using a slightly modified form of the Avestan word for "hundred," the eastern group is referred to as *satem*, the western by the Latin word *centum*. The discovery of the Anatolian and Tocharian languages led to rejection of this grouping, especially because the palatals show up as velars far to the east in Tocharian (see 4.1); but since the time of Bradtke's publication, interrelationships are determined largely by phonological and grammatical criteria, with attention to words when they are pertinent.

Other phonological characteristics were added to that based on the reflexes of palatals, such as the following.

1 Labio-velars are attested as such only in the centum languages in a distribution that provided added support for Bradtke's classification.
2 Most shared characteristics extend over only a portion of the two larger groupings; for example, *s* shows up as [š] after *i u r k* in Indo-Iranian, Slavic and to some extent in Baltic.
3 The distinction between aspirated voiced stops and simple voiced stops was not maintained in Iranian, Slavic, Baltic, Albanian and Celtic.
4 *t + t* shows up as *ss* in Germanic, Italic and Celtic.

More and more such characteristics common to specific dialects were examined, with the aim of determining subgroups. The family then was sketched in its development, much like a known language that had been differentiated into subgroups; Latin and the Romance languages provided the obvious pattern for treating such a language family. A parent language comparable to Latin, earlier referred to as primitive Indo-European but now (in view of the possible pejorative implications of the adjective "primitive") as Proto-Indo-European (PIE), was not only reconstructed but also treated for its daughter languages and their interrelationships.

1.4.1 Investigations in dialect geography

In the meantime the principles of the neogrammarians had led to a further kind of investigation. Those principles implied that languages would exhibit the results of regular and consistent change; but standard languages, like literary German and English, obviously did not. As a simple example, the English pair *fox* : *vixen* is irregular in its initial consonants when contrasted with the German cognate pair *Fuchs* : *Füchsin*. Observing that such irregularities often were not found within dialects, linguists set out to examine specific dialects, partly in an effort to support the principles.

Such investigations led to observations on the establishment of change in language, and on the differentiation that gives rise to subgroups. It is a general axiom that languages are constantly changing; the axiom may be substantiated by examining any text of an earlier period. Yet not all the results of every change are maintained. The reasons for these effects were now disclosed. Languages are maintained by societies in which individuals for the most part wish to participate without appearing as odd; in western societies of the present, allowance is, however, made for adolescents, who fix on idiosyncratic speech known as slang. Accordingly, changes in language are maintained or rejected in accordance with the prestige of the groups that make those changes. Further, such changes are spread on the basis of the prestige accorded specific speech communities. The validity of these observations has been demonstrated time and time again. It may be exemplified most simply by noting lexical items, like the word *tonic* for a specific kind of beverage in Boston and the surrounding areas in which Boston enjoyed prestige (Kurath *et al.* 1939: 28), or French *jument* "mare," which spread from Paris, replacing reflexes of *caballa* and *equa* throughout central France.

Languages of the central area of prestige, also labeled focal, influence those of neighboring areas. At the outer limits of one prestige area its influence may overlap with that of another prestige area; such border areas may show characteristics of two focal areas. Also, specific areas may not maintain their prestige over an extended period. In Italy during the late Middle Ages, Florence enjoyed higher prestige than did Rome; until Rome once again gained highest prestige in the country during the nineteenth century, the language of Florence determined the standard of Italian. These conclusions on language interrelationship reflecting change were first demonstrated geographically. Similar obversations were also made on the basis of social and professional groupings, as in Friedrich Kluge's works on the language of sailors and the language of students. The procedures and conclusions were then applied to earlier periods as well; information on their application to the various Indo-European languages and to the proto-language is capably presented by Porzig (1954: 17–52).

While the information for determining focal areas and the range of their influence, as well as their shifts through time, is not as abundant for earlier periods as for a language like French, Italian or German today, attempts were made to identify them. In 1908 Meillet published the first work on "The Indo-European dialects." Porzig's more comprehensive work of 1954 identifies characteristics and the extent of the areas in which they were maintained. As information on the members of the family has increased, details on geographical and social alignments have been assembled, such as the following. Through its intellectual prestige, Athens came to be a focal area and maintained that status throughout the fourth century BC even though political domination was centered at this time in Macedonia; it was Attic Greek then that was extended throughout Alexander's empire. And in India the Brahmins remained the class of prestige; their language, Sanskrit, influenced the languages wherever Hinduism was the dominant religion, even in Dravidian-speaking areas. Such geographical dialects and social registers allow us to determine the interrelationships among the various languages and the bases for their dominance.

1.4.2 Models of relationships among languages and inferences on the Indo-European homeland

Increased scrutiny of shared characteristics and innovations demonstrated that Schleicher's tree model rarely applies; the model reflects situations where groups separate and never again are in contact. While some such situations are documented, such as the colonies sent out from Greek cities, languages generally are not extended in this way. Extension accompanying expansion of population with incorporation of neighboring groups is far more frequent, or even simply extension of a language over languages of less prestige. The interrelationships resulting from such patterns of extension are far better reflected in the wave model proposed in 1872 by Johannes Schmidt. The validity of the wave model rests on the observation that adjacent languages and dialects share characteristics on the basis of intercommunication. If a sound change like that of palatal *k* to a sibilant takes place in a prestige or focal area, and similarly morphological, syntactic and lexical innovations, the results may be adopted by adjacent dialects. The wave model likens the process to a wave set up in a body of water and extending until the effects of the impetus are weakened.

Study of characteristics of the languages in this way revealed the history of the early period and led to the assumption of a parent language, comparable to Latin for the Romance group. But the location of the speakers of that language, generally referred to as the home or homeland, was less evident. Since archaeology of the time amounted to little more than treasure hunting, the evidence had to be taken from the data revealed in the languages. Terms for items that might be located in specific areas were sought out. Among these is the word for "honey", since the location of bees could be pretty well identified. Similarly, the words for the "sal-

mon", for the "beech tree" and other items. Yet the evidence for the
distribution of the items represented by these words was so inadequate that
other criteria came to be involved.

Most troublesome among these nonlinguistic criteria was another dominant concern of the century, nationalism. Not only national prestige, but
also political boundaries, played a part in locating the homeland; since
Indo-European linguistics had its center in Germany, the home of the
Indo-Europeans was also assumed by many to be there. Even more
insidiously, in view of the elementary understanding of biology, races were
identified with nations, thereupon the two in turn with languages and
cultures. Further extension of these proposals by ambitious politicians, like
Wilhelm II of Germany, or highly unscrupulous successors, like Adolf
Hitler, has poisoned the discussion to this day. Today, still, even straightforward and well-documented statements of comparison, as between the
culture of the Greeks and that of the Hebrews, may be taken as prejudiced.
Yet it is clear that some social group, of whatever size or coherence, at one
time spoke the relatively unified language labeled Proto-Indo-European
and that this group maintained a specific culture. Some more assured data
have now been provided through much-improved techniques of archaeology; but since the crucial data assembled by archaeologists for the
preliterate period of Proto-Indo-European cannot be directly associated
with languages, there is no unanimity on the location, or on the extent of
unity of Proto-Indo-European, nor on the dispersal of its speakers.

1.5 The Culture of the Society speaking Proto-Indo-European

Towards the end of the nineteenth century the increasing confidence in
conclusions based on linguistic study led to a concerted attempt to determine the culture of the early community. Competent as they were in
philology, many of the historical linguists concerned themselves with cultural as well as linguistic study. In his "History of the German[ic] language" (1848) Jacob Grimm included essays on both areas.[10] His early
chapters deal with agriculturists, cattle, falconry and so on; they were
followed by chapters on the characteristics of the languages, and then on
the literature and tribal groupings. Similar concerns with cultural and
philological matters occupied the other prominent linguists. Schleicher
carried on fieldwork in Lithuania. Sievers edited early writings. At the
same time specialists in culture provided cultural accounts that drew on
linguistic findings. In 1845 Adalbert Kuhn (1812–81), founder of the first
journal devoted to Indo-European linguistics and philology, published an
essay "On the history of the Indo-Germanic peoples in the most ancient
times." His account was based on evidence in the languages and the early
texts. The publication indicates that there was no sharp break between
attention to language and culture by individual scholars.

Even at this early period of Indo-European studies, much linguistic evidence was identified that gave leads on the culture. There was only one term for metals, reflected in our term "ore"; accordingly scholars assumed that the Indo-European community was emerging from a neolithic stage. Somewhat similarly, a general term for "artisan," Greek *téktōn*, etc., suggested that the society was not yet specialized technologically. Moreover, terms for the plow and for domestic animals indicated some practice of agriculture, not a purely hunting–gathering culture. By 1883 a prehistorian, Otto Schrader, published a major work on "Language comparison and proto-history." Lavishly praised by leading linguists, among them Brugmann, it appeared in a second edition, translated with the title: *Prehistoric Antiquities of the Aryan Peoples* (1890).[11] Schrader followed this work with an "Encyclopedia on Indo-European antiquity" (1901), which was expanded in a second edition (1917–29). Making use of numerous articles and monographs, extensive presentations in this way aimed to provide thorough treatments of the early culture.

The procedure of deriving cultural information from the language is known as palaeontology. Often ingenious, inferences had their problems: for example, there was sufficient evidence to reconstruct an etymon for our word "goose"; but one cannot be certain that the reference was the same as it is in historical times. Other difficulties resulted from using items that had limited distribution for identifying the homeland; the etymon for "beech" is notorious because, if accepted for the proto-language it provides evidence that the homeland was west of a line extending from the Baltic to Odessa, since the tree so named did not flourish to the east of that line. But the corresponding word refers to the oak tree in Greece. And in the languages of the east the word is not attested, even with changed meaning, so that it cannot with certainty be attributed to the proto-language. Statements on the putative early culture then came to be criticized, and the practice of linguistic palaeontology discredited.

Yet it is unfair to accuse Schrader and his fellow-prehistorians of inferences based solely on reconstructed terms. Schrader is very cautious in his inferences, stating flatly that we cannot reconstruct "the primitive culture of the Indo-Europeans" by linguistic research (1890: 149). He also insisted on the use of "prehistoric research and history," which to some extent can be obtained from texts. Unfortunately, the earliest of these then available, the *Rigveda*, consists largely of hymns and prayers that include little information on other matters than religion. And our first major history, by Herodotus, describes cultures of the fifth century BC, if in the area associated with early Indo-European peoples. His Book 4 on the Scythians presents many facts that seem relevant for the early culture; but the disparity in time, and the tendency of Herodotus to write a good story, led many interpreters to doubt his accounts, some even calling him the father of lies.

Other evidence was also called into question. Scholars examined the culture of areas relatively unaffected by the industrial culture of the time, areas such as Serbia. Here extended families still flourished, in social units and way of life not unlike those depicted by Homer and Hesiod. Yet, today as well, anthropologists dispute the validity of conclusions concerning earlier periods drawn from descriptions of such cultures as that of the Bushmen of southern Africa, and also about their maintenance of an earlier way of life. There is little question that Milman Parry through his investigation of epic verse in the Balkans in this century illuminated the poetic practices of Homer's day (1971). Nonetheless, the work of the late nineteenth-century prehistorians came to be more and more rejected. The large work dealing with many facets of culture, including such practices as music, that was assembled to celebrate the seventieth birthday of Hermann Hirt (1936) may be occasionally mentioned still, but is today not accorded much credence.

In short, the aim to determine the culture of the Proto-Indo-European community was vigorously pursued for some time, but the conclusions were held to resemble fiction more than fact. As a further result, they did not contribute to solving the problem of the homeland. Greater assurance came to be expected from the rapidly developing field of archaeology.

1.6 New Data and New Stimuli Resulting from Archaeological Discoveries

Discoveries in three areas at the beginning of this century provided data that contributed information on two previously unknown groups, Anatolian and Tocharian, and also on Greek of around 1500 BC. These discoveries led to fuller understanding of the early dialect situation as well as that of the parent language, and opened new perspectives for dealing with the early culture.

The most important new materials were obtained by excavations in Anatolia, especially those at Boğazköy from 1906 to 1909 that uncovered cuneiform tablets with inscriptions in the language now known as Hittite (see Pedersen 1931: 164–6). The cuneiform could be read immediately, but no Indo-European language was expected for Anatolia of the second millennium BC; and, written as they were in a syllabic script, the materials were long opaque. The texts were not identified as Indo-European until 1915, and then not immediately accepted as such. When finally accepted as Indo-European more generally in the 1920s, they came to be recognized as our oldest texts in the family, some dating back to 1750 BC.

Among two important disclosures, they did not have sibilants in place of palatals like the eastern dialects, and they showed *h* in some of the forms for which Saussure had posited consonants that were attested in none of the languages (1879; Kuryłowicz 1927). As we note in greater detail below, Saussure had assumed two elements that had been lost, which he represented by *A* and *Q*. By positing these in earlier forms of roots like *(s)tā-* – "stand," i.e. *(s)teA-* and *dō-* "give," that is *deQ-*, he proposed that these roots had been parallel with those like *sed-* "sit," *leg-* "pick up." Saussure did not try to identify the elements phonetically, but simply posited them as "increasing" the quantity of short vowels, as in the roots cited; hence his label "coefficient." Since in some forms they were represented in Hittite by symbols transcribed with *h*, the coefficients could now be regarded as phonemes.

These two characteristics as well as others modified previous assumptions on the dialect division and on the phonology of the proto-language. Moreover, the contributions of the Anatolian languages to our knowledge of the early post-dialect period and the culture have continued, as more and more materials are being discovered, also in other dialects of the branch now known as Anatolian, especially Luwian.

About the turn of the century manuscripts of two languages now labeled Tocharian were found in caves in Chinese Turkestan (see Pedersen 1931: 194–6). Written in a form of the *Brāhmī* script and consisting chiefly of translations of Buddhist texts, the material could readily be translated. The two dialects differ remarkably from other Indo-European languages; phonologically, they contributed further to the solution of the proposed split into satem and centum dialects. For, like Hittite, they did not exhibit sibilants in place of the palatals. It was now apparent that the shift from palatals to sibilants had taken place in one section of the Indo-European community, much as other changes affected only a portion of the family. Besides raising questions about its own earlier location, discovery of Tocharian so far to the east complicates assumptions on the homeland.

The third major addition of early texts came from Crete and coastal sections of southern Greece. Archaeologists uncovered tablets in a previously unknown syllabic script labeled Linear B. As for Hittite, the syllabic script and the expectation of no Indo-European language for the area at the period of writing long obscured the texts. The tablets remained unread until Michael Ventris in 1952 demonstrated them to be Greek. Chiefly records for tax purposes, they are limited in their linguistic and cultural contributions. But they provide data on Greek of almost a millennium before the language in which the Homeric poems have come down to us. They also enlarge our understanding of the penetration of Indo-European speakers into the Hellenic peninsula and beyond (Ventris and Chadwick 1973).

However limited the cultural information they added, these three discoveries changed markedly the conclusions concerning Proto-Indo-European that had been reached on the basis of previously known data. As the materials became more widely accessible, scholars revised their views also on the language and culture of the period shortly after the dispersal of the early speakers of the Indo-European languages. Moreover, archaeological techniques were massively improved after the Second World War, in part through the new possibility of dating discoveries by means of carbon 14. While in the absence of textual discoveries the new techniques do not permit identification of specific peoples with sites excavated, they make available materials that allow us to arrive at a much more secure picture of the early cultures than was possible through use of linguistic palaeontology. In this way they establish with more hope of certainty the aims of reconstructing the proto-culture and the proto-language, because the archaeological data provide perspective for interpreting the linguistic conclusions. These will be our major concern in later chapters. Here we may sketch briefly the general contributions resulting from the new material.

1.7 REVISED VIEWS OF THE LANGUAGES

In the course of time the information derived from the materials in the Anatolian branch have affected our entire view of Proto-Indo-European. The first major contribution brought about modifications of the phonological system. Kurylowicz in 1927 pointed out that many items in which the sounds transliterated by *h* are attested correspond to those for which Saussure had posited coefficients, subsequently called laryngeals. As a result the entire phonological system of Proto-Indo-European was recast and earlier possible systems came to be proposed. Further, the morphological system of Hittite is more comparable to that of Germanic than to that of the reconstructions based largely on Sanskrit and Greek. With greater reluctance, Indo-Europeanists have taken up the position that the simpler system may more closely resemble that of the parent language, which in turn had been elaborated by a central community consisting primarily of speakers of pre-Indo-Iranian, pre-Greek and pre-Armenian. In addition, since Hittite is strictly verb-final, the syntactic description produced by Delbrück for Vedic Sanskrit gradually came to be accepted as also valid in large part for the syntactic structure of Proto-Indo-European. Its OV structure is without question today.

In short, many problems in the grammar proposed for the proto-language could be explained on the basis of the new Anatolian data, supported in some respects by the materials in Mycenaean Greek. The Tocharian languages, on the other hand, had undergone such extensive changes, in part by influence of agglutinative languages, that they provide little information for reconstruction of the proto-language.

1.8 REVISED VIEWS ON INTERNAL RELATIONSHIPS AMONG THE DIALECTS AND SUBGROUPS

If Tocharian provided little data for reconstructing the early language, it included crucial data on the relationships proposed among the Indo-European languages. For, unexpectedly in a language of the east, the palatal tectals (*k' g' g'h*) did not show up as sibilants. Accordingly, the previously assumed major division between satem languages in the east and centum in the west was nullified. Since in addition the Anatolian languages maintain the tectals, the entire conception of dialect relationships had to be recast. We now propose that the shift of tectals was carried out in a central area that included Indo-Iranian, Armenian, Albanian, Slavic and for the most part Baltic; but it did not extend to the western group nor to the border areas in the east. Moreover, the sound change may have taken place after the Anatolian languages had separated from the other groups – an assumption that may be proposed with less confidence. But the Tocharian data have led to a view of the language area in which Indo-European languages were spoken comparable to the view concerning later language groups like that of Latin and its Romance language reflexes.

The more realistic view of dialect relationships leads to increasingly assured proposals on the relative locations for the various Indo-European dialects. Changes may have been carried out in portions of the area. For example, with reference to the centum : satem division it now became clear that unshifted tectals in the Baltic languages indicate that these languages were on the borders of the area in which that change was carried out, so that some unshifted residues were maintained. The realistic view of the Baltic group was amplified by the observation that it shares innovations with the Germanic languages, such as the formation of "eleven, twelve." In both groups the neologisms for these numerals consist of compounds corresponding to "one left, i.e. additional, two left."

Similar conclusions were proposed for the other groups. While problems remain, the picture of the early dialect situation today is far more detailed and credible than that of the late nineteenth century.

1.9 REVISED VIEWS OF THE EARLY CULTURE

The new, early materials are somewhat disappointing in their contributions on the culture of their speakers. The early Anatolian texts are short, patterned after religious and secular texts of the Mesopotamian world. Rather than a religion that might be taken as an early form of that portrayed by the Greeks, or recorded in the Vedas, the practices and gods of the Hittites are essentially taken over from the Hurrians. In this way they support the finding that the speakers of Indo-European languages readily took over customs and beliefs from other peoples.

One might have expected, however, to find evidence for the Dumezilian conception of Indo-European society with major divisions into a priestly class, a warrior class and a class devoted to production of economic necessities. That conception is often referred to as the "new comparative mythology." It is based heavily on Vedic society with support from early Celtic society, and buttressed by sporadic evidence for similar alignments in the other groups; but lacking evidence among the Anatolian speakers, and even more so among the Tocharian speakers, the view requires further attention.

In other respects as well, interpretation of the new materials for their contributions to knowledge on the early cultures profited more from the information in the other dialects than they modified it. We will note something of the cultural situation in chapters 11 and 12.

1.10 CURRENT AIMS OF INDO-EUROPEAN LINGUISTICS

The rapid advances in archaeology have put the spotlight at present on determining the culture and homeland of the Indo-Europeans, while discussions on the language are left to specialists. Remarkable information on cultures at a number of excavated sites may be coordinated with well-established information from the language and early texts, leading prehistorians to propose one or another site as the homeland. Yet, as the diversity of sites so proposed indicates, the evidence from archaeology is by no means decisively in favor of any one location.

On the grounds that the practice of agriculture was developed in the Middle East, and then spread into Anatolia, Renfrew has associated its further extension into Europe with the Indo-Europeans (1987). On the same basis he has proposed as location for the homeland of the family the Çatal hüyük area of central Anatolia, taking it as the center from which agriculture was spread to Europe. The assumption that agriculture was being introduced at the time when Indo-European languages were being established in Europe accords well with views taken from study of the languages. Already in the middle of the nineteenth century, linguists had concluded that the speakers of Proto-Indo-European were at an early stage of an agricultural economy; but that stage is proposed for the fourth millennium and somewhat earlier, while Çatal hüyük flourished in the seventh. The gap of several millennia does not suggest support for Renfrew's assumption; moreover, the civilization of Çatal hüyük is totally different from that we may reconstruct for the presumed Indo-European speakers of the time. Further, as Diakonoff has pointed out, the internal situation in Anatolia at the end of the seventh millennium provides evidence against a continuous development of the peoples there to the advanced situation determined for the Balkan area in the fourth millennium.

Diakonoff has proposed that the Balkans are a highly plausible area for the homeland (1984). He does not argue vigorously in favor of that hypothesis, but maintains that the Balkans provide as much evidence for the assumption as do any of the other sites.

He has also argued strongly against the hypothesis of Gamkrelidze and Ivanov (1984) concerning a homeland in eastern Anatolia. As basis for their assumption they emphasize the ready availability of the means of transportation that were highly important for the extension of the peoples and their languages. Almost a half-century ago Specht pointed out that the terms for these items, the wheel, the wagon and so on, have the morphological characteristics of the proto-language at the time of its break-up into the dialects (1944); accordingly, the terms may have been introduced upon adoption of the new technology from the nearby Mesopotamian area. However, there is no archaeological evidence for large-scale extension of peoples from eastern Anatolia in the fifth and fourth millennia. Moreover, some of the conclusions of Gamkrelidze and Ivanov relying on names for fauna and flora have not been well received. Their proposed location for the early homeland has accordingly been met with objections.

Gimbutas places great weight on archaeological data that she has identified with Indo-European speakers, fixing on evidence from mound burials to propose a homeland north of the Black and Caspian Seas (1970). Such burials are well attested in the early texts, as at the end of the *Iliad* as well as the *Beowulf*, and also in the report of Ibn Fadlan on the Scandinavians in Russia (Brønsted 1960: 280–4). Moreover, the contents of the tombs can readily be correlated with conclusions derived from the languages. And the mounds themselves are located over much of the area occupied by Indo-European speakers. But Gimbutas's proposals have been vigorously criticized for her assumption of a series of invasions from the Pontic area into Europe. Prehistorians today lay much more weight on less spectacular extensions of peoples and languages at that early time. Moreover, a matter that is essentially nonpertinent has been poorly received, and has reduced credence in Gimbutas's conclusions; she has painted an idealistic picture of the civilization in Europe at the time before the Indo-Europeans supposedly invaded. By that picture the peoples were peaceful; they enjoyed an advanced civilization, flourishing under a matrilineal social system. This conception of hers has been viewed as unrealistic; coupled with her reliance on invasion theory, her assumptions on the homeland have been rejected by many scholars, such as those cited earlier in this section. On the other hand, because of a less fanciful view of the earlier culture in Europe and less insistence on spread of the Indo-European languages by invasions, assumption of a homeland in essentially the same area, as presented by Mallory (1989) and by Anthony, has not been accorded the same criticism.

Other archaeologists assume the development and expansion of indigenous peoples in the eastern European area. Insisting on the absence of archaeological evidence for culture change in the fifth to third millennia, Häusler assumes a homeland in east-central Europe. It may be well to recall that Brugmann suggested that the homeland was located somewhere in a long "strip of land extending from France through Middle Europe to Iran" (1897: 22). Subsequent scholarship has attempted to determine a more precise location. Whatever the outcome of the different proposals, the intense concern with culture and homeland provides the major aims of current discussion on the family, certainly among nonspecialists.

Among linguists attention to all components of the language has continued. The phonological system is being vigorously discussed, following the hypothesis of glottalics in the proto-language (Vennemann 1989). Also views on details of the laryngeal theory are still disputed, though the theory is now widely accepted. Moreover, the syntactic and morphological systems are being re-examined, especially with reference to the typological structure of the earlier form of the proto-language. The revised views of the language have reopened the question of relationship with other language families: on the one hand, a genetic relationship with the large number of families that Holger Pedersen labeled Nostratian, now generally called Nostratic (1931: 335–9); on the other hand, areal relationships with projected neighboring families, such as the Finno-Ugric, the Caucasian and the Afro-Asiatic.

These aims extend the inquiry into the early period far beyond those of the standard handbooks. They also require re-evaluation of much of the evidence, and scrutiny of the new data, especially in the Anatolian languages. While the handbooks of Brugmann, Delbrück and Meillet among others can scarcely be surpassed as sources for data and their interpretation at the time each of these works was published, the new data coupled with expanded methodological procedures require revised interpretations and updated handbooks for the dialects at the early period and for the proto-language itself. The aims of Indo-European linguistics today then parallel those of the beginnings of its study, but extend over many more facets of the language and the culture thanks to vastly increased information and the impressive results of virtually two centuries of study.

2 Methods

2.1 EARLY METHODS BASED ON THOSE DEVELOPED IN THE SCIENCES, ESPECIALLY COMPARATIVE ANATOMY, AND ON MANUSCRIPT STUDY

This chapter is designed to sketch the development of the methods of historical linguistics. Statements on the methods as currently applied may be consulted in special works like that of Hoenigswald (1960) or in the handbooks on historical linguistics. No satisfactory historical linguistic study was carried out before the beginning of the nineteenth century, and accordingly linguists had to develop appropriate methods for the new field. Like other new sciences, historical linguistics then looked to those that had developed useful methods. The greatest help came from comparative anatomy.

Anatomical study had advanced greatly in the eighteenth century, thanks in large part to Linnaeus. He laid the foundations of biological classification by selecting characteristic items for identification of species and genera, thereupon families and larger groupings. For classifying the higher orders of flowers he selected the reproductive organs, for birds their beaks, for animals their teeth and toes. The method had been so successful that by 1812 Georges Cuvier (1769–1832) could apply it to fossils, in his influential book, *Recherches sur les ossemes fossiles de quadrupès*.[1] It was a small step to apply the method to selected items of languages.

Bopp, as we have noted, applied such comparison to verb forms after his period of study in Paris. The methods developed in anatomy could be readily transferred to the research on early languages. Characteristic items had long been identified in Greek and Latin grammar. Categories recognized for verbs were: voice, tense, mood, number and person. These categories had also been noted by the Indian grammarians. Setting the forms side by side demonstrated their relationship much as had the comparison of anthers, pistils and other characteristics among species of flowers. What distinguished Bopp from earlier scholars who compared

Sources for this chapter: Lehmann (1967), especially for the selections by Grimm, von Raumer, Lottner, Grassmann, Verner, Saussure; Meillet ([1925] 1967); Hoenigswald (1960); Greenberg (1963); Lehmann (1992) on glottochronology; Baldi (1990).

24

related words was his attention to systems. As the title of his monograph of 1816 indicates, he compared the conjugational system of Sanskrit with the systems in Greek, Latin, Persian and Germanic. This approach raised the monograph far above previous works pursuing random comparison; it also justifies his distinction as father of comparative linguistics. The comparative method was now installed in linguistics through Bopp's innovative work.

The method was further established when Jacob Grimm in 1822 applied it to the consonantal system of Germanic in relation to the other Indo-European languages, chiefly Latin and Greek, with some attention to Sanskrit. Having recognized Rask's accuracy in setting up relationships among the consonants, Grimm in a quickly produced second edition of his 1819 volume on Germanic phonology systematized the relationships in tables (1822: 584; Lehmann 1967: 52). It is instructive to review his presentation in these references. The rules in his format are succinct lists presenting the essential facts.

Greek	P.	B.	F.	T.	D.	TH.	K.	G.	CH.
Gothic	F.	P.	B.	TH.	T.	D.	-.	K.	G.
OHG	B.	F.	P.	D.	Z.	T.	G.	CH.	K.

Labeling the positions for such items "grades," he accounted for the differences through "sound shifts." And he supported the comparisons with numerous examples, such as the following: "Initial position: . . . pes, pedis; Gk poûs, podós; Skt padas; Goth. fôtus; OHG vuoz." In this way he secured acceptance of the rules that he determined for classes of items, as well as for the comparative method itself. His rigorous and systematic treatment of the consonants also brought him the title father of historical linguistics.

Adoption of the method from comparative anatomy was accompanied by views that were not completely appropriate in the study of language. For a long time language was referred to as an organism rather than as a social convention. Although that view has now been corrected, other biological terminology for classification has been maintained. Languages are still classified into "families," and successive stages of a given language are referred to as "daughter languages." Biological terms are also maintained for chronological relationships, as in the term "descended from." From time to time linguists have pointed out that languages comparable in space or time cannot literally be classified in this way; for infants acquire their language independently, refashioning it in accordance with the versions they hear rather than having a preceding version imposed on them. But the terms "genealogical" or "genetic" classification are thoroughly installed, and apparently impossible to dislodge.

The methods applied in the study of language also benefited by comparison that was pursued in the course of manuscript study. In the large-scale attention to early texts that was carried on during the early nineteenth century, philologists sorted out earlier and later manuscripts. For this purpose they determined specific characteristics, identifying them in one manuscript or in a set of manuscripts. For example, a large number of manuscripts were found for Wolfram von Eschenbach's *Parzival*. These were examined for patterns of spelling, of rhymes, of vocabulary and other criteria. The manuscripts were then classified into two large groups, labeled D and G. The process of determining the groupings is similar to determining relationships among dialects, as of ancient Greek or medieval Iranian. The manuscripts were plotted by use of genealogical trees. And since virtually all older texts were preserved only in manuscripts produced after the time of their authors, efforts were made to reconstruct the *Vorlage*, or original manuscript. It is not remarkable that philologists like Jakob Grimm applied similar procedures to the data of ancient languages.

Another procedure came to be very productive in linguistic study: examination of selected materials for general description, followed by identification and study of residues. The procedure is typical in chemistry, which as we have noted influenced the phonetician Brücke, and may well have provided a pattern for comparison of sets.

2.1.1 Statements on related items by means of rules; the comparative method

As a further step, the general findings are presented in rules comparable to chemical formulae. Such rules were stated by Grimm, in various degrees of abstraction. The most abstract version posits three classes of obstruents: *T*enues, *A*spiratae, *M*ediae. Voiceless spirants as well as aspirates were labeled aspiratae. Since the tenuis *k* became the Germanic aspirate *ch*, the aspirate *gh* became the Germanic media *g*, and the media *g* became the Germanic tenuis *k*, the rule is presented with three points on a circle labeled *T*, *A*, *M*. The set of rules was so impressive that the term "law" was unfortunately applied to it. The term is still maintained in historical linguistics, even for minor correlations. The field would profit by returning to Grimm's own term "rule."

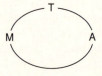

As a final step, the earlier forms for the elements of any such set are proposed. This step was not taken until Schleicher introduced it in his *Compendium*. From the time of its publication, the items have been reconstructed in the parent language, now known as Proto-Indo-European.

The comparative method (CM), as such treatment of comparable elements in related languages came to be known, is the fundamental procedure in historical linguistics. Through additional application it was formulated with increasing rigor. Already Grimm's immediate successors determined more accurate classes of sounds than the tenues, mediae and aspiratae that he assumed on the basis of classical linguistic study. And, as we have seen in the identification of the "law of palatals" (see 1.3.2), with increased understanding of phonetics the method came to be extended to study of forms that initially did not seem to be related. It also was applied in the study of morphology, syntax and the lexicon. Its refinement was achieved largely by application to Indo-European linguistics, which in turn acquired improved understanding of its field through increasing precision in treating the data. But it has been demonstrated to apply equally in other language families (see Baldi 1990). By it comparable items in related languages are examined for similarities and differences; earlier forms, that is *etyma*, are then reconstructed.

2.2 THE COMPARATIVE METHOD AND ITS PROGRESSIVE REFINEMENTS

To understand the success of the comparative method we may examine Grimm's procedures and other investigations that were carried out after his statements on the phonological system of the Germanic languages. Such scrutiny is also useful because in recent proposals to set up large groupings similar to those labeled "stocks" by Sapir, the method applied has been likened by its users to the comparative method, though others have severely criticized their procedures. A clear understanding of the comparative method is accordingly essential.

2.2.1 Procedures observed by Grimm with reference to the Germanic consonants

In support of his rules, Grimm provided an exhaustive set of examples, as may be noted in his presentation (1822: 585–8; Lehmann 1967: 52–5). Following his example, if one proposes a rule like $p > f$, all instances of p at its stage of the language must be examined as well as all instances of f at its stage. Further, as did Grimm, the items must be carefully scrutinized by environment; Grimm examined the consonants in question both for initial and for medial position. In short, when applying the comparative method, all ascertainable elements on either side of a rule must be determined in the languages under consideration, thereupon examined and accounted for.

Moreover, Grimm set out to find unambiguous examples: for example, he laid great weight on words that included two of the items, such as Greek *podós*, Gothic *fôtus* "feet"; and he looked for "suspicious deviations," accounting for some of them through borrowing, such as Old High German *scrīban* from Latin *scrībere*.

He, of course, was equipped to deal only with the classical languages, and to some extent with Sanskrit and Lithuanian; but as handbooks were produced that provided access to other Indo-European languages, Indo-Europeanists applied these procedures throughout the members of the family.

Grimm also dealt with the "exceptions, i.e. instances where the proposed comparisons fail" (Lehmann 1967: 56–7). To illustrate the fruitfulness of this procedure, we may note that the "imperfection of the aspirations in most languages" troubled him. Grassmann, of course, found a better explanation for the problem than to consider the set of aspiratae "imperfect."

Grimm also noted the "lack of initial Gothic *p*." So did Schleicher and many others throughout the century; they pointed out in addition that few examples of the expected etymon *b* in Proto-Indo-European could be found. A proposed solution has been advanced only in the present generation.

And Grimm has a special note on the "contradiction to the comparison" in words like Greek "*patếr*, Gothic *fadrs* (?)," wondering whether the Greek should not have been "*pathér*." (His question mark after Gothic *fadrs* would later be replaced by an asterisk before it. Only one form is attested in Gothic: *fadar*.) Verner later solved this "contradiction."

The care with which Grimm proceeded is noteworthy, both for its consequences and the instruction it should give anyone using the method. As we have already noted, subsequent linguists took it upon themselves to examine the exceptions, much as chemists examine residues. When specialists in other language families apply the comparative method to reconstruct forms, they must be as careful in its application as was Grimm. Later Indo-Europeanists enjoy the possibility of even greater support for their reconstructions through the availability of capable descriptions of the many Indo-European languages, but they must apply similar care to achieve credibility.

We have noted in the first chapter (1.3.2) how such care led to the solution of the exceptions that Grimm recognized. Further, how the solution of each set of exceptions was accompanied by improved understanding of language, first of all, phonetics. But we have also seen that "the lack of initial Gothic *p*" was not amenable to solution in this way. This problem was mentioned by successive Indo-Europeanists, but was only recently provided with a solution. The proposed solution, not accepted by all Indo-Europeanists, relies on generalizations achieved in typological study by examining the phonological systems of the many languages that have been studied (Vennemann 1989: 65–263; Djahukian 1990). For the time being, we are concerned with noting the importance of recording "exceptions" and accounting for them when using the comparative method; but we will return to the problem of "Gothic initial *p*" below.

2.2.2 Procedures with reference to the vowels

Grimm virtually threw up his hands in despair with reference to the vowels. After surveying them he concluded "that the vowel relationships are uncertain and subject to various influences, but that their distribution and alternation are not arbitrary, rather, resulting from deeply established laws that have not yet been disclosed" (Lehmann 1967: 48). He held out for hope from the "law of the ablauts."

As late as the publication date (1854) of the first volume of his dictionary Grimm could only provide the following definition for ablaut: "permutatio vocalium literarum, regulated conversion of the vowel of the root into another; a noble and essential capability of the German language [i.e. the Germanic dialects], different from umlaut" (I: 69). The definition of umlaut was not due in the dictionary until the twenty-third volume of 1936; fully understood at this time, its definition requires virtually an entire column. Its coinage is credited to Klopstock, who introduced it with reference to all change of root vowels, including those that Grimm ascribed to ablaut (1854–1954 XXIII: 1011). Even though Grimm differentiated the two processes, determining the "law of the ablauts" required far longer than solution of the consonantal problems. A full account of that determination would be extensive; see chapters 5 and 6 below. Here, results yielded for linguistic methodology by its study may be briefly noted.

Grimm's difficulties with the vowel system arose from a twofold complexity. Like the Germanic obstruents, the vowels showed differences that could be expressed in grades, as the ancient Indian grammarians had done. With *i* as example, vowels manifest three grades, Sanskrit *i, e, ai* (often transliterated *āi* with a macron over the *a*), the comparable grades for vocalic *ṛ* are *ṛ ar ār*. And morphemes containing no resonant had the grades –, *a, ā*. Operating as they did on a purely descriptive basis, the Indian grammarians regarded the first, for example, *i* as the fundamental vowel, and treated the two others as strengthened forms. Guna, the first grade of strengthening, yielded *é*; vṛddhi (vriddhi) yielded *āi*. In this way the proposed vowel grades may be aligned as Grimm did the obstruents.

But the bases for the two sets of "grades" differ also in their complexity. The proposed consonant grades are relatively transparent for description and explanation, because the changes that had taken place were relatively recent. The Old High German change (yielding Grimm's third grade) is dated around the end of the fifth century of our era, the Germanic change (yielding his second) about a thousand years earlier. But the vowel changes that led to ablaut relationships were far earlier, having taken place some time before the development of the various Indo-European dialects. Like the results of many sound changes, they came to be used as morphological markers. For example, the guna grade was so employed in the present tense of thematic verbs, e.g. Greek *leípō*, and the lowest grade in the aorist, as in Greek *élipon* "I left." When such patterning is installed in a language, it may be extended, as the contrast between the simple noun and the form with plural *-s* has been in English. The complexities of such extension of the early vowels after changes had taken place were so great that a half century of devoted study was required to sort them out. The investigations that succeeded in this achievement also contributed to assurance in the comparative method.

Much of the eventual clarification of Indo-European ablaut is attributed to Hermann Hirt (1865–1936), who sketched the steps that led to his views (1921–37). The first step in clarification for the nineteenth-century Indo-Europeanists came when Bopp realized that for historical explanation it would be necessary to posit the guna form as basic (1836). For, as Hirt pointed out, deriving guna and vriddhi forms of roots like **ped-* "foot" from **pd-* would seem to be creating vowels from zero. Bopp's observation led to the eventual rejection of Sanskrit as equivalent to the parent language. And the guna form was now taken as historically prior; but Bopp did not make further advances in the understanding of ablaut.

The next major step came when Adolf Holtzmann (1810–70) proposed a cause for the vowel variation (1844). He aligned it with shifts in accent. However, the relationship remained unclear because he and others found it difficult to determine the precise relationships between accent and vowel grades. The forms for "I know, we know" indeed show the expected relationship in the Sanskrit perfect *véd-a*, *vid-más*; but their Greek cognates, do not, i.e. *oîd-a*, *íd-men*. Similarly, "I go, we go" indeed show the appropriate relationship with the accent in Sanskrit *é-mi*, *i-más*, though not in the Greek cognates *eî-mi*, *í-men*. Many more such difficulties might be cited. The two languages considered oldest then failed to provide unambiguous support for Holtzmann's proposal; and the other dialects that preserved a variable accent, Baltic and Slavic, added further difficulties.

The situation was not clarified until Verner proposed his solution for the voiced fricatives corresponding to Proto-Indo-European voiceless stops, as in Gothic *fadar*. When he pointed out that this correlation applied if the accent stood on the vowel after the voiceless stop, it became clear that at one time Germanic had a variable accent like that of Sanskrit. The phonological explanation has strong morphological support; for example, the past tense of verbs with medial voiceless stop, like PIE **wert-* "turn, become," have consonant variation in Old High German that is parallel to the position of the accent in Sanskrit, i.e. *ward*, *wurtum*. Verner's article, then, as a further contribution showed the way to the solution of Indo-European ablaut. It demonstrated that some dialects, notably Vedic and Proto-Germanic, maintained the earlier accent, but that others, such as Greek, redistributed it in accordance with accentual principles in their own language.

In this way it contributed further to assurance in the comparative method, for it demonstrated decisively that, after a sound change or any change takes place, the results may be determined even when they are redistributed on other grounds. Generally, these grounds are morphological, though they may also be lexical. In view of such redistribution, mere examination of subsequent forms may fail to disclose the earlier situation. The patterning in a language some centuries and millennia later may differ markedly from the situation at the time when a sound change has taken place.

This finding is repeatedly disregarded, as in the evidence for treatment of Sievers's law. For recent material, such as distribution of umlaut in German, the situation can be readily determined, if at some pains (Paul 1916–21 II: 9ff.) A sentence of Paul's on page 9 is especially worth notice: "Although it was only by chance originally that plural forms [of the noun] were distinguished from the singular by means of umlaut, this has gradually developed into a characteristic feature of the plural." We can determine such developments for umlaut in German; it is far more difficult to do so for early or reconstructed languages. But if we choose to deal with them, we are required to apply the same rigorous procedures that have been applied in determining the redistribution, as of German umlaut vowels.

Shortly after the publication of Verner's article, Brugmann published the statement that provided the theoretical basis for the explosion of fruitful historical studies in the last quarter of the nineteenth century (1878). From this point the comparative method in careful use merits the characterization "proofed procedure," as Diebold put it (1987: 25). Such use yields accurate solutions when the data to which it is applied are taken from the same chronological period; further, when they are parallel in environment. These provisions are by no means trivial, as Hoenigswald's careful elaboration of the method indicates (1960); but when they are observed, the results may be regarded with great confidence.

2.3 THE METHOD OF INTERNAL RECONSTRUCTION

The second central method in historical linguistics relies on data in only one language rather than comparison of comparable data in three or more languages. The method of internal reconstruction (IR) is based on the fact that sound change takes place by specific environments. Items parallel morphologically may nonetheless include differing environments, or may differ in form: for example, parallel Indo-European roots like *b^her- "bear" and *b^hed^h- "dig" differ in environment through the presence of two aspirates in the second; roots like *ag- "lead" and *$(s)tā$- "stand" differ in form from the canonical CVC structure of Indo-European roots, such as *sed- "sit."

If Grimm's rules had been applied, *b^hend^h- would be reconstructed from Gothic *bind*-; but Sanskrit was considered closer to the parent language, and accordingly the contrast between the Sanskrit root *bandh*- and the Gothic form was considered an exception in Germanic. Grassmann found the decisive evidence for this so-called exception by noting that the forms varied in Sanskrit and Greek, rather than by relying on Germanic; for example, the future of *bandh-* in Sanskrit has an initial aspirate, e.g. *bhantsyati*. It is also clear that strict reconstruction from Germanic alone, that is internally, would have resulted in the correct form of the root in Proto-Indo-European. In short, by internal reconstruction the problem could have been solved.

But rather than Grassmann's solution, a rigorous analysis of irregular Indo-European roots provided the first and ultimately most impressive demonstration of the method. That demonstration was produced by Saussure when he was a student in Leipzig (1879). Assuming that Indo-European roots have a canonical form consisting of Consonant–Vowel–Consonant, Saussure examined especially those roots that failed to meet the pattern. Among these were some of the most widespread, such as **ag-* and **(s)tā-* cited above. Applying his conclusion to these as well, Saussure proposed that at an earlier stage they also had CVC structure; and he proceeded to reconstruct the missing C. Long viewed as a daring step that could not really be accepted, Saussure's proposal was demonstrated to be accurate when in 1927 Kurylowicz determined that the missing C in some words is attested in Hittite, where it is transliterated with *h*, for example Hittite *hark-* "hold," Latin *arceo* "enclose", Hittite *haran*, Old High German *aro* "eagle" (see also Kurylowicz 1935: 27–76, 253–5). After this demonstration, internal reconstruction was accepted as a second important method for historical study.

The comparative method was supported by comparable procedures in other sciences, as we have noted. If we wish to account for the development of the method of internal reconstruction, we may ascribe it to observations on language patterning. Sound changes take place by phonological environments. These may not coincide with the structure of morphological classes, as illustrated by the examples above of Proto-Indo-European roots. When applying the method to them, a standard or canonical form is proposed, such as CVC. Thereupon deviations are noted, such as the root **ag-*, which includes only VC elements. Finally, one proposes possible explanations and reconstructions. These are provided by drawing on one's knowledge of structures and processes in language generally, that is, from typological investigations.

Somewhat similar procedures have been fruitful in manuscript study. For example, one of the most highly regarded biblical manuscripts, the Codex Sinaiticus, includes a strange sequence in I Maccabees 5.20. The text there has the equivalent of "six or three thousand" where it should have "eight thousand." The problem was solved when it was proposed that this codex, like many others, was written down from dictation. The reader presumably could not make out the writing of the earlier manuscript, and said "six or three," which the scribe conscientiously put down. Knowledge about the production of manuscripts led to the solution.

The method is most effective when one can determine canonical forms.

As we have seen, the canonical form of roots in Indo-European is CVC; in Semitic, on the other hand, it is CCC. Some Semitic roots consist of only two consonants; for many of these a further consonant is posited, and then the posited consonant is reconstructed on the basis of modifications it has left on other elements of forms. Similarly, the consonants that Saussure reconstructed for Proto-Indo-European left modifications in some roots. For example, the length of vowel in *(s)tā- is ascribed to compensatory lengthening on loss of the earlier consonant; French *tête* "head" from Latin *testa* provides an example of such compensatory lengthening. And the *a*-vowel of *ag- is similarly ascribed to the earlier consonant; for the typical vowel of Indo-European roots is *e*, but in the neighborhood of some laryngeals it was colored to *a*. Similar processes have been attested in other languages. In applying the method, one calls on such information in the effort to achieve a credible hypothesis.

While the method is applicable to attested languages, it is especially useful for reconstructed languages. In attempts to relate them to other reconstructed languages, such as the repeated proposals of relationship between Indo-European and Afro-Asiatic or similar proposals about Amerindian languages, internal reconstruction is the primary method for arriving at the structure of the languages when the two proto-languages were closer to one another. The results then may be treated with the comparative method. However, internal reconstruction is also highly important in attempts to account for phenomena in one language family, such as ablaut in Proto-Indo-European.

2.4 FURTHER APPLICATIONS OF THE METHOD OF INTERNAL RECONSTRUCTION

After the publication of Saussure's monograph of 1879, linguists were equipped with the two important methods of historical linguistics. Furthermore, solution of the so-called exceptions to Grimm's law, as it was now called, gave them great confidence for clearing up the problems posed by earlier study. Chief among these was the vowel system, and ablaut.

In 1876 Osthoff provided one advance by proposing vocalic liquids – *r̥* and *l̥* for the proto-language. Having seen his article in manuscript, Brugmann reconstructed vocalic nasals in a publication of the same year (1876; cf. Lehmann 1967: 190–5). Shortly thereafter, Sievers proposed that such vocalic elements varied with consonantal counterparts in accordance with their environment (1878; cf. Lehmann 1967: 210–16); the formulation is known as Sievers's law, also as the Sievers–Edgerton law. For instance, with /y/ as example, the vocalic variant shows up in the Sanskrit first person plural *i-más* of "go," the consonantal variant in the third person plural *yánti*. Using data assembled by Benfey, Sievers demonstrated additional variation after long versus short syllables, as in Sanskrit *aryá* : *kāviá*, both with the suffix -*ya*-; after a long syllable the -*iy*- variant of -*y*- appears, transmitted as *-i-* in *kāviá-*. A similar situation was assumed for the other resonants, but the patterning was not worked out definitively until Edgerton's articles of 1934 and 1943. Still, in the meantime the role of the resonants in root structure, and further in conjunction with ablaut, was brought to general attention. At the same time it was now assumed that the basic vowel of most roots was *e*.

The vowel *e* (or its reflex, e.g. Gothic *i*) is found in the present forms of verbs, though other forms were marked by different vowels, as in Gothic.

Infinitive		Past singular	Past plural
wisan	"be"	was	wēsun
sitan	"sit"	sat	sētun

It had already been determined that PIE *e* had become *i* in Gothic, and *o* had become *a* in Germanic. The Indo-European variation then was between *e* and *o*, and a lengthened form of *e*. Moreover, forms were also found in which the root vowel had been completely lost, as in **nist-* "nest," a compound of the particle **ni-* "down" and **sed-* "sit." The problem now was to determine the bases of the variation.

The varying vowels were accounted for by assuming a series of vowel changes in the Proto-Indo-European period. The changes were ascribed largely to accent shifts. In referring to the variants, the term "grade" has been maintained. The terms applied for specific grades have also been kept, even though they, especially in abbreviations, are often confusing; here only a selection of that terminology is given.

Patterns with *e* are said to be in *Normal* grade. When the *e* is lost, as in *nists*, the pattern is referred to as in *Zero* grade; since this is *Nullstufe* in German, the symbol *N* can be troublesome in treatments of ablaut. As explanation, it was proposed that in the zero grade the vowel has been lost because a stress accent stood on a different syllable from that of the base. Such a process is readily observed in languages with a strong stress accent, as in English words that formerly had unstressed vowels in final syllables, e.g. *duke*, *lived*, and so on. In much the same way, the *-e-* of **sed-* is presumed to have been lost when the accent was placed on the initial particle; the *-d-* was then devoiced before consonants, yielding **nist-*.

The lengthened grade (*L*) is the result of compensation. Some scholars assume that in nominative forms of many nouns a syllable has been lost, e.g. Greek *patḗr* from **patére*, cf. nom. pl. *patéres*; others attribute the lengthening to loss of final *s* or other consonant (Szemerényi 1970 [1989]: 121–3). This grade then came to be extended in various morphological forms, like the etymon of Gothic *setun* (generally written without macron on *e*, since the letter never represents a short vowel in Gothic).

Accordingly, the two processes giving rise to zero grade and to lengthened grade could be ascribed to approximately the same period of the proto-language when it had a strong expiratory stress accent. However, the early dialects, such as Vedic Sanskrit, have musical accent rather than stress. As a result a pitch accent was proposed for the pre-dialect stage of the proto-language. Stress accent was in force during an earlier period, but then was replaced by pitch accent. The shift of *e* to *o* was attributed to pitch accent. Forms like the Greek perfect *dédorka* "I saw" have the accent on the reduplicated syllable rather than on the root, as in the present *dérko-mai* "I see." On the basis of these and other forms, it was assumed that *e* became *o* when a syllable lost its principal pitch accent but acquired a secondary accent. The *o*-grade is then referred to as *Deflected*.

In summary, the following grades are the chief that have been proposed, with selected examples:

Normal	e	ew	ey	er
Zero	–	u	i	ṛ
Lengthened	ē	ēw	ēy	ēr
Deflected	o	ow	oy	or

Other explanations as well have been proposed for the alternating vowels, as we will see later. Here our primary concern has to do with the application of the two methods, CM and IR, in efforts to account for problems in the phonological system of the proto-language and its dialects. The only data available for determining the earlier structure consist of forms that exhibit the results of the changes. These forms were analysed for patterns and subpatterns that provided leads for explanation on the basis of increasing knowledge of languages.

In view of possible misunderstanding of data and misinterpretation of historical methods, we point out again that distribution of the ablaut variants in the dialects may have no relationship to the earlier cause of the changes. Like the distribution of umlaut vowels in German today (see section 2.2 above), ablaut patterns came to be associated with morphological classes. Deflected grade, for example, was associated with the preterite singular of strong verbs in Germanic; in Greek it was associated with the singular forms of the perfect. In order to determine the original conditions under which the changes took place, an enormous amount of work was performed by Indo-Europeanists in the nineteenth century. Even then, some situations remained unclear until laryngeals were determined as part of the phonological system of the proto-language at the time when the vowel variations known as ablaut were being brought about. The explanations achieved, both for the processes by which the ablauting vowels originated and their subsequent distribution as well, were determined by use of the comparative method, and to a lesser extent by the method of internal reconstruction.

2.5 GLOTTOCHRONOLOGY

In 1951 Morris Swadesh proposed an additional method by which he aimed to determine time depths and the extent of relationships between languages. The method is applied to the lexicon. On the grounds that it too undergoes change, Swadesh advanced the hypothesis that over a period of a thousand years a specific proportion of the core vocabulary of any language would be lost. If so, related languages would not share cognates for such words after a given period of separation. As examples, we may note that German *Tier* is not a cognate of English *animal*; nor is *Hund* a cognate of *dog*. English came to restrict the cognate *deer* to the most common large wild animal so that it was "lost" in its earlier use; and *dog* was generalized from a word of unknown origin, reducing *hound* to a term for a special kind of dog. Similar examples might be cited from other languages. By Swadesh's hypothesis, if one could determine the rate of lexical loss from languages known for the period of a millennium, a means would be available to compute the degree of relationship among languages attested only today.

Initially Swadesh provided a list of slightly over 200 words for the core vocabulary. The words were to be found in every language. He therefore excluded some items, such as "snow," for which no word could be expected in languages of tropical islands. Critics objected to some other words he included. A list of 100 words was then proposed. Both lists were tested on many languages. From the tests it was concluded that approximately 80–85 per cent of core-vocabulary words are maintained over a period of 1,000 years (see Embleton 1991).

Taking the figure 80 per cent for the purpose of ease of computing, we can conclude further that two related languages would share 64 per cent of their core vocabulary after separation of 1,000 years. If two languages are found that agree in this way, for example Spanish and Portuguese, it follows that they became distinct languages about AD 1000.

Initially attractive, glottochronology came to be treated sceptically. We know, for example, when Iceland was settled, chiefly from Norway; but if we compare the core vocabularies of the two languages, the results are far lower than the actual date. Glottochronological results indicate that Icelandic was separated from Norwegian four to five hundred years ago, but the actual time is more that twice as great. We can account for the results through the continuation of close contacts between Iceland and Norway, and through the conservative maintenance of the ancient literature among Icelanders; that is, we can explain the situation sociolinguistically. Yet if the method were to be universally valid, such a requirement is troublesome. We do not know the social relationships among many languages of the past, and accordingly we might not be able to correct the results as we can for Icelandic.

Other difficulties were pointed out, such as the cultural spread of some supposedly basic words, such as "sun"; it might occupy a privileged position in a spreading religion, and accordingly be extended or maintained among numerous languages. Moreover, languages may not be parallel in core vocabulary; rather than two words for demonstrative senses, e.g. *this*, *that*, languages may have as many as five. Formerly English itself, with *yon* and derivatives, included three. Eliciting the expected comparable term may then be impossible.

Nonetheless the simplicity of the method is so attractive that it continues in use, especially for languages poorly or not at all attested in the past. For these it has been especially helpful in initial subgrouping, as for Austronesian (Baldi 1990: 146–7) and Australian languages (Baldi 1990: 399).

Dolgopolsky reduced the list further for purposes of determining distant relationships (1986); for at time depths over 6,000 years the number of words in two languages for which relationships can be found in the Swadesh lists is so small that the proportion identified is about the same as that of chance. Dolgopolsky hoped to avoid that problem by determining a small number of carefully selected words, such as *two*, *louse*, *tooth*; he assumed that these words are rarely borrowed from other languages and that accordingly they are relatively permanent in all languages. As we note further below, 2.8, even some of those words are problematic.

Applied with care, as among the Romance languages or the ancient Greek dialects, the method of glottochronology may provide additional insights into their interrelationships. The severest critics object to it by applying it rigorously as if it were a method in the physical sciences; but in linguistics, social and psychological relationships always must be taken into account, as we have noted for Icelandic. With sufficient study, the effects of them may be determined, and the glottochronological results may then be more realistic. Nevertheless, since the social and psychological conditions for early and for prehistoric languages are difficult to reconstruct, the method is unfortunately least useful for situations we would most like to determine.

2.6 TYPOLOGY

As we have noted, typological studies were prominent before attention turned to historical study in the second decade of the nineteenth century. From this time the problems of the Indo-European family occupied the major energies of the foremost linguists. Moreover, when concentrating on history, these linguists were little concerned with typology, where one collects and examines selected patterns without attention to their history. Typology then came to be neglected until recently, except by a few linguists.

Typological studies aim to determine generalizations about languages and, on the basis of these, to propose specific language types. Such generalizations may be directed at the structure of language, or pursued for further correlations, as between language and culture; less fruitfully they may be correlated with race, as was done by some linguists in the last part of the nineteenth century.

The few nineteenth-century typologists did not continue the massive collections of the eighteenth, which received their final formulation in Adelung's *Mithridates* (1806–16). By contrast, they were almost exclusively concerned with morphology. On the basis of morphological structure they proposed various types. Languages with little or no inflection, like Chinese, were called analytic. Languages with considerable inflection, like Greek, were called synthetic. A kind of intermediate structure was called agglutinative; in agglutinative languages, elements, including inflections, are added to bases, but the relationship is not tight as it is in inflected languages. Japanese and Turkish are examples: for example, the Japanese base for the verb *ageru* "raise" is *age-*; its past is *age-ta*; its causative is *age-sase-ru*, for which in turn the past is *age-sase-ta*; the simple negative is *age-nai*; the negative of the causative is *age-sase-nai*, and so on. Similar examples from Turkish could be cited, as could examples from other agglutinative languages, like Quechua.

The concern with history, influenced at least to some extent by the ideas of evolution, led some linguists to propose explanations for the types found at a given time. Since Proto-Indo-European, as reconstructed on the basis of Sanskrit and Greek, is highly inflected, and many current Indo-European languages have little or no inflection, some scholars concluded that inflected languages are simplified in the course of time towards uninflected structure. Chinese and Vietnamese among other languages would then be highest in development.

Holding that current English is more efficient than Old English, Jespersen published as one of his first books a sketch of English, entitled *Progress in Language*. Its minimal inflection today led him to conclude that it had reached a high stage of development. Yet his article of 1949, "Efficiency in linguistic change," is not only "an old man's aftermath," but also a wise man's view of language as a social and cultural possession. While still maintaining that the changes during the history of English led to greater efficiency, he now sees reasons for some of the complexities in language and does not consider monosyllabic structure to be the sole test of efficiency (*Selected Writings of Otto Jespersen*, n.d.: 153–345, 381–466).

Other linguists took the reverse path; Marr, the dominant linguist in the Soviet Union, placed inflected languages highest and uninflected languages lowest in the scale. This position was abruptly rejected by Stalin when the communist government took over in China. These results may suggest that nineteenth-century typological study scarcely achieved great success, or high prestige in linguistics, even though a succession of brilliant linguists concerned themselves with it, from Wilhelm von Humboldt to Edward Sapir.

Devoting much of his only book to typology, Sapir applied semantic as well as morphological criteria (1921). Yet his approach had little response. After some attempts to improve it, Greenberg in 1963 turned to syntax, proposing correlations of selected syntactic constructions with basic sentence structure. These have provided the basis for important observations on change in language. Greenberg's generalizations assumed three basic elements in sentences: *S*ubjects, *V*erbs, *O*bjects. The possible arrangements of these would permit six types: SOV, SVO, VSO, VOS, OSV, OVS. By some estimates the first type is attested in the greatest number of known languages, nearly 50 per cent; the proportion of SVO languages is somewhat less. VSO languages make up fewer than 10 per cent. The remaining types are found in only a few languages. Accordingly, it is useful to speak of OV and VO languages, especially because in many languages subjects are not essential.

Each of these two classes of language manifests further characteristics among common patterns like the use of adpositions, comparison of inequality, relative clauses, the position of genitives and adjectives with regard to their heads, etc. (see Lehmann 1978). For example, OV languages typically include postpositions rather than prepositions, comparatives of the pattern "The pen sword than mighty" in contrast to the VO "The pen is mightier than the sword," as well as preposed relative clauses, etc. These observations are highly significant for historical study, because languages undergo syntactic change as well as changes in other components. In such changes patterns are often not totally lost, but replaced in most occurrences. If, then, a language like Classical Latin includes among its adpositions some postpositions, as in frozen phrases like *mēcum* "with me," we may conclude that at an earlier stage its structure was OV. That conclusion may be pursued in examination of earlier texts, such as the plays of Plautus, where we find it supported; it is also supported there by residues of the other characteristic OV constructions. Typological investigations in this way have provided the basis for applying internal reconstruction in the important area of syntax, with extensive correlations for reconstruction of morphology.

Similarly, findings useful in historical study have been determined concerning phonological structure: for example, languages with nasal consonants have *m* and *n* in their inventory if this includes ŋ; but the two may be present without it. Accordingly, if in even a small body of material for a given language there is evidence for ŋ, one may conclude that the other two nasals were also present in the language.

Such phonological findings led to the explanation proposed by Gamkrelidze and Ivanov and Hopper for the "lack of initial Gothic *p*" < Proto-Indo-European *b*. In glottalic sets, the voiceless labial stop is poorly attested, if at all. Accordingly, these three linguists proposed that the series in Proto-Indo-European was glottalic. Since the series concerned has been reconstructed as *b d g*, by a further inference these were reconstructed as voiceless glottalics, *p' t' k'*. This proposed explanation requires many further adjustments of the conclusions reached by the nineteenth-century linguists concerning Proto-Indo-European and its various branches.

Some Indo-Europeanists have virtually rejected out of hand the possible usefulness of conclusions reached on the basis of typological findings. In the strict neogrammarian tradition change is assumed to take place without exceptions. Recognition of apparent exceptions, and even more the procedure of basing inferences on them, is distasteful for such linguists. Moreover, successors of the neogrammarians who confine their attention to language as an abstract social system, following Saussure, or to an ideal language of an ideal speaker–listener in an ideal speech community, following Chomsky, cannot deal with actual language. Befogged as they are in the "hypotheses-beclouded atmosphere of the workshop," they fail to understand language in its social settings and use. In spite of their objections to inferences based on the findings of typology, its application has led to improved understanding of early stages of Proto-Indo-European and has also provided explanations for residues in the early dialects as we note in chapters 9 to 11.

2.7 TYPOLOGY BASED ON VIEWS OF LANGUAGE AS A STRUCTURE

The search for universals in the eighteenth century sought language characteristics without relating them to a total structure of language. In the nineteenth century and early part of the twentieth century, attention was given almost entirely to morphology, though, as we have noted for Bopp, to morphological structure, not simply to single items in morphology. Pater Wilhelm Schmidt proposed to classify languages by position of the genitive with regard to its head (1926); it might follow the head of the construction, as generally in French and Spanish, or precede it, as in Turkish and Japanese. Including under the term "genitive" also phrasal expression, as in "purchase of houses," English has about 90 per cent of its genitives following the head; those that precede are almost exclusively animate nouns, such as "the neighbor's houses." Others did not agree on the assignment of such importance to the position of the genitive. Yet Schmidt must be credited for assuming a basic pattern for language, and noting correlations with it. Many current proponents of typology deal with language as a whole.

2.7.1 Contentive typology

By one typological approach, linguists of the former Soviet Union treat language by examining content in conjunction with form. They refer to this approach as "contentive." Contentive typology recognizes three major language types: accusative, ergative and active–stative, generally referred to simply as active. These show specific characteristics in vocabulary and syntax as well as in morphology (Klimov 1983).

Accusative languages, for example, include transitive and intransitive verbs; ergative languages, by contrast, include factitive and agentive verbs; and active languages include active and stative verbs. Assuming that the accusative-language classes of transitive and intransitive verbs are clear from English, we may propose typical verbs for the two classes in ergative languages; "eat, come" would be agentive; "build, drive" would be factitive. While the cases in ergative languages differ from nominative vs. accusative, the accusative and ergative types are similar in having government relationships between verbs and nouns.

Active languages, by contrast, express such relationships primarily through agreement; active nouns require active verbs and inactive nouns require inactive verbs: for example, "boy" as well as "eat" and "come" would belong to the active class, "chair" as well as "stand" and "block" would be inactive. Moreover, active languages may include different lexical items for meanings like "stand," the active verb corresponding to "arise," the inactive to "be erect."

Each type includes further characteristics, distinguishing especially the active from the accusative/ergative. Further, as has been stated earlier, since languages change, we find examples of inconsistent languages in respect to contentive criteria as well as in other respects. Such inconsistencies provide means for proposing earlier patterning, as has been done spectacularly for Proto-Indo-European.

2.7.2 Syntactic typology

A second approach takes syntax as the central component of language, and the government relationship of verbs with objects as primary distinguishing characteristic. The approach focuses on order, or by Bloomfield's term arrangement, as noted in the examples above. While the verb–object relationship is primary, it is related to many other characteristics: for example, object clauses, or complements as they are generally called today, have their position and also their structure determined by language type. Since complements stand before verbs in OV languages, they often are concluded by nouns meaning "fact, situation" and the like; infinitives on the other hand, are less favored in OV languages and are rare. An example like the following is typical: "He the boat buys | fact: she expects." By contrast, VO languages make heavy use of subordinating conjunctions, as in *She expects that he is buying the boat*. They also include infinitives, as in *She expects him to buy the boat*.

Such observations are important for historical purposes: for example, the various Indo-European languages show a variety of infinitive endings; in Sanskrit they end in *-tum*, in Latin they end in *-re*, in Germanic in *-onom* > *-an*, etc. Accordingly we cannot reconstruct an infinitive for Proto-Indo-European. Its lack is one of the bases for assuming that Proto-Indo-European was an OV language, which do not typically contain infinitives.

We may cite many more such characteristics (Lehmann 1978: 24–6). Some have to do with morphology: for example, OV languages express modality and tense/aspect after verb stems, VSO languages before them. The early Indo-European languages included complex verbal endings, such as those indicating active voice, present tense, subjunctive mood, third person, singular number, e.g. Greek *paideúēi* "he may educate" vs the passive *paideúētai* "he may be educated," etc. These have been replaced in current Indo-European languages by auxiliaries and other words that stand before the verb, as the English translations illustrate.

The number of such correlations that have been identified may illustrate that syntactic typology relying on arrangement of verb and object is useful for understanding change in language. Syntactic typology does not, however, include correlations with the lexicon, except for devices to distinguish transitive and intransitive verbs; for that reason it does not deal with content, as does the typology discussed above. But to the extent that "meaning" is expressed syntactically, as by government, syntactic typology is not purely morphological as was nineteenth-century typology.

2.7.3 Head/modifier marking typology

A third typological approach relies heavily on location of "marking" (Nichols 1986). Constructions like phrases and clauses are taken to consist of head and modifier. In a phrasal construction like *Jean's cat*, *cat* is head and *Jean* is modifier. One of these constituents is typically marked. In English it is the modifier. In many languages it is the head; in Biblical Hebrew, for example, nouns functioning as heads in such constructions stand in the so-called construct form rather than the absolute.

In sentences the verb is taken to be head of the clause. Accordingly, verbs are heavily inflected in head-marking languages. By contrast, in modifier-marking languages, such as English, verbal inflection is scanty. Biblical Hebrew, by contrast, has massive verbal inflection.

The active class of verbs is heavily inflected in active languages. Nichols has proposed that the typology positing them should take note of their marking characteristic. By her view, rather than the three proposed contentive types, the role of marking should be taken as primary. Whatever the reaction to this proposal, the correlations found for marking may be useful for making inferences about poorly known languages. If such languages have considerable inflection of the verb, one may draw conclusions about other morphological and syntactic characteristics.

These brief characterizations of three typological approaches are designed to sketch their usefulness for historical study. Many languages are now being investigated for their typological structure, yielding further insights into these and other typological findings, as concerning the phonological component. The contributions of typology to Indo-European linguistics will be presented further below, especially in chapter 10.

2.8 EXTENSION OF THE TRADITIONAL METHODS

In sum, historical linguists have at their disposal three methods: CM, IR and glottochronology. Of these CM is most highly regarded and most widely used; but it can be applied only when data in three or more related languages are available. IR has been applied with impressive results, but the data needed for its use in a language are often unavailable. Glottochronology has severe limitations.

Besides these methods, historical linguists make use of the findings of typological study, both to identify patterns that provide possibilities for explanation and patterns that lend credence to conclusions that have been advanced through application of the three methods. Linguists have always examined their conclusions with reference to patterns in other languages; but the patterns so used have often been atypical, taken from languages that the individual happened to know. The findings of typological study are based on examination of all languages for which data have been secured; accordingly, they provide much more secure bases for such purposes.

In view of the limitations of the methods, linguists concerned with languages for which data are not available from early periods, or those seeking to determine relationships more than six millennia ago, have attempted to extend the established methods. Through such extension they set out to determine "remote relations" and "macrofamilies" or "super-stocks." The procedures employed have been called "multilateral" or "mass comparison." Applications of the approach are now being vigorously continued; see, for example, Lamb and Mitchell (1991: 125–350).

In using multilateral comparison, cognates are selected where they are available in any language of families assumed to be related. In illustrating the methodology, Dolgopolsky examines items in seven "language families": Indo-European, Hamito-Semitic, Kartvelian, Uralic, Altaic, Chukchee-Kamchatkan and the Sumerian languages (1986:30). Selected for their permanence in language, the items are fifteen: "two, who/what, tongue, name, eye, heart, tooth, finger/toe nail, louse, tear (noun), water, dead," first-person marker, second-person marker, and verbal negation. He then looks for cognates in any one language of the families concerned: for example, the item "name" is well-attested in Indo-European, as in Sanskrit *nāman*; for Hamito-Semitic Dolgopolsky cites Arabic *ʔism*; for Sumerian *inim* "word" and so on. It is assumed that the resemblance is adequate for proposing relationship among those items. But, in contrast with the comparative method, no attempt is made to compare similar items, such as all Sanskrit, or even Proto-Indo-European, words beginning with *n*, or all Arabic, or even all Proto-Hamito-Semitic, clusters of *sm*, nor to account for all the lexical items meaning "name" in each of the languages held to be Nostratic.

Moreover, even the highly selected fifteen items are open to general forces affecting language, including language loss. Terms for "tongue, eye, tooth" are open to taboo; and in active languages more than one designation is likely for "water." Accordingly, the approach is totally different from the comparative method as it has been applied in the Indo-European languages and to other families.

On the other hand, it is important to observe the care with which results of comparison are tested in reliable historical studies; a review of problems in the history of study of the Indo-European languages and their solutions is highly salutary. Nostraticists make general assumptions, such as taking the same vowel *e* as basic in all the families. By contrast, the vowel relationships in the Indo-European languages were extensively examined to arrive at current analyses. To illustrate the difficulties, as well as the error of assuming the vowel *a* as basic in Indo-European, Hirt pointed out that any of the five short vowels of Greek may correspond to Sanskrit *a* (1921: 1).

Sanskrit		*Greek*	
ájati		ágei	"leads"
catvằras		téttares, písures	"four"
jámbhas	"tooth"	gómbhos	"nail, peg"
nákta-		núks	"night"

It is scarcely credible to assume that, over the much longer interval assumed between Proto-Nostratic and the various proto-languages of numerous families assumed to be reflexes of it, we would be able to posit retention of the same vowels in each of those proto-languages.

Moreover, the families selected as originating in Nostratic are not the same among all Nostraticists. Some are dubious: for example, the "Altaic panel" brought to the workshop on linguistic change and reconstruction methodology in 1987 came to the conclusion that "Proto-Altaic, at best [is] a premature hypothesis and a pragmatically poor foundation on which to build a sustained research program. . . . [Further,] that perpetuating the term "Altaic" probably does more harm than good" (in Baldi 1990: 479, 481; see also Miller in Lamb and Mitchell 1991: 293–327). Yet, as noted above, Altaic is one of the "language families" used for reconstructing Nostratic.

Similar doubts have been expressed in dealing with the Amerindian languages. In spite of a time depth of more than ten millennia, all but Eskimo-Aleut and Na-dene are taken as reflexes of the same proto-language. The hypothesis of a single origin has attracted massive criticism, as well as acclaim among journalists and nonlinguists, but is also strongly upheld by its proponents (see Baldi 1990: 23–6 and Ruhlen in Lamb and Mitchell 1991: 328–52).

In view of the concern, Matisoff was invited to discuss "mass comparison" (1990: 106–20). Citing examples from languages other than Amerindian or the supposed Nostratic, Matisoff illustrates the inadequacies of mass comparison with examples from languages of southeast Asia.

He reiterates the finding from applications of glottochronology that loss in languages obscures cognates so completely in 6,000 or more years that they cannot be distinguished from accidental resemblances, whether among roots or grammatical morphemes. The verbal endings or expression of negation utilized by Dolgopolsky would then be open to the same difficulties as is the highly reduced set of core words.

In discussing the problems, Matisoff points out with examples that large parts of the core lexicon or basic vocabulary and grammar of a language may be remodeled under the influence of languages with which it comes into contact; see also Austerlitz (in Lamb and Mitchell 1991: 353–64). For Indo-Europeanists it may be well to recall that Bopp proposed a relationship between Indo-European and Indonesian, as no-one would do today. Matisoff then reiterates, if at times with some vehemence, the position maintained by Indo-Europeanists on the basis of previous claims that the procedures used by the Nostraticists and others dealing with remote relationships are limited in their applicability, if at all reliable.

Yet for Indo-European purposes it must be noted that Shevoroshkin and Ramer propose that "Nostratic data" provide a "new understanding of Proto-Indo-European phonology" (in Lamb and Mitchell 1991: 189). Among "problems" they consider solved by reference to Nostratic is the assumption of three tectals rather than two, the source of two laryngeals and the "phonetic" nature of the Indo-European stops (*ibid.*) Such contributions would indeed be welcome, not only for Proto-Indo-European but also for other families in the Nostratic "macrofamily." For acceptance of such "solutions," however, the method of multilateral comparison will have to meet the objections of its critics.

2.9 GENERAL PRINCIPLES OF HISTORICAL-LINGUISTIC STUDY

Research in all fields dealing with social institutions, including language, has demonstrated that such institutions undergo change that limits the period for reliable results through use of any conceivable method for positing items or institutions of six and more millennia in the past. Strong support for such a conclusion may be taken from the modifications that have been accepted for Proto-Indo-European after the availability of data from the Anatolian languages. Little older than the data provided by the Vedas, or even the earliest Greek texts, the Anatolian data have led Indo-Europeanists to modify greatly the reconstructions previously proposed, as will be clear in subsequent chapters. In changing so rapidly, linguistic and other social data differ starkly from biological or physical data, which are now being dated by means of remarkable new methods. By contrast, unless we have data from early periods, the relationships and genealogical classifications that may be determined with any certainty for social institutions have very specific chronological limitations.

Thanks to records from the second millennium before our era, we can reconstruct Proto-Indo-European to a credible degree. Few other language families are privileged with similar early records, so that reconstruction of earlier stages encounters severe difficulties. The conclusions of specialists in such families may be examined in essays of Baldi (1990) and Lamb and Mitchell (1991). Even for the long studied Afro-Asiatic languages the specialists cannot provide a "dependable picture of Proto-Afro-Asiatic" (Baldi 1990: 573; see however Hodge in Lamb and Mitchell 1991: 141–77). Until such a "picture" is available, attempts to relate Indo-European with Afro-Asiatic are highly tentative.

Claims for further genealogical relationships with the Indo-European family must therefore be examined with care. Such attempts must be scrutinized for their chronological applicability as well as the bases on which the reconstructions in other language families have been made. Proto-Indo-European reconstructions rely primarily on strict application of the comparative method, with support from the method of internal reconstruction. The accepted reconstructions are results of the procedures tested during two centuries of rigorous linguistic study.

2.9.1 Descriptive grammars used as bases in historical linguistics

In their study Indo-Europeanists and historical linguists in general rely on grammars that have been produced for descriptive purposes. The grammars of Greek and Latin are based on those produced in classical times; from medieval times similar grammars were produced for the European languages, such as Aelfric's for Old English. Based on a long tradition, the grammars are referred to as traditional.

Traditional grammars identify the sounds of a language, often devoting considerable space to examination of the writing system for proper interpretation of the sound system. They then go on to deal with the morphology, distinguishing between inflectional and derivational morphology, with primary attention generally to inflectional. Thereupon they deal with the syntax, when such a section is included. The lexicon is treated separately. The first edition of the Brugmann and Delbrück *Grundriss* (1886–1900) and Meillet's *Introduction* of 1937 among many other grammars, such as that of Leumann *et al.* (1963–79) for Latin and that of Schwyzer (1939–50) for Greek, follow this format.

In some linguistic study of the past decades, departures have been made from the format of traditional grammars. A deep or underlying syntactic structure was posited, the rules of which were thereupon aligned with those of surface syntactic structure; morphological and phonetic structures were derived by additional rules. In contrast with traditional grammars, the phonological, morphological and syntactic components were closely correlated. A distinct (autonomous) phonemic structure was omitted; instead, systematic phonemes, determined in part by syntactic criteria, are posited.

The approach led to different interpretations, especially of phonological phenomena: for example, by a phonemic approach, Edgerton, following Sievers, assumed a sound change in Proto-Indo-European by which /y/ in specific environments was represented as [i], in others as [iy], and in still others as [y] (1943). Thereupon in the dialects or possibly even in late Proto-Indo-European, the allophones [i] and [y] became distinct phonemes, /i y/. Under a systematic approach, the alternations in Vedic and other dialects were depicted by phonetic rules. Similarly, morphological phenomena were derived from syntactic structures rather than accounted for in a distinct morphological component.

Recently, younger linguists in the generative school who have dealt extensively with actual languages have returned to a format like that of traditional grammar. For example, Sadock states explicitly of his approach:

> The idea that grammar consists of parallel organizational principles is really quite a traditional point of view. This orientation resembles, in broad outlook, the sort of view that underlies descriptive grammars of the last century, where one finds the discussion divided into more or less independent sections called something like "phonology," "flexion," "word building," and "syntax."
>
> (1990: 5)

Phonology and morphology then are treated as distinct levels, or in Sadock's term "realms," as are syntax and logical semantics (i.e. relationships among linguistic elements rather than those between linguistic elements, e.g. *horse*, and objects in the outside world). The lexicon is handled apart from these realms, containing "the basic vocabulary for each of the modules and information as to the structural properties of each lexical item with respect to the several autonomous components" (*ibid.* 29). As part of the interface, it plays a central role "in associating representations from different modules" (*ibid.* 36). No underlying form or deep structure is proposed.

Apart from greater attention to formalism, this format is very similar to that of traditional grammar. With some shift of terminology, the approach is that of the eminent historical linguists, Brugmann, Delbrück, Sievers, Meillet and others.

It is clear then that the standard handbooks can continue to be utilized with assurance. The segments that have become obsolescent were superseded largely by the discovery of new information, like that provided for phonology by the Anatolian languages. Historical-linguistic study will continue to rely on the methods developed and improved over the course of two centuries. Modifications in the format for representing the results are advantageous if they assist in understanding the data in their development.

3 The standard handbooks

3.1 HANDBOOKS FOLLOWING THE NEOGRAMMARIAN MANIFESTO

The formulation of strict theory and the solution of many problems that had baffled the early Indo-Europeanists prepared the way for a large number of publications in the last half of the nineteenth century. By the end of the century the field had attracted many capable and highly trained scholars. They were editing the important texts and producing handbooks, many of which are used today after numerous editions.

For the first time in its long tradition, the *Rigveda* was published, to the initial consternation of the Brahmins; subsequently, on recognizing that they could no longer count on oral preservation by means of dedicated young men, they were grateful to Max Müller and others who kept their sacred text from loss. We still make use of Müller's text with its representation of the *Rigveda* in both the pada or word-by-word form and the samhita or phrasal form, as well as of the transliterated text by Aufrecht. Editions of other important texts have also remained definitive, such as Sievers's of the manuscripts of the Old Saxon *Heliand*, and his edition of the Old High German *Tatian*, among careful editions of central texts in many of the languages. Moreover, grammars, dictionaries and other monographs on specific topics were being published. Journals were established to circulate the latest findings: in addition to Kuhn's, the journal of the Indogermanische Gesellschaft, with its review section that led to an annual bibliography. Similar developments could be cited in other countries, France, Great Britain, Italy, Russia, the Scandinavian countries, the United States, though there is no question that Germany, especially Leipzig, was the center of linguistic and Indo-European studies.

The time was right for production of syntheses, or in the German term *Grundrisse* "compendia." These were undertaken in a variety of fields, such as Germanic, Indic, Iranian and Romance studies. For Indo-European linguistics the responsibility was assumed by two scholars, Karl Brugmann and Berthold Delbrück. The field was and remains highly

Sources for this chapter: Brugmann (1897–1916); Delbrück (1893–1900); Hirt (1921–37); Meillet (1937); Szemerényi (1970 [1989]).

fortunate in their decision to undertake the reponsibility. Their work will never be surpassed because of the accuracy of its information and its care in presenting it, as well as cautiously proposed hypotheses in attempts at explanation. To evaluate these properly, we must note the principles they applied, as well as the difficulties they were faced with.

3.1.1 Brugmann's systematic approach

Probably the most important principle is a self-imposed limitation of the authors. In the first paragraph of the preface to the second edition of his *Grundriss* Brugmann states that a scientific grammar should be presented from a historical point of view (1897: ix); but he continues that the time is not yet at hand for such a presentation, and accordingly he has selected a systematic approach. That is to say, he does not determine the older as opposed to the more recent phonological characteristics of the proto-language, and similarly the morphological data; instead, he simply lists all the elements that can be determined. In much the same way Meillet states that his *Introduction* is not a grammar (1937: viii). He too provides a sketch of the phonological and grammatical material. This approach has been maintained in the standard handbooks, through Hirt's, even though he called it a grammar, to the presumable replacement by the Winter publishing firm under the editorship of Kurylowicz, now Mayrhofer, and the recent "Introduction" of Szemerényi. Although these handbooks are important, and will remain so, those using them need to understand the fundamental principle adopted by their authors with regard to their presentation.

In treating some elements the traditional linguists may point out archaic features: for example, the inflection of root nouns is known to be older than that of the thematic nouns, and similarly the root verbs as opposed to the thematic verbs. However, Indo-European is treated as a kind of storehouse. Elements are identified by form. If there are formal differences, as in declensions, the elements or sets are treated under a different rubric. As a result, Brugmann arrived at a huge list of phonological elements and also a large number of nominal inflections; the other handbooks include almost as many, as we note below (see 7.1).

A further matter of presentation has to do with citation of authorities. In his preface to the first edition (1886), Brugmann states that the field is already too extensive to allow presentation of the various points of view that have been expressed, or to list every scholar who has made any contribution. Rather, he has decided to present what he considers correct or probably correct. Such firmness a century ago arouses feelings of envy today, when one compares the subsequent publications, many of whose authors take great pride in their contributions and expect to be included in bibliographical lists. Szemerényi takes a totally different approach. He criticizes both those like Meillet who list bibliography in appendices and also Brugmann, who, according to him is selective in his references. He presumably solves the difficulty by listing all references that are credible, whether agreeing with his own views or not (1970 [1989]: xii). By his view this procedure is more honest and more useful to the reader. But a page or more of highly abbreviated references on a specific point creates its own problems, especially when the references are to collections for which no editor is listed. While adequate bibliographies take a good bit of space, any attempt to evade them puts great burdens on users. Yet, even more than in Brugmann's day, bibliographies in handbooks cannot be complete because of the huge volume of publication.

Although Brugmann did not provide exhaustive bibliographies, he made a point of citing unsolved problems, both so that others might set out to solve them and in awareness of the advances that had been made earlier by such attention. At least in his view, his own hypotheses were advanced to prompt additional attention by others.

3.1.2 The format and theoretical bases of the *Grundrisse*

The content, and arrangement, of a compendium like that Brugmann undertook with Delbrück were also a matter of considerable concern to him. The first edition, published in five volumes from 1886–1900, follows a straightforward framework, in which the phonology, the inflectional and derivational morphology and the syntax are distinct, the last presented by Delbrück. Within a decade, however, Brugmann questioned that framework, so that the second edition was entirely his own; as one result, the three volumes on syntax that were published from 1893–1900 were not redone and have not been superseded. In his second edition Brugmann intended to provide a syntactic treatment, but was unable to achieve more than a treatise on "the simple sentence" that was published posthumously (1925). However, his first two segments were massively expanded, especially the morphology, which came to consist of four volumes, including not only a presentation of the forms but also of their uses or functions. The decision to deal with their uses in connection with the forms took over a great deal of the material from the former sections on syntax. Delbrück's role would therefore have been greatly diminished; he turned to other interests, producing important studies on Germanic syntax.

The shift in presentation must have resulted from a great deal of thought, which is formulated in the prefaces to the second edition (1897) and to Brugmann's "Short comparative grammar of the Indo-Germanic languages" (dated 27 October 1903). In view of inaccurate impressions concerning linguistics at the time, some additional points might be noted.

First, it is often stated that linguistic study neglected syntax before some fancied year, say 1957 or 1964. The statement may be countered by examining the allotment of space in the "Short grammar" but even more so Delbrück's massive treatment in the first edition of the *Grundriss*, following his several monographs on syntax. The "short comparative grammar," after an introduction of 31 pages, and 248 further pages devoted to phonology, including sentence intonation, followed by 342 to morphology, including uses of forms, allotted 83 pages to syntax that dealt largely with sentence structures.

Moreover, in presenting his views on language, Brugmann states repeatedly that the sentence is the basic linguistic unit, going so far as to say that "all scientific consideration in the study of language is study of the sentence [*Satzlehre*], because speaking is always done in sentences" (1904a: 623, see also 281–2). He goes on to point out that linguists deal with words and phrases as well as sentences for adequacy as well as clarity of presentation; yet words are by no means frozen, for among other things speakers manipulate the language according to their own views, as coinages of new words like "the teens" illustrates (1904a: 281). Brugmann's view of language is therefore not unlike that of linguists today.

Further, he deals with language as a structure. Meillet is generally cited for his characterization of language as a structure in which everything is interrelated, and Saussure is credited with guiding linguists to a structural approach. Brugmann, however, states pointedly in the preface he wrote in 1903 that "language is a highly complex human activity in which the most varied factors are coordinated in mutual dependence on the whole, and in which basically everything is conditioned by everything else" (1904a: viii). He could scarcely have stated more emphatically a structural conception of language. We may also recall that Friedrich Schlegel in one of the earliest publications in the Indo-European field was primarily concerned with determining the innermost structure of language. The view of language as a structure is therefore by no means recent, but was held through the entire period of Indo-European linguistic study, even though it may not have been applied by all Indo-Europeanists.

Yet it is also important to be aware of restrictions that Brugmann imposed on himself, and of his realization that his work would be superseded just as his own replaces that of predecessors – those of Bopp and Schleicher.

In keeping with his structural conception of language Brugmann quotes approvingly a criticism of the neogrammarian approach by Schuchardt, who is often held up as an early representative of the opponents to neogrammarian theory. In the quotation Schuchardt asks about the purpose of the "thousands of sound laws" if they are stated in isolation and not related to "higher orders"; for linguists must look for universals, and also apply their findings to clarification of human and cultural interrelationships. In this way Brugmann, while presenting details and individual facts, kept in mind the wider purposes of Indo-European linguistics. Though he graciously gives credit to Schuchardt, the position is essentially the one he had presented in his essay of 1878 on regarding language realistically.

In dealing specifically with Indo-European linguistics, Brugmann states as his goal the study of the development of all languages in the family from the earliest ascertainable periods – the time of the proto-society – until today, in all their differentiation (1897: 29). Yet in view of the breadth of such a field, Indo-European studies actually restrict themselves to the earliest periods of the individual languages, and to the proto-language, leaving later developments to specialists in the various subgroups.

Concentrating so specifically on Brugmann, this section may seem to be representing only one scholar of the time and his views. However, both the *Grundriss* and the short grammar were adopted by Indo-Europeanists as standard handbooks, and have remained so, indicating their representative status. The basis for their acceptance was not only Brugmann's amazing knowledge, coupled with his capacity for careful and accurate presentation. He also continued to deal with general linguistic problems. Published in academic series, his monographs are unfortunately overlooked by subsequent linguists who examine the same topics. Thus his monograph on "Expressions for totality" of 1894 is not cited in Sapir's brief monograph on the same topic (1930). And the monograph on deixis (1904b) is similarly disregarded by current scholars publishing on the topic. Because Brugmann was well informed and imaginative in his treatment of such theoretical matters, much that he published has not been superseded even though new data have been made available since his publications.

3.1.3 Shortcomings of Brugmann's *Grundriss*

The *Grundriss* has shortcomings, in part because of decisions made by its author. As he hoped, these have been noted and addressed by his successors. One of the earliest shortcomings to be treated by them is the reconstruction of elements whenever there seemed to be reflexes in the ancient dialects. It was apparently Brugmann's strict reliance on the comparative method, coupled with his systematic approach, that required reconstruction if parallel items are found in several languages. His structuralism also contributed to this result, for he assumed parallelism among the items in a set. For example, since there was evidence for a fourfold set of obstruents at each position of articulation, e.g. *t th d dh*, when dental fricatives were proposed, a similar fourfold set was reconstructed, *þ þh ð ðh*. Somewhat similarly, a complete panoply of long vocalic resonants was reconstructed for the proto-language (1897: 92). As a result, the phonological system includes a large number of members. Applying structural principles somewhat differently, Meillet reduced the inventory of phonological units considerably (1937: 85–126).

As a second shortcoming, Brugmann's treatment of ablaut leaves much to be desired; he himself was unhappy with it. Here the basic problem consisted in reconstruction of all elements for the proto-language without positing earlier stages, once again in accordance with his systematic approach. The proto-language then is a kind of storehouse. Hirt criticized

Brugmann for his inadequate treatment of ablaut, and took as one of his own major aims solution of ablaut variation and its sources, to provide thereupon a somewhat different set of vocalic elements for the proto-language. And shortly after Hirt published his phonological conclusions (1921), Kurylowicz related the widely disregarded coefficients (laryngeals) to problems in vocalism (1927), providing clarification of at least some of the major difficulties and eventually a far simpler vocalic system.

3.1.4 Further handbooks

Nonetheless, by the time of publication of the last volume of the second edition of the *Grundriss* (1916), Indo-Europeanists had available a secure collection of data, with hypotheses on difficulties, and stimuli to further publication. Brugmann's compendium is clear and comprehensive. Anyone dealing with a problem could go to it for details on related data and proposed solutions. Although the First World War interfered with scholarship, it seemed as though Indo-European studies had reached almost a definitive stage as the major figures of the neogrammarian move-ment were leaving the scene. Hirt's grammar in seven volumes is largely a rearrangement of the data in Brugmann's *Grundriss*, except for Hirt's contributions on ablaut (1921–37). Meillet's introduction is a carefully composed parallel to Brugmann's short grammar (1937, 8th edn). Szemerényi's introduction is restricted to phonology and inflectional mor-phology (1970 [1989]). The presumable replacement to Hirt's grammar by the same publisher under initial editorship by Kurylowicz consists of a series of unrelated volumes (1968, etc.). All these handbooks are essen-tially comparative compendia like Brugmann's. The more recent include some new data, as on the Anatolian languages and the laryngeals. But much of their work simply recapitulates that of Brugmann.

Since Brugmann's collections of data and his formulations represent a careful compendium of a century of intense devotion to Indo-European studies, the *Grundriss* and the short grammar have by no means been replaced. Details have been modified, and supplemented, by data from the Anatolian languages, from Tocharian and from Mycenaean Greek, and occasional other welcome sources, such as the Celtic inscriptions of Spain. Taking these into account, linguists today may use the formulations of Brugmann and his contemporaries for reanalysis by improved theoretical methods, applied with a historical approach.

3.2 THE INDO-EUROPEAN FAMILY

By the last quarter of the nineteenth century the members of the family had been identified, and fairly well documented. The classification had not been straightforward, for especially one reason: linguists placed undue weight on the lexicon in sorting out the interrelations. For this reason

Armenian had long been considered an Iranian dialect, in view of its many loanwords from Persian. It was only in the last part of the century that Hübschmann pointed to distinctive characteristics that were unique to Armenian, such as changes in obstruents somewhat comparable to those in Germanic. The basis for his recognition should have made it clear once again that characteristics of the grammatical system, including the phonological component, are far more reliable than are lexical elements in establishing genetic relationships. Yet even today scholars who seek distant relationships rely heavily, some exclusively, on the lexicon.

At about the same time Albanian came to be better known. It also includes many borrowings, and in addition is attested only from the nineteenth century, apart from a few earlier texts; accordingly it was long overlooked. But distinct characteristics were now noted in it, such as the change of PIE *e* to *o*, and the presence of voiced stops after nasals where the proto-language has voiceless, as in *dhëndër* "son-in-law" from PIE **gomH-ter-*. Once again phonological criteria indicated a distinct subgroup. By the end of the century then, eight subgroups or dialects were recognized for the family: Indo-Iranian, Armenian, Balto-Slavic, Albanian, Greek, Italic, Celtic, Germanic.

Views on their interrelationships, however, were disputed. Italic and Celtic were often classed together; they share phonological features, such as the shift of g^w in some forms to *b*, as in Latin *bōs*, Old Irish *bō* "cow" and also morphological features, such as *s*-forms in the preterite. Moreover, the Osco-Umbrian dialects of Italic show intriguing similarities with the Britannic dialects of Celtic and the Latin–Faliscan with the Goidelic. Some scholars then assumed one subgroup, Italo-Celtic, in the post-Indo-European period, but this view has never been widely maintained.

Such a view has, however, been persistent with regard to Balto-Slavic. Brugmann assumes such a subgroup as one of the eight he posits. Among other shared characteristics, treatment of vocalic resonants is parallel in each. Both also share an innovation in having a definite declension of the adjective made by suffixing PIE **-yo-*. Both make the genitive of *o*-stems with a form parallel to the ablative **-ōd* ending as maintained in Sanskrit. Both use PIE **to-* rather than **so-* in the demonstrative. The shared characteristics therefore are greater than those in the rejected Italo-Celtic. Yet the question of Balto-Slavic unity is unsettled even today, even though individual scholars maintain strong views on each side of the question.

Determining the various subgroups accordingly required a great deal of attention, yet the eight subgroups of Brugmann's handbooks, nine if Baltic and Slavic are regarded as distinct subgroups, have been maintained. Other languages, such as Thraco-Phrygian and Venetic, are so poorly attested that they provide few data for comparative studies. The chief efforts involved in dealing with them have to do with interpretation of the texts rather than seeking additional insights into the parent language.

Besides identification of the various subgroups, their interrelationships were also examined. Brugmann was aware that shared characteristics might be ascribed either to maintenance of earlier composite subgroups or to areal relationships. Yet apart from the classification into satem and centum subgroups, he cautiously avoided hypotheses on other early groupings.

But he assumed a society that maintained the proto-language, and he contemplated the possible locations of their homeland. In his view the earlier assumption of a homeland in Asia was giving way to one in Europe, or in the border regions of southwest Asia and Europe. Yet he saw little hope of more specific location for that homeland than somewhere in a broad band from France through central Europe to Iran (1897: 22). By Brugmann's view, somewhere in this area the speakers at one time communicated in one language that might be viewed something like the Bavarian dialect of German; he apparently chose Bavarian in the knowledge that it was by no means without variation in his day. His conception of Proto-Indo-European is then comparable to a dialect continuum, in Diakonoff's term.

Moreover, Brugmann also assumed differentiation already within the proto-language, with changes in some areas developing spontaneously or through influence from other languages. The change of tectal stops to sibilants in the satem languages he ascribed tentatively to the effect of indigenous speakers who gave up their own language in favor of an Indo-European (1904a: 25). While later Indo-Europeanists may differ from Brugmann in details, as concerning the homeland, he had achieved a position that is remarkably close to that held today, though scholars today attempt to be more precise in identifying the early location.

Brugmann also held that, as the number of speakers increased and their territory was expanded in size, the proto-language came to be differentiated to the groups that are historically attested. Those speaking proto-languages like Proto-Indo-Iranian and Proto-Greek in turn gradually differentiated their language, in time to the varieties we know. Brugmann was well aware of the findings of dialect geography that had been secured through several decades of work; following them, he assumed that Proto-Indo-European had developed somewhat as had Proto-Germanic or as did Vulgar Latin into the Romance languages.

There is little to criticize about Brugmann's assumptions in view of the materials available at his time. Even before all volumes of the *Grundriss* were published, however, Hittite and Tocharian materials had been discovered that were to modify its conclusions. Hirt and Meillet were aware of the two new subgroups, but did not modify Brugmann's basic conclusions about the proto-language nor about its characteristics with data from them. Publication of the texts, and thereupon analysis of the characteristics, took some time, so that the data from the two additional subgroups were only available shortly before Brugmann's death, long after the initial publication of Meillet's *Introduction* and not long before Hirt's initial volume was published in 1921. Modifications in the classification of the subgroups and their early interrelationships were then left to others.

3.3 BASES OF THE PHONOLOGICAL SYSTEM

The reconstructed phonological system proposed at the end of the nineteenth century was based on straightforward application of the comparative method. If distinct elements were found in three or more languages, especially Greek, Sanskrit and Latin, a reconstruction was made for Proto-Indo-European.

Moreover, a symmetrical system was assumed, and all points in it filled. There was accordingly no hesitation about positing PIE *b* even though Schleicher and already Grimm had recognized its infrequency, especially in initial position. And since palatal and velar series of stops were reconstructed, nasals were proposed alongside them, not only consonantal but also vocalic, short and long. Brugmann took a further step; he distinguished an [o] that varied with [e], as in Greek *pod-*, Latin *ped-* "foot," from one that did not, as in Greek *óis*, Latin *ovis* "sheep"; the nonablauting element he represented with **å*. This reconstruction provides another example of his systematic approach.

The various handbooks include copious examples, providing them for the phonological entities in medial as well as initial position. And the entities are listed in varied arrangements, as well as with varied diacritics, as for the palatal tectals. Since these are readily reconciled, we may follow the arrangement and representation adopted by Szemerényi for summarizing the phonological system (1970 [1989]: 37).

3.3.1 Vowels, diphthongs, and resonants

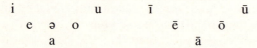

Diphthongs with *i* and *u* as second member were assumed for long and short *e, o, a*, though Szemerényi accepts only *āi ōi*, and *ēu ōu*, and these only in inflectional endings.

In addition, six resonants were posited, two semivowels *w y*, two liquids *l r*, and two nasals *m n*, though Brugmann and others also posited palatal and velar nasals. Moreover, all of these were assumed to have long and short vocalic variants: those for *w y* are *u i*; the others are short and long vocalic versions of however many further resonants were posited. Szemerényi includes short and long vocalic *r l m n* in his section on the phonology (1970 [1989]: 46–52), listing them as well in his phonological system (*ibid.* 71–2).

All of these phonological elements were determined by use of the comparative method, with no attention to their distribution; when it was taken into consideration, as by Meillet, the number of elements was reduced. If we disregard palatal and velar nasals, the set consisted of eleven vowels, eight further vocalic resonants, twelve diphthongs and six consonantal resonants. In the chapters on phonology, we will examine the evidence for these elements, and also modifications in approach that reduce their number even beyond the reduction by Meillet.

3.3.2 The obstruents

The obstruent system proposed in the standard handbooks is also based entirely on the comparative method. Yet it too is extended in several sets, in spite of limited evidence.

Aspirated voiceless stops are assumed almost entirely on the basis of items in Indo-Iranian, such as Sanskrit *ratha-* "chariot." It is cognate with Latin *rota*, Lithuanian *rātas*, Old High German *rad* "wheel," none of which include evidence for aspiration. Some, though not all, cognates of Sanskrit words with voiceless aspirate after *s* do include such evidence. The set of voiceless aspirates then was reconstructed largely in accordance with the systematic principles applied by Brugmann among others.

Another problem in reconstruction concerns the tectals. When we survey the various languages we find evidence for palatals, velars, and labio-velars. Yet no dialect provides evidence for all three. In general, the palatals, e.g. k', and the velars, e.g. k, exhibit the same reflexes in the centum languages, i.e. k; but the velars, e.g. k, and the labio-velars, e.g. k^w, exhibit the same reflexes in the satem languages, e.g. k. The handbooks, with the exception of Meillet's, posit three sets for the proto-language. Meillet proposes for Indo-European the system of the centum languages, assuming that palatal variants arose in these before front vowels. Kurylowicz is virtually alone in assuming that the labio-velars arose from velars in the centum languages; by his hypothesis the parent language includes only palatals and velars (1935: 1–26). Even today, consensus on the Indo-European system has not been reached, although that proposed by Meillet accords best with assumptions based on findings of dialect geography.

A third problem concerns fricatives. The sibilant s is extensively attested, and also a voiced variant before voiced stops; Brugmann then proposed for sibilants, *s sh z zh*. Later handbooks do not, listing only *s*, with two allophones, [s] and [z].

A further problem that has been extensively treated has to do with the analysis of consonant combinations in words of the common vocabulary, especially two, those for "earth" and "bear." Sanskrit *kṣam-* has as cognate in Greek *khthṓn* "earth," in Latin *humus*, in Old Church Slavic *zemlja*. In accordance with the procedure of reconstructing an etymon for every distinct element, an interdental fricative ð was added to the set of obstruents. Since in the word for "bear" Greek has a voiceless stop cluster, e.g. Sanskrit *ŗkṣa-*, Greek *árktos*, a voiceless member of the set was also reconstructed. Brugmann then lists a second set of fricatives, aspirates as well as simple elements: *þ þh ð ðh*. Because of the small number of words including any of these, the set has always been treated hesitantly. As we will see below, Hittite provided data that are generally assumed to have resolved the problem.

The total set of obstruents proposed by Brugmann is as follows:

	Stops					*Fricatives*		
	Voiceless	*Voiceless aspirates*	*Voiced*	*Voiced aspirates*	*Voiceless*	*Voiceless aspirates*	*Voiced*	*Voiced aspirates*
Labials	p	ph	b	bh				
Dentals	t	th	d	dh	þ	þh	ð	ðh
Palatals	k′	k′h	g′	g′h	s	sh	z	zh
Velars	k	kh	g	gh				
Labio-velar	kʷ	kʷh	gʷ	gʷh				

Szemerényi omits the fricatives other than *s*, taking *z* to be a variant of it and the dental fricatives to be results of combinatory phenomena.

3.3.3 Accent

As we have noted above, Verner's solution to the third set of exceptions to Grimm's rules demonstrated that Germanic had had a variable accent. Exact parallels with Vedic were found in the preterite of strong verbs. Among examples are Old High German *zeh : zigum*, Vedic *didéśa : didiśimá* "indicate, point out" from the PIE root **deyk-*. The demonstration of variable accent with Germanic data was significant, because Greek indeed had variable accent but with its own rules; similarly, Lithuanian and the Slavic languages with variable accent did not match that of Vedic.

From Indic grammarians it was known that the Vedic accent was musical, that is, it was a pitch rather than a stress accent. Because the Germanic dialects have a strong stress accent that was fixed, their accentuation no longer provides evidence to corroborate that in Vedic; but the pitch accent of Greek and Balto-Slavic supports the assumption that Vedic accent represents that of late Proto-Indo-European in type as well as variability. Moreover, the maintenance of unaccented vowels in the early dialects, including Germanic, is in accord with the treatment of vocalic elements in languages with pitch accent; Germanic then indirectly supported the assumption that Proto-Indo-European had a variable pitch accent.

Brugmann and his contemporaries dealt with accent as found in three segments: syllables, words, clauses/sentences. Evidence for accent in each was taken largely from the accentual systems of Vedic and Greek, supplemented by inferences from poetic meter, and from treatment of vowels.

3.3.3.1 Syllable accent

In dealing with syllabic accent, attention was given to the difference between acute and circumflex accent, as in Greek and Lithuanian. It was recognized that evidence in Greek could be taken only from final syllables because of the shift to restriction of accent on one of the three final syllables of words. Evidence also from Vedic led to the identification of acute accent as a high pitch followed by falling pitch on the next syllable. Named *Stosston* "falling accent," it contrasted with circumflex, referred to as *Schleifton* "slurred accent," which was assumed to involve a shift from high to low within the syllable. To account for these patterns, the notion of mora was introduced. A mora is defined as the length of a short vowel.

Short vowels could have only acute accent. Long vowels and diphthongs might consist of two or three morae; two-morae vowels or diphthongs could receive either the acute accent or the circumflex, but only the circumflex fell on three-morae vowels and diphthongs. All three-morae syllables were assumed to be secondary, lengthened because of the loss of a following vowel or resonant, or because of vowel contraction, e.g. Greek accusative *bôm*, Vedic *gâm* "cow" < PIE *$g^w\hat{o}um$*.

Reconstruction of the accent system in Indo-European remains one of the most difficult phonological problems because the branches have shifted to a variety of systems. While Proto-Indo-European had free accent that might fall on any syllable, in the dialects other than Vedic the position of the accent is restricted to certain syllables. Moreover, most of the dialects have shifted from a pitch to a stress accent. In the attempt to determine the accent in the proto-language, the notion of mora has been maintained; but long vowels are assumed to consist of only two morae. The difference between acute and circumflex accent is assumed to lie in the segment of the vowel that has higher pitch – if the initial, acute or falling, if the second, circumflex or rising accent.

3.3.3.2 Word accent

In treatment of word accent, the most important issue is its location; for within paradigms it could shift. In the oldest inflection of verbs, the athematic, the base is accented in the singular, the ending in the plural, cf. Sanskrit *ás-mi*, *s-más* "I am, we are." Similarly in the perfect; that shift is ultimately responsible for the difference in vowel and final consonant in English *was* : *were*, cf. Greek *oîda*, *ísmen* "I know, we know." Recent concerted attention to accent has clarified the patterns in nominal inflection (Szemerényi 1970 [1989]: 170–1). The location of word accent has been pretty well determined; it is disputed only when data are lacking for individual words or morphological sets.

3.3.3.3 Sentence accent

Clause and sentence accent presents a further problem because writing systems do not indicate it. Yet the accentuation of the finite verb in Vedic provides a clue. In independent clauses the finite verb is unaccented when not initial. Since verbs stand in final position in unmarked clauses and sentences, it may be concluded that clause and sentence accent was characterized by a drop in pitch on their final elements.

This conclusion could be supported by the position of alliteration in Germanic verse. A long line consists of two half-lines; alliteration in each indicates the location of metrical stress. The first half-line may have two alliterative syllables, but the second has only one; its last section invariably does not include an alliterative syllable, suggesting that the long line was based on a simple sentence, as it often is in the earliest Germanic verse, where stichic lines are common. Finite verbs are typically placed in the last metrical position (non-alliterating) of the second half-line. Since metrical principles often maintain archaisms, it could be assumed that verbs occupy this position because they were unaccented when so placed; further, that the Germanic clause ended with a falling accent, much like the Vedic clause.

As an example, we may cite the runic inscription on one of the horns found at Gallehus, which is noteworthy also because of its maintenance of unstressed vowels; it is generally dated about AD 325.

Ek	Hlewagastiz	holtijaz	horna	tawido
I	Hliugast	of Holt	horn	made

By the time metrical principles were formulated in the Germanic area, accent occupied the first syllable of words. Choice of the initial sound for the two nouns and the descriptive epithet in this inscription, which has the form of a Germanic long metrical line, indicates location of the stronger accents, and conversely the lesser accent on the verb.

Other elements in the clause as well were used to make inferences about sentence intonation, and also word accent, in the proto-language. As in many languages, particles are weakly stressed. They typically stand in second syntactic position in the clause or sentence, as Wackernagel pointed out in an influential article of 1892. When Indo-European shifted from its OV order, the finite verb was placed in second position in declarative clauses, in accordance both with its lack of accent and with the second position for unaccented items. On the other hand, in typically marked syntactic patterns such as commands and questions, verbs stand initially and are accented.

Through approaches like those indicated here, the accentual system of late Proto-Indo-European was pretty well determined. But the patterning of some derivatives from roots suggested that at an earlier stage the language had stress accent, not pitch. In this way, as noted earlier, the loss of vowels, as in **nist-*, could be accounted for.

Since pitch and stress accentual systems are generally distinguished sharply, the shift from one system to another may seem difficult to support. In his explanation of the difference between the two types of systems, Roman Jakobson concluded that an accent system is perceived as based on pitch if the extent of accent covers only a part of the syllabic element, or one of two or more morae; if, by contrast, it covers the entire syllabic element, it is perceived as a stress accent system. The distinction between the two types may then not be great, so that shifts from one to the other type need not seem inexplicable.

As these statements may suggest, the brief treatment of accent in Brugmann's *Grundriss* (1897: 946–54) was generally accepted, but expanded and supplemented by further understanding of suprasegmental phenomena in language.

3.4 MORPHOPHONEMIC VARIATION OF VOWELS; ABLAUT

One of the characteristic features of the Indo-European languages is the vowel variation in derivatives from a root. Found especially in the verbal system, it applies to derived nouns as well, as in examples like *sing*, *sang*, *sung*, *song*. Accounting for it long baffled linguists, as we noted in Grimm's attention to the consonants but his despair about the vowels. The difficulties for the early linguists resulted from various causes. Among them, the assumption of Sanskrit as representing in great part the parent language long hindered proper understanding of its system, especially the vowels. In Sanskrit one vowel, *a*, in short and long form corresponds to three in Greek, short and long *e a o*, and to two in many of the other subgroups. No rules to account for a putative shift of *a* to the vowels of the other dialects could be determined; yet the prestige of Sanskrit was long weighted more heavily than the inability to account for division of **a* to **e a o*.

Moreover, in their own efforts to account for the variation of vocalic elements in roots, the Indian grammarians assumed a set of "grades" with *i*, *u* and the other vocalic resonants as basic vowels for many roots, and from *a* or even zero in other roots. Since the vowels of the Germanic languages, or of Latin, could often not be directly correlated with those of Greek, and certainly not those of Sanskrit, the problem long escaped even the beginnings of a solution.

Only when the "law of palatals" made it clear that Sanskrit had once included an *e* vowel did the earlier system become apparent (see 1.3.2). By the "law," velars are replaced by palatals before Sanskrit *a* that corresponds to *e* in other dialects; examples are the reduplicating syllables of the perfect in *cakára* from the root *kṛ-* "make" and *jagáma* from the root *gam* "go." The earlier forms would have been **ke-kor-e* and **gʷe-gʷom-e* > Proto-Indo-Iranian **ge-gom-e*. The law is an example of a discovery that occurs to a numbers of scholars at approximately the same time. Linguists had become aware of the importance of scrutinizing elements in relation to one another, as illustrated by the solutions of the exceptions to Grimm's law. While Pedersen gives priority of discovery to his countryman, Vilhelm Thomsen (1931: 290), Hermann Collitz claimed it. Besides illustrating the advanced state of Indo-European studies, the discovery made it clear that Indic at one time had the *e*-vowel and that it could no longer be taken as primary source for reconstructing the parent language. In this way it was Indo-Iranian that provided decisive evidence for assuming earlier *e a o*. A five-vowel system was then proposed for the parent language.

Moreover, *e* was taken as basic vowel of roots, as by Saussure in 1879. Theories to account for the vowel variations in ablaut were then proposed, especially by Hirt although publication on ablaut by others as well was voluminous. In the course of time a consensus was pretty well reached on the changes that had taken place, as of *e* to *ē*, *e* to zero, and *e* to *o*, as well as the sets of forms incorporating the changed elements. Moreover, the changes were ascribed to shifts in accentuation. Yet many problems remained in determining the interrelationships of the attested vowels.

In attempts to solve some of these, an additional ablaut grade, the so-called reduced grade, was assumed in addition to zero grade. And because roots and bases that included laryngeals remained opaque, long vowels resulting from merger of laryngeals with short vowels could not be clearly distinguished from long vowels that resulted from lengthening by ablaut; they had fallen together in the parent language. Accounts of the morphophonemic variations in the vowel system were therefore highly complex. Rather than present these here, we limit ourselves to these generalizations and treat ablaut below as it is currently understood.

Apart from the results of ablaut, we distinguish relatively few morphophonemic changes in the parent language. Meillet assumed "autonomy" of the word, so that there are few modifications in sequences other than for enclitic particles. A pitch accent would not bring about massive changes of unaccented elements, whether medial or final. Suffixes on verbal and nominal stems then remained transparent until accentual shifts in the dialects led to losses of weakly stressed vowels, with resultant blurring of morphological elements.

3.5 DERIVATIONAL MORPHOLOGY

The structure of words in the early dialects, and in the proto-language, was early understood, in large part thanks to the capable analysis of the Indian grammarians. A word typically consists of a root, a suffix, and an ending (*désinence*, in Meillet's term, 1937: 147). A small number of nominal and of verbal roots have no suffix before the ending; labeled root nouns and verbs, these are assumed to be archaic. They belong to the most frequent items of the vocabulary, such as names of body parts or major natural bodies, like the sun and moon, and verbs indicating movement, such as "come" and "go". Later in the dialects, most of these also came to have suffixes.

Root and suffix form a unit, which Benveniste called theme, Hirt base. The commonest suffix came to be the vowel *e/o*, which is known as the thematic vowel. As noted above, we use the term base. The base expresses lexical meaning; the ending indicates grammatical meaning, e.g. -*m* on masculine nouns the accusative case, on verbs the first person singular.

The language contained a large number of suffixes. Attempts have been made to determine their significance, as by Persson (1912), though after a length of time suffixes tend to develop their own values, which may be quite distinct from their former meaning. Using evidence only from today, for example, it would be difficult to support a relationship between the suffix -*dom* in such words as *kingdom* with the noun *doom*. The function of a suffix in any one dialect may also come to differ from its function in another; the verbal -*ske/o*- suffix, with inchoative meaning in Latin though not in Indo-Iranian and other dialects provides an example.

There were no prefixes in the proto-language. Short adverbial elements or particles may seem to be prefixes, such as the *ni*- in *nist*- "nest," but their accentuation indicates that they are elements of compounds. The language included one infix, *-n-*, which is prominent in verbal derivation. In addition, reduplication was prominent for derivation and especially for verbal inflection.

3.5.1 Derived forms based on ablaut variants

The ablaut variations and the numerous suffixes permit a large number of derivations from any one root; Meillet gives a well-chosen group of examples (1937: 157–65). Here we cite only some forms of the root *sem*- "one, same":

e-grade	Greek *hén* "one",	Gothic *simle* "once"
zero grade	Greek (*s*)*mía* "one",	Armenian *mi* "one"
o-grade	Greek *homós* "same",	Gothic *sama* "same"

Saussure's assumption of the structure CeC for Indo-European roots was generally maintained. But the classic analysis of roots accompanied by possible suffixes was provided only in 1935 by Benveniste. We will present his analysis below (5.1.1, 6.4.1).

3.5.2 Derived forms based on two or more roots

In addition to simple words made up of roots and suffixes, compounding was well established. For the parent language two types of compounds are especially prominent (see also 7.2.2). One type is called *possessive*, or by the Sanskrit term, *bahuvrihi*, literally "much-rice." The meaning of such compounds is "one who possesses something," as here "much rice." They then are exocentric, that is, compounds whose basic meaning differs from that of either of the elements it includes. Few are found in English, such as *Blue-beard* "one who possesses a blue beard," rather than a kind of beard as *blue-bird* refers to a kind of bird.

The second prominent type in the proto-language is called *synthetic*. Compounds of this type represent syntheses of sentences, e.g. Latin *artifex* "artist," literally "art" + "maker." The second element is verbal; the whole is comparable to a clause signifying someone who makes things. These compounds are endocentric; the function of the compound is the same as that of the second element.

In the dialects a different type of endocentric compound came to be most prominent: those like *blue-bird* in which the first element modifies the second; an example is the Greek *akró-polis* "peak-city." They are also endocentric, but, unlike the Indo-European synthetics, the second element is nominal.

Derivational morphology of the parent language is then well understood; the forms that are attested are thoroughly described in the *Grundriss* as well as in later publications. The chief unsolved problems have to do with the origin of specific patterns; solutions may never be possible, because of the well-known fading of the meanings of the suffixed material.

3.6 INFLECTIONAL MORPHOLOGY

The system of inflections was earliest accounted for, as we have noted with reference to Bopp. The reasons are various. Among them, Greek and Latin morphology was thoroughly described and well known by all scholars at the beginning of the nineteenth century. Further, the discrepancies between the morphological systems of these two languages were disclosed on the availability of Sanskrit. Also its inflections are transparent. An inflectional system for Indo-European was then proposed that was a composite of Sanskrit and Greek for the verb. Since the Greek noun is inflected for only five cases, the ampler paradigm of Lithuanian nouns was taken as supporting the assumption for the parent language of the eight found in Sanskrit; Slavic, and Latin with six cases, provided further support. Once again the procedure of assuming the largest possible set was followed.

3.6.1 Nominal inflection

The noun was then assumed to have had eight cases, three numbers and three genders. Some data suggested caution in constructing totally parallel forms in singular and plural; in Vedic, for example, the oblique cases are poorly attested. However, a large system that gradually lost elements was taken as characteristic for the parent language, and accordingly eight plural as well as singular forms were accepted. No more than three dual forms could be assumed.

The paradigm in grammars of Sanskrit was determined by economy in presenting forms; in the dual the instrumental, dative and ablative share one form, as do the genitive and locative. Accordingly, the arrangement is as below, illustrated by the Sanskrit root noun "foot"; in words for which a vocative is made, the form is like that of the nominative.

	Singular	*Dual*	*Plural*
Nominative	pā́t	pā́dau	pā́d-as
Accusative	pā́d-am	pā́dau	pad-ás
Instrumental	pad-ā́	pad-bhyā́m	pad-bhís
Dative	pad-é	pad-bhyā́m	pad-bhyás
Ablative	pad-ás	pad-bhyā́m	pad-bhyás
Genitive	pod-ás	pad-ós	pad-ā́m
Locative	pad-í	pad-ós	pat-sú
Vocative	–		

For the parent language a set of endings was determined that was added to roots and bases of whatever structure. Some modifications were thereupon introduced, as in the nominative singular of Sanskrit with loss of the final -*s*. Further, when preceded by vowels or resonants, the endings came to merge with segments of preceding bases. Accordingly, by the time of the later dialects nominal inflections with a variety of endings developed. These provide a complex set of declensions among the dialects, such as the five of Latin, in which the original inflection is still relatively transparent. Yet even in these dialects, losses of elements, mergers of suffix and ending and the falling together of various patterns obscures the earlier parallelism. Simplification of final clusters leads to the loss of the stem consonant in the Latin nominatives, e.g. *lapi*(*d*)*s* "stone," and with lengthening, *pē*(*d*)*s* "foot"; vowel weakening leads to the obscuring of the stem vowel in *lupus* "wolf" in contrast with Greek *lúkos*, etc. In the course of time, the losses of final syllables in Latin and other languages with stress accent led to massive reductions of nominal inflection.

Adjectives exhibit the same number of forms as nouns, but differ from them in possible inflection through the several genders. Moreover, comparison comes to be restricted to them. Personal and demonstrative pronouns also parallel in inflection the nouns. The endings affixed to them differ in part from those of the nouns, leading to further complexities in the dialects as noun, adjective and pronoun paradigms come to influence one another. The numerals belong to a special class. They will be discussed in 7.8.

3.6.2 Verbal inflection

In accordance with the principles applied by Brugmann and his successors, the verb is fitted out in the standard handbooks with all the categories found in the central dialects. As a result, three voices were reconstructed: active, middle and passive, in spite of the defective paradigm of the passive in the early dialects. Similarly, seven tenses were reconstructed on the basis of Sanskrit, especially with attention to Greek. These are present, imperfect, future, aorist, perfect, pluperfect, future perfect.

Moreover, four moods were proposed: indicative, subjunctive, optative, imperative. Some Indo-Europeanists have included a fifth, the injunctive; the term was devised because the forms are like those of the indicative but the meanings like those of the subjunctive. Its forms are those of the imperfect or aorist, without augment; found only in early texts of Indo-Iranian and Greek, it is now accounted for as a residue of an earlier pattern. Further, as for the noun, three numbers are reconstructed: singular, dual and plural. And finally, three persons.

Finite forms were inflected for these categories. In addition, participles and nominal forms were made from verbal roots and bases; the nominal forms subsequently developed into the infinitives of the several dialects.

3.6.3 Non-inflected elements

Besides these two large sets of inflected forms, the standard handbooks also posit uninflected forms: adpositions, conjunctions, adverbs and particles. The adpositions were placed after nouns, as in Latin *mēcum* "with me," and hence were postpositions; they are maintained as residues in many of the early dialects. The conjunctions, like Latin *-que* "and" were postposed or treated as clitics, like its Greek cognate *te*. The adverbs are often frozen noun forms that provide modifications of verbal or sentential meaning, as for indications of time (today, tomorrow) or place (here, there). The particles carry functions such as indicating nominal relationships, negation and discourse marking.

3.7 SYNTAX

Views on the syntax of the parent language owe a great deal to Delbrück's studies, which drew their conclusions from analysis of Vedic prose (esp. 1878, 1888, 1893–1900). He determined that Vedic sentences were verb-final, a position he also assumed for the proto-language. In addition, he described other syntactic constructions, such as nouns with adpositions; in the earliest Vedic texts these are postpositional, not prepositional. The various constructions were treated as unrelated, however. Confining their attention to the Indo-European family, Delbrück and other linguists at the time did not arrive at a structural conception of syntax.

Syntactic treatments, when included in the standard handbooks, provide syntactic patterns, generally by morphological criteria. Two types of sentences are acknowledged: verbal and nominal. In nominal sentences the verb "be" is generally expected, though in Latin one may find nominal sentences like *Puer bonus* rather than *Puer bonus est* "The boy is good." Brugmann discusses nominal as well as verbal types, continuing with detailed examination of their constituents (1925). In his introduction to this work, he states that "the structure of the sentence at the time of Proto-Indo-European society still remains hypothetical" (1925: 9). He had attempted to arrive at it by conjectures on sentence utterances by primitive man, besides examining the constituents of sentences in the dialects.

Brugmann's treatment of the "simple sentence" consists almost entirely of examples, with no generalizations about the parent language (1925). Meillet's crisper treatment may be characterized as a summary of Delbrück's findings (1937: 355–77). Distinguishing nominal and verbal sentences, with the help of numerous examples, chiefly from Greek, he examines the role of government and agreement. He also notes the devices for expressing negation and interrogation. And, finally, he treats coordination, indicating that it is marked especially by particles. We can have no objections to his conclusions; but he too deals with syntactic constructions independently, so that no relationship is recognized among them. As a notable example, the comparative pattern in which the ablative case of the standard is placed before adjectives in contrast with the comparative pattern of the late dialects is disregarded. An understanding of it, as well as the general structure of syntax, came only through typological studies of the past three decades.

The syntactic treatments in the standard handbooks then are useful for collections of data. But in spite of a great deal of attention to syntax from the last quarter of the nineteenth century, they bear witness to Hirt's mournful statement: "one assembles a series of facts but doesn't know what to do with them" (1931–4 III: vi).

3.8 THE LEXICON

By the end of the century the word stock of the parent language had been well determined. Meillet includes in his *Introduction* a chapter "on the vocabulary" (1937: 378–417). The more extensive accounts by Walde and Pokorny (1927–32), Pokorny (1959) and Buck (1949) provide detailed information on the reflexes in the various dialects. Monographs deal with selected segments of the vocabulary, for example Delbrück's treatment of kinship terms (1889), now amplified by Szemerényi's (1977). Analysis of the lexicon yields information on the early speech community, which is essential for determining its location and also central for proposing earlier stages of the language.

After a section on roots, Meillet discusses sets of "isolated words" that provide indications concerning the social status and the civilization of the people who spoke Proto-Indo-European (1937: 389). The sets include kinship terms, names of animals and plants, words having to do with religion, some generalities, parts of the body, adjectives and finally numerals. With a different aim, Specht in 1944 sorted out by their form the corpus of words assumed for Proto-Indo-European, in an attempt to determine those that are older, both for insights into the developing structure of the language and the stages in the civilization of the speakers. Such lexical studies are highly important, though unfortunately their value has not been recognized, especially by archaeologists.

We will not discuss them further here, except to point out the very real contributions of a century and more of lexical study. What is now necessary is informed attention, often to individual items. An exemplary study was provided by Scharfe (1985: 543–8), in which he demonstrated that the assumed word for "king," as in Meillet (1937: 392) and many other handbooks, early Sanskrit *rā́j-*, is a ghost word. The three occurrences in the *Rigveda* of *rā́ṭ* Scharfe demonstrates to be the nominative of a feminine noun meaning "power, strength"; its oblique forms are based on the "weak stem" *ū́rk-*, as in the accusative singular *ū́rjam*. When attested as second member of a compound in later Vedic texts, as in *deva-rāj*, Scharfe takes it to mean "ruling (over the gods)." Scharfe's demonstration has important consequences: it shows that the proposed word for "king" is attested only in Latin *rēx* and Old Irish *rī* so that no Proto-Indo-European etymon can be reconstructed; it removes one argument for closer relationship between Italic, Celtic and Indic; and it demolishes any support for a larger social organization in the early period that was ruled by a "king."

Scharfe's finding may illustrate the kind of contribution that is now possible, and welcome, in contrast with massive new insights during the nineteenth century. It also indicates that those insights may have led to error by failing to observe key evidence; many treatments of the society speaking Proto-Indo-European assume kings among their social institutions. Similar painstaking and imaginative analyses are especially important in view of the data contributed by the Anatolian languages, as well as those from Tocharian and Mycenaean Greek with occasional new material in the other dialects.

3.9 HANDBOOKS THAT MAY BE CONSIDERED FUNDAMENTAL IN CURRENT STUDY

The grammatical treatments by Brugmann (1897–1916), Delbrück (1893–1900), Hirt (1921–37) and Meillet (1937) remain useful, though superseded in parts. Similarly, the large dictionary of Walde and Pokorny (1927–32), revised and arranged in accordance with the order of the Latin alphabet by Pokorny (1959–69, reissued 1989), and the thesaurus of Buck (1949) are important as sources of data. Moreover, the handbooks based on these, among them those of Adrados (1975) and of Szemerényi (1970 [1989]), and Watkins's lexicon (1985), as well as the grammar inaugurated under the editorship of Kurylowicz (1968) and now continued under the editorship of Mayrhofer, provide useful summaries of earlier findings, with some revisions. Labeled here the standard handbooks, they aim at description of Proto-Indo-European at a late stage, shortly before its separation into the numerous branches. Moreover, their conclusions are based largely on use of the comparative method.

After the discovery of Hittite supported conclusions based on use of the method of internal reconstruction, increasing efforts have been made to determine earlier stages of the proto-language. Many of these have checked their hypotheses by means of the generalizations determined in typological study. The handbook by Gamkrelidze and Ivanov (1984) is the most comprehensive such work. It was preceded by monographs on sections of the grammar, among them my *Proto-Indo-European Phonology* (1952) and *Proto-Indo-European Syntax* (1974) as well as by many articles included in its lengthy bibliography (1984: 974–1113).

In addition to the increased confidence in results arrived at by the method of internal reconstruction, these later works make use of methods for subgrouping languages achieved by work in dialect geography. The resulting procedures have supported the view that the extensive set of inflections found especially in Sanskrit and Greek may have arisen in a central subgroup, and that peripheral branches like Anatolian and Germanic may be more conservative in maintaining the inflectional system of the proto-language. Further, the Anatolian verbal system has been taken as providing insights into the still earlier system of Pre-Indo-European, through its maintenance of residues and through different redistribution of forms from those in the dialects attested previously.

Moreover, we now deal with the proto-language from a historical point of view, in contrast with Brugmann's systematic approach. Under this approach we seek to arrive at a system of all grammatical components, not only the verb system, as did Bopp in 1816, or of the phonology and morphology, as have Brugmann and others. In the current effort the comparative method is therefore applied also to syntactic patterns. Accordingly, a grammar of Proto-Indo-European today would reconstruct the three systems: phonology, morphology and syntax.

4 Revisions on the basis of new data and new principles

4.1 NEW DATA AFFECTING THE TRADITIONAL VIEWS

By the early decades of this century Indo-European studies were equipped with large and well-considered presentations on the parent language, the early dialects and the cultural background of their speakers. These were based on theoretical views that had been expressed most forcefully at the beginning of the neogrammarian movement, but, as noted in chapters 1–3, also earlier, at the beginning of the nineteenth century. Indo-Europeanists were concerned with structure, indeed innermost structure. They sought to determine that structure by mastering the data. The data of the early texts were to be treated like information obtained about spoken languages of the present. Respect for data kept them from publishing revisions of hypotheses simply by examining those proposed by their predecessors as bases for intellectual gamesmanship. And when new information was provided, as after the discovery of Tocharian, the Anatolian languages and Mycenaean Greek, the articles and monographs that treated them did not begin with a section on some "theorist" or some specific "theory"; rather, they presented the data and then proposed their interpretation on the basis of long-accepted procedures and theory.

This is not to say that theoretical works were lacking. They were generally produced by eminent scholars after long concern with many languages. The outstanding Sanskritist, Jakob Wackernagel, produced two volumes on syntax that still ought to be mastered by anyone concerned with this section of grammar (1926–8). The somewhat more daring Havers published an explanatory treatise on syntax (1931). Starting from a different tradition, Trubetzkoy laid the groundwork for treatment of phonology (1939). Among those treating methods, Meillet, when invited to give a series of lectures in inaugurating the program of the newly founded Institute for the Comparative Study of Culture in Oslo, presented an excellent exposition of the comparative method in its relationship to typological comparison, illuminating at the same time application of these

Sources for this chapter: Meillet ([1925] 1967); Gamkrelidze and Ivanov (1984); Bammesberger (1988); Vennemann (1989); Klimov (1977); Lehmann (1991).

procedures to data that takes into consideration the varied social situations in which language is used ([1925] 1967).

Meillet's insistence on dealing with actual speech, like Brugmann's, and his pointed statements on the variety of language in accordance with specific social communities, would scarcely have pleased his former teacher, Saussure, nor many linguists today. In one of his crisp sentences he may even exaggerate the differences among varieties within language: "Rien ne diffère plus d'un état de langue qu'un autre état de langue" (1925: 111). There can be little question that he chose the term *langue* deliberately a decade after publication of Saussure's subsequently celebrated series of lectures. The different varieties recognized by Meillet are neither specimens of parole nor of performance, but actual languages maintained by actual language communities. And since the Caucasian languages, rather than his example of varieties within his own French language, were to be the research area of the new institute, Meillet welcomed the proposed undertakings, because they would "provide precise and comprehensive information on states of language, and in this way lead to renovation of theoretical principles [doctrines]' (1925: 116). We may be grateful that in the country which carried out the most notable political revolution of modern times this term had not been extended to revisions in intellectual approaches.

Meillet's unsurpassed little monograph should be well known by every linguist, both because of its highly thoughtful conclusions and because of the accuracy of his predictions on the results of detailed concern with specific languages. Some of the most highly regarded linguistic study of recent years was carried out in accordance with Meillet's insistence that varieties of languages, such as the social registers of English, be studied. Moreover, some of the most fruitful theory of recent times has resulted from examination of the very Caucasian languages to which he referred. The monograph might be characterized as an updated and enlarged version of Brugmann's manifesto, with more specific attention to actual data than Brugmann allowed himself in his brief statement. Like Brugmann's statement, it may seem to center on historical study, but the insistence on detailed attention to current French and to investigation of the Caucasian language – among other language – areas indicates that Meillet is dealing with all linguistic study.

It was into this highly informed and theory-based linguistic situation that the new data from Anatolia and Chinese Turkestan were introduced. Linguists have been fortunate that some of their colleagues could read, understand and interpret the data.

The early fortunes of the Anatolian materials might virtually be the subject of a thriller. Their discoverer, Winckler, was reportedly too ill to do much with the texts he excavated at Boğazköy in 1906; until his death in 1913 his considerate colleagues did not encroach on his prerogative for their publication and interpretation. Thereupon, since the texts were in cuneiform, Assyriologists undertook to read and interpret them.

Interpretation was not hastened by the statement published in 1896 by the highly regarded classicist, Paul Kretschmer, that no Indo-European language could be expected in the future from Asia Minor. When the young Assyriologist, Friedrich Hrozný, published an article in 1915 proclaiming "The solution to the Hittite problem," followed up by a monograph in 1917 on "The language of the Hittites, its structure and its membership in the Indo-European language family," the Indo-Europeanists did not believe him. He provided incontrovertible evidence, such as the nominative *watar*, genitive *wetenas* "water"; even the presence of a heteroclitic noun comparable to Latin *iocur*, *iocinoris* "liver" or cognate with English *water*, Norwegian *vatn* did not convince all the sceptics. Further, the social disruptions caused by the First World War were not helpful in bringing about an accurate understanding of the new data.

A strange development hampered the potential contributions of one of the most brilliant linguists of the time, Carl Marstrander. He turned his attention to the language, relying for his data on the brief texts that Hrozný had provided in transcription. Marstrander's monograph of 1919 included advances beyond Hrozný's publications, though its adventurous undertaking to interpret the phonology was something of a disaster. After this single publication, Marstrander dropped his concern for Hittite, quite inexplicably. The reason – which we learned from him during personal conversations in 1951 – may provide an insight into at least one apparent irrational development in scholarship. A colleague urged Marstrander to provide some business to an impecunious bookbinder. In impetuous generosity, Marstrander took over all his Hittite materials for binding. That night the bookbinder's shop burned to the ground.

Another early scholar, Forrer, lost credit through imaginative suggestions, such as that the people named Ahhiyava in the texts were Achaeans, a suggestion that after two generations has again found some supporters. Giving up his interest, Forrer turned to Mayan studies in central America, where he was effectively separated from scholarship.

It was only when the highly regarded Ferdinand Sommer dealt with the texts in accordance with the painstaking procedures developed in study of the classical languages that Indo-Europeanists accepted the identification of Hittite as a member of the family. Thereupon capable young scholars, notably Johannes Friedrich and Albrecht Götze, dedicated themselves to concentration on the language. And a few years later the brilliant young Polish scholar, Jerzy Kurylowicz, published an article identifying some Hittite words that included the sound transliterated by *h* which he related to Saussure's coefficients (1927). The implications of his discovery eventually led to the refashioning of many of the conclusions that had been presented in the standard handbooks, though conservative scholars long resisted them. Yet after publication of the article, accounting for Hittite and the other Anatolian languages came to be one of the major pursuits of Indo-European study.

In the meantime knowledge of the two Tocharian languages had advanced steadily. The texts were readily understood, being largely translations of Buddhist works, which were written in the already known *Brāhmī* script (see 1.6 above). Specialists then needed to edit and interpret them, thereupon to produce grammars and other handbooks. Advances encountered problems that were social and political rather than linguistic; the Tocharian B texts were in Paris, the Tocharian A texts in Berlin; but when eventually published, the material could be used. It was soon clear that the texts were not only recent, from the seventh to the ninth centuries of our era, but also limited in value for comparative Indo-European purposes through heavy modification of the language by languages of agglutinative structure. Although full of intrinsic interest as languages greatly modified in structure and lexicon, Tocharian A and B contributed to Indo-European studies largely through their evidence that disproved the centum : satem classification, besides posing the intriguing problem of how an Indo-European branch came to be located in far-off Turkestan.

In somewhat the same way the Mycenaean inscriptions that Michael Ventris demonstrated to be Greek in 1953 have great intrinsic value for this subbranch, but scarcely provided surprises with reference to Proto-Indo-European. One kept hoping for written evidence of laryngeals, not least because of a number of unidentified syllabic signs. Yet the awkward Linear B representation of early Greek, provided in short texts produced chiefly for tax and administrative purposes, furnished only relatively minor contributions, such as evidence for retention of labio-velars as opposed to the *p t k* of the later language.

In short, it was the Anatolian languages that led to revisions of the proto-language as presented in the standard handbooks. No-one in the academic world can be surprised that these came slowly.

4.2 THE IMPACT OF HITTITE

While other members of the Anatolian branch, such as Luwian, contributed insights into the proto-language, for some time the chief materials available were Hittite. It is to these that we owe improved understanding of the early period of Indo-European. We may note specific modifications in the system that had been previously accepted.

4.2.1 The laryngeal theory

An entirely new set of phonological elements had to be assumed for the proto-language. In keeping with the terminology that had been introduced for Saussure's coefficients, these were called laryngeals (see 5.4), and their assumption, the laryngeal theory. As for any phonological items no longer central in the inventory of a language, evidence for them was not extensive. Reconstructing the actual number and their phonetic make-up aroused vigorous debates. Some posit three laryngeals, others four, still others very many or only one. We examine the bases for the varied positions later.

4.2.2 Elimination of the voiceless aspirated stops

The set of stops proposed as voiceless and aspirated was now eliminated, on the grounds that some of the reflexes identified earlier in Sanskrit resulted from clusters of voiceless stop and laryngeal, the others from positional variants of the voiced aspirates and laryngeals. Their elimination as distinct entities in the proto-language had many consequences for the remaining system. No-one with any background in phonology would assume a set consisting of voiceless stop, voiced stop, voiced aspirated stop, the dental set of which might be represented *t d dh*. The problem was reviewed by Indo-Europeanists, and came to be a happy hunting-ground for others who somehow learned of the situation.

4.2.3 Clarification of ablaut

Treatments of ablaut had been highly complex, in part because of morphophonemic differences between the so-called inherited long vowels and the long ablaut vowels resulting from short vowels by compensatory lengthening. Saussure had concluded that the inherited long vowels arose from contraction of a short vowel and following laryngeal. Hittite now provided evidence for his explanation.

Besides assuring the inclusion of laryngeals as a distinct set, the new evidence supported assumption of a root structure consisting of Consonant–Vowel–Consonant. Roots like **dhē-* "place," **(s)tā-* "stand," **dō-* "give" could now be put in a class with roots like **sed-* "sit" or **leg^h-* "lie" on the basis of textual evidence. As a result the entire ablaut situation was clarified. Widely attested changes like that of *e* to zero, or to lengthened *ē*, or to *o* were assumed to have occurred in early stages of the proto-language; eventually, the highly complex vocalic formulae and their interrelationships as presented in the standard handbooks could be replaced by simpler statements.

4.2.4 Effects on the treatment of the morphology

The recognition that the so-called original long vowels resulted from contractions of laryngeals with short vowels also clarified inflectional and derivational morphology. In inflection, the feminine nouns ending in long *ā*, as in the Latin first declension, were now seen to be the result of a laryngeal suffix that had contracted with the preceding vocalic element. This conclusion upheld Schmidt's assumption that the ending was orig-inally a marker of collectives (1889). A further inference was made that the marker came to indicate feminine gender because in an agrarian society the female animals were those preferred and accordingly predominant within herds. By this inference the few masculine *ā*-stem nouns in Latin were also accounted for; *agricola* "farmer," *nauta* "sailor," *poeta* "artificer" did not actually stand for an individual, but rather for collectives, and thereupon their members. Moreover, it became clear why the same suffix was used to mark nominative singular feminines and nominative/accusative plural neuters. Schmidt had equated them formally, but reasons for the twofold use had remained obscure even though some neuter plurals were translated as collectives (see 7.3).

An even more spectacular clarification resulted in the verbal system. Verbs with nasal infixes had been analysed as belonging to three separate classes. In Sanskrit these had sequences consisting of *-na-*, *-nu-* and *-nā-*, which had been distinguished as classes 7, 5 and 9 (Whitney 1896: 228–9). It now became clear that the verbs with long *-nā-* were found in bases that ended in one of two laryngeals. In a paper presented at the Linguistic Society of America in 1953 I proposed that the base of many *-nu-* verbs ended in another laryngeal; I never submitted the paper for publication, but some time later Martinet published the same hypothesis. If one accepts the analysis, the three Sanskrit classes are readily interpreted as members of one original class. The assumption concerning the bases was supported by various other developments.

4.2.5 Effects on the treatment of syntax

In syntax it now became clear why a singular verb was used after a neuter plural subject. At the time the rules for congruence were established, the "neuter plural" was not really viewed as a number of distinct items or individuals but rather as a collective.

In a less widespread pattern, found in older Germanic dialects, a neuter plural anaphor was used to refer to a group consisting of males and females (Lehmann 1957). The pattern is another residue from the period when the ending indicated a collective.

As these statements illustrate, the incorporation of laryngeals into the phonological system of Proto-Indo-European has, in Vennemann's words, "dramatically changed our view not only of the phonology but also of the morphology and lexicology" (1989: xi). We can continue to use the stores of data compiled in the systematic treatments of the standard handbooks, especially the reliable information assembled by Brugmann and Delbrück, as well as by the notable authorities who produced almost definitive grammars for the dialects, among them Wackernagel's for Sanskrit, Schwyzer's for Greek and Leumann's for Latin. However, we must update those sections that represent the situation before an accurate understanding of Proto-Indo-European phonology was achieved.

4.3 MODIFICATIONS IN METHODOLOGY

In addition to the new data provided by the discovery of the Anatolian languages, a clearer understanding of the structure of language contributed to an improved treatment of the proto-language. The methodology applied represents an extension of the structural view that the early Indo-Europeanists had adopted, stimulated by generalists like Friedrich Schlegel. Bopp and his successors dealt with the morphology in this way, assisted by increasing knowledge of the presentation of the Indian grammarians, especially Panini. It was only at the end of the century that a comparable approach was applied to phonology. More recently, the approach has been introduced in the treatment of syntax.

4.3.1 Comment on theory and terminology

In view of the massive attention to methodology and linguistic theory, as well as the varied use of terms, a brief statement on definitions of key terms and on theory may be useful at this point. The term "structuralism" has come to be used in linguistic study for the approach prevalent among a group of largely American linguists during the third, fourth and fifth decades of this century. Moreover, when used by many it has a derogatory implication, suggesting that linguists in the period limited their treatment of language to external form with no attention to meaning. Without discussing the merits of this implication, we may recall that "structure" for Schlegel and early Indo-Europeanists did not represent the external shell of language. Indo-Europeanists throughout the nineteenth and the twentieth centuries have dealt with forms and meanings, as well as their values in the systems of communication used by societies speaking languages of the Indo-European and other families.

Further in linguistic study, the term "generative" linguistics has come to be used for an approach that succeeded the so-called structural linguistics. The term "generative" was properly applied to grammar, where its most highly regarded proponent equated it with "explicit". Like many popular movements, generative grammar has acquired its own mythology. Its devotees credit it with introducing formalism into linguistics. It has pre-empted terminology like "transformation," subsequently to downgrade it. The mythology has developed in spite of specific pronouncements on his aims by Chomsky. In popular as well as academic statements he has indicated that he is chiefly concerned with mental processes involved in the use of language, and with the descriptions of the accompanying manipulations, descriptions equivalent to what others call grammars. As in the paragraph on "structuralism," I am not concerned here with the usefulness of generative grammar/linguistics, nor of the validity of its several versions. I simply indicate that some terminology in generative grammars was used earlier, and in a different sense.

The term "transformation," for example, was introduced into generative grammar from structural grammar. There it was applied to processes long studied in approaches to language, as for interrelating passive with active sentences. Since the focus of generative grammar has now been shifted, it may be important to recall that in its early phase the term "transformation" was applied to a special kind of rule that related one set of rules (e.g. those "generating" an active construction) with another set of rules (e.g. those "generating" a passive construction). Before its introduction into structural grammar, the term "transformational" was applied by logicians in their treatment of language. Even sketching its use there would extend this section unduly; anyone interested can find a concise presentation in the works of Carnap.

Besides noting the need to be aware of the varied applications of terminology, linguists must also be clear about the use of formalism and claims made for it. Generative grammar is often credited with its introduction and use in current linguistic study. That claim can more properly be made for computational approaches. Computer manipulation of language preceded the earliest publications in generative grammar, and obviously would have been impossible without careful formalism. The use of formal procedures and of formalist terminology like that noted above was based on symbolic logic developed in the nineteenth century and elaborated in the twentieth.

Yet far more important than views about the recent application of formal procedures in treatment of language is the background of formal approaches. They deal with language by assuming categories. In western approaches to language Aristotle is generally credited with the theory and formulation of categories. And one of the important contributions of Indian grammar to nineteenth-century linguistic study came from its highly developed formalism that was possible through use of categories. Linguists today still praise its elegance, which can now be readily examined in the admirable presentation of Panini's grammar by Sumitra Katre (1987). In short, categories have long been features of eastern as well as western treatments of language.

However an individual may interpret the term "categorial grammar," grammars from the time of Bopp and earlier deal with language through categories. Terms like "indicative, subjunctive, aorist, nominative, comparative" refer to categories – morphological categories. Terms like "tenues, mediae, aspiratae" refer to categories – phonological categories, maintained from the time of Latin grammarians. Terms like "prótasis" and "apódosis" refer to categories – syntactic categories. We may sharpen the use of categorial terms, or introduce others. The terms "tenues, mediae, aspiratae" were replaced in phonological study. And in dissatisfaction with the term *árthron hypotaktikón* "hypotactic article" as marker of what seemed to him a specific type of clause, August Grotefend introduced for such a construction the term "relative clause" in his *Principles of a New Theory of Syntax* (1827); the "article" introducing them has subsequently been called a relative pronoun. Categories then have been recognized in treatment of all aspects of grammar.

The role identified for a specific category, as well as theories of language, are not exempt from the change found in all social conventions. Since 1827 Grotefend's "new theory" has been replaced by many "new" theories. Each theory, and its proponents, may claim for themselves the worn adjective "new" and even others, like "more rigorous," or they may even express proprietary claim to terms applied in linguistic study. Whatever the claims, of greater importance is knowledge of the application of a specific term in a specific work and, of course, any advantage gained by its use. The perspective that results from awareness of earlier approaches and terminology is also of no slight benefit in any academic undertaking.

4.3.2 Phonological theory

The major development in the treatment of the sound component of language had to do with categories of sounds, and their interrelationships. As is well known, besides the perceived, articulated sounds, classes were proposed that were labeled "phonemes". The classes, like the long-applied morphological classes, are abstractions. Scholars vary in associating them with more concrete manifestations, some preferring articulatory values, others mental. Whatever the basis, the entities of any reconstructed item, e.g. PIE *dem-* "build," cf. Greek *dómos* "house," correspond to phonemes in current treatments of language; each of the entities is determined largely by relationship with others, such as /d/ : /n/, as in PIE *nem-* "arrange," cf. Greek *nómos* "law."

The classes may be distinguished for subclasses, often called allophones. Phonemes may also be analysed for distinctive features; nasality is such a feature in distinguishing between /d/ and /n/. It has long been clear that in "sound change" only one distinctive feature is generally involved: for example, when *bant* became *batt* in Old Icelandic, the primary distinctive feature involved was nasality.

Phonological theory was energetically pursued in the fourth decade of the twentieth century. Trubetzkoy's *Grundzüge* presents many of the findings. After the author's death, Jakobson discussed more explicitly the application of distinctive features. Subsequently other considerations have been examined, as of accentuation; the works of Allen (e.g. 1973) are especially valuable for Indo-Europeanists. Treatments of phonology with reference to the parent language or to the early dialects today apply modern phonological theory, even if they are not always explicit in identifying it.

4.3.3 Morphological theory

Western grammatical tradition centered on morphology, developing procedures for representing it structurally through paradigms. The term "paradigm" is equivalent to structure, or substructure. Items in a selected set, for example nouns, or nouns of a subtype, such as those with bases ending in *e/o*, are arranged by a selected principle, in the list-like patterns that are well known. The procedure yields convenient summaries. It has proved to be so successful that recently a historian of science, Thomas A. Kuhn, applied it to scientific approaches, providing means for scientists to sort out varying ideas and terminology while securing for himself wide acclaim.

Semantic criteria are the principal means used to build paradigms. In nouns, for example, the dative case refers to a paradigmatic category indicating a recipient, usually, though not exclusively, an animate recipient. Stated differently, cases are defined by identification of specific functions. Like other grammatical categories, cases may be expressed with differing forms: for example, in Latin the dative singular form of "wolf" is *lupō*, of "spirit" *animae*, of "tower" *turrī*. In spite of the formal differences, these forms are equated in a paradigm because they stand in comparable relations to other forms within the set to which they are assigned. Such identification is extended beyond one language: for example, the genitive of "wolf" in Latin, *lupī*, is equated with that in Greek, *lúkou*, with that in Sanskrit, *lukasya*, and so on.

The procedure has been so long applied that linguists may fail to observe its bases: for example, some linguists who do not hesitate to equate totally different morphological entities like Latin *-ō*, *-ae*, *-ī* have condemned use of the same procedure in dealing with syntax. Further, they apply the comparative method in equating as datives forms as different as Latin endings *-ō* and *-ae*, but consider the method inapplicable in dealing with syntax.

Those objecting to the use of similar procedures in syntax also fail to note that the meanings, or in Saussure's term – values – of such morphological entities may not be equivalent. Apart from the vocative, Latin has five cases, Greek four, Sanskrit seven; the value of any one case in each of these languages is determined by the total membership within its paradigm: for example, in Greek the genitive is used more widely than is the genitive in Latin, or that in Sanskrit, as in absolute constructions. Yet in spite of such differences in value, the cases in these languages are given the same labels. While the procedure is useful, it is also hazardous when "theoreticians" discuss categories like the genitive, or the passive, or broader spheres like aspect through a broad array of languages and even language families without distinguishing the position of such categories in the individual languages that are treated.

Yet the paradigmatic procedure is advantageous in permitting disregard of formal and semantic differences after the general parameters for determining a set are selected. It may be useful to recall that similar procedures are used in phonology; for example, the bilabial voiceless fricative as in *Fuji* is classed with /h/ in Japanese, though its value as well as its form differs from [h]. Similarly, the glottal stop in pronunciations of such words as *bottle* is classed as a member of the English phoneme /t/.

Strict paradigms are not used in derivational morphology, on the grounds that its formations are too irregular. Nor did Panini use them for inflectional morphology. Some grammars and grammatical sketches have followed him in providing such a treatment of inflectional morphology. For languages with minimal inflection, this type of nonparadigmatic approach may be successful; for highly inflected languages like Sanskrit, presentation through paradigms provides greater clarity. The use of paradigms has seemed so successful to some linguists that they apply them in languages lacking inflection, such as Japanese; grammars that they produce list phrases consisting of noun and postposition in paradigms.

Others have appropriated the term "case" for semantic sets that are in no way distinct in form: for example, used with the widely cited English verb "break" the noun preceding the verb in the following sentences is assigned to different cases, as labeled:

The boy broke the window.   AGENT
The stone broke the window.   INSTRUMENT
The window broke.   TARGET

Each of these nouns is subject of a sentence; in languages indicating grammatical case, like Latin, each would be in the nominative case as the appropriate grammatical form for a subject. It is clear then that the extent of a paradigm based on "case" in this way is determined largely by semantic criteria. The procedures applied to determine such categories are even more comparable to those used for determining syntactic sets than are those of morphologically based grammars; but, in addition, determination of syntactic sets involves the formal device known as arrangement or order.

4.3.4 Syntactic theory

Probably the greatest advance in syntactic study today has resulted from increased attention to formal criteria that are specifically syntactic. The standard handbooks classify syntactic entities largely by semantic criteria: for example, the noun after the verb in the following sentences is assigned different syntactic analysis as indicated, even though it maintains the same form.

She gave *the dog* to her son.   DIRECT OBJECT
She gave *the dog* a bone.   INDIRECT OBJECT

In syntactic study today the same identification would be given, if such terminology were requested, but the grounds for that identification would be more overtly formal, based on syntactic devices such as order, congruence, possible rearrangement as in the alternative form of the second example:

She gave a bone to the dog.

Such rearrangements have long been used in syntactic analysis. In recent study they have been labeled transformations, with various implications, as we have noted.

Moreover, when the standard handbooks discuss syntax, they deal with morphologically identified forms, going on to describe their uses in syntax. It was Brugmann's decision to prepare the second edition of the *Grundriss* in this way that led to its production without the participation of Delbrück. As one example of morphologically based syntax, the standard handbooks discuss separately syntactic patterns like the accusative with the infinitive, as in:

We expected her to come.

Typically at some other section they deal with so-called object clauses, as in:

We expected that she would come.

By contrast, in current syntactic treatments, the two constructions may be treated in relation to each other, under the rubric *complement*. For Modern English there would be another construction under this heading, as in:

We expected her coming.

The arrangement of a current treatment of syntax would then differ from that of Brugmann and others using his approach, such as the impressive treatments of Latin by Szantyr and of Greek by Schwyzer and Debrunner.

Identification of syntactic patterns by syntactic criteria has led to a highly important finding, for which Greenberg merits principal credit. Syntactic constructions determined by comparable application of formal devices, such as government, are associated in sets somewhat like paradigms: for example, verbs and adpositions are so associated because both govern objects. It was Greenberg's important contribution to point out correlations, such as that in languages with verbs preceding their object (VO languages) the adposition would also be preposed before its object as a preposition, as in English, Classical Greek and Biblical Hebrew among many languages. On the other hand, in languages in which verbs follow their object (OV languages), the adposition is postposed as a postposition, as in Japanese, Quechua and Turkish among many languages. In this way a "paradigm" of syntactic constructions has been assembled. See Lehmann (1978: 19–26) for a fuller set.

A further syntactic construction belonging to the government paradigm is that of comparison of inequality. Languages that, like English, place verbs before their objects include comparison of inequality constructions like its, in which an adjective precedes the standard, often with an intervening pivot, as in:

The dog is bigger than the cat.

Here the standard *cat* is placed after the adjective *big* with an intervening pivot *than*. Somewhat like verbs and adpositions, adjectives govern a standard in comparison of inequality constructions.

On the other hand, languages that place verbs after their objects include comparison of inequality constructions that place the adjective after the standard, often with a pivot, as in the Japanese equivalent of this English sentence:

Inu	wa	neko	yori	ookii
dog	ptc	cat	from	big

And as in Japanese there may be no distinctive form of the adjective in comparison, as there is in English with the *-er* suffix.

The identification of such syntactic paradigms is highly important for the study of poorly attested languages or of proto-languages because of the inferences one may make on the basis of any one member of such a paradigm. For such purposes we determine the more highly characteristic members of the paradigm. In the government paradigm the basic sentence structure may not be the most useful to seek out because sentence order is often modified, especially in poetic texts. For example, Milton begins *Paradise Lost* with a sentence in which the object precedes the verb; yet by analysis of his prose, as well as our general knowledge of English, we do not classify his language as OV. However, it would be most unusual, almost impossible, to find a comparative construction like that of Japanese in Milton's writings. As a result, in examining early texts, of which the earliest are chiefly poetic, for example the Sanskrit Vedas, the Greek Homeric poems, we look for such constructions and draw conclusions about the syntactic structure from them.

To illustrate the advances in recognition and explanation of syntactic patterns we may cite an example from the authoritative grammarian of Hittite, Johannes Friedrich. In his early sketch on Hittite and the Anatolian languages, Friedrich includes the following statement concerning syntax (1931: 35):

> With regard to the syntax of the noun it may be mentioned that comparison of adjectives in contrast with other old Indo-European languages is not expressed by means of special formants but rather by a syntactic method; one says "A is large towards B" for "A is bigger than B". "A is big among all" for "A is the biggest of all."

And in his grammar of a generation later he cites the Hittite pattern in transliteration: *nu-wa-kan* ANA ERIN*MES*-KA ERIN*MES*-IA *mekki* (1960: 127). He then provides the translation, which I reproduce in English: "now (are) my infantry troops more numerous than your infantry troops (literally: more numerous near [beside] your infantry troops)." From the discussion above it is clear that he missed the crucial feature of order, for the adjective *mekki* is placed after the standard without marking for comparison and without a pivot.

Friedrich also notes the presence of postpositions in Hittite, but like the standard grammars of Indo-European his is concerned with the cases they may govern rather than with any further inferences about the type of syntax (1931: 36; 1960: 129–30). And in treating the syntax of verbs, he is especially concerned with the lack of moods and necessity of using particles to express modalities (1931). Further, in his grammar he deals with categories and the uses of forms without discussing the order within the clause (1960: 135–45). He then misses the most important feature of verbal and clausal syntax, and also its interrelationship with the comparative and postpositional constructions he has identified.

From our knowledge of syntactic structure today we equate the pattern of the Hittite comparative construction with the arrangement of the finite verb and other constructions, like the use of postpositions, to identify the language as OV in syntactic structure. Further, having arrived at that conclusion, we recall the observations on the verb-final order of clauses and other syntactic constructions in Vedic, as described in Delbrück's excellent monographs and in his volumes of the *Grundriss*. Thereupon we apply the comparative method to reconstruct the syntax of the proto-language as OV. Further, the knowledge that our two oldest attested Indo-European languages have OV structure permits us to account for residues of the OV syntactic structure in the other dialects, such as postpositions surviving even to Old English, and to Classical Latin in expressions like *quoad* "as far as, until," and of OV comparative constructions in Old English and other early Germanic verse. The retention of many such OV patterns in the various dialects supports us in our reconstruction of the proto-language as OV in structure by use of the comparative method (see 9.5.1, 9.6.1).

The procedures have been severely criticized, even with unscientific stigmas. The pointlessness of one major criticism has been indicated above. It has been stated that the comparative method does not apply to syntactic constructions. The statement ignores bases of syntactic analysis as well as the essence of the method.

Criticisms have also been published regarding the presence of exceptions, especially regarding congruence patterns, as of adjectives, that are proposed for types of language. Such criticisms totally ignore the findings of linguistics and other social as well as human sciences. There are no rules governing every item in a language or any other social convention. Any description seeks to provide as broad generalizations as possible. Clear-headed linguists have long consoled themselves for their limitations with expressions like "grammars leak"; even particle physicists have come to understand the limitations of human knowledge.

In short, if one wishes to assemble more than lists, whether in syntax, morphology, phonology or the lexicon, one proposes structures. Since all social conventions are open, and constantly undergo change, realistic generalizations cannot be made without exceptions; like physical scientists, linguists no longer assume that they can provide absolute explanations. Scientists in all fields deal with items and structures, and attempt to provide generalizations that account for as many phenomena as possible. The students of language who posit ideal language as their concern would be well advised to abandon such a concept.

4.3.5 The lexicon

The lexical items of a language are those most difficult to control. Scholars in all civilizations have recognized the problems by adopting external methods for listing them. In Chinese civilization, for example, specific shapes of the writing symbols have been selected for the purpose. Dictionaries for languages written in alphabets are somewhat easier to produce and use. Yet their shortcomings in relying entirely on external form have prompted scholars to devise other approaches. The most successful of these resulted from the linguistic study of the eighteenth century, when words were arranged in selected classes of meaning. This type of dictionary is still in use. For English it is generally referred to as a thesaurus, the typical one credited to a nineteenth-century scholar, Peter Mark Roget (1779–1869).

In Roget's thesaurus general classes were selected, the broadest reduced to six: abstract relations; space; matter; intellect; volition; affections. These then are subdivided into ultimately a thousand classes. All words are listed under one of these thousand classes, some with multiple uses under more than one.

For languages of the past, the procedure seems unduly capacious. Carl Darling Buck applied a somewhat similar method in selecting twenty-two classes, under which he arranged his highly useful "selected list of words in the principal Indo-European languages" (1949). His work was preceded by others in the nineteenth century. In recent Indo-European studies the work of Specht has been most useful (1944, 1947).

Specht arranged the words he selected under rubrics that he assumed would be of importance in a culture of the fourth and third millennia. Those rubrics are as follows: natural objects; the animal world; the plant world; parts of the body; family and domestic concerns. It is clear that the classification is in the first instance semantic; but Specht also determined formal criteria. The essential words in these sets are typically inflected under patterns that had been identified as archaic: for example, inflections of nouns as well as verbs came to have the *-e/o-* or thematic suffix after the root; but many of the words that Specht sought for the stage of culture that concerned him lack the thematic suffix. In his study then he found, not entirely without precedent, a correlation between basic words and formal treatment.

The study accordingly permits proposing chronological layers for the lexicon of the proto-language. One of Specht's most useful findings concerns his last set: terminology for wagon construction. In contrast with words for his five classes of basic items in early culture, the terms have thematic inflection. It was a simple matter to conclude that these terms were created at a late stage of the proto-language.

Once again a structural approach demonstrated its usefulness. The lexical sets, or structures, are relatively loose, especially in comparison with morphological paradigms. Yet the parallelisms exhibited by the members of such sets have led to important conclusions. The procedure may be applied beneficially throughout the lexicon.

4.4 EFFECTS ON THE PHONOLOGICAL COMPONENT

In the remainder of this chapter we sketch the effects of the new information and improved theory on the various segments of the grammar of the proto-language. For phonology we place these in order of their determination.

Like other segments, phonology is treated as a structure consisting of substructures. The first of the substructures to be analysed rigorously was the set of resonants: /w y r l m n/.

4.4.1 Systematization of the resonants, with effects on the vocalic system

Already in the early neogrammarian period Sievers recognized that allophones of the resonants vary in accordance with preceding phonemes: for example, the Gothic infinitive for "save" is *nasjan*, the preterite *nasida*, reflecting the alternation in the proto-language. The sounds written *j* and *i* are reflexes of PIE /y/. When such a reflex stands between consonants, it is vocalic; when before a vowel, consonantal. Sievers accounted for further reflexes in Germanic through his observation. In accordance with procedures of the time, the observation is referred to as Sievers's law (one of the "laws" credited to him).

While Sievers was an excellent phonologist – according to some he recognized the phonemic principle – he did not apply the systematization to determine the allophones of the six resonants in all environments. Then in 1932 Franklin Edgerton produced such a systematic treatment, developing it further in 1943. Concentrating especially on Vedic, Edgerton proposed that each of the resonants had three allophones, for /y/ [i y iy]. He also determined the environments in which they appeared. Sievers's observation in its amplified form is now often referred to as the Sievers–Edgerton law.

The observation has various consequences. The most important, and most troublesome, especially to conservative scholars, has to do with the vocalic system. By phonemic principles the vowels *i u*, formerly included in the vocalic system of the proto-language, are no longer identified as members of that system. The short-vowel system is then reduced to three, *e a o*, plus *ə*. Some scholars resist this interpretation of the system, especially since there are further consequences.

4.4.2 Recognition of the laryngeals

The second important modification of the standard phonological system was the introduction of laryngeals. As noted above, the identification that Kurylowicz made in 1927 concerning the presence in some Hittite forms of *h* where Saussure had posited coefficients led to acceptance of laryngeals for the proto-language.

Only in 1935 did systematizations resulting from the identification appear. Then two of the most brilliant recent linguists, Benveniste and Kurylowicz, published highly important monographs. These monographs dealt to a large extent with the laryngeals and the consequences for grammar of the proto-language through their assumption; those consequences will occupy us further below. Here we may note that Benveniste posited three laryngeals, Kurylowicz four. The chief bases for their recognition are as follows:

1 Although inconsistent, Hittite texts distinguish between the use of one *h* and two in medial position. The distinction parallels that in use of symbols for stops, where one indicates a voiced stop, two a voiceless. Accordingly a voiced and a voiceless laryngeal were assumed.
2 The assumed laryngeals are associated with vowel "colors," the voiced with PIE *o*, the voiceless with *a*. Roots like **ag-* "lead" could now with full confidence be reconstructed with initial consonant and vocalic *e*. Some roots like **ed-* "eat" were reconstructed on this basis with an initial laryngeal; since this laryngeal did not color the vowel, a third one was proposed, generally reconstructed as a glottal stop.
3 While the voiceless laryngeal represented by *h* was written in texts and assumed for roots with PIE *a*, some *a* vowels were found in words cognate with Hittite words lacking *h*. To account for these, Kurylowicz posited a fourth laryngeal. Benveniste disregarded the evidence for a fourth set, and posited only three, as do many linguists today.

As we have noted above, the assumption of laryngeals had numerous consequences for the proto-language. Here we recall only the dismissal of voiceless aspirated stops and the reduction of the set of stops to three

(4.2.2). The resulting system was difficult to maintain, if the elements symbolized by b^h d^h g^h g^{wh} were assumed to have the articulation of their reflexes in Sanskrit. Voiced aspirated stops with no contrasting voiceless are generally recognized as rare or non-existent in natural languages. Accordingly, proposals were made regarding a plausible system of obstruents.

4.4.3 Revision of the obstruent system

Various suggestions were made on such a more likely system, but for the time being we will put off discussion of them. They aroused little attention until in 1973 linguists proposed that the obstruent system of Proto-Indo-European included glottalics.

Proponents of glottalics argue strongly for their conclusions on the basis of the skewed system sketched above. But no-one accepted such a system; Indo-Europeanists either retained the fourfold system of Brugmann and his predecessors or they defined its allophones realistically. If the allophones are so defined, the only usable evidence from the Indo-European languages is the defective situation of b. Before noting the consequences, we might mention that some linguists, such as Szemerényi, do not admit that its situation is defective (1970 [1989]: 153).

Assuming that it is, the proponents argue from our knowledge of phonological systems that when there is such a situation, which they identify as a gap, the missing labial is voiceless, not voiced. Further, the gap is most likely in systems where the labial and other elements of the series are glottalic. Accordingly, they propose a series of voiceless glottalic stops in place of the (b) d g g^w proposed earlier. As a result, the previously assumed p t k k^w must be reinterpreted. This set is taken to have two allophones, one aspirated, the other unaspirated. The third series, b^h d^h g^h g^{wh} is similarly interpreted as having aspirated and unaspirated allophones. For further discussion of the theory see 5.2.2.

Of special interest in this chapter is the basis of modifications of the standard views. The basis for restatement of the resonants is revised phonological theory. For the proposal of laryngeals it is new information in the Anatolian languages. For the restatement on the obstruents support is found in typological study. We will deal in greater detail with each of the subsets in chapter 5, after noting changes in views regarding other segments of the proto-language.

4.5 EFFECTS ON THE MORPHOLOGICAL COMPONENT

The differences from earlier treatments of morphology are more extensive in Pre-Indo-European than in Proto-Indo-European. They concern both verbal and nominal inflection, with modifications introduced largely on the basis of evidence found in Hittite.

4.5.1 Nominal inflection

As we have noted, in 4.2.4, Schmidt concluded a century ago that the ending indicating feminine singular and neuter plural (-*a*) was originally the same. The conclusion had the implication that the category of feminine gender was late in Indo-European. When Hittite was analysed, no evidence was found for feminine gender. The threefold gender distinction ascribed to the proto-language might therefore be reduced to two, with further implications for nominal inflection. Yet because of differing views on the reasons for the relatively simple inflection of Hittite as opposed to the complex declension of Sanskrit – whether due to maintenance of the earlier inflection or to loss of forms – agreement has not been reached on the earlier nominal inflection. Some scholars still assume the feminine for Proto-Indo-European, with loss in Anatolian.

The problems involve number as well as gender. The plural of Hittite nouns is highly defective, with fewer forms than the singular; dual forms are entirely lacking. Here the evidence is in favor of conservatism of the earlier system in Hittite. Plural forms of the oblique cases of nouns in Vedic, as well as duals, are also poorly attested. Consequently, we may assume that Hittite reflects an earlier system with little inflection in the plural that was in part remedied in early Indic. With that point of view the extensive nominal paradigms proposed for the proto-language largely on the basis of Sanskrit and Greek would be revised, on the grounds that they are late developments limited to one subgroup, that speaking Proto-Greek and Proto-Indic.

4.5.2 Verbal inflection

The Hittite verbal conjugation provided even more problems. In contrast with that of the other earliest attested dialects it is very simple. There are only two tenses, present and preterite, and only one mood besides an unmarked indicative, the imperative. And as a major problem, there are two conjugations, one with the present first person singular ending in -*mi*, the other in -*hi*. In addition, there is a present that ends in -*ha*, referred to as a middle.

The problem was long treated by efforts to reconcile the strikingly different systems of Hittite and of the other Indo-European languages. The Hittite *mi*-conjugation was readily equated with the basic verbal paradigm of the other dialects. And the *hi*-conjugation was perceived to have similarities with the Indo-European perfect. But the differences were adequate to cause disquiet. A highly convincing solution has been proposed by Soviet linguists, summarized by Gamkrelidze and Ivanov (1984: 293–302). Drawing on typological findings, it proposes a structure of an earlier stage of Proto-Indo-European from which the two systems developed.

4.5.3 Other problems

One of the striking characteristics of Hittite is the large number and conspicuous use of particles. Accounting for them in their uses belongs to the sphere of syntax. But as a morphological class they are not paralleled by a similar set in other subgroups except to some extent in Vedic and the Homeric poems. As a result, an explanation must be given for their prominence.

Moreover, compounds are rare, almost non-existent in Hittite. The situation contrasts strikingly with that in the other languages.

In sum, there are differences in morphology, especially from the proto-language reconstructed largely on the basis of Sanskrit and Greek. Other dialects, such as Germanic, also have a morphological system, especially for the verb, that is simple, in some ways like that of Hittite. As a major problem concerning the system of the proto-language, we must determine whether it had a structure like that of Hittite, with subsequent expansion in many dialects; or, on the other hand, a complex system like that of Sanskrit and Greek, with losses in most of the other dialects. The topic will be discussed further below.

4.6 EFFECTS ON THE SYNTACTIC COMPONENT

It was readily recognized that the verb stands in last position in the Hittite clause. Hittite word order is therefore equivalent to that determined by Delbrück in Vedic Sanskrit. Other syntactic characteristics as well correspond to those expected in OV languages, such as the presence of postpositions.

The basic syntactic structure of Hittite and of the proto-language was then clear. Yet syntax was still treated by Indo-Europeanists on a nonstructural basis. Items were identified morphologically, and then interpreted, as we noted for the second edition of Brugmann's *Grundriss*. Accordingly, traditional Indo-Europeanists failed to understand the syntactic constructions of Hittite.

One of the special problems concerns relative clauses. In OV languages, relative clauses precede their head. Further, they may lack a marker associating them with that head; or if the marker is included in the relative clause, it may attract the head to its clause. Instead of relative clauses on the pattern, "the man who came to dinner . . . ," an OV language may apply the pattern, "which man to dinner came, that one. . . ." That is to say, the equivalent of the relative pronoun in an OV language may be a topic marker within the relative clause, associated or not with an anaphoric particle in the principal clause. Hittite has relative clauses of this pattern. So does Vedic, even though they were poorly understood.

The presence of such constructions as residues in other early languages as well as Hittite provides grounds for reconstructing the syntax of the proto-language through use of the comparative method. The availability of Hittite data in addition to that of Vedic and early Latin gives us evidence for such reconstruction in much the way earlier treatments have reconstructed the phonology and morphology of the proto-language.

4.7 CONTRIBUTIONS OF FURTHER TYPOLOGICAL APPROACHES

The assumptions based on recognition of syntactic structures have been amplified by recent typological study, as we have noted in 2.6 and 2.7. While Proto-Indo-European itself was an OV language of accusative type, it includes patterns that have been identified as characteristic of active languages. One such characteristic is the lack of a verb for "have." As we have noted earlier, because active languages rely heavily on agreement, expression of transitivity is weak, if found at all. Instead of a transitive verb "have," possession is indicated by means of locatives or datives, as in the Latin *mihi est* (*liber*) construction "to-me is book = I have a book."

To provide an understanding of recent treatments of Pre-Indo-European, the active type may be sketched briefly. The lexicon occupies a central position, with content words classified either as active (animate) or stative (inanimate). Verbs are divided into two classes, active or dynamic, e.g. "eat, roar, plant," and stative or inactive, e.g. "stand, be tall, be green." Nouns similarly belong either to the active or animate class, e.g "child, lion, hunter," or to the inactive or inanimate, e.g. "chair, house, hill." Clauses and sentences have two principal patterns: active and inactive. Active sentences are bound together by pairing animate nouns with active verbs, inactive sentences by pairing inanimate nouns with inactives or statives.

The basic structure has numerous additional consequences, of which we cite a few here. Inflection of nouns is poor, especially of inactive nouns. Inflection of verbs, on the other hand, is rich, especially of active verbs. Particles are prominent, filling some of the roles that cases do in accusative and ergative languages and also indicating modality of verbs.

Over the last decade a number of linguists have proposed that Pre-Indo-European was an active language, with residues in Proto-Indo-European. In this way they account for the defective nominal inflection in the plural, as well as the absence of feminine gender; the earlier contrast was between animate (Proto-Indo-European masculine) and inanimate (Proto-Indo-European neuter). Further, the long-standing problem of the origin of the perfect and its relationship with the middle is clarified; both have developed from the earlier stative conjugation. Moreover, we can now account for the great variety of verbs for "have" in the various dialects, as well as for the Latin *mihi est* construction; each dialect needed to develop a verb for "have" as is typical in accusative languages. The fullest account of this view of Pre-Indo-European has been provided by Gamkrelidze and

Ivanov (1984: 308–19). We will examine the conclusions further in chapter 10.

By another typological approach, languages are classified as either head-marking or dependent-marking (Nichols 1986). Head-marking languages indicate syntactic relationships with devices applied to heads of constructions, as in Hebrew, e.g. *B'nai B'rith*, Hebrew *bənē bərith* "sons of the covenant," where *bənē* is marked through modification from the absolute plural form *bɔnīm*. Dependent-marking languages, on the other hand, indicate such relationships with modifications applied to subordinate or dependent segments, as in English, e.g. *Mary's sons*, *sons of Mary*. In head-marking languages, the equivalent of *sons*, rather than of *Mary*, is marked by some device. Active languages are strongly head-marking. Nichols then subsumes contentive typological classification under that of head/dependent-marking. Although other linguists as well examine languages in this way, analysis of active structure has provided important insights, especially into Pre-Indo-European, as we note in greater detail in chapter 10.

4.8 ATTENTION TO THE LEXICON

While the lexicon is least structured of the components of language, it may also be examined for structural classes. As we noted above with reference to Specht's conclusions, words may be sorted out by the level of culture of the society using a language. Indo-Europeanists have long pointed to the presence in the proto-language of only one word for "metal," a word represented in Modern English as *ore*. The lack of words for specific metals suggests that the culture of the community at a late stage of the proto-language was neolithic. Other evidence bears out the conclusion.

Languages may then be analysed for layers, representing cultural stages. Such analysis is comparable to that introduced into archaeology at the beginning of this century, by means of which successive stages of habitation and culture may be determined. Specht's use of the approach provides highly important information on the state of the society at which the technological developments enabling increased mobility were introduced. By determining stages of development in a language, such as the introduction of thematic inflection, items may be identified for relative chronology, and then linked to archaeological discoveries that may be identified for absolute chronology.

A different kind of insight into lexical problems resulted from the hypothesis that at an earlier stage the language was active. While nouns and verbs are assigned to either an active, animate or an inactive, inanimate class, some items may be viewed as both animate and inanimate. Indo-Europeanists have long been puzzled by the presence of two words for some items, such as fire and water. Assumption of active structure provides a clarification. Fire and water, like other objects and activities, may be viewed as either an active process or as an inanimate thing. In consideration of such a view, words of both classes may be in use for them. When the structure of the language changes, as to accusative, only one term for each item may be retained. The Greek *pûr* of neuter gender, as well as the English word *fire*, may be accounted for as reflexes of the inactive noun, Latin *ignis* and its cognates as reflexes of the active noun. The conclusion finds support in that *Agnis*, the Sanskrit word cognate with *ignis*, is the name of the god of fire. Other such lexical items have been similarly explained as residues of the earlier active type.

Structural attention to the vocabulary has in this way clarified views on the technology and the culture of the speakers, and also long-standing problems like the presence of two words for meanings like "fire, water, lie, sit." We examine such findings in chapter 11, noting possible evidence for determining the homeland of the society of Indo-European speakers.

4.9 AVENUES TO THE NEW INSIGHTS

Indo-European studies today have profited from three advances beyond the possibilities available to specialists during the nineteenth century. Improved understanding of the data in the attested languages has been achieved through a more rigorous structural approach. Important new material, especially in the Anatolian subgroup, has provided information on earlier stages of the Indo-European family. And the general study of language, by which characteristic patterns and interrelationships have been identified, has enabled clarification of structures and problems that earlier Indo-Europeanists could not solve.

The possibilities made available by these three advances have not been exhausted. Careful examination of texts, even those long studied, may lead to further understanding of the early period and may provide further insights into early stages of the proto-language. Additional data are being provided through archaeological finds that supplement our information derived from the languages and the texts. As typological investigations continue, they disclose more characteristics of specific types of languages and of those types in change, so that we can more accurately interpret our data. Accordingly, the revised view of the proto-language in its society that is now being proposed is by no means closed.

5 Phonology 1: Proto-Indo-European

5.1 THE PHONOLOGICAL SYSTEM OF PROTO-INDO-EUROPEAN

Following the publication of Meillet's *Introduction* in 1937, Indo-Europeanists agree in general on the phonological system of the proto-language. It has been determined by application of the comparative method, the results of which are treated phonemically. The phonemes are also examined for their morphological roles, especially in verbal roots and bases. In contrast, the system given in the older standard handbooks is based essentially on phonetic analysis, extended by the procedures that Brugmann labeled purely systematic (1897: ix).

This chapter presents the currently assumed system, with attention to positions that were held in the past, as well as to disputed analyses and the bases for the disagreements. Since our view of the morphological patterning follows the formulations of Benveniste (1935), which represents a rigorous version of the root theory propounded already by Saussure (1879) and elaborated by others, including Meillet, we sketch it briefly.

5.1.1 Indo-European root structure

The morphemes with most distinct structure are verbal roots. Morphological analysis in the last century determined that these generally consist of the sequence *Consonant–Vowel–Consonant*. Saussure employed such a sequence in 1879 for determining coefficients. The position is summarized by Meillet (1937: 173–82) and Schrijnen and Fischer (1921: 272–88). Hirt, as we note below, considered roots to be abstractions of linguists; instead, he proposed bases that he considered full words in the early period of Proto-Indo-European.

Benveniste contributed to our understanding of Indo-European morphological structure by proposing rigorously determined extensions of

Sources for this chapter: Brugmann (1897: 72–622; 1904a: 51–108); Meillet (1937: 82–145); Lehmann (1952); Gamkrelidze and Ivanov (1984: 5–151); Mayrhofer (1986: 88–177); Szemerényi (1970 [1989]: 39–72).

roots that he called theme I and theme II (1935: 147–73). Adopting Hirt's term, we call them bases; they are also referred to as stems (see Lehmann 1952: 17–18). These are as follows. (C here stands for any consonant, i.e. obstruent, laryngeal or resonant; *e* is the typical vowel in normal grade, and accordingly we use it in the illustration. We leave to chapter 6 treatment of the two possible extensions of base II: CC-*é*C-C- and CC-*n*-*é*C-.)

Root structure:	C*é*C	
Bases:	I	II
	C*é*C-C	CC-*é*C-

As example of the three patterns we may use forms from the root **ter-* "cross over, overcome" (Pokorny 1959: 1074–5):

		ter- as in Sanskirit *tárati*
	ter-x-	tr-ex-
	as in Hittite *tarhzi*	as in Latin *trāre*

By Benveniste's statement any form extended beyond these three constructs and the two extensions of base II is a nominal base.

The verbal roots and bases serve to distinguish subclasses among the phonological elements. We find sequences of the types TRET and TERT, though not RTET or TETR, nor ETRT or TRTE (where T represents obstruents, i.e. stops and the fricative /s/; R represents resonants /w y r l m n/; E represents vowels). We assume accordingly these three subclasses, distinguishing them by their position in bases: obstruents stand only at the boundaries of bases; resonants may also, but not outside an obstruent; vowels are nuclei of bases.

Using the further cover symbol H for laryngeals, we find sequences of the type HET, THER, TEHR, TERH, TETH. As these sequences indicate, laryngeals may stand before or after resonants in bases, but not before obstruents initially. Since the distribution differs from that of the other elements, we posit laryngeals as a fourth subclass. Most treatments today assume three laryngeals, which we symbolize as /χ ɣ ʔ/; others, including that here, assume a fourth laryngeal, /h/. Below we examine evidence for these assumptions, as well as alternative assumptions, including those in the standard handbooks.

5.1.2 The phonological system of Proto-Indo-European

The phonological system for the stage of Proto-Indo-European presented here is as follows:

1 Obstruents:	p	t	k	k^w
	b	d	g	g^w
	b^h	d^h	g^h	g^{wh}
	s			

2 Resonants:	m	n		
	w	r	l	y

3 Vowels:			ī		ū
	e	e	o	ē	ō
		a		ā	

4 Laryngeals: x   γ   h   ʔ

The standard symbols for the elements of subsets 1 and 2 of the obstruents are maintained deliberately, with superscript ^{h} in subset 3 the only modification. All the handbooks, including the dictionaries and the grammars for individual dialects, use them; alteration of symbolism then merely causes confusion. Interpretation of the phonetic entities signaled by the symbols may readily be carried out as is done for languages spoken today. By the glottalic theory *b d g g^w* are written as voiceless glottalics, (*p'*), *t'*, *k'*, *k'^{w}*; since the correspondence is regular, the symbols in the handbooks can readily be interpreted as representing glottalics.

An accentual system of high pitch, symbolized by the acute mark á, and of low pitch, symbolized by the grave mark à when useful to indicate, is further assumed. Low pitch is generally not indicated here. Nor do we discuss at this point distribution of accent in paradigms.

Further, the distribution of consonants demonstrates that sequences we identify as words were distinguished by signals labeled junctures, that is, word, clause and sentence boundary signals. Clauses and sentences were distinguished by boundary signals consisting of pitch and modified duration.

Most of the dialects treat final syllables of words differently from internal syllables. In Greek, for example, only /n r s/ among the consonants are permitted to stand finally. In Germanic and other dialects final syllables exhibit various kinds of losses. The proposed word juncture will be indicated by a space rather than by an additional symbol. Some lexical items lacking accent are added to accented words with no such juncture, the so-called enclitics or clitics. These carry low pitch, and may be distinguished by the grave mark.

Differences among representations and interpretation of the various symbols will be discussed in the sections below.

5.2 THE OBSTRUENTS

In view of our primary concern with the theories by which the elements are determined, and of the availability of numerous examples of the phonemes in many handbooks, only one example will be given for each phoneme.

Evidence for the obstruents: *initials only! No Anatolian or Tokarian*

p:	Skt *pitár-*, Gk *patér*, Lat. *pater*, Goth. *fadar* "father":	PIE p$_e$ter-	
t:	Skt *tráyas*, Gk *treîs*, Lat. *trēs*, Olr. *trī* "three"	PIE treyes-	
k:	Skt *kraviṣ-*, Gk *kréas*, Lat. *cruor*, Olr. *crū* "meat, blood"	PIE krew-	
kʷ:	Skt *kás*, Gk *tís*, Lat. *quis*, Goth. *hʷis* "who"	PIE kʷis	
b:	Skt *bálam* "strength", Gk *bélteron* "better", Lat. *debilis* "weak"	PIE bel-	
d:	Skt *dīrghás*, Gk *dolikhós* "long", Goth. *tulgus* "steadfast"	PIE d$_e$lgʰ-	
g:	Lith. *gérvè*, Gk *géranos*, Welsh *garan*, OHG *cranah* "crane"	PIE ger$_e$n-	
gʷ:	Skt *gámanti*, Gk *báske* "go", Lat. *veniō*, Goth. *qiman* "come"	PIE gʷem-	
bʰ:	Skt *bhárāmi*, Arm. *berem*, Lat. *ferō*, Olr. *berim* "I bear"	PIE bʰer-	
dʰ:	Skt *dhárṣati*, Lith. *dresù*, Goth. *ga-dars* "I dare"	PIE dʰer-	
gʰ:	OCS *gadajǫ*, Gk *khandánō*, Lat. *pre-hendō* "I guess, seize"	PIE gʰer-	
gʷʰ:	Skt *gharmás*, Gk *thermós*, Lat. *formus*, ON *varmr* "warm"	PIE gʷʰer-	
s:	Skt *saptá*, Gk *heptá*, Lat. *septem*, Olr. *secht n-* "seven"	PIE septm̥	

Three major situations among the obstruents have been topics of concern. Since the phonological system was initially based largely on that of Sanskrit, a set of voiceless aspirated stops was proposed. Moreover, from the time of the earliest linguists, including Jacob Grimm, the small number of items attesting /b/ was pointed out. Third, the number of tectals was generally assumed to be three for each series, a palatal, a velar and a labiovelar. We discuss these problems.

5.2.1 The voiceless aspirated stops that were formerly assumed

As we have noted, evidence for this set was based almost entirely on Sanskrit. After initial *s* some Greek words exhibit the voiceless aspirated stop, as in *skhízō*, Sanskrit *chinátti*, Gothic *skaido* "cut off." Since other proposed aspirates have unaspirated reflexes, the aspirated reflex after *s* may be a result of the environment. Medially after *s* as well, Greek may exhibit a voiceless unaspirated stop, as in *ostéon*, Sanskrit *ásthi* "bone." Support from Greek for positing Indo-European voiceless aspirates is therefore weak. Moreover, relatively few examples are found even in Sanskrit; Szemerényi lists ten, and a few more after *s* (1970 [1989]: 70). And in some of these the etymology is obscure, reducing even further the possible number of Indo-European words with such stops.

Pursuing a brief note of Saussure's (see 1921: 603), Kurylowicz proposed that many of the Sanskrit voiceless aspirated stops resulted from voiceless stop followed by aspirated laryngeal (1935: 46–54, 254–5). A clear example is the root for "stand," generally written *stʰā-*. According to the laryngeal theory the long vowel resulted from contraction of *-e-* with a following *a-* coloring laryngeal, so that the early root was *teh-* with movable *s* initially. When the root was in zero grade, the laryngeal came to stand directly after the *-t-*, as in the third person singular Sanskrit *tí-ṣṭh-ati*, coalescing with it to produce an aspirated stop in Indic. From the reflex in the zero grade the aspirated stop spread to other forms of the root.

Kurylowicz proposed further that the voiceless aspirated stops became phonemic when reflexes of voiceless stop plus /h/ merged with devoiced variants of the voiced aspirates. This statement has been dealt with sceptically (Szemerényi 1970 [1989]: 56, 69–71, 109, 152–3; Mayrhofer 1986: 92). As a third source, some Sanskrit words including voiceless aspirates were introduced from non-Indo-European languages, e.g. *phala-* "fruit." The clusters of stop and *a*-coloring laryngeals and devoiced allophones of voiced aspirates could have developed into separate phonemes through merger with such borrowings.

However the voiceless aspirated stops arose in Sanskrit, they are assumed for the proto-language only by those maintaining the approach of the standard handbooks.

5.2.2 The infrequency of *b* and the glottalic theory

The standard handbooks, from the time of Schleicher, simply record the infrequent employment of *b*. Only in recent times have further conclusions been made on the basis of its infrequency. Before considering these we may mention that Szemerényi finds its frequency normal (1970 [1989]: 153). He admits that relatively few *b* are attested initially, but considers the medial attestations to be in accordance with expected frequency.

Pedersen did consider the frequency of *b* irregular, and proposed as explanation that it had developed from earlier *p* (1951). He supported this assumption by noting that the voiceless stop often has lesser frequency in phonological systems. The proposal would, of course, modify the entire set of stops assumed for the proto-language. It was received respectfully, in view of Pedersen's eminence, but in general ignored.

From the 1960s there has been great interest in phonological universals. A conference in 1961 was followed up by an extensive study directed by Joseph Greenberg; concurrently other investigations were being carried out, as at the University of California at Los Angeles. On the basis of these studies and also attention to aboriginal languages, as by Kuipers (see 1968) and linguists in the Summer Institute of Linguistics, typical patterns of phonological elements were determined, leading to an extensive typology. In the early 1970s some of the conclusions were applied to the phonological system of the proto-language.

Starting from the observation of the infrequent *b*, Gamkrelidze and Ivanov, and Hopper in 1973, proposed that the assumed voiced stops had developed from glottalic voiceless stops (see 4.4.3). As a supporting phonological argument they referred to a statement by Jakobson in his paper at the Oslo Congress of Linguists that no phonological system with members consisting of voiceless, voiced and voiced aspirated stop, e.g. /t d dh/, has been attested, and further that such a system is highly unlikely. The observation was widely approved, although Djahukian among others rejects it (1990). We may also note that after the voiceless aspirates were eliminated from the proto-language, Indo-Europeanists no longer proposed that the elements represented with added *h* were voiced aspirates. Even before the end of the nineteenth century the distinguished Indo-Europeanist, Walde, had argued for fricative articulation (1897). This interpretation was adopted by the vigorous Germanist, Prokosch (1939). Yet proponents of the glottalic interpretation still state that before proposal of the "glottalic theory" the *dh* set was interpreted as a voiced aspirated stop.

The glottalicists have also supported their proposal with morphological arguments, such as the structure of affixes, in which the voiced stops (in their interpretation glottalic voiceless stops) are relatively infrequent. By their view, when glottalics are found in a language, they are poorly employed in derivational and inflectional morphology. Further, they attempted to account for the absence of roots like *deg-, by their view **t'ek'*-, on the grounds that two glottalics would not be permitted in a root. Yet Wedekind in an impressive article points out that African languages, especially those of Ethiopia, have no such constraints (1990). He also suggests that glottalics may seem to be unusual for Indo-Europeanists, but demonstrates that they are widespread in other language families.

Moreover, it has long been observed that roots consisting of voiceless stops and aspirated stops, e.g. **b^{h}et*-, **teb^h*- etc., are not attested. The glottalicists have suggested that their interpretation of these is superior to those given previously. Like the previous proposals, their argumentation rests on dissimilatory effects. By one previously proposed explanation the basis of the dissimilation was fortis articulation. Under the glottalic theory the basis is nonglottalic stop articulation, that is, weaker grounds.

Arguments in favor of the glottalic theory are purely typological. Some efforts have been made to ascribe glottalic stops in Armenian dialects and in Sindhi to retention from the proto-language, but these have not been widely accepted; rather, in both languages the glottalics are assumed to be recent. The theory has also been rejected by nostraticists.

By the glottalic theory the threefold set of stops in each of the four locations would consist of a glottalic, the member represented by traditional *b d g g^w*, and of voiceless and voiced stops, each with aspirated allophones: /p t k k^w/ [p p^h t t^h k k^h k^w k^{wh}] and /b d g g^w/ [b b^h d d^h g g^h g^w g^{wh}]. New symbols have been proposed for the glottalics in place of the standard (*b*) *d g g^w*, i.e. (*p'*) *t' k' k'^{w}*. Reaction to the theory has been varied; see especially Vennemann (1989: 85–263) and Djahukian (1990).

As noted above, some efforts have been made to support the theory by ascribing phenomena in the early dialects to retention of the glottalics. By one of these Winter suggested that long vowels before voiced stops in Baltic and Slavic occur when the stop developed from a glottalic (rather than from the stop with aspiration), e.g. Lithuanian *ė̃du*, Latin *edō* "eat," Lithuanian *sėdė̃ti*, Latin *sedeō* "sit" (1978: 431–46). Among the dozen or so reflexes of the situation, about a third are exceptions, e.g. Lithuanian *pãdas* "sole of shoe," Russian *pod* "ground," Greek *podós* (genitive) "foot." Some scholars have accepted the suggestion enthusiastically, notably Kortlandt, who labeled the proposal "Winter's law" (in Winter 1978: 447). Others have argued against it with equal vigor (Szemerényi 1970 [1989]: 162–3).

Examining a different situation, I have proposed that the aberrant treatment found in some reflexes of the dental initially may be ascribed to its glottalic articulation (1986b). Found in initial cluster with *l*, as in Latin *longus* < **dlongus*, cf. Greek *dolikhós*, the assumed glottalic was lost; it was also lost in Baltic, e.g. Lithuanian *ìlgas* "long". Further, in this way we may account for the so-called Sabine *l* of Latin; in a number of words the assumed dental glottalic stop shows up as *l*, e.g. *lacruma* "tear" < **dacruma*. While there is no previous explanation of these changes, this proposal has largely typological support.

In the most extensive reconsideration of dialect developments with reference to the glottalic theory, Vennemann has reinterpreted the obstruent structure in the Germanic dialects (1984: 1–45). Distinguishing between the northern dialects and the southern, especially Old High German, he uses the theory to propose a direct development from the Indo-European system to those in the two sets of Germanic dialects. There would not then be a first Germanic consonant shift and a second that applies only to High German, but a separate treatment from the time of Proto-Indo-European. Like the other reappraisals of dialect situations in the light of the glottalic theory, Vennemann's has had a varied reception.

Other typological information fails to support the model: for example, on the basis of observations in many languages, glottalics have been identified as the least marked members of the stop series. Apart from the labial gap in the set of voiceless stops, they are generally maintained in phonological systems. In view of this universal, Krauss has asked why they should have been changed in the proto-language (1990: 150).

Moreover, Szemerényi has pointed out that ejectives have been attested chiefly in the Americas and in the Caucasus, with some attestation in Africa, but only in Ossetic and East Armenian of the Indo-European languages, both located in the neighborhood of the Caucasian languages (1970 [1989]: 159–62).

The glottalic theory faces additional problems, such as the massive changes its assumption requires throughout the Indo-European dialects. Formerly, Germanic and Armenian were identified as the only dialects undergoing considerable change of obstruents. By the glottalic model these branches are relatively conservative, and the other dialects have modified the obstruent system.

In addition, Szemerényi asks how voiceless ejectives could have become voiced (1970 [1989]: 162). Since the glottalic theory is relatively recent, such questions may be answered eventually. Its acceptance, as noted by Vennemann (1989: 107–15), will no doubt depend on whether more unexplained phenomena in the various dialects can be accounted for by it. Until they are, Vennemann's characterization is valid, that, unlike the laryngeal theory, it accounts for only the data to which it is applied (1989: xi). That evaluation is scarcely surprising, because the theory is essentially concerned with phonetic interpretation rather than with modification of the phonological system. Under the theory there are still three manners of articulation, and the same oppositions as for the traditional triad exemplified by *t d dh*.

5.2.3 The tectals

The standard handbooks apart from Meillet's propose three tectals – palatals, pure velars and labio-velars (Brugmann 1897: 542–622; Mayrhofer 1986: 101–9; Szemerényi 1970 [1989]: 60–9). Yet none of the dialects show reflexes of more than two. Albanian, to be sure, contains a threefold set; but its reflexes are recent and scarcely provide cogent evidence for Proto-Indo-European. The three sets assumed for the proto-language result from strict application of the comparative method, in accordance with Brugmann's systematic approach. Using the phonemic approach in applying the comparative method, Meillet assumed two tectals, velars with palatal and pure velar allophones, and labio-velars (1937: 91–5).

The assumption of two sets recognizes the distribution in the centum languages and that in the satem languages; neither group provides a threefold contrast, as do, for example, English *tin* : *thin* : *sin*. Meillet assumes the centum set for the proto-language, since there is evidence in the satem group for a change involving palatalization. By his view the centum languages are the more conservative in their treatment of the tectals. This assumption finds support in Tocharian and Anatolian; they include only one set, although evidence has been found to demonstrate that earlier forms of each also included more tectals.

Under Meillet's assumption there was a sound change in a central area of the late proto-language – the so-called satem languages – by which velars before front vowels became sibilants. Those before back consonants merged with the labio-velars, which lost their labial coarticulation. His view may be supported by the observation that the coarticulated labio-velar stops were unstable; in Greek, which includes evidence for their maintenance in the Mycenaean inscriptions, they developed to simple stops in three positions: to dentals before high front vowels *i*, *e*, as in *tís* "who," cf. Latin *quis*; to labials before *a*, *o*, as in *poû* "where," cf. Latin *quō*; to velars before *u*, e.g. *kúklos* "wheel," where Old English *hwēol* maintains evidence for earlier velar plus labial articulation. In Germanic and Italic the labio-velars often developed into clusters.

In seeking to support the assumption of three sets of tectals, Mayrhofer cites the following group (1986: 103):

Greek	*Sanskrit*
kléos	śrávas "glory"
kréas	kravís "raw meat"
príasthai	krī- "buy"

Yet these lists require only two sets; for neither Greek nor Sanskrit has three different reflexes. The different reflexes in individual pairs can be ascribed to allophonic variation in the proto-language; *k* before *l* may have been palatal. If there had been three distinct tectals, it is highly unlikely that every dialect would maintain only two.

Proper treatment of the situation involves consideration of the early Indo-European languages as members of a dialect continuum. In a central area, spirantization of the palatal allophones took place, extending throughout Indo-Iranian, Armenian and Albanian. But the change did not affect all potential palatal tectals in Baltic and Slavic. Among examples are Lithuanian *pēkus*, Old Prussian *pecku*, vs. Sanskrit *páśu* "cattle, herd"; Old Slavic *svekrŭ* vs. Lithuanian *šẽšuras*, Sanskrit *švášuras* "brother-in-law" (see Brugmann 1897: 545–7, who cites many more examples as well as sources with additional lists). The distribution of shifted and unshifted palatals is typical of a change in a dialect area, for example, that of the High German stops; here the sound change took place in the south and spread to the north, with increasing numbers of residues at greater distances from the focal area. Outside the influence of the focal area, the shift was not adopted; pre-Old High German voiceless stops shifted to voiceless fricatives in *schlafen* "sleep," *wasser* "water," *machen* "make," but not in the Low German *slapen*, *water*, *maken*. The area between High German and Low German shows irregular adoption of the voiceless fricatives, much as Baltic and Slavic do of the palatalized fricatives.

In short, if one deals with the late period of the proto-language realistically, the reflexes in the various dialects can readily be explained by assuming two sets of tectals, as Szemerényi concedes (1970 [1989]: 153–6). That they were open to combinatory change can be demonstrated by their treatment in Sanskrit, where only one reflex of the three proposed variants is found before *s* (Brugmann 1897: 545). A phonemic presentation of the system then must follow that of Meillet.

5.2.4 The proposed interdental fricatives

Another problem whose solution depends on one's theoretical position concerns consonant clusters, as in Greek *téktōn* "carpenter," Sanskrit *tákṣan* "artisan," Latin *texō* "weave," Old Slavic *tesla* "axe," Old High German *dehsala* "axe," where the reflexes in Latin and Germanic indicate a voiceless cluster. By contrast, in Greek *khthṓn*, Sanskrit *kṣam-*, Old Slavic *zemlja*, possibly Albanian *dhe* "earth," some reflexes, like the Slavic here, indicate voiced initial. As these and other examples illustrate, some cognates may have only one consonant, as in Latin *humus* "earth," Old English *guma* "(earthling,) man." Moreover, Hittite with *te-kán* and Tocharian with *tkan, kem* "earth" have simple stops.

Since these words have different reflexes from those in which *s* followed *k*, as it does in Greek *áksōn*, Sanskrit *ákṣas*, Latin *axis* "axle", by Brugmann's systematic approach a further set of fricatives was proposed for the proto-language, interdentals: *θ θh ð ðh*. The voiceless and voiced reflexes as cited above suggested voiceless and voiced fricatives that were identified as interdental; the two aspirated items filled out the set in accordance with systematic practice (see Brugmann 1897: 561–2, 790–3).

Yet the number of forms in which the clusters are found is small, and accordingly the proposal of an additional set of fricatives has seemed cumbersome. Various explanations have been advanced. Benveniste dealt with the items with reference to his root theory. There is no evidence for a root **tek-* "weave" nor for an extended base **tk-eC-*; accordingly, he assumed single phonemes, which he reconstructed as the affricates k^s, g^z, g^{zh} (1937: 139–47). While morphologically cogent, his assumption of a further infrequent set of tectals suffers from the same weakness as the assumption of interdental fricatives in the standard handbooks.

I have taken them to be clusters of homorganic velar and dental, e.g. *kt*, *gd*, *gd^h*. The two elements always have the same manner of articulation, both voiceless, as in "artisan," or both voiced, as in "earth," and so on. While the order of the two elements is not significant, since dialects may exhibit either, I have written them conventionally in the order found most frequently, velar plus dental (1952: 99–100). Others write them in the converse order (Mayrhofer 1986: 151–8, with bibliography; see also Szemerényi 1970 [1989]: 54). While this sequence is supported by the Hittite and Tocharian reflexes, a cluster of dental plus velar seems more likely than the reverse. Current treatments may vary in this way in details, but they differ in their theoretical position from earlier explanations in not adding further phonemes to the stock in the parent language.

5.2.5 Summary of the theoretical positions affecting the assumption of obstruents

By the purely systematic approach, Brugmann and the standard handbooks assume separate entities for phonological sets found in only one of the earliest attested dialects, as when they posit voiceless aspirated stops on the basis of Sanskrit alone, with some support in Greek. This approach has now been abandoned. Efforts are made to account for the situation in the aberrant dialect, as Kuryłowicz did for the proposed voiceless aspirated stops; unless there are reflexes in the other dialects that can better be explained by assuming additional sets, such as the laryngeals, the proto-language is reconstructed on the basis of the majority of dialects.

Similarly, the earlier assumption of additional sets, as for the tectals that do not exhibit minimal pairs in any one dialect, is less widely held; some nostraticists claim, however, that their evidence requires a threefold set (Shevoroshkin and Ramer 1991: 189–90). The older assumption represents a phonetic approach. Meillet adopted a phonemic approach in assuming only two sets of tectals. Like him, Indo-Europeanists and other historical linguists today reconstruct phonemes within a phonological system. They then propose allophones, such as palatalized velars before front vowels.

By another current approach, findings from examination of all studied languages have been assembled to determine phonological universals. The conclusions are applied in reconstructing credible systems, in proposing the phonetic characteristics of individual phonemes and in checking reconstructed sequences.

As a result of these steps, greater realism has been achieved for providing credible systems, and identifying the allophones of the phonemes. Moreover, whatever the reaction to conclusions, the bases for them are explicitly stated. Accordingly, in reviewing interpretations of the attested data, and also in examining possibilities for further analysis and comparison, even those with different views can identify the grounds for the conclusions and explanations that have been provided. Indo-Europeanists who fail to agree with interpretations of any of the problems, or with the methodology on which they were based, may support their views either through use of additional data or improved approaches.

5.3 THE RESONANTS

The greater precision that was observed by linguists after the clarification resulting from Verner's article of 1875 led to the understanding of the system of resonants in the proto-language. The consonantal members had been assumed without difficulty; but because of merger of some *l* with *r* in Vedic, there was at one time question whether the proto-language included an *l*. The problem was soon resolved.

The following are examples of the consonantal members:

y:	Skt *yugam*, Lat. *jugum*, Goth. *juka*, Lith. *jùngas* "yoke"	PIE [yug-]	ᚲᛋᚾᚲᚠ
w:	Skt *veda*, OCS *vědē*, Gk (*w*)*oîda*, Goth. *wait* "I know"	PIE [woyd-]	ᛈᚱᛁᛏ
m:	Skt *mātár*, OCS *mati*, Gk *mḗtēr*, Lat. *mater* "mother"	PIE [mēt-]	ᛗᚨᛈᛁᚱ
n:	Skt *návas*, Lith. *naũjas*, Gk *néos*, Lat. *novus* "new"	PIE [new-]	ᛏᛗᚾᛐ-
r:	Skt *rudhirás*, Lith. *raũdas*, Gk *eruthrós*, Goth. *raudai* "red"	PIE [rewdʰ-]	ᚱᚠᚾᛒ-
l:	Skt *riṇákti*, Gk *leípō*, Lat. *linquō* Goth. *leihʷan* "leave"	PIE [leykʷ-]	ᛗᛁᚼᛈ-

As we have observed above, the early dialects also included forms of these in which the resonant appeared as a vowel, for example, *i* in the first person plural of "I know": *y* [i] Sanskrit *vidmá*, Greek *ísmen*, Gothic *witum* "we know". In the interpretation of these forms, the relationship between accent and vocalism became apparent after the publication of Verner's article. Thereupon in 1876 Osthoff posited for the proto-language vocalic r̥, as in the participial form *dhr̥ṣṭá-* "daring," Greek *thrasús* "bold," Old English *gedyrst* "daring," parallel to the vocalic variants *i* and *u*. Since Indian grammarians had recognized it in long as well as short variant, the proposal was readily accepted. Later in the year Brugmann proposed vocalic nasals as well. These are not maintained in any dialect, but have reflexes either of short vowel or short vowel plus nasal, as in Sanskrit *matás*, Lithuanian *miñtas*, Greek *autó-matos*, Latin *com-mentus* from the root **men-* "think", with the zero-grade form *mn-* [mn̥] in these words. The proposal illustrates Brugmann's imagination, as well as his attention to structures and substructures.

A further step was taken by Sievers in the following year; see 4.4.1. To account for the variation in Gothic inflections, as in the second person singular present of *nasjan* "save" in contrast with that of *sōkjan* "seek," he proposed that in the proto-language the resonants had varying representations, in accordance with the weight of the preceding syllable. When standing before the ending *-is*, the resonant was consonantal after short syllables, as in *nasjis* "thou savest"; but when after long syllables, it was vocalic plus consonantal, as in *sōkeis*, a reflex of earlier **sōkijis*. Sievers extended the observation also to Vedic.

Sievers's observation was presented informally; but it was soon labeled a law, noted also for other Indo-European languages and accounted for as the result of allophonic variation in the proto-language. Schrijnen and Fischer state that "the Indo-European sounds *r*, *l*, *m*, *n* are accordingly comparable to *i* and *u*' (1921: 266). By the assumption, Indo-European *w* and the other resonants varied in the proto-language between consonantal, e.g. [w], vocalic, e.g. [u], and vocalic plus consonantal expression, e.g. [uw], in accordance with the adjacent elements and also with the weight of the preceding syllable.

The variation in Germanic that Sievers accounted for was examined extensively in Vedic. In Vedic poetry, vocalic elements of the resonants count as syllables metrically, in contrast with the consonantal elements: for example, in the Strophic hymn to Varuna, *Rigveda* 7.86.4, the n of the fourth word must be read with vowel plus consonant after the long preceding syllable, i.e. *-mn̥n-* even though it is written as a consonant:

sr̥já, vatsáṃ ná dā́mno, Vásiṣṭham.
free calf like from-rope Vasistha
"Release Vasistha, like a calf from a rope."

Only in this way is the line metrical. The metrical rule does not apply throughout the *Rigveda*, however, because Vedic poetry was composed over an extended period of time; later verse does not show the variation of resonants that is found in earlier verse. Moreover, seven of the ten books of the *Rigveda* are compilations maintained by individual families, and there is little likelihood that the hymns even in these were composed by the same author who preserved the early system; this situation is even less probable in the first, ninth and tenth books whose compilers are more diverse. It is then unrealistic to expect that the variation of resonants in the proto-language is preserved.

In seeking evidence for the basis of the variation in the proto-language, it is important to examine the older verse, that of the so-called Archaic and Strophic periods of the *Rigveda*. But even in these periods, suffixes including resonants, especially *y*, have specific morphological values, and as such they tended to be frozen. Accordingly, since the variation was brought about early in the proto-language, metrical exploitation of them may not be in accordance with the initial situation. Examination of their readings may then reveal more about metrical practices by authors than about the situation at the time of origin of the threefold variants. It is well known also of Homeric and other poetry that poets, while making use of their own language, may archaize in selected patterns for various reasons, among them to secure greater esteem in following a poetic tradition. The proto-language situation then must be reconstructed with the help of residues, not only in Vedic but also the other dialects.

In 1934 Edgerton published an initial essay on the resonants, interpreting them from a phonemic point of view. He followed up this study with an extended essay in 1943. At this time he provided specific formulae for the treatment of the resonants, amplifying Sievers's conclusions, as we may illustrate with /y/.

1 If standing between vowels, if after pause (|) or single consonant and before vowel, e.g. /a/, or after vowel before pause or a consonant (C), the allophone was consonantal, e.g. [y], as in the formulae: aya, |ya, ay|, ayC, aCya.
2 If standing between consonants, where pause equals a consonant, the allophone is vocalic, e.g. [i], as in: CiC, |iC, Ci|.
3 If following two consonants (or consonant and pause), or after long vowel (i.e. short vowel and laryngeal) plus consonant and before vowel, the allophone is vocalic + consonantal, e.g. [iy], as in: CCiya, āCiya, |Ciya.

Examples of y for each of its allophones are as follows:

Sanskrit *yakṛt*, Lithuanian *jēknos* (plural), Latin *jecur* "liver"; Sanskrit *vidmá*, Greek *ísmen*, Gothic *witum* "we know," Latin *videō* "I see"; Sanskrit *pátriyas*, Greek *pátrios* "pertaining to the father."

The six resonants exhibit parallel variation in this way. On the basis of Edgerton's detailed demonstration of the specific environments for each allophone, the formulation is now often referred to as the Sievers–Edgerton law.

This analysis of the resonant subsystem in the proto-language has numerous consequences. As one that troubles some linguists, it requires positing either six "consonantal" members of the system or six "vocalic" members. Most treatments published after Edgerton's formulations posit consonantal /y w r l m n/. In accordance with phonemic theory, there then are no *i u* phonemes in the vocalic system of Proto-Indo-European. Moreover, since long *ī ū* result from coalescence of short resonant plus laryngeal, there are also no long high vowels before coalescence of vocalic allophones with laryngeals. The vowel system then seems to be reduced in membership, though the reduction is only at the phonemic level, not the phonetic.

A phonological system for the proto-language may, on the other hand, be constructed at the phonetic level, as was done by Brugmann and his contemporaries. One then must accept for the system a full panoply of short resonant vowels and long resonant vowels, or variants of these as devised by some Indo-Europeanists; Hirt included in such variants a second schwa, the so-called schwa secundum. Some Indo-Europeanists still maintain Brugmann's rich system, though with less thorough inclusion of all the vocalic segments he proposed. If proceeding in this way, they need to state their assumptions; for operating with random procedures in dealing with scant data or even more so with reconstructions does not inspire confidence in proposed explanations.

Two further methodological observations are of interest in dealing with the resonants. One of these concerns the detailed compilations made by Seebold (1972). Examining only the variations involving the semivowel resonants, *y w*, he treated the *Rigveda* as a unitary text, though occasionally recognizing older hymns. Moreover, he viewed Indo-European in accordance with the standard handbooks, positing schwa rather than laryngeals. Operating under these premises, he arrived at generalizations by which he attributed the variation largely to metrical conventions. As might be expected for a diverse body of texts, the generalizations still have numerous exceptions. Seebold finds these normal, though he is sharply critical of Indo-Europeanists who cite Vedic examples in support of their formulations of the situation in the proto-language. Unfortunately, Seebold's attempt to account for the variation by assuming a phonological system lacking laryngeals deprives his massive effort of any hope of usefulness for Proto-Indo-European. It is a striking example of a painstaking work rendered futile because it is based on erroneous presuppositions.

A second point has to do with the dismissal of a phonemic approach in linguistics, initiated by Halle (1962) and widely held, at least until recently, by followers. By this assumption the description of a language proceeds directly from syntactic representations to phonetic expression; the procedure involves the assumption of "systematic phonemes" but not as members of a distinct component as in standard linguistics. The futility of this procedure was amply demonstrated by the formulation of the Great English Vowel Shift in accordance with it. Nonetheless its adoption has confused scholars, who persist in applying it to other phonological situations, such as that of the resonants in Proto-Indo-European. If any of these do, they must begin from representation of the S (sentence), which some even deny the possibility of reconstructing for the proto-language (Lightfoot 1979: 165). Any application of the assumption then is unfortunately a waste of time. In pursuing autosegmental approaches, some younger linguists from the generative-transformational tradition are now treating phonology much as did eminent earlier linguists like Sievers. The return to reality is refreshing.

We maintain the system of six resonants for the proto-language, with the three variants for each as determined by Edgerton. We also accept the consequences resulting from this system, such as removing /i u/ from the Indo-European phonological system, positing instead /y w/ with [i u] as allophonic subclasses.

5.4 THE LARYNGEALS; SEE ALSO 4.2.1

As indicated above, notations in Hittite that are represented by *h* in transliteration of the cuneiform symbols agree in some forms with the entities that had been posited and labeled coefficients by Saussure in 1879; in a note of 1879 by the Semitic linguist, Möller, they were relabeled laryngeals, a term that has been maintained. The two terms reflect differing methodological approaches. For Saussure, the entitites were distinguished by their increase in quantity of the preceding *e* to *ē, ā* or *ō*; hence the label, coefficient, as if for a mathematical abstraction. Möller equated them with laryngeal consonants in Semitic, and for that reason he introduced the term "laryngeal" into Indo-European.   *phonemes!?*

The evidence in Hittite was long overlooked, even though the language was recognized as Indo-European in 1915; yet social problems of the time unfortunately hampered correlation between the earlier assumption of laryngeals and the Hittite consonants written with *h* until 1927, when Kurylowicz published his article linking the two. Its implications were not perceived even then, so that modification of the phonological system to include laryngeals has only been gradually accepted. In this section we will deal largely with their representation, and with phonological evidence for assuming them. In chapter 6 we examine further the evidence from morphophonology and morphology.

5.4.1 The number and representation of the laryngeals

The notations in Hittite and the reflexes of the assumed laryngeals permitted wide interpretation. Although Saussure had posited two coefficients, and others raised the number to three, Hittite (by the conventional transliteration) employs only one letter, *h*, to represent them. Yet medially some words include double *h* with reasonable consistency, e.g. *pahhur* "fire" in contrast with others like *mehur* "time, point of time"; cf. the cognates Greek *pûr* "fire," Gothic *mel* "time." Double writing of *p t k s* was found to

? how reg?

be <u>used</u> to distinguish voiceless obstruents from voiced (Sturtevant 1942: 34, fn. 6). Sturtevant then proposed that the same orthographic principle applied to *h* and *hh*, concluding that two laryngeals were distinguished in Hittite notation. Total agreement regarding his proposal has never been reached, inasmuch as the distinction between single and double notation does not apply to resonants; if the convention for *h* is comparable to that for resonants rather than to that for obstruents, the distinction between single and double *h* would not be distinctive. Those accepting Sturtevant's proposal, on the other hand, posit two <u>velar fricatives</u> on the basis of the distinction: /χ ɣ/.

not same!

Hittite *h*, *hh* are the only unambiguous representations for the <u>laryngeals</u> in any of the Indo-European languages. Other evidence for the <u>coefficients</u>, however, had been assumed to consist in neighboring vowels. Assuming one vowel, *e*, for roots, Saussure had ascribed *a* as in roots like **ag-* "lead" to coloring of the *e* by the laryngeal. Hittite indeed includes forms that support the assumption, such as *har(k)-* "have, hold," Latin *arceō* "hold, enclose." The laryngeal /x/ then was confidently posited in the proto-form of the root for PIE **ag-* "lead," even though no Hittite cognate is found. Yet, as we have pointed out, Kurylowicz noted a further distinction in the texts. In <u>some Hittite forms</u> which paralleled forms in the other dialects with *a*, *h* never is written, such as *taya-* "steal," Sanskrit *(s)tāyús* "thief." He therefore posited two *a*-coloring laryngeals.

The modification of *e* in roots like **ag-* further suggested that vowels in roots with *o* might also be the result of coloring, as in Latin *pōtāre* "drink," Hittite *pahs-* "swallow, drink". If so, a third laryngeal is required. The *o*-coloring apparently resulted only when the laryngeal coalesced with the vowel. The laryngeal in question is /ɣ/. When it does not coalesce with a neighboring vowel, as in *mehur* "time," and in *hekur* "summit, peak," cf. Sanskrit *girís* "mountain," it is represented by *h*.

Similarly, in accordance with the principle requiring CVC, roots beginning with *e*, such as **ed-*, Latin *edō* "eat," would also have had an initial consonant. As a consequence, a fourth laryngeal was assumed for the proto-language. This is identified as the glottal stop.

Indo-Europeanists have varied in their interpretation of the evidence. The majority maintain three laryngeals, in accordance with the <u>threefold coloring</u> of neighboring vowels. Others assume only two, basing their views on the Hittite notation. Still others insist on only one, in view of the unclear notation in Hittite. And some, as presented here, maintain the four that Kurylowicz posited.

Differences have also existed concerning the treatment of the reconstructed elements. As had Saussure in 1879, the two notable treatments in 1935 by Kurylowicz and Benveniste take them as <u>abstract elements</u>, symbolized with schwa and <u>subscript</u> numerals; those confining themselves to assuming abstractions today use *h* <u>with subscript numerals</u>. Sapir, on the other hand, who came to know Kurylowicz during his fellowship at Yale, proposed phonetic entities as well as symbols corresponding to the four we use here; he was followed in this practice by Sturtevant (1942). Such representations reflecting phonetic values are useful for securing credible explanations of the phenomena in which laryngeals were involved.

5.4.2 Impact of the laryngeal theory on views concerning Indo-European phonology

Assumption of laryngeals greatly modified the view of the phonological system provided in the handbooks. As noted in 5.2.1, Kuryłowicz ascribed some of the previously assumed voiceless aspirated stops to a coalescence of voiceless stop with following laryngeal and accounted for others as secondary developments. As a result, this set of stops was removed from the system of Proto-Indo-European. Since voiceless aspirated stops appear only in Sanskrit, this explanation requires the assumption that laryngeals were maintained into the early dialects.

In discussing the vowel system, Indo-Europeanists had long distinguished "original" long vowels from those resulting from ablaut. In contrast with the long ablaut vowels that alternate with short *e*, the "original" long vowels are found in roots where they correspond to *e* plus consonant. The roots *$d^h\bar{e}$*- "place," *$d\bar{o}$*- "give" and *$(s)t\bar{a}$*- "stand" are notable examples; rewritten *d^heʔ-*, *dey-*, *teh-*, these correspond to the canonical root pattern noted for the proto-language, as in *sed*- "sit," *leg^h*- "lie" and so on. They also differ from the lengthened grade forms of roots with -*e*- in having schwa in unaccented syllables rather than zero. Because both sets of the long vowels are the result of phonological developments, *$\bar{e}$ $\bar{a}$ $\bar{o}$* as posited in the handbooks cannot be assumed for an early stage of the vocalic system, that is before development of the long vowels resulting from ablaut lengthening and of those resulting from coalescence with laryngeals.

Moreover, at least some long *$\bar{\imath}$* and *$\bar{u}$* resulted from coalescence with laryngeals. As one example, the suffix -*h* indicating a collective was the marker for the feminine singular and neuter plural in *$\bar{a}$* that Schmidt recognized in 1889, as in Sanskrit *sénā* "army"; it also coalesced with -*i*, as in *vṛkī̆*- "female wolf," establishing *$\bar{\imath}$* as a phoneme in Proto-Indo-European. In view of this observation, long *$\bar{\imath}$*, *$\bar{u}$*, like the "original" long vowels, would have developed only in late Proto-Indo-European, upon loss of laryngeals.   *new form of Indo-Hittite hyp-*

Further, since two of the three vowels, *a*, *o*, resulted from coloring by laryngeals in roots, questions also arose about the number of short vowels in the proto-language. Some Indo-Europeanists maintain that original short *a* and *o* existed in the language before the additional *a*, *o* arose through coloring by laryngeals. The question has not been resolved to this day. But clearly the period of few or only one phonemic vowel was early.

Since Anatolian is the only branch that includes notation for reflexes of the laryngeals, we may assume that they were being lost already in late Proto-Indo-European. Assumptions on the time of loss rely heavily on the vowel variation known as ablaut. We will examine that at length after presenting a sketch of the vocalic system of the proto-language (6.2–4). As this sketch indicates, the presentation here assumes that laryngeals had already been lost in some positions in Proto-Indo-European, so that the vowel system was moving to the structure that is evident in branches such as Greek and Baltic.

Interpretations vary considerably on the time of loss of the laryngeals in various environments. It is apparent that they were maintained relatively late when in the neighborhood of resonants. The evidence is difficult to sort out, however; even recent examination by specialists has not arrived at generally accepted solutions. To some extent the problems fall on specialists in individual branches. Because the evidence for laryngeals is in general difficult to determine, the system proposed for them in the proto-language depends in great part on the solution of the problems in the early dialects. Publication has been enormous. As recent surveys demonstrate (Bammesberger 1988; Vennemann 1989), general agreement remains elusive.

5.5 THE VOWELS

The short vowels *e*, *a*, *o* are assumed for the late stage of the proto-language on the basis of examples like the following:

PIE *e*: Sanskrit *bhárāmi*, Armenian *berem*, Latin *ferō*, Old Irish *berim* "I bear," PIE *b^her-*;

PIE *a*: Sanskrit *ájāmi*, Armenian *acem*, Greek *ágō*, Latin *agō* "I drive," PIE *ag-*;

PIE *o*: Sanskrit *aṣṭaú*, Latin *octō*, Old Irish *ocht* "eight," PIE *okt-*.

As we have noted, upon formulation of the "law of palatals" shortly after the time of publication of Verner's article, the vowel system centering on *a* that had been proposed previously on the basis of Sanskrit was totally rejected (3.4). Forms like the Sanskrit first person singular perfect *cakára* "I have made" were especially clear, since the reduplicated *ca-* must at one time have had the consonant *k* of the root; -*e*- was the reduplicating vowel here, as demonstrated by such dialects as Greek and Latin, so that the preceding tectal was palatalized and then became the Sanskrit affricate [č]. And in accordance with Brugmann's statement that PIE *o* became Sanskrit *ā* in open syllables before resonants, the third person singular *cakára* is also explained. Its ending in late Proto-Indo-European was -*e*, in contrast with -*ha* of the first person that provided a closed syllable before *o*. The first person singular form is then regularly *cakára*, with PIE -*o*- becoming Sanskrit -*a*- in a closed syllable.

In addition to these three short vowels and the allophones [i u], the schwa vowel has been posited on the basis of Sanskrit *i* in contrast with *a* of the other dialects in unaccented syllables. Because schwa as proposed in the standard handbooks is either a reduced vowel plus laryngeal, or a vocalized laryngeal, the element posited here, i.e. $_e$, represents such a central vowel that is generally unstressed.

PIE $_e$: Sanskrit *pitar-*, Latin *pater*, Old Irish *athir*, Gothic *fadar* "father," PIE *p_et-.

These four vowels will be discussed further in the next chapter, when earlier stages of the proto-language will be sketched in explanation of the ablaut phenomena. It is obvious from the example given here in support of assuming PIE *a* that at least some of the short *a* vowels are secondary.

Evidence for the long vowels is as follows:

PIE *ē*: Hittite *te-ih-hi* "I place", Greek *éthēka*, Latin *fēci* "I did," PIE *$d^hē$-;

PIE *ā*: Sanskrit *ásthāt*, Doric Greek *hístāmi*, Latin *stāre* "stand," PIE *$(s)tā$-;

PIE *ō*: Lithuanian *duóti*, Greek *dídōmi* "give", Latin *dōnum* "gift," PIE *$dō$-.

Because the vowels in each of these roots are now assumed to have originated in short vowel plus laryngeal, before their coalescence such long vowels could not be assumed for the proto-language. We examine the origin of these, and their sources in greater detail in the next chapter.

Examples of the two remaining long vowels are as follows:

PIE *ī*: Sanskrit *jīvás*, Lithuanan *gývas*, Latin *vīvus* "alive," PIE *$g^wī$-;

PIE *ū*: Sanskrit *ábhūt* "became", Greek *éphū* "grew", Old Latin *fūī* "was," PIE *$bhū$-.

In these examples as well as the above there is evidence for an earlier laryngeal after short variants of the vowels, as we will see in the next chapter. But again there is a question of earlier long *ī*, *ū* that we must also consider later, as in words like PIE *mūs* "mouse." The problem is without solution because we have no cognate forms of "mouse" without long *ū*.

The system of vowels proposed must then be determined for a specific stage in the proto-language. To account for the data of the Anatolian languages, as well as for the ablaut phenomena, we must determine such stages by examination of unexplained residues and of the patterning that requires the assumption of laryngeals. The system proposed in this chapter is that of a late stage of Proto-Indo-European.

5.6 PROCEDURES APPLIED IN DETERMINING THE SEGMENTAL SYSTEM OF PROTO-INDO-EUROPEAN

The segments of the phonological system of the proto-language are reconstructed through use of the comparative method. In view of the numerous branches of the family, and because of the uncertainty of their earlier grouping, different conclusions may be reached on the number of those segments and on their identity. The assumption by the early Indo-Europeanists of a system like that of Sanskrit illustrates the difficulties. Only intensive investigations uncovered the evidence for the phonological system now assumed.

Moreover, the relative chronological period of the system must also be taken into account. When Hittite came to be described, an assumption was made that it was a sister language of Proto-Indo-European rather than a member of a separate branch much like the Indo-Iranian branch, or the Celtic or others. Proponents of this assumption then maintained the term Indo-European for a supposed proto-language that flourished after Hittite broke away; the early stage was labeled Indo-Hittite. One motive for the hypothesis was the possibility of retaining the phonological system of the handbooks for Proto-Indo-European, and positing a system with laryngeals only for Proto-Indo-Hittite. Associated especially with Edgar H. Sturtevant (1875–1952), the Indo-Hittite hypothesis lost its last major supporter with the death of Warren Cowgill (1929–85). The system proposed here takes the Anatolian branch, of which Hittite is a member, as comparable to the other branches that have been known longer.

After it is determined by the comparative method, the system is checked against results obtained through application of other procedures, such as the method of internal reconstruction as well as examination of the functioning of the elements in morphology and syntax. As the law of palatals demonstrates, virtually any reconstruction by the comparative method can be cross-checked by examination of irregularities or residues in any one dialect. The "irregular" reduplication of velars in such forms as Sanskrit *cakara* would alone be adequate to reconstruct *e* for the proto-language. We may recall as a further example the possible use of internal reconstruction for Germanic forms like *bind* that yields the accurate Indo-European root. The evidence provided by such veiled patterns illustrates the validity of the views expressed by Brugmann and Meillet on language as a system in which all parts are interrelated. And the parallel treatment of sets like the resonants, or the voiceless stops, in bases, with the same allophonic members for all elements of such sets, i.e. /y/ [i y iy] to represent the treatment of the resonants, /t/ [t t^h] to represent the treatment of the voiceless stops, furnishes another illustration of systemic structure.

Finally, testing the proposed system by means of observation of as wide a range of phonological systems as possible, that is, through the results of typological study, supports the proposed conclusions or suggests problems with them. The glottalic theory provides possibly the most dramatic example in linguistic study to the present of a major departure from a long-assumed set of consonants for a proto-language without the addition of new data, such as the information supplied by Hittite for laryngeals. But, as stated above, it should also be noted that the departure represented by it lies in assumptions concerning phonetic characteristics and not concerning the number of obstruents nor the relationships among them; that is to say, the glottalic theory does not require changes in the phonological system.

5.7 THE ACCENTUAL SYSTEM; SEE ALSO 3.3.3

Determining the accentual system has provided some of the greatest difficulties in reconstructing Proto-Indo-European. On the one hand, the evidence is poor. Only in Vedic have early texts been preserved with their accentuation from the time they were composed. A second source of evidence is found in Greek texts, but from a much later time than their actual production. Accentual patterns were recorded only from the third century BC, when it became difficult to remember the accentuation of Homeric and other texts. Moreover, rules for the position of the accent had changed from those of the proto-language, restricting its position to one of the three last syllables. The accentual systems of the other dialects are from later periods: that for Latin from about the beginning of our era; those for Germanic, Baltic and Slavic, as well as other dialects, even later. Each of these dialects has modified the accentuation considerably.

A second major problem arises from the varied views regarding accent. Phonologists have attempted to determine the distinguishing features of accentual systems, but these are not as readily ascertainable as are the features of segmental phonemes. There is general agreement on a distinction between accentual systems based on stress and those based on pitch. Moreover, languages in which stress is distinctive generally distinguish syllabic units with a vowel as nucleus, while those with pitch distinguish units of length for which the theoretical unit, mora, has been introduced. But difficulties arise in determining contours, whether of syllabic or word accent, or of clausal accent. As the term "suprasegmental" implies, accentuation consists of features accompanying the segmental string; these features consist of differences in pitch, in stress and in duration, of which one or more are prominent in a given language.

In chapter 3 we have noted that the standard grammars have arrived at the system of accentuation proposed for the late period of the proto-language largely on the basis of Vedic and Greek, with some reference to Baltic, Slavic and Germanic. The results may be outlined.

1 The location of the primary accent is variable, as in Vedic; restriction to the last three syllables of words, as in Greek, is secondary.
2 The accent is characterized by pitch, not stress.
3 Accentual processes may be determined for syllables and for words, and to some extent for phrases and clauses. Words have one prominent accent, which was represented by high pitch.

Views on details differ, depending on whether they are more heavily based on Sanskrit or on Greek. All agree that if the accent fell on a short vowel, it consisted of high pitch. But scholars who rely largely on Greek and Baltic, propose that long vowels or diphthongs may have either acute or circumflex accent. In accordance with evidence from Greek, with some support from Baltic, an acutely accented long element had heightened pitch on its second element; one with circumflex accent on the first element. Since there is no evidence for such contours in Sanskrit, scholars who rely on Sanskrit do not propose them for the proto-language.

4 Accentuation of phrases and clauses may be noted on the basis of modifications from an expected accent, as when an acute accent may be expected on a final syllable in Greek but is represented by a grave accent. Phrasal accent is also clear from the treatment of clitics, that is, elements lacking an inherent accent. Clausal accentuation may be noted from the treatment of finite verbs in independent clauses.

These statements may indicate the essential features of accentuation in Proto-Indo-European. It should be noted that some Indo-Europeanists have proposed different views from those sketched here, for instance Kurylowicz (see Szemerényi 1970 [1989]: 81). As the number of publications dealing with accent may indicate, comment on the less widely accepted or the rejected theories of Indo-European accent would require a great deal of space.

We may note still that considerable attention has been given to determine the bases for location of the accent (see Szemerényi (1970 [1989]: 171, 269); Kiparsky 1973; Garde 1976; Kiparsky and Halle 1977). Two large classes are found for both nominal and verbal inflection: the accent may be fixed on one element of words, or it may be variable.

If fixed, the primary accent may be located on the first syllable or on the stem-syllable of nouns and verbs: for example, among the present classes in Sanskrit, the first class has the accent on the first syllable, as in *bhávati* "becomes," the sixth class has the accent on the stem syllable, as in *tudáti* "strikes."

If variable, the primary accent may fall on the beginning and suffix syllables, or on the beginning and the end syllables of nouns. In verbs without a stem suffix, the so-called athematics, it falls on the first syllable in the singular present, on the final syllable in the dual and plural. The singular then has normal grade, the remaining forms have zero grade, as in Sanskrit *ásmi* "I am," *smás* "we are." The earlier distribution of the accent is often clear from the ablaut grades, as in the Greek perfect forms *oîda* "I know," *ísmen* "we know," even when the location is no longer the same. The comparable Gothic forms, *wait* : *witum*, may similarly be used for such conclusions.

These examples may illustrate some of the problems involved in reconstructing the accent system of words and phrases. Since it is closely associated with morphological structure, we will leave further discussion of accentuation for chapters 7 and 8.

5.8 THE PATTERNS OF SENTENCE ACCENTUATION

The accentuation of the simple sentence may be determined from Sanskrit and Greek, with support from other dialects. The first hymn of the *Rigveda* begins: *ágnim ī́ḷe* "Agni I implore"; the verb stands in final position in the clause and is unaccented. A similar order is found in the initial clauses of the *Iliad*: *mênin áeide* "wrath sing = sing of the wrath" and of the *Odyssey*, *ándra moi énnepe* "man to-me tell = tell me of a man"; the subsequent accentuation of Greek requires accents on the verbs. We may conclude that the declarative clause ends on low pitch, signaling final intonation. The conclusion is supported by metrical practice in Germanic verse.

In early Germanic verse the verb also stands finally in the clause, and typically fails to alliterate; an example is the fourth line of the Old High German *Hildebrandslied: sunufaturungo   iro saro rihtun* "son and father   their gear readied." On the basis of the three dialects, we may reconstruct the accentual sentence pattern and intonation of independent clauses as consisting of high pitch on its early elements and falling pitch to mark the end of the clause.

By contrast with declarative clauses and sentences, questions and exclamatory expressions may be marked for *pluti* "(swimming) intonation" in Sanskrit. This expression implies continued length of a vowel to three morae with high pitch. Because the pitch does not drop in such expressions, we conclude that early Sanskrit had a characteristic intonation pattern to indicate expectation or request. The pattern may also have been maintained in Germanic verse, where verbs in subordinate clauses may alliterate, that is, have high pitch. The same practice is observed in Sanskrit if subordinate clauses precede the principal clause. We may then conclude that the characteristic intonation patterns marked both principal clauses and subordinate clauses, as well as questions and exclamations.

5.9 REMAINING PROBLEMS THAT MAY BE CLARIFIED BY RECONSTRUCTING EARLIER STAGES OF THE PROTO-LANGUAGE

The assumption of the phonological system as provided here still leaves problems. The most difficult lie in vowel patterns of root and base structures, that is, in the ablaut interrelationships. The distribution of short and long vowels coupled with absence of vowels within roots, bases and inflectional elements is difficult to understand when we propose for all stages of the proto-language a system of pitch accent. In keeping with procedures of historical linguistics, such a situation can only be explained by determining the structure of the language at an earlier time. The procedures for providing such explanations were gradually developed in the course of the nineteenth century, in attempts to account for the ablaut phenomena.

These phenomena were greatly clarified when laryngeals were assumed. It became clear that laryngeals were members of the phonological system as the ablaut system developed, but were gradually lost. Solution of the problems with the vowel system then required reconstruction of the stages of both subsystems, as we note in the next chapter.

6 Phonology 2: Pre-Indo-European

6.1 STEPS TOWARDS RECONSTRUCTION OF THE PRE-INDO-EUROPEAN PHONOLOGICAL SYSTEM

Achievement of an understanding of the vowel system and its variations known as ablaut provided the key to reconstructing earlier stages of Proto-Indo-European. Through that achievement, probably the greatest difficulty in Indo-European studies was overcome. In the process the results of earlier sound changes had to be examined for their interrelationships. These were obscured by subsequent changes, such as umlaut. They were also difficult to untangle because the short vowel system of Proto-Indo-European, as late as Schleicher's *Compendium*, was assumed to consist of the three vowels *a i u* in keeping with those of Sanskrit. In comparing these with the vowels of the other dialects *a* was found to correspond to the five vowels *i e a o u*, but no pattern of correspondence could be determined.

Moreover, the ablaut interchanges had been utilized to distinguish morphological categories, and accordingly extended to new patterns; for that reason the phonological environments in which the vowel changes giving rise to ablaut had taken place were determined only slowly and through painstaking analysis. Additional problems were caused by the losses of laryngeals, which were members of the phonological system when the original ablaut changes had taken place. Solving these problems to achieve an understanding of ablaut required the efforts of several generations of Indo-Europeanists.

The course of their work illustrates the gradual improvement of linguistic methodology, including the importance of appropriate formalism. Before we reconstruct the earlier phonological system some of the important findings in that effort will be briefly sketched here as examples of successive refinements of the theoretical bases by which our current views of the proto-language and its earlier stages were achieved.

Sources for this chapter: Sturtevant (1942); Lehmann (1952); Polomé (1965); Lindeman (1987); Bammesberger (1988); Vennemann (1989).

117

6.1.1 Identification of distinct processes and stages in earlier phonological systems

The initial studies in Indo-European linguistics, as well as the terminology present a flat picture of the language in the early period of the Indo-European family. In the late eighteenth century Klopstock's term *umlaut* "change of sound" was used to refer to the alternations that are found in vowels of the Germanic dialects, those in *men* vs *man* as well as those now known to be the result of changes in the proto-language, e.g. *gave* vs *give*. Until such processes were sorted out, it was not possible to distinguish stages of the early languages or results of distinct processes at different stages. The efforts to account for the ablaut phenomena in the last part of the nineteenth century and the beginning of ours opened the way to determining the phonological systems of Proto-Indo-European and finally Pre-Indo-European, especially its vocalic and accentual patterns.

As a major step in clarifying earlier processes and stages, Jacob Grimm distinguished the alternations resulting from changes in Proto-Indo-European from the alternations brought about within Germanic, adopting for the alternations due to Proto-Indo-European changes the word *ablaut*. Klopstock's term *umlaut* was maintained for the changes within Germanic. In this way steps were taken that led to examination of the early periods of the various dialects in accordance with successive stages. The procedure is essential for a realistic representation of Proto-Indo-European and the separate dialects in their developments.

Moreover, it gradually became clear that the Sanskrit vowel system was not that of the proto-language. The need to assume the short vowels *e* and *o* as well as *a* resulted from lessons learned in solving the exceptions to Grimm's law. As we have noted in 3.4, it became clear to a number of linguists in the 1870s that earlier forms of Sanskrit had included the *e* vowel because of the combinatory changes of velars before that earlier *e*, through the so-called law of palatals. As in solving the maintenance of voiceless stops after fricatives, e.g. Gothic *standan*, the law demonstrated further that sounds had to be examined in their environment and not simply as individual entities.

Moreover, Verner's article of 1875 demonstrated the importance of observing patterns of accentuation. When his finding was applied to the alternating ablaut vowels, it was recognized that the roots of ablaut lay in the position and shifts of position of the earlier accent.

Furthermore, the importance of observing phonological and morphological structures was re-emphasized by Brugmann's assumption in 1876 of vocalic *m* and *n* in the proto-language. Because none of the dialects preserved vocalic *m* and *n*, which had developed into vowels like *a*, or combinations like *um*, *un* in Germanic, Brugmann's proposal was based purely on considerations of structure. While it met with considerable resistance initially, it received strong support from the parallelism among the six resonants that it implied. Sievers then formulated his law concerning their pattern of variation, demonstrating further the usefulness of a structural approach.

Another important step was taken by Hirt, in assuming bases rather than only roots. In his view, roots were abstractions determined by linguists, while bases represented words in the earlier stages of Proto-Indo-European. Building on the three previously mentioned advances, Hirt proposed bases in which an accented *e* was the original vowel; if the base included a resonant, e.g. **bhéndh-*, upon loss of the accent the resonant became vocalic, whether a nasal or a liquid or a semivowel. The system of vowels and resonants, and their variation within bases, was then determined, as well as the causes of the variation.

However, as Hirt pointed out, the ablaut patterning that he proposed was not without its problems. Distinctions such as that between long vowels resulting from the process that led to lengthened grade, like the long *e* in Gothic *gēbum* "we gave," and those vowels that resulted from merger of short vowel plus laryngeal – the so-called original long vowels – like the long *e* in Greek *títhēmi* "I place," had to be identified to understand the processes of ablaut and successive stages of the vocalic system. Hirt's grammar, like the other standard handbooks, deals with a phonological system of late Proto-Indo-European in which these vowels had merged. That is to say, their handbooks present the results of a series of changes rather than successive phonological systems in which the ablaut changes had occurred. To be sure, the ablaut interchanges, and the location of original vowels in specific morphological categories like the present indicative singular, revealed covert differences between the original long and the lengthened grade vowels; but until the origin of "original long vowels' in short vowel plus laryngeal was known, positing two variants of long vowels seemed like an awkward solution. Hirt did propose successive stages of accent; but since he did not posit laryngeals, the vowel systems at these stages were difficult to determine.

In examining the earlier changes and their stages, one must be aware of twofold uses in the handbooks of central terminology. The terms *ablaut* and *umlaut* are used both to refer to the processes that brought about the changes, and also to the alternations resulting from the changes: for example, the vowel of *men*, German *Männer* is referred to as an *umlaut* vowel. But at the same time the term *umlaut* is used to refer to the process by which Proto-Germanic *-a-* was fronted and raised to yield *ä/e*. In spite of objections to such twofold uses, that practice has continued. Twofold use is also found for the term *change*, that is, for a change itself and also for an "exchange" resulting from a change as between *men* and *man*. The specific use of each term in a given context must then be identified, whether it refers to a process or to the result of such a process. Careless use of the central terms unfortunately increases the difficulty of distinguishing the changes in the phonological system of the proto-language and the early dialects.

6.1.2 Identification of distinct stages in the morphological system

Much like early linguists who presented a flat picture in phonology, Franz Bopp related the morphological items in other dialects to Sanskrit forms rather than proposing early forms of the "common source" that Jones had assumed. But, in the half century after his publication of 1816, he and other Indo-Europeanists began to sort out the changes in the morphological system, most dramatically by means of the reconstructed forms that Schleicher introduced. The forms reconstructed for the proto-language helped to clarify the chronological stages of development between Proto-Indo-European and its dialects.

Treatment of the morphology as well as the phonology was not adequate, however, until such changes were projected in earlier periods of the proto-language as well; for the prominent morphological categories were often marked by differences in vowels resulting from ablaut, as in the present Sanskrit *dádhāmi*, Greek *títhēmi* "I place" and the aorist middle Sanskrit *ádhita*, Greek *étheto* "he placed." Until laryngeals were posited, the earlier stages of the vowels in these forms could not be determined. That is to say, the interrelationships between the forms of the morphological system at the various stages had to be determined in order to understand the vowel and resonant systems in their development.

6.2 CLARIFICATION OF ABLAUT THROUGH ANALYSIS OF MORPHOLOGICAL STRUCTURES AND ASSUMPTION OF LARYNGEALS

Because ablaut is treated in the standard handbooks by using the vowel system of the late proto-language, its presentation is highly complex. Painstaking analysis, as by Hirt, distinguished the characteristic forms. However, they were arranged under different classes of bases, rather than accounted for by the sound changes that took place; the arrangement relied heavily on later application of the vowel grades in morphological purposes. Nonetheless the bases that Hirt posited alongside roots permitted improved clarification of ablaut, as we may note after sketching his presentation.

6.2.1 Hirt's classification of Proto-Indo-European roots and bases

Hirt distinguished between monosyllabic and disyllabic bases, each of which include light and heavy members (1921–37 II: 104–6). His monosyllabic light bases have a simple vowel, *e* as in **sed-* "sit" and **nem-* "take," *a* as in **ag-* "lead," *o* as in **okʷ-* "see." Monosyllabic heavy bases, by contrast, have a long vowel, *ē* as in **dhē-* "place," *ā* as in **(s)tā-* "stand," *ō* as in **dō-* "give."

It is clear today that the heavy bases at one time had a simple vowel; that vowel was followed by a laryngeal while obstruents or resonants were final in the light bases. **dhē-* is now analysed as **dheʔ*, **(s)tā-* as **(s)teh-*, **dō-* as **deɣ-*, all with laryngeals that contrast directly with obstruents, as in **sed-* or with resonants, as in **nem-*. The distinction between the two types of bases at the time when the ablaut changes took place is accordingly unnecessary; it rests on the difference between them in late Proto-Indo-European, long after the time at which the vowel changes took place that led to the ablaut relationships. If we maintained Hirt's terms, we could state that all bases were light at the time of the ablaut changes.

Hirt's disyllabic bases are comparable to the monosyllabic, the light having short vowels in both syllables, e.g. **deme-* "build," the heavy having a long vowel in the second syllable, e.g. **bhewā-* "become." Hirt provided formulae to illustrate them; in the formulae, as given here, X stands for any consonant, R specifically for resonants. Among light examples are EXE-, EXEX-, EXER-, EREX-; among heavy examples are EXĀ-, ERĀ-. The basis of the distinction is now clear. The so-called heavy bases result from contraction of short vowels with laryngeals; at an early period the heavy disyllabic bases would have been parallel with the light EXEX- and EREX-.

The assumption of laryngeals then eliminated the distinction between light and heavy bases. Using H as cover symbol, the three examples given above of heavy bases in Hirt's notation would be EXAH-, ERAH-. In this way we simply rewrite Hirt's formulae and bring about complete parallelism between the two sets of light and heavy bases. Moreover, instead of complex phonological patterns that are assigned to groups of bases, we may explain all the ablaut changes that took place by indicating modifications of one vowel: *e*; but we should note that the assumption of one vowel is schematic for the purpose of simplifying the understanding of the ablaut situation in early Proto-Indo-European.

The explanation of ablaut as resulting from a series of changes in a period of the proto-language that included laryngeals therefore requires the assumption of various stages in the proto-language. It also entails the abandonment of Brugmann's purely systematic presentation in favor of one that is historical.

6.2.2 The classification of roots in Indic grammar

The identification of laryngeals also clarifies the Indic classification, which, as in Whitney's handbooks, refers to roots; these correspond in general to Hirt's bases. Instead of light and heavy bases the Indian grammarians distinguish *aniṭ* and *seṭ* roots.

The terminology is typical of Paninian grammar: *an-* signifies "without," *sa-* signifies "with"; *i* indicates the suffix; and *-t* is comparable to our symbols in logic, closing the grammatical designation. The *aniṭ* roots are those without the Sanskrit *-i* that was derived from Proto-Indo-European schwa. Since by the laryngeal theory this schwa corresponds to a laryngeal, the *aniṭ* roots are those without final laryngeal, e.g. *d^hewg^h-* "milk," given as *duh* by the Sanskrit grammarians. The *seṭ* roots are those with laryngeal, such as Hirt's **bhewā-* "become," written with laryngeal as **bhewʔ-*. Because, as noted above, the Sanskrit grammarians identified roots in the zero grade, their notation for the base of "become" is *bhū*.

The difference between the two types of roots may be illustrated by citing infinitive forms in Sanskrit; that of *duh* "milk" is *dogdhum*, while that of *bhū* "become" is *bhavitum*. Contrasts between such forms illustrate that the *seṭ* roots of Sanskrit are those with laryngeal as final element, which regularly became Sanskrit *i*. In this way assumption of the laryngeal theory clarified the Sanskrit classification for historical purposes as well as the formulations arrived at by Hirt and others.

6.2.3 The changes of vowels that led to the ablaut alternations

Determination of the laryngeals then provided clarification of the phonological system of the period at which the sound changes contributing to ablaut had taken place. Whatever the extent of time between that period and the period for which we reconstruct Proto-Indo-European, three simple vowel changes provided the variants that subsequent exploitation for morphological purposes extended throughout the nominal and especially the verbal inflectional systems as well as to derivational forms.

By one change *e* was lost; this was the basis of the so-called zero grade. An example is the compound resulting in Gothic *nists*, < **ni + *sd-* "nest < (place to) sit down."

By another change, *e* was lengthened; this change was the basis of lengthened grade. An example is the form of the root **sed-* in the preterite plural in Gothic *sētum* "we sat."

By the third change, *e* became *o*; this change was the basis of deflected or *o*-grade. An example is Old Irish *suide* < **sodyom* "seat," Latin *solium* "throne."

6.2.3.1 Subsequent modifications obscuring the results of the changes

Modifications of the sounds within words by neighboring sounds were very prominent in late Proto-Indo-European and the early dialects: for example, the *-d-* of **ni-sd-* was modified to *-t-* in keeping with the following voiceless *s*. By a different process the *-s-* was lost with lengthening of the preceding vowel in Latin *nīdus* "nest." Through such processes the earlier situation was often obscured. The modifications were determined only by long and careful analysis in the nineteenth century.

The modifications have been especially difficult to determine in roots that contained laryngeals. When the vowel of such roots was lost, only the nonlaryngeal consonant might remain, as in Sanskrit *dadmás* "we give" in contrast with *dádāmi* "I give." Further, it is possible to distinguish only by morphological means, if at all, the source of long vowels in laryngeal roots, as for Greek *dôron* "gift." They may be the result of lengthened grade, or "original long vowels," lengthened upon merger of short vowel with the laryngeal.

Moreover, roots that had initial *a*-colored laryngeal, such as **ak-* < **xek-* "sharp, pointed," seem to have ablaut interchange between *a* and *o*, as in Greek *oksús* "sharp" as opposed to Latin *acus* "chaff;" but the *a* developed from *e* in the noun upon loss of the initial laryngeal after the *e* had changed to *o* in the adjective. The ablaut change is then that of *e* to *o*.

More such complexities will be discussed later in this chapter. These examples may be adequate to indicate the reasons for the lengthy presentation of ablaut classes in the standard handbooks, which simply list the patterns that may be found in the late proto-language. When we posit laryngeals at the time of the ablaut changes, the processes are shown to be very simple. Yet because the handbooks have not been replaced, it is important to understand their formulations.

6.3 SUBSEQUENT MORPHOLOGICAL REARRANGEMENT OF THE RESULTS OF ABLAUT CHANGES

As with many changes, the results of the ablaut changes were exploited for morphological purposes. As one example, they were used to distinguish verb stems in the perfect from those of the present, a distinction maintained in the Germanic strong verbs, e.g. Gothic *giban* : *gab*. To exemplify the situation by means of a subsequent parallel, the initial umlaut changes in Germanic had nothing to do with morphological categories; back vowels were fronted whenever they stood before *j* or short and long *i*. However, because some noun plurals were indicated with endings containing *-i-*, the umlaut vowels came to stand characteristically in plural forms of nouns; accordingly, umlaut came to be a marker of noun plurals, as in *men*, German *Männer*, *feet*, German *Füsse*, mice, German *Mäuse*, and many other nouns. We assume similar exploitation of the ablaut changes for grammatical purposes in the proto-language. The *o*-grade in the perfect singular and in causative verbs, for example, is so used because of specific forms that had undergone the change of *e* to *o*, and thereupon came to be patterns for an entire morphological class.

When such extension takes place, the original situation is obscured. For when morphological markers are established, they are extended with no reference to the etymological situation; in German, umlaut vowels came to be plural markers, and thereupon nouns like *Nagel* "nail" that had no etymological basis for the umlaut nonetheless were modified, as in *Nägel* "nails." We have noted above the difficulties that we would face if we attempted to account for the origin of umlaut in English, or in German, or in the Scandinavian languages through distribution of its results in any of them today. Ablaut presents us with similar problems. Many points are now clear. Yet for others the evidence is lacking to decide in favor of one or another proposed explanation. Our only responsible procedure requires us to propose a hypothesis that permits us to account for the most characteristic or the largest number of sets of forms, and then to deal with exceptions. This procedure encounters objections, especially when critics disregard essential elements, such as the laryngeals, or the variants of resonants, or the accent. Such critics may also cite one or more exceptions to oppose an explanation; but it is fruitless to seek or to demand total explanation for prehistoric data in keeping with the extreme version of the neogrammarian principle. Inevitably we must seek the most plausible explanations that account for the largest number of examples.

In the history of clarifying the ablaut situation of Proto-Indo-European we must credit Benveniste for making use of the new phonological information to revise the treatment of Indo-European roots. Hirt also merits credit for assembling large stocks of data that took earlier studies into account. Schrijnen and Fischer (1921: 272–88) and others in turn presented a compact version of Hirt's views; Meillet also provided a succinct summary (1937: 153–68); but only after roots and bases could be represented with laryngeals did the origin and subsequent extension of ablaut become clear.

Benveniste's clarification illustrated once again the importance of dealing with specific stages of language, and of treating proto-languages in their historical development. When solving any of the outstanding problems, such as the dissimilation of aspirates, as was done by Grassmann, or the voicing of fricatives, as done by Verner, it is clear that the solution rested on assuming earlier and later stages of the languages concerned, even though they were unwritten and reconstructed languages. But as we have also noted, Brugmann and his contemporaries resisted proposing stages for the proto-language. After Kurylowicz's article of 1927 their approach could no longer be maintained.

We will present a statement of ablaut in its successive stages. But first it is useful to note in greater detail the morphological patterns that provide evidence for laryngeals, as in the bases proposed by Hirt. Morphological sets of well-defined structure provide secure evidence in support of the laryngeals posited on the basis of phonological evidence, as stated in the preceding chapter. Besides accounting for morphophonemic alternations, the posited laryngeals clarify the structure of roots and bases in Proto- and Pre-Indo-European.

6.4 THE LARYNGEALS AND THEIR RESIDUES IN PROTO-INDO-EUROPEAN AND THE EARLY DIALECTS

A great deal of study was devoted to the laryngeals in the years after Kurylowicz's publication of 1927. Many of the early works are no longer cited, especially by those who have recently accepted the theory. Among important treatments incorporating previous findings is Sturtevant's monograph of 1942, in which earlier monographs are cited, like that of Couvreur, as well as many articles, among them Sturtevant's own. Subsequent findings are admirably presented by Polomé (1965), which after twenty-five years still provides an excellent statement of the evidence and efforts to interpret it, with full bibliography to that year. Later works may be determined from the essays edited by Bammesberger (1988).

As these essays indicate, publications continue to appear, some providing little more than autobiography, others dealing primarily with one or more early dialects rather than the proto-language. Such works will be left to specialists in the respective dialects. Since the evidence for laryngeals is fragmentary, interpretation depends heavily on the methods applied by individual scholars. More information occasionally becomes available, as by discovery of additional texts in Anatolian languages. Yet as has been long observed, after corroboration of Saussure's conclusions through the distinct reflexes in Hittite, evidence must also be taken from the branches other than Anatolian, in view of the many problems with the texts available in the Anatolian languages and with their writing systems. The non-distinctive evidence, however, in the branches other than Anatolian, and the obscuring of the original situation through subsequent modifications, provide occasion for endless disputes. Referring to all interpretations, or even to summaries, would obscure presentation of the basic situation.

6.4.1 Clarification through precise formulation of root and base structures

Benveniste's presentation of Indo-European root and base structure, here given with the two extensions of base II, is central to assured positing of laryngeals.

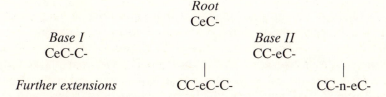

$$\text{Root} \atop \text{CeC-}$$

Base I   Base II
CeC-C-   CC-eC-

Further extensions   CC-eC-C-   CC-n-eC-

The constraints against presence of specific consonants limit the number of roots. Moreover, the structure of roots and bases limits the suffixes that may be added; a root like *sed- "sit," for example, would not be extended to any of the four additional verbal bases except by laryngeal. Such constraints are highly useful in identifying the phonological elements in affixes.

Yet many roots are open to extension by a wide array of suffixes; the -C- and -eC- in *base I* and *base II* may be represented by many consonants, including laryngeals that are difficult to identify: for example, suffixes with three different laryngeals may have been added to the root *pel- "fill": ʔ as in Latin *plēnus* "full," *h* or *x* as in Sanskrit *pr̥ṇā́ti*, γ as in Sanskrit *pr̥ṇōti* "fill." If we cannot identify the specific laryngeal on the basis of criteria determined in the course of research on the laryngeals, we simply posit an unidentified laryngeal in such etyma.

6.4.2 Residues of the laryngeals identified through morphophonemic criteria

Six patterns are especially useful for identifying the earlier presence of laryngeals.

6.4.2.1 *The "original" long vowels*

An important set of residues for clarification of ablaut is that of the "original long" vowels, as in roots like *dhē-, *dō-, *(s)tā-. These were distinguished from long vowels resulting from lengthened grade in ablaut through morphophonemic alternations. The lengthened grade vowels alternate with short vowels, such as *e* and *o*; the "original" long vowels, on the other hand, alternate with schwa indogermanicum, which is given the longer label when it is useful to contrast it with schwa secundum discussed below, but is usually referred to simply as schwa. Moreover, the reduced form of the original long vowels is simply the laryngeal in zero grade. I maintain the label "schwa" here in part to call attention to the patterns cited in the handbooks in which laryngeals may now be posited, and also in part because current Indo-Europeanists assume one of two different replacements, either vocalic laryngeals or the vowel $_e$.

6.4.2.2 *Schwa indogermanicum*

As a corollary of the morphophonemic variation of original long vowels, schwa was recognized to be their weakened form: for example, in a disyllabic heavy base like *bhewā- "become," the weakened form of -ā- in Sanskrit is -i- , as in *bhavitum* "to become"; similarly, in *genē- "give birth to" the weakened form of -ē- is -i-, as in Sanskrit *jánitas*, and also in *dhē- "place," as in Sanskrit *hítas* "placed." It was concluded that schwa indogermanicum represented the weakened form of each of the three long vowels that had not developed from vocalic resonants. However schwa indogermanicum is interpreted today, it provides evidence for laryngeals.

Since schwa indogermanicum had high frequency, it gives us information about a large number of forms. However, as Indo-Europeanists have long pointed out, not all Sanskrit *i* that may seem to be derived from schwa indogermanicum can be ascribed to the early language; many spread through morphologically induced extension to forms in which they are not etymologically expected. Accordingly, we cannot simply posit a laryngeal wherever Sanskrit and the dialects have reflexes that were formerly ascribed to schwa in Proto-Indo-European.

In the branches other than Indo-Iranian, schwa indogermanicum generally yielded *a*; cf. Greek *patḗr*, Latin *pater*, Gothic *fadar* and Sanskrit *pitar-*; but in Greek some reflexes show *e* and *o*. Their appearance is especially notable in the verbal adjectives of the frequently cited heavy bases, i.e. *thétos*, *státos*, *dótos*. Two interpretations have been proposed: by one the reduced *ₑ* was indeed colored by the laryngeal, so that Greek preserves evidence of different laryngeals in such forms; by the other interpretation, the expected *a* was modified by analogy with noncontracted forms as illustrated in the roots. Arguments have been cited in favor of each view. I favor the first.

6.4.2.3 *Long vocalic resonants*

In Sanskrit *bhavitum* and similar forms, the base stood in zero grade only in the second syllable. If, however, both syllables stood in zero grade, the base would have been reduced to **bhw* + laryngeal (schwa indogermanicum by earlier analysis). The vocalic variant of *-w-* would then have resulted. In this way the Sanskrit verbal adjective *bhūtas* from Proto-Indo-European **bhewā-* is accounted for. That is to say, when a laryngeal rather than schwa is posited, the long vocalic resonant is explained as resulting from contraction of its short counterpart with following laryngeal. The long vocalic resonants (or variant notations as posited by Hirt, among others) then provide evidence for laryngeals much as do the original long vowels.

While in some dialects, such as Germanic and Baltic, the proposed long resonants have the same segmental reflexes as do the short resonants, the laryngeals have left other residues. In Baltic, a difference was preserved in accentuation; reflexes of the long resonants have acute intonation in contrast with circumflex on the short. The differing reflexes in the various dialects indicate that the laryngeals were maintained in at least some environments into the post-Indo-European period (see Kortlandt 1988 and the bibliography he cites).

6.4.2.4 *Long diphthongal roots*

In the same volume as an article of Johannes Schmidt's examining Indo-European *ēi*, Wilhelm Schulze published a widely cited article on Indo-European *āi*-roots (1885). He pointed out their morphophonemic variation, as for the root *pā* "drink." Beside the root with its long *ā* vowel, some derived forms with unaccented root syllables contain long *ī*, e.g. Sanskrit *pītí* "a drink," *pītá* "drunk." Moreover, further forms, such as Sanskrit *pāyanam*, lead to the conclusion that the earlier vocalic element of the root was a long diphthong. Schulze went on to list more than twenty such roots, and added a section on Indo-European *āu*. Since he was a scholar with assured reputation for accuracy coupled with conservatism, his identifications were accepted without question.

The article is an excellent example of the procedures at the time; it also provides possibilities for explaining other reflexes of the roots. Schulze correctly questioned the interpretation of the "long diphthongs" by Saussure in his monograph of 1879 as consisting of *ayA-* : *ī*; but he provided no explanation of his own.

It is clear that the so-called long diphthongal roots are bases of roots that ended in laryngeals, and were suffixed by resonants. Thus the root of "drink" would now be reconstructed *peγ-* on the basis of *-o-* vowels in Greek and Latin, e.g. *pōtus* "drunk." By yielding reflexes of long vowels in some forms, of long resonants in others, and still other reflexes of interest, the so-called long diphthongs provide excellent evidence of laryngeals in various environments. As in *pōtus*, Greek *thêlus* "female," *khêtos* "need" and so on, in some environments they have reflexes of long vowels. These environments have been identified, so that the long diphthongal roots provide information on where laryngeals were maintained, and where they were lost.

Among further examples, Schulze lists Gothic *daddjan* "suckle" as a reflex of Indo-European *dhāi-* "suck." He equates it with Sanskrit *dháyati*. It is clear that the laryngeal left a reflex in Germanic that led to "lengthening" which resulted in the sequence represented as *-ddj-* in Gothic, *-ggj-* in North Germanic dialects, and doubled *-jj-* and *-ww-* in the West Germanic dialects. In this way Schulze's article, and those of other scholars in the systematic tradition represented by Brugmann, provide data that can be further investigated, and often now explained.

6.4.2.5 *Sanskrit verbs of classes 5 and 9*

Long vowels appear in the *to*-form of roots like Proto-Indo-European *pew-* "cleanse," i.e. Sanskrit *pūtá-*. The Vedic present of this root is made with nasal infix, i.e. *punấti* "he cleanses." By Benveniste's analysis (1935: 170–1), this form is a reflex of PIE *pw-n-ex-ti*, that is to say, of the extended base *pw-ex-* with nasal infix. The zero grade of the extended base, *pwx-*, resulted in lengthened vowel, as of *pūtá-*, before the *-to-* suffix. By interpreting the morphophonemic variation in accordance with the data presented above, the ninth verb class of the Sanskrit grammarians may be explained as made from bases with laryngeal suffix.

The three classes with nasal infix in Sanskrit were derived from the same base pattern in the proto-language: CC-*n-é*-C-; they differ only in the last element of the base. Class 7 has bases in which the suffix contains an obstruent in contrast with the laryngeal of class 9. In class 5 the suffix seems to contain *w*; as noted above, however, in a paper presented to the Linguistic Society meeting in 1949 I suggested that at least some class 5 verbs suffixed the ɣ laryngeal, which I thereupon proposed to be a labio-velar (cf. Polomé 1965: 33–5). In origin, class 5 is then parallel with class 9, in having a laryngeal as suffix; the difference between the two classes results from the difference in suffixed laryngeal.

-C- = ɣ	Class 5	śṛṇóti	"he hears"
-C- = Obs.	Class 7	rinákti	"he leaves"
-C- = x/h	Class 9	punáti	"he cleanses"

The laryngeal theory then has clarified the three nasal classes of the Indian grammarians. Although many verbs of classes 5 and 9 can provide evidence for laryngeals, *-no-* and *-nā-* came to be treated as specific verbal morphemes in Sanskrit and thereupon could be affixed to bases that did not have a final laryngeal. Classes 5 and 9 give us valuable information for laryngeals, but like all morphological data they must be interpreted for phonological inferences with care.

6.4.2.6 *Lengthened vowels in first elements of compounds*

Among further morphological evidence is the lengthening of short vowels in the first element of many compounds: for example, the negative of an adjective based on the participle of *ʔes-* appears in the *Rigveda* with long initial *ā-*, i.e. *ásat* "not true" from the proto-language form *ṇ-ʔs-at*. Since the negative prefix should have short *a*, we account for the length through contraction with following laryngeal. Through analysis of such forms we can identify elements with initial laryngeal.

The morphological evidence obtained from the patterns noted in this section can be compared with evidence from other patterns that will not be treated here, such as (1) initial *z* in some words in Greek; (2) prothetic vowels before *r* initially in Greek; (3) Germanic lengthened *w* and *y*, with development of obstruent plus the resonant in North and East Germanic. Discussion of these would extend this section unduly. A catalogue of all the evidence by environment in each branch has been provided by Beekes (1988: 59–105). While details in any such list may be interpreted differently by others, it may be consulted for information on patterns and sequences for which at least some scholars have agreed on the earlier presence of laryngeals. The evidence proposed on phonological grounds gains credence when it can be supplemented by that derived from morphophonemic and morphological patterning.

6.5 RELATIVE CHRONOLOGY AS REFLECTED IN THESE FORMS AND ITS PERTINENCE FOR ABLAUT

Through analysis of the forms noted above as representing distinct processes, we may determine the chronology of changes that led to them, as well as the relative time of origin of the various ablaut grades.

6.5.1 Zero grade earlier than loss of laryngeals

We illustrate the relative chronology of zero grade with reference to maintenance of laryngeals by citing forms in which a reduced element has been lengthened before the division into dialects.

Sanskrit *ásat* is a compound made up of the negative particle **ne*, as reflected in Sanskrit *ná* "not," Gothic *ni*, Old Church Slavonic *ne*, etc., and as second element, Proto-Indo-European **sént*, the participial form of **ʔes-*, as in Sanskrit *sánt*, Doric Greek *hent* "being," etc. The compound would have been accented on the final syllable, as is Sanskrit *adánt* "toothless." The first element **ne-* would then have been in zero grade, i.e. *n̥*, as would the root, i.e. **ʔs*. But the laryngeal of the root had not been lost, so that the zero-grade *n̥* was lengthened, yielding the Sanskrit long *ā* (that later became accented).

We may conclude from such forms that the laryngeals were maintained after the loss of vowel in zero grade. We conclude conversely, that zero grade reduction took place at an earlier stage of the language than did coalescence of the maintained laryngeal with the reduced vocalic *n̥*. Similarly, in past perfect participles like Sanskrit *bhūtas*, the laryngeal was maintained until both zero grade in PIE **bʰew-* and zero grade in the suffix *-ex-* resulted in the vocalic form of *w* followed by *-x-*; the vocalic form [u] of the resonant was thereupon lengthened on loss of the laryngeal. Examples like *bhūtas* then demonstrate that the laryngeals were maintained after reduction of the root vowel, as well as after zero grade of the suffix.

6.5.2 Zero grade earlier than lengthened grade

In accordance with the accepted explanation, lengthened grade arose by compensatory lengthening. Nominative forms like Sanskrit *pitā́*, Greek *patḗr* "father" are assumed to have lengthened grade on the accented syllable because of loss of a following vowel, *e* or *o*, that is, because of zero grade of that vowel (Hirt 1921–37 I: 36–49), or upon loss of *-s* (Szemerényi 1970 [1989]: 121). The further syllable was not lost in the accusative, e.g. Sanskrit *pitáram*, Greek *patéra*. We conclude then that lengthened grade was brought about after vowels were lost through lack of accent; that is, lengthened grade was initiated later than zero grade. Conversely, zero grade is therefore chronologically earlier than lengthened grade.

6.5.3 Deflected grade later than zero grade

Deflected grade is explained by loss of primary accent on a vowel and replacement by a secondary accent. If in derivation the accent fell on an affix rather than on the root, the root vowel under such secondary accent changed to *o*, as in Greek *nomós* "pasture," *nomeús* "shepherd" in contrast with the vowel of the accented root in the verb *némō* "I pasture." Since the loss of principal accent in such words did not result in zero grade, this process must have taken place after zero grade was no longer being brought about by shift of accent. As we see in the next section, the process implies further a change in the kind of accent, from an earlier stress accent to the pitch accent found in Sanskrit, Greek and other dialects.

The change in deflected grade also affected vowels that had been lengthened, e.g. Greek *patḗr*, *apátōr* "fatherless." Accordingly, the period of deflected grade must be later than that of lengthened grade.

6.5.4 Summary of relative chronology of ablaut

On the basis of such forms we can determine the relative chronology of the vowel changes that are represented in ablaut. As first change, loss of vowels led to zero grade. Next, accented vowels were lengthened upon loss of an element in the following syllable. This process provided the vowels of lengthened grade. Last, some *e* *ē* changed to *o* *ō* in deflected grade. Since we find deflected-grade vowels beside *a* which was colored by laryngeal, as in Greek *oîtos* "fate" as opposed to *aîsa* "fate," we assume that the initial laryngeal of roots like **xey-* > **ai-* "allot to" was maintained after the change to *o*-grade. It thereupon colored the *e* to *a* in those forms that had not undergone deflection. That is to say, the laryngeals were maintained until all the processes recognized under ablaut had been carried out.

6.6 THE ROLE OF ACCENT IN ABLAUT

As Indo-Europeanists came to recognize in the nineteenth century, and as pursued at length in the formulations of Hirt, the ablaut changes were due to shifts in accent. After publishing numerous articles and monographs on accent and ablaut, Hirt provided his conclusions in several places of his Indo-European grammar (1921–37, I: v–vi, IV: 348–55, V: 28–9). Criticizing some of his predecessors for "projecting everything on a single plane" (IV: 348), he assumed a series of chronological stages.

As we have noted above, Hirt proposed that in the earliest stage, the accent was one of stress. It was during this period that unstressed vowels were lost in zero grade. Hirt also proposed an intermediate stage, where vowels were merely reduced, on the basis of which he posited a further ablaut grade, which he labeled reduced (R) (1921–37, II: 76–102). The characteristic vowel in this grade was labeled schwa secundum; it had front and back variants, represented by ι and z or $\check{\iota}$ and $\check{u}$. With schwa secundum Hirt accounted for reduced vowels that cannot be explained as reflexes of schwa indogermanicum. For example, Latin has *a* in forms in which other dialects have *e*, e.g. *magnus*, cf. Greek *mégas* "large." Other examples are the third allophone by the Sievers–Edgerton law; Hirt here proposed ι plus resonant in contrast with vocalic plus consonantal resonant, e.g. ηm, etc. Hirt also assumed schwa secundum plus vocalic *r l m n* rather than long resonants. The forms cited in support of schwa secundum have been more economically explained by means of laryngeals and the Sievers–Edgerton law; accordingly, schwa secundum is no longer posited. I have shown that the assumed reduced vowels and absence (zero) of vowels were in complementary distribution, and that, accordingly, we do not need to posit such a distinct stage or reduced grade (1952: 23).

It was also during the period of stress accent that some vowels were lengthened in lengthened grade. Hirt cites parallels in modern languages for both types of change; these are so well recognized that it is unnecessary to repeat his reasoning with further documentation here.

At a later stage there was an "accent revolution" by Hirt's term (1921–37, IV: 355). By the proposed revolution in early Proto-Indo-European, pitch came to replace stress. During this stage, an *e* that lost principal accent became *o* under a secondary accent. In support of this view Hirt cites Russian, where the name Gorbachev provides an excellent example of ‹e› pronounced as *o* under accent.

In this way Hirt, making use of the findings of a large number of predecessors whom he acknowledges, presents a credible and accurate statement on accent in the proto-language. He is troubled, however, about the incidence of *a*-vowels, which does not accord with his views on accent. Unfortunately, he failed to include Hittite among the languages that he used for comparative purposes. He was aware of the new discoveries of additional Indo-European languages; but in the publications he produced in the decade available to him after 1927 he did not make use of them for fuller understanding of the proto-language; and he took no account of the explanations provided by Kurylowicz. If he had, his perplexity about the role of *a* might have been allayed.

As we have seen, the *a*-vowels that perplexed Hirt were occasioned by neighboring laryngeals after the changes that led to ablaut had taken place. The *a*'s then did not provide counter-evidence for his theory. Applying this information, we may accept Hirt's conclusions concerning the accent of Proto-Indo-European in its successive stages.

The assumption of a pitch accent in late Proto-Indo-European is supported by the situation attested in many of the early dialects: Vedic Sanskrit, Greek, Baltic, Slavic and early Germanic.

The assumption of an earlier stress accent is demonstrated by the previous loss of vowels in specific, well-defined environments. We therefore maintain the conclusions on accent stated by Hirt, which are strengthened when, by adding laryngeals, we revise the phonological system he assumed. To illustrate the resulting clarification we may review briefly the presentation of ablaut as given by Hirt, and thereupon sketch the situation modified under assumption of the laryngeal theory.

6.7 PRESENTATION OF ABLAUT BY HIRT

Treatments of ablaut before recognition of laryngeals list the Proto-Indo-European vowels by the grade they represent, as the English term "vowel gradation" may suggest (Hirt 1921–37, II: 4–102). The original vowel, i.e. *e*, is said to stand in full or normal grade, in translation of the terms *Voll-* and *Normal-stufe*; the abbreviation N is typically used for this grade. The term may contribute to confusion, since it is applied also to *o*, though that is recognized as standing in *o*-grade or deflected grade, a translation of *Abtönung*. As we have seen, *o*-grade is last in a series of changes in the early language; tables, like that below, accordingly ignore the historical sequence. Because Hirt assumed the two further normal grade vowels, *a* and *o*, even though they were poorly attested in roots, he listed their ablaut grades as well, as indicated in the chart below.

A further grade with these two timbres in long vowels [*e: o:*] is referred to as lengthened grade, in translation of *Dehnstufe*. In English texts it is represented by L, though the abbreviation D may also be found.

As we have noted, Hirt also includes a reduced grade, in his terminology *Reduktionsstufe*, referred to with R. I view that as a variant of zero or null grade, which are translations of *Nullstufe*, referred to with Z. As his treatment shows, the two stand in complementary distribution. The gaps in the chart under Z correspond to items listed under R.

By Hirt's approach, light bases may have six variants. Heavy bases, on the other hand, have only three: $\bar{e}\ \bar{o}\ \partial$. The two sets of bases as proposed by Hirt are not presented separately in the chart below, on grounds that were given in 6.2. After listing the proposed grades of a monophthongal light base, we illustrate them with forms of PIE **ped* "foot," taking examples from Latin, Greek, Gothic and Sanskrit; the examples of heavy bases are from the root **d^hē- < d^he?-* "place".

	N	N$_o$	L$_e$	L$_o$	R	Z
e-series	e	o	$\bar{e}$	$\bar{o}$	e	–
o-series	o	o	$\bar{o}$	$\bar{o}$	o	–
a-series	a	o	$\bar{o}$	$\bar{o}$	a	–
ē-series	$\bar{e}$	$\bar{o}$				∂
ō-series	$\bar{o}$	$\bar{o}$				∂
ā-series	$\bar{a}$	$\bar{o}$				∂

Lat. *pedem*	Gk *póda*	Lat. *pēs*	Goth. *fotus*	Lat. *pedis*	Skt *upabda-*
Gk *títhēmi*	*thōmós*				Skt *hita-*

The situation represented in the chart is greatly simplified when all the vowels are reduced to *e*, as they currently are after the recognition that laryngeals must be assumed during the period of ablaut. The first set given as the *e*-series is then adequate to represent all the other sets as well.

In Hirt's presentation, the bisyllabic bases are highly complex because either syllable may stand in any of the grades, as illustrated below, with one form from Lithuanian in addition to the languages given above (Hirt 1921–37, II: 103–71). The possibility of lengthened grade in bisyllabic bases has been considered, but in general rejected; accordingly, it is not included here. By such a presentation of Hirt's analysis, the bases exhibit six grades, as illustrated with *b^hewā-* "become" and *genē-* "beget".

N + R	R + N	Z + N	Z + R	R + R	Z + Z
Skt bhávitum	Lith. buvo	Lat. -bā-	Skt -bhva-	ábhūt	Gk phúsis
Gk genétēs		gnésios	Skt jātás	Gk gígnomai	

For the bisyllabic bases as well as the monosyllabic, the presentation is greatly simplified when the final item of the bases is given as a laryngeal, as in the bases *b^hew-x-*, *gen-ʔ-* rather than as a long vowel.

The forms provided as illustrations of Hirt's position represent stages of the language long after that in which the changes took place. As did he, it is possible to align selected forms at any subsequent stage, much as we can align modern English *sit*, *sat*, *set*, *seat*, *soot*, and so on to demonstrate Indo-European ablaut. But without historical analysis, such illustrations fail to represent the original alignments and their causes. While we are grateful to Hirt for his contributions to the understanding of ablaut, we depict the earlier situation much more simply, aided by the assumption of laryngeals.

6.8 ABLAUT EXEMPLIFIED BY ROOTS INCLUDING EACH SUB-CLASS OF CONSONANTS

As we have stated above, ablaut was brought about by three vowel changes. Following the traditional assumptions we can represent these by supplying the canonical forms of roots, and thereupon the zero, lengthened and deflected grades. These forms for well-known roots are as follows.

Normal	Zero	Lengthened	Deflected	
*sed	*sd	*sēd	*sod	"sit"
*b^her	*b^hr	*b^hēr	*b^hor	"bear"
*heg	*hg	*hēg	*hog	"drive"
*d^heʔ	*d^hʔ	*d^hēʔ	*d^hoʔ	"place"

Reflexes of these forms can be provided from the dialects. For *sed* "sit" we have already cited such forms; the Germanic verb provides three of them: the normal grade form in the Gothic infinitive *sitan*, the deflected in the preterite singular *sat*, the lengthened in the preterite third person plural *setun*. The zero-grade form is found in the Gothic noun *niss*.

For *b^her- we may cite for the normal-grade form the Greek present *phérō* "I bear," for the zero-grade the noun *dí-phros* "chariot-board," for the lengthened grade the noun *phṓr* "thief," and for the deflected grade *phóros* "tribute"; it may be noted that the lengthened-grade vowel underwent deflection in the subsequent period of pitch accent.

For *∂eg- "drive" we may cite for the normal-grade form Sanskrit *ájati* "drives," for the zero grade the Greek participle *aktós* "led," for the lengthened grade the Sanskrit *ājíḥ* "combat," and for the deflected grade Greek *ógmos* "furrow, path."

For *$d^he\partial$-, traditionally written *dhē*- we may cite for the normal grade the Hittite first person singular present *te-eh-hi* "I place" (where the *h-hi* is the personal ending and the glottal stop of the root is not expressed), for the zero grade Greek *thetós* "placed," for the deflected grade Ionic Greek *thôkos* "seat."

In this way we can cite reflexes of the various ablaut grades in support of the assumptions stated above. As these and other illustrations indicate, the forms exemplifying ablaut grades have been appropriated for various purposes, and appear in various morphological sets. Similar reflexes could be cited for the extended roots, that is, the bisyllabic bases posited by Hirt. As more complex forms they would require somewhat more elucidation; but the essential principles for their formation are like those of the unextended roots.

6.9 A COHERENT VIEW OF THE INDO-EUROPEAN PHONOLOGICAL SYSTEM IN ITS DEVELOPMENT

Our examination in this chapter and in the previous chapter of the development of the Proto-Indo-European phonological system may illustrate the recognition that it is a coherent set of segmental and suprasegmental elements that have been modified and rearranged, much like the elements of any language over a period of time. We have not dealt with some of its characteristics, such as the interrelationships of words in sentences. Two points may be briefly mentioned.

6.9.1 Movable *s*- as evidence for phrase groups

When we compare selected cognates from dialect to dialect we find doublets, one variant with preposed *s*, the other without it: for example, the Avestan verb corresponding to Sanskrit *páśyati* "sees" is *spasyeiti* "sees." An example of such a noun is Greek *tégos*, *stégos* "roof, house," of which the Germanic form has no *s*-, as in German *Dach* "roof," English *thatch*, while the Lithuanian form *stógas* "roof" does – and so on in other branches. Although several explanations have been proposed for the *s*, the only likely one accounts for it through mistaken word division.

Examples of mistaken word division could be cited from various languages; they are ready at hand in English, with pairs like *newt* made from an older form of *eft*. Since in English a typical word preceding these nouns is *a/an*, speakers may mistake the word boundary, and pronounce the noun with the *-n* of the indefinite article. The Middle English word *napron*, borrowed from French, was conversely modified to *apron*, and similarly *nadder*, German *Natter*, to *adder*.

In Proto-Indo-European a form ending in *-s* would commonly have preceded the verb. Accordingly, a mistaken word division may have been made, giving rise to the Avestan form from the alternate root **spek-*. On the basis of such forms we conclude that Proto-Indo-European sentences were spoken in phrases, much like the modern Indo-European languages. The alignment of words in Vedic Sanskrit, as well as in texts like the Old High German phrase book, supports this general assumption, and provides evidence for reconstructing phrasal rules.

6.9.2 Sentence intonation represented through distribution of accent

Somewhat similarly, sentence structure is displayed for us by distribution of accent. If as we have noted in the previous chapter, verbs stand finally in Vedic sentences, they lack an accent. Since the accent is one of high pitch, we may conclude that sentences were marked by final drop of pitch, much as in many current Indo-European languages: for example, Hymn 71 of the seventh book of the *Rigveda* begins as follows:

ápa	svásur	Uṣáso Nág	jihīte
away (from)	sister	Dawn Night	departs

"Night departs away from her sister Dawn."

The lack of accent on the verb contrasts with that on the verb in the subordinate clause of the fourth stanza, which we may interpret as maintaining the pitch level:

abhí yád	vāṁ viśvápsniyo	jígāti
for so-that	you having-all-food	it-may-come

"so that it (the chariot) may come for you filled with all food"

Sustained accent was apparently a boundary signal at the ends of subordinate clauses, in contrast with falling accent at the ends of principal declarative clauses.

As we have stated above, these conclusions are supported by Germanic alliterative verse, in which the verb is placed at the end of the line unless it is emphasized by initial placement. Words in final position also fail to alliterate, indicating that they have less phonological prominence, presumably from a fall in accent; but verbs placed initially may alliterate, indicating that they carry accent, as in *Beowulf* 6: *egsode eorlas* "terrified the warriors." Their patterning is comparable to the initial verb in the second line of Hymn 71:

riṇákti kṛṣṇír aruṣáya pánthām
yields black to-red path
"Blackness yields the path to the sun."

We then have means to reconstruct structural characteristics of sentences as well as phrases in Proto-Indo-European speech.

The assumption of a contrast between declarative sentences, on the one hand, and some questions, requests and the like, on the other hand, is supported by indication of the special accentuation in early Sanskrit known as pluti, which indicates maintenance of pitch as opposed to falling pitch. We assume on the basis of these patterns in Vedic and those in Germanic alliterative verse two distinctive intonation patterns for the parent language, final falling pitch for principal declarative clauses and level accent for dependent clauses as well as some questions and requests (see 3.3.3, 5.8).

6.9.3 The phonological system in its successive stages

Finally, we may illustrate the coherence of the phonological system in its successive stages. We have noted how that system, as represented in the early period of Indo-European studies, including the compendium of Schleicher, was depicted almost as an exact reflection of the Sanskrit system. Internal analysis, following Verner's insights, led to corrections, both of the vowels and the basis of ablaut variations. Combined with Saussure's proposals on root structure, the phonological system came to be portrayed as that of a language which underwent shifts of accent and, accordingly, also shifts of its vocalic system as well as its system of resonants and laryngeals.

We have followed these back to earlier stages from the attested texts. Here, by contrast, we propose the initial system that we can reconstruct; we pursue it through the shifts in phonology in the successive stages of the proto-language, noting that the system as given is highly abstract. If, for example, we represent the [i] vowel by means of the symbol /y/, as in Proto-Indo-European /bʰydʰ/, the representation of the segment may seem forbidding; but the pronunciation would be very similar to that of English *bid*. We illustrate the various stages by archaic forms especially from the *Rigveda*.

To illustrate the earliest stage that is readily reconstructable we must recall that the Indo-European phonological system consisted of sets of phonological elements, of which the set of obstruents, of laryngeals and of resonants each shares specific characteristics. If, for example, we construct forms from the base represented as **bheid-* or **bheyd-*, maintained in English as *bite*, we would expect Proto-Indo-European equivalents to the injunctives attested in Vedic: *bhinát* and *bhét* "he splits." (The form *bhét* is not attested with an accent, but that is a matter of its position in the Vedic verse.) It is clear from the first form, a class 7 present injunctive, that the vowel is associated with the accent. The vowel is also associated with the accent in the form *bhét*, which is an aorist injunctive. But the obstruents, and the resonant, are independent, pronounced according to their relationship to other segmental phonemes.

We may examine similar forms with a laryngeal, as of the base represented in Indo-European dictionaries as **bʰewā*, and by us as **bʰewx-*. Here the two corresponding injunctives are the present *bhúvat* and *bhūt* "becomes." (It would serve our purposes better if a different form from *bhúvat* were attested, because the accent has been rearranged in the present; this is not true of subjunctive forms like the second plural *bhūtás* from **bʰwxtés*. Here the vowel is associated with the accent.)

6.9.3.1 The earliest reconstructable stage

From the independence of obstruents, laryngeals and resonants but not the vowels, we may conclude that the language is better represented by not proposing any vowel; rather, when a vowel-like segment appears, it results from a suprasegmental element that we may call syllabicity. For recent support of this view, first presented in Lehmann 1952, see the review of Gamkrelidze and Ivanov (1984) by Palmaitis (1988: esp. 284). That is to say, in the earliest reconstructable stage of the proto-language we do not reconstruct any vowels, but only the three sets of consonants and the nonsegmental phoneme syllabicity. I have represented this with a caret $/\wedge/$, and refer to this stage of the language as stage A. If we propose the second person singular subjunctive for "become" at this stage we would write it $/bwxt\wedge s/$. The word would have been pronounced [buçtás], hardly a difficult form for most speakers.

6.9.3.2 The stage with phonemic stress accent

In stage B stress comes to be phonemic. If maximum stress is aligned with syllabicity, the allophone is [e]. That is to say, a vowel now is added to the segmental system, even though it still is an allophone of syllabicity. Side by side with maximum stress, minimum stress is found associated with resonants. When it is they have a vocalic allophone, e.g. [i u r̥ l̥ m̥ n̥]. It is during stage B that the vocalic system comes to be expanded. When a syllable with maximum stress stands before a syllable that loses its syllabicity, the [e] is lengthened, providing [eː] beside [e].

In stage C the allophones of syllabicity become phonemes. The language then has a system of phonemes that may be expressed by /e eː ₑ/. In the neighborhood of vowel-coloring laryngeals, these have allophones that may be represented with those of /e/ [e a o].

6.9.3.3 The stage with phonemic pitch accent

In stage D a pitch accent replaces the previous stress accent. If at this stage a vowel with primary accent loses it, the vowel is shifted to [o]. Some of the [o] vowels fall together with those colored by the voiced velar laryngeals. At this point the vocalic system develops to that of stage E, where the previous allophones of vowels become phonemes.

In stage E the vowel system consists of three low phonemes in short and long form, as well as the reduced vowel: /e a o eː aː oː ₑ /. The vowel system is then substantially that of the late proto-language. Now on the promotion of the laryngeal-colored vowels to phonemes, laryngeals are lost when adjacent to these vowels, contributing further instances of the vowels /a o eː aː oː ₑ]. At the same time, loss of the laryngeals in the neighborhood of [i u] leads to the additional vowels /iː uː/. The system now is that of the late proto-language as provided earlier.

6.9.3.4 The phonological system in Proto-Indo-European

In the phonological stage of the proto-language, stage F, which was presented in chapter 5, the system continues to change, largely by continued loss of laryngeals in specific contexts, and by disruption of the allophones of the resonants, so that these become phonemes. Further changes lead to the phonological systems of the individual dialects.

In much the same way, the earlier stages had undergone changes in the consonantal system. If one accepts the glottalic theory, in one of the earlier stages the glottalics would have become voiced stops. The change must have taken place before the proto-language, because, as we have noted, all the branches have voiced stops or reflexes of them as in Germanic and Armenian; in no dialect are glottalics attested as reflexes of the Indo-European glottalics.

Moreover, laryngeals must have been lost in some positions in an earlier stage, as when standing after a vowel before a consonant, so that these lengthened syllabic nuclei fell together with the long vowels resulting from lengthened grade. At this stage as well, vocalic *i* and *u* would have been lengthened in the same environment, so that the proto-language included long *ī* and *ū*.

The phonological system was in this way undergoing change, much as does any spoken language. As we reconstruct the early stages of the language, however, it is increasingly difficult to relate changes as of the obstruent system with those of the vocalic and accentual systems. It is important, on the other hand, to relate the phonological changes with those in the morphological system, as illustrated in the next two chapters.

7 Morphology 1: the nominal elements

7.1 VIEWS ON MORPHOLOGY AT THE BEGINNING OF INDO-EUROPEAN STUDIES

When Bopp and his successors began their work in comparative Indo-European linguistics, morphology was well understood. The classical languages were thoroughly mastered on the basis of handbooks that included nominal and verbal paradigms as well as descriptions of uninflected parts of speech. Sanskrit grammars provided a clear pattern for portrayal of a somewhat more complex set of verbal forms than either Greek or Latin. And concern since the time of Leibniz with all known languages provided information on types of morphology and categories, as its characterizations brought to their high point in Adelung's *Mithridates* may illustrate.

The first volume of the *Mithridates*, published in 1806, begins by presenting samples of various Chinese dialects among "monosyllabic languages." It then continues with "polysyllabic languages," among them Sanskrit (*ibid*. 134–76). After citing considerable bibliography on Sanskrit, including publications produced before those of Jones and contemporaries, Adelung briefly characterizes the language, pointing out among other traits that nouns have seven cases besides the vocative, and verbs have ten classes. Later in the volume (*ibid*. 459–68) he deals with Osmanli Turkish, again citing a large bibliography dating from 1599 to 1780. Here too his characterization is accurate though informal. Inflectional and derivational elements at the ends of words are said to be very "manifold." Substantives do not indicate gender nor take articles, but have six cases; and verbs are said to be the most difficult part of the language, some forms seeming to be "phrases." In short, languages were described for form; categories were identified. The functions expressed through such forms and by the categories and subcategories were determined. This brief sketch may indicate that procedures were available for analysing the data of the various Indo-European languages, classifying them, and comparing the results to find the common characteristics.

Sources for this chapter: Bopp (1820); Johannes Schmidt (1889); Delbrück (1907); Wackernagel (1926–8); Benveniste (1935); Specht (1944); Lehmann (1958); Kurylowicz (1964); Gamkrelidze and Ivanov (1984); Adrados (1988a); Beekes (1985).

It was also clear that the Indo-European languages were inflectional, rather than agglutinative like Turkish or monosyllabic like the Chinese dialects. Adelung had pointed out that Sanskrit lacks a suffix like Turkish *ler* that indicates the plural of nouns (1806: 463); instead, the categories of gender, number and case are expressed in the Indo-European languages through composite endings. It remained for August Wilhelm von Schlegel to inaugurate labeling of language types with his terms synthetic and analytic; but even earlier it was apparent that the structure of the Indo-European languages was different from that of the two other types noted above. Bopp then proceeded to provide increasing information on the forms, categories and functions of an increasing number of branches of the Indo-European family in the three editions of his comparative grammar (1833, 1857–61, 1868–71).

7.1.1 Nominal classification by form; number, gender, case

Following the long traditions of Greek and Latin grammar, Bopp and his successors classified words by the inflections they undergo. These inflections correlate with grammatical classes, nouns, pronouns, adjectives and so on. For nominal inflection, gender, number and case provide the sets of categories. These were recognized as largely grammatical, not natural categories; but the two overlap, the grammatical often coinciding with natural categories. In number, for example, one rose is represented with a noun in the singular, Latin *rosa*; two with a noun in the plural, *rosae*. That correlation does not apply to some nouns; the singular *littera* means "letter (of the alphabet)" while the plural *litterae* means "a letter, an epistle." There may also be contrasts between grammatical and natural classes; the Latin first declension, which is generally feminine, includes masculine nouns like *agricola* "farmer" and *nauta* "sailor." In the second declension the nouns ending in *-us* are identified as "mostly masculine," though "most names of trees and plants" are feminine, e.g. *fāgus* "beech," *ficus* "fig tree." Yet the terms "masculine" and "feminine" were maintained, opening the way to misunderstanding of grammatical classification.

The partial overlap of natural and grammatical classification supported a lingering assumption that the categories have some natural basis: for example, the use of the feminine gender for names of trees and plants in the Latin second declension could be explained on the basis of their productiveness. Wackernagel (1926–8: 37–44) discusses the course of the argumentation, pointing out that Herder and Grimm, on the one hand, saw the origin of gender distinctions in an effort at natural classification, while Brugmann viewed it as grammatical. Wackernagel sympathized with Herder and Grimm, on the grounds that speakers of the languages in their earlier stages differ from those today in their attitudes towards language and its use; but Indo-Europeanists today would consider the grammatical function primary and the relationships with natural categories secondary. By this view gender is a congruence category.

The treatment of case differs from that of gender and number because some of the cases are clearly grammatical, namely the nominative, accusative and genitive; and the vocative essentially makes up a complete clause. By contrast, the four others are referred to as concrete, that is, ablative, dative, instrumental, locative. As the names of these cases suggest, they have often been assumed to have an origin in localistic reference; the ablative case then would indicate "place from," the dative "place to," the instrumental "place or object by means of," the locative "place at." Even though Kurylowicz recognizes that "case-forms with grammatical (syntactical) functions are attested at every stage of the history of a language," he states firmly that "all cases go back to forms denoting spatial relations" (1964: 202).

Although scholars differ in their views on the " 'localistic' theory of cases" (*ibid.*), the chief problem in the treatment of case results from the lack of distinction between formal categories and semantic categories. Throughout the nineteenth century, and even later, nominal forms were identified by inflectional categories, such as dative and ablative, and these were assumed to have a characteristic function, with possible secondary uses. Grammars then might include sections discussing the ablative use of the genitive, or of the dative, and so on. The problem is especially acute in grammars of languages with few case forms, like Greek and Germanic; grammars of these languages may be especially confusing in describing uses of forms with the names for the items within paradigms. Procedures for distinguishing between form and function, such as those devised by the ancient Indian grammarians, would lead to greater clarity.

7.1.2 Kāraka categories and underlying cases

The standard treatment of western handbooks was doubly unfortunate because the Indian grammarians had devised an elegant procedure to distinguish between the forms and the functions. The forms are labeled by their position in the paradigm; the functions are treated as *kāraka* categories, comparable to underlying cases (Lehmann 1974: 10–12, 190–8). Delbrück was aware of them but also somewhat disquieted by them (1893: 173–5). There are six: four based on the Sanskrit root *kṛ* "make, do" and two on the root *dā* "give." *Kartar* "doer, actor" corresponds to the underlying case "agent." *Karman* "action" indicates the aim of the action, represented as "target" in Lehmann (1974). *Karaṇa* "tool" indicates the means or instrument. *Adhikaraṇa* "placing on, at," etc. indicates place or time of action; underlying case systems typically include a slot for time as well as place of action. *Saṁpradāna* "giving to" indicates the recipient of an action. *Apādāna* "giving away" indicates departure or separation through action. Only in recent times has the distinction between surface and underlying cases been consistently observed in western linguistics, after an influential article by Fillmore (1968: 1–88). But many subsequent treatments of underlying case are inferior to those of the Indian grammarians in applying some of the inflectional labels for underlying cases. The very application of the term "case" for function is unfortunate. As in Paninian grammar, the functions are better treated as categories.

By linguistic theory the value of any form or any word is determined by oppositions in a structure. Indian grammar applied this principle. Forms are identified by formal characteristics, and thereupon their functions are determined; the *kāraka* categories represent a well-considered set of these. From time to time western grammars have attempted to be explicit about the difference between form and function, providing distinct labels for formal elements as opposed to their meanings. Bloomfield, for example, was precise about the distinction, introducing the terms *tagmeme* for the smallest unit of form and *episememe* for the meaning of such a form; but the distinctions may seem cumbersome and are often neglected, as in discussion of case forms. If, however, the structure of a language is to be understood, and applied capably for comparison, the meanings of forms in a given language must be clearly identified apart from the sets of forms themselves, and appropriate labels applied to keep these two features of language distinct.

7.1.3 Classification for nouns, pronouns, adjectives

In Indo-European grammars, the larger formal classes are accurately identified. A distinction is made between nominal and verbal elements on the basis of inflectional categories; in addition, non-inflected or indeclinable elements are identified. Nominals in turn are classified in three subgroups: nouns (sometimes labeled substantives), pronouns, adjectives. In addition, numerals are treated with reference to nominals. Depending on their treatment in a given language, the cardinals after three or four are classified with nouns, the ordinals and the first three or four cardinals with adjectives; other numerical items, for example "once," "twice," etc. are treated as adverbials.

These subgroups are distinguished by the categories they admit. Nouns are characterized for a specific gender, and also for number and case. Personal pronouns, by contrast, are not characterized for gender. Further, in the first and second person different stems are used in the plural, so that we may conclude they are not distinguished for number even though they are so listed in many grammars; it has often been pointed out that "we" is not the plural of "I," or that "I" can have no plural. Most of the other pronouns – demonstratives, interrogatives, indefinites and, when they appear, relatives – include inflection for gender; accordingly, they may be associated with adjectives, although there are some distinctive pronominal endings. Adjectives may be inflected through more than one gender, but in other respects they, like nouns, are inflected for case and number.

These subclasses were posited by the earliest Indo-Europeanists, for they were evident in Greek and Latin in addition to the newly studied Sanskrit, which served as models for the remainder of the family.

Accordingly, there was no hesitation concerning the subcategories to be assumed for nominals. Since Sanskrit includes eight cases, eight were accepted for the family. This set, as illustrated below, has been maintained in many handbooks. Those branches which, like Greek and Germanic, exhibit fewer cases were taken to have lost earlier distinctions. Latin with its six cases then was interpreted as supporting the set based on Sanskrit, as were Baltic and Slavic. Only recently, especially after the discovery of Hittite, has a set of eight cases for the proto-language been questioned.

Similarly, three genders and three numbers were posited on the basis of Sanskrit as well as of evidence in other dialects. Besides forms and categories, functions were noted: for example, the nominative case was recognized as filling the function: subject of a sentence. A variety of functions was ascribed to the accusative case: object of verbs and prepositions, extent of time, direction of motion, among others.

For any nominal, then, the form and the functions were determined. These are treated at great length in the handbooks; for example, in Brugmann's short Indo-European grammar (1904a), gender is discussed on pages 354–62, then the case endings for nouns are presented (*ibid*. 373–99), followed by similar treatment of the pronouns, and thereupon by exposition of the meanings of number and cases (*ibid*. 413–46). Szemerényi's presentation corresponds to Brugmann's, differing only in details (1970 [1989]: 164–203, with copious bibliography).

7.1.4 The case endings according to the standard handbooks

The standard handbooks list the endings by case and number (Szemerényi 1970 [1989]: 169). Except for the neuter nominative/accusative plural, which has the ending -$(e)h$, the same array of endings is reconstructed for each of the three genders. In the nominative singular neuter, the ending is that of the accusative, except that some nouns have zero (-0) ending.

It is most economical to list the cases by the order followed in Sanskrit grammar; for in the dual the nominative, vocative and accusative have the same ending; so do the instrumental, dative and ablative; a third ending is found in the genitive and locative. The accusative forms are given here in phonemic notation; they may be vocalic or consonantal, depending on their environment.

The case endings

	Singular	Plural	Dual
Nominative	-s, -0	-es	
Vocative	-0	-es	-i(H), -e
Accusative	-m	-ns	
Instrumental	-bh/mi	-bh/mis	
Dative	-ey	-bh(y)/mos	-bh/m-
Ablative	-ē/ōd	-bh(y)/mos	
Genitive	-(e/o)s	-ōm	-ou(s)
Locative	-i, -0	-su	

An illustration of the inflected forms of nouns for the proto-language can best be given with a root noun. These may undergo combinatory changes. For illustrative purposes the noun for "foot" is highly suitable in having few such changes; other examples may be noted in Meillet (1937: 254–6). Evidence for the Indo-European inflection is difficult to support with data from some sub-branches because many root nouns have been shifted to declensions with a vocalic suffix; in Gothic, for example, the word for "foot" is included in the *u*-declension, as in the forms *fotus*, *fotum*. And even in the earliest dialects there have been modifications, as comparison of the forms in Sanskrit, Greek and Latin indicates.

	PIE	Sanskrit		Greek	Latin
Singular					
Nominative	*pṓ(t)s	pát		poús	pēs
Accusative	*pédm	pádam		póda	pedem
Instrumental	*pedé	pádá			
Dative	*pedéy	padé		podí	pedī
Ablative	*padés	padás			
Genitive	*padés	padás		podós	pedis
Locative	*pedí	padí			(pede)
Plural					
Nominative	*pédes	pádas		pódes	pedēs
Accusative	*pédns	padás		pódas	pedēs
Instrumental	*pedbhís	padbhís	Myc.	po-pi	
Dative	*pedbh(y)ós	padbhyás			pedibus
Ablative	*pedbh(y)ós	padbhyás			pedibus
Genitive	*pedṓm	padám		podôn	pedum
Locative	*petsú	patsú		posí	

Among notes to the reconstructions, it may be pointed out that the nominative singular here is reconstructed by the comparative method. Szemeréni, by contrast, reconstructs PIE *pēs*, accounting for the long *o* of Greek and Gothic, and implicit in Sanskrit, through deflection of *e* to *o* in compounds, with consequent extension of the *o*-grade throughout the paradigm in Greek (1970 [1989]: 173). Further, as here, lengthening of the root vowel in the nominative singular is assumed. And the Mycenaean Greek form, even in its defective writing system that fails to include final consonants or to indicate voicing of stops, indicates that some early Greek dialects included a form corresponding to the instrumental.

Other problems in reconstructing the Proto-Indo-European paradigm might also be discussed. The forms are provided here largely to illustrate the difficulties facing anyone who sets out to undertake such reconstruction. As a major problem, in accordance with the requirements of accent shift those forms with accent on the ending should have zero grade of the root. But through paradigmatic regularization either *e* or *o* was generalized. Root nouns with internal resonant, like PIE *weyk-* "village," have zero grade in such forms, as illustrated by Sanskrit *víśam*, Old Slavic *vĭsĭ*, presumably maintaining the form of the root when the accent fell on endings. For roots like *ped-* we may assume regularization already in the proto-language.

7.1.5 Stem classes of nouns

As in the dialects, noun stems in the proto-language had various suffixes, chiefly resonants but also *-s*. These combined with the endings, so that a variety of inflections arose: *i*-stems, *u*-stems, nasal stems, liquid stems, *s*-stems. The forms may be consulted in the handbooks. In the early dialects noun inflection came to be highly complex because the stem-suffixes often combined with endings to yield new suffixes.

Combinatory changes of endings, such as those in the root nouns and stems ending in resonants and *-s*, are not brought about in the thematic inflections, especially with *e/o* as thematic vowel, as forms of "wolf" in several dialects may illustrate: Sanskrit *vŕkas*, Greek *lúkos*, Latin *lupus*, Lithuanian *vilˇkas*, Gothic *wulfs*. The final consonant of each of these forms is unmodified by the ending. It is not surprising then that thematic inflections replaced the root inflections increasingly throughout the nominal and also the verbal paradigms of the dialects.

Paradigms came to be regularized, as in Latin, where the third declension includes all stems but the thematic and a small number of *u*-stems in the fourth declension and a few relic forms in the fifth. Late Latin, as well as the later forms of most of the other dialects, simplified inflection even further, leading to the noun systems in the languages today that in many branches have little or no inflection.

7.2 DERIVATIONAL MORPHOLOGY OF THE NOMINALS

The structure of nouns as well as the categories of inflection occupied the attention of Indo-Europeanists from the early publications, if only because it is closely associated with markers of inflection. Nouns were assigned to classes by pre-desinential affixes. While, as we have noted, these are not found with root nouns, by the time of the earliest texts most nouns can be analysed into three elements: a root; a derivational affix; an affix of inflection, often referred to as ending. The term "ending" may also to used to include the derivational affix, and accordingly for clarity the term "desinence" may be preferred for the third or inflectional element.

The segments consisting of the first two elements are referred to as stems or themes, the derivational affixes as stem vowels. Because the ablauting variants *e/o* are especially frequent, the term "thematic vowel" is used specifically for them; nouns and adjectives with these stem vowels are referred to as thematic. In the earliest dialects, notably Sanskrit, *i-* and *u-* stems make up large classes; but they become less distinct in later periods, merging with declensional classes formed characteristically in the dialects, as we have noted above.

7.2.1 Derivation by means of additional affixes

Moreover, in the dialects, and already in the proto-language, new derivational affixes arose. Some of these came to have characteristic meanings, such as *-ti-*, which marked abstract nouns. It is difficult to determine more precisely the class meanings of the early derivational affixes, though some have been proposed, for example that the *u-*stems are prominent in religious terms.

The new derivational affixes are presented at length by Brugmann (1897–1916, 2.2: 130–574) as formants, with treatment of their manner of formation and their class meaning when it can be determined. Much of Brugmann's extensive presentation consists of lists, including the words attested in individual dialects. In this way discussion of derivational morphology came to resemble listing in dictionaries rather than structural descriptions. Such presentations are also available for the dialects, as in the comprehensive grammars of Sanskrit by Wackernagel, of Greek by Schwyzer, of Latin by Leumann, and major grammars of other dialects as well as specific handbooks on derivation (for further references, see Lehmann 1969). They may be consulted for the derivational processes of the branch concerned, generally with information on the earlier situation.

Through comparing the older examples in these languages, the meanings of some suffixes may still be ascertained. Persson in a comprehensive work set out to determine the consonant suffixes, known as determinatives or root-determinatives, and also their distribution (1912). Benveniste produced an exemplary study of the determinative *-dh-* which may well have come to be a tense marker for the Germanic dental preterite (1935: Lehmann 1942, 1943), as the determinative *-s-* did in Indo-Iranian, Greek, Armenian and Slavic. And in 1948 Benveniste attempted to distinguish the functions of the nominal suffixes, PIE *-ti-* and *-tu-*. While he proposed contrasting meanings for them, the evidence is minute, even for similar studies in subsequent periods.

Ready examples may be provided, as by English *-hood* : German *-heit*,

English *-dom* : German *-tum*, or by recently produced affixes, such as *-ware* or *-burger*. The first two examples here are suffixal variants of nouns, of which the second is still maintained as "doom"; the two last are clipped elements of words. Either of these clipped suffixes may illustrate how segments may be abstracted almost by chance and used for devising new words. For example, the suffix *-ware* was appropriated in devising new terms for the new computer technology. In keeping with an ambivalent attitude to the mysterious device, its makeup was referred to as *hardware*. Since the hardware was useless without directions, these were developed and came to be known as *software*, and the pattern was set. More specific applications used for instruction were dubbed *courseware*. No-one was taken aback by such further creations as *lingware*; the suffix was established. Yet without accurate knowledge of the situation in which it arose, we would be hard-pressed to account for the new suffix *-ware*.

Determining the origin and development of suffixes even in material as recent as that of Germanic is far more difficult, though the course of some is clear. The Gothic suffix *-assus*, for example, is based on use of the prominent Indo-European suffix *-tu-* to derive abstract nouns from verbs ending in *-atjan*, with *-at-tu-* becoming *-assu-*. Identified as an independent suffix, it was then used after other words than the verbs in *-atjan*, as in Gothic *ufarassus* "abundance," based on *ufar* "above." When added to verbs like *fraujinon* "rule over," the abstract noun had the form *fraujinassus** "mastery" (starred because it is attested only in oblique case forms in our fragmentary Gothic texts), and the suffix came to be perceived as *-nassus*; its cognate is maintained in English *-ness*. Clipped once again in Gothic as *-inassus*, it was added to verbs like *blotan* "worship" to form nouns like *blotinassus** "worship." For references see Lehmann (1986a: 76).

Suffixes then can be developed by several processes. Words may be appropriated, or selected sequences may be cut off, and generalized. As any treatment of derivational morphology will demonstrate, many such suffixes came to be highly productive in the Indo-European dialects.

7.2.2 Derivation by compounding

The lexicon was also expanded by means of compounding, the types of which were noted in 3.5.2. Extensive, especially in late Sanskrit and Greek, compounding is surprisingly infrequent in Hittite, almost absent there. Where present in languages, it reflects syntactic patterns, usually those of the earlier periods; for compounds are essentially reduced phrases or clauses. Current publications on derivational morphology set out to explain the compounds of a language in this way. When established, a compound pattern often reflects syntactic patterns of a previous stage of the language (Lehmann 1969).

In a comprehensive study Risch found that synthetic compounds make up 60 per cent of all attested compounds in early Greek (1944: 5).

Consisting of noun followed by verb root or stem, they indicate individuals performing an action, such as Sanskrit *mantra-kŕt* "one who makes poems," Greek *logopoiós* "one who makes words, a poet," Latin *artifex* "artist." As these examples indicate, they observe the pattern of the Indo-European sentence, in which verbs stand after objects.

The second most frequent type in the early dialects are known as possessive or *bahuvrihi* compounds, after their Sanskrit designation; the two individual Sanskrit elements meaning "much rice" as here compounded have the meaning "one who has much rice." These compounds reflect the clause pattern in active structure to indicate possession, as maintained in Latin in the *mihi est* construction, for example, line 71 of the *Aeneid*: *sunt mihi bis septem Nymphae* "I have twice seven Nymphs." As in the earlier pattern, no verbal element is necessary. Possessive compounds differ from synthetics in having the accent on the first member, as in Sanskrit *gó-magha* "having an abundance of cattle."

A third type of compound is additive; less widely used, it is found in the teens, as in Latin *tredecim* "thirteen," the meanings of the two components are added to provide the overall meaning. These compounds reflect processes of coordination for nominal elements.

Moreover, compounds comparable to synthetics are found in names, e.g. Vedic *Trasá-dasyus*, literally "one who causes enemies to tremble," Greek *Archélaos*, literally "one who rules people," Old Persian *Xšayāršan* "one who rules men, *Xerxes*." While earlier scholars interpreted the first element as an imperative, I accounted for the order of the elements through marking (1969).

In setting out to account for synthetic compounds, such as Sanskrit *go-ṣá* "one who gains cattle < cattle gain," Jacobi proposed that they were reflexes of an earlier relative clause pattern (1897). By our view, as noted above, they are abbreviated forms of the clause, reflecting in their OV order the unmarked clause pattern of Proto-Indo-European and the early dialects.

This explanation may be supported by the relatively small number of compounds used primarily in names, e.g. Greek *Agélāos* "he who leads men," Old Persian *Dārayavauš* "he who has wealth," in addition to those cited above. As proper nouns, these compounds represent the VO order of marked clauses in the proto-language and may be accounted for as marked variants of synthetics.

Like the usual synthetics and bahuvrihis, the marked synthetics are not maintained as productive types in the dialects. We account for the loss of these types in part through regularization of accent, in part through shift of the sentence order to VO patterning. While the clause order was changed, adjectives were maintained before nouns in many dialects, as still in Modern English in contrast with French. Descriptive compounds like *bluebird* then remained productive, illustrating once again the relationship between compound patterning and order of syntactic elements.

In sum, nominal derivation was prominent in the proto-language, initially through suffixes that characterized declensions. Thereupon extended suffixes were used, as were specific types of compounds.

7.3 PROBLEMS IN THE TREATMENT OF NUMBER

The handbooks, including the third edition of Szemerényi's, maintain the treatment of the Indo-European nominal system as worked out during the nineteenth century. But already in the last part of the century some problems in reference to the system were pointed out. In an impressive study on "The plural formations of the Indo-European neuters" (1889), Johannes Schmidt dealt with irregularities in morphological and syntactic alignment of neuter plurals. By one of the irregularities, subjects in the neuter plural are accompanied by singular verbs, especially in Greek. Moreover, as we have noted, some nouns ending in *-a* of the Latin first declension are inflected like feminines though they refer to males, e.g. *agricola* "farmer" and *nauta* "sailor"; the comparable nouns in Greek have *-s* added in the nominative, e.g. *naútēs* "sailor, *neanías* "a young man." Schmidt concluded that, rather than a neuter plural, the form was actually a collective singular.

Although Schmidt was highly respected and the book well received, his conclusions did not modify the general views on number and gender in the proto-language. Handbooks provided explanations in keeping with Schmidt's conclusions for masculine nouns like Latin *agricola* "farmer" and *nauta* "sailor" of the first declension in Latin through the assumption that the members of such occupations were viewed collectively rather than as individuals. In this way the irregular masculines seemed to be explained with no further need to account for the ending. Oddly, acceptance of the explanation did not lead to adoption of Schmidt's explanation for the neuter plural.

Problems are also evident in the plurals of Sanskrit nouns. In the older Vedic poems the endings in *-bh-* . . . and the locative *-su* are treated for purposes of sandhi (juncture) like distinct words rather than inflectional elements. Moreover, forms other than the nominative, accusative, genitive plural are infrequent. Further, the plural form of the accusative is much like the singular, with the addition of *s*; the accusative singular ending *-m* presumably changed to dental articulation in keeping with following *-s* to yield the accusative plural *-ns*. These problems also were treated as individual irregularities.

The availability of Hittite put the situation on a totally different plane. The language does not include feminine gender. Also the presence of laryngeals provided the key to the ending explained earlier by Schmidt. Rather than a collective suffix *-a*, the ending was a laryngeal, *-h*. This conclusion is supported by the neuter plural ending of consonant stems, and of *i-* and *u*-stems in *-i*, which Sturtevant already equated with Indo-

European schwa (1942: 44), in this way supporting the identification as a laryngeal. On the other hand, traditionalists sought in various ways to maintain the view of number and gender given in the handbooks; they assumed that the feminine gender had been lost in Hittite. But the lack of different plural endings provided difficulties for an assumption that Hittite had reduced the set of inflections (Gamkrelidze and Ivanov 1984). Use of the same endings in the two numbers suggests that the formation of the plural is late.

7.3.1 The earlier nominal system

In a paper of 1958 I proposed a totally different view of nominal inflection for an earlier stage of Proto-Indo-European from that of the handbooks. By this view, nouns in that earlier period added inflectional affixes that had a specific lexical meaning rather than grammatical meaning as in Sanskrit and the other dialects. The laryngeal -*h*, which indicates a collective meaning, is one of these affixes. Similarly, -*s* suffixed to a noun indicated an individual. This view of the early system has been essentially adopted by Gamkrelidze and Ivanov (1984). It is supported by the recent recognition that at that stage the language was active. Such languages have minimal inflection of nouns, and may lack plural forms. As we have just noted, plural forms of the oblique cases are infrequent and irregular in the oldest Vedic texts. Clues to the earlier system survived in such residues, also in the Latin masculines in the *a*-declension.

It is useful to observe how conclusions may be drawn from residues in the morphological system, much as von Raumer, Grassmann and Verner, on examining the phonological residues identified by Grimm, provided explanations for them. Yet the results obtained by investigation of phonological residues are readily accepted, while treatment of morphological residues is viewed less favorably in the standard handbooks. The evidence is equally cogent. Our only grounds for positing a variable pitch accent in early Germanic, for example, are the consonant variations that Verner linked with the accent. The aberrant syntactic pattern by which neuter plurals are accompanied by singular verbs in Greek provides equally strong evidence for deriving their form from a singular collective. And the masculines with the -*a* ending support the view that the earlier system did not include marking for number, as corroborated by Hittite. The conclusions proposed for the earlier morphological system are then as fully supported as are the phonological reconstructions based on the explanations of Grassmann and Verner. In both systems residues are useful for determining earlier patterns.

7.4 PROBLEMS IN THE TREATMENT OF GENDER

Schmidt's book of 1889, much of its content previously published in articles, included the implication that the threefold system of gender in the early dialects was late; for, if the neuter plural was formerly a feminine collective, the evidence for a neuter gender was virtually eliminated. Its only other characteristic – use of the accusative singular form in the nominative – was hardly an adequate basis to assume a separate gender; inanimate objects represented by the neuter would be used infrequently as subjects. Moreover, the residual masculine nouns in -*a* suggest that the collective was not necessarily feminine.

It is hardly surprising then that a linguist of Brugmann's penetration published an article in 1891 "on the problem of the origin of grammatical gender." He returned to the problem later, as in a lecture at Princeton (1897) and in his handbooks. His view is summarized in the *Grundriss* 2.1: 593–4 (1897–1916). There he states that "gender distinction is clearly related to stem formation of nominals. . . . The masculine and neuter gender lack any expression in stems from an earlier period of Indo-European, and are distinguished only by inflectional formation of the nominative and accusative; but by contrast, in the feminine gender the stem formants -*ā*-, -(*i*)*i̯ā*-, -*ī*-, -*ē*- (-(*i*)*i̯ē*-), -*ī*- -*ii̯*-, -*ū*- -*uu̯*- are directly involved."

It does not require great insight to note that in all these examples the stem formant is lengthened by a laryngeal. Accordingly, the distinctive marker of the subsequent feminine gender nouns is not the stem vowel but rather a following laryngeal that was not maintained as a consonant in the dialects. After the acceptance of laryngeals for the phonological system, we can carry Brugmann's excellent analysis further, and conclude that the feminine as well as the neuter and masculine "lack any expression in stems from an earlier period of Indo-European." Instead of the threefold gender proposed for early Proto-Indo-European, we must posit three endings: -*s*, -*m*, -*h*.

Having expanded Brugmann's conclusion in this way, we can scarcely be surprised to note that Hittite has no evidence for feminine gender. The -*h* that marked collectives was lost as a consonant in Hittite before gender was introduced as a grammatical category. Unfortunately, we cannot determine whether preceding vocalic elements, also of resonants as Brugmann's list indicates, were lengthened in Hittite, because vowel quality is dubiously represented in the writing system. Any evidence to account for the introduction of grammatical gender must be taken from the other branches.

For such explanation we must note that gender is a congruence category. That is to say, it functions in associating other elements with nouns. In an OV language, relationships between attributive elements and nouns are clear from their position; the attributive elements precede the nouns they modify. We may make such an assumption for the early period of Proto-Indo-European. Modifiers preceding nouns were suffixed for their semantic value, and accordingly might have any of the possible endings, presumably often zero ending; this pattern is attested in early Sanskrit, where the demonstrative *sa* often has no *-s*. Since there was no grammatical opposition between forms with these endings, modification was determined by position. Similarly, in predicative position, the relationship between noun and its modifier would have been clear on the basis of the position and the semantic value of the endings.

As I pointed out in 1958, however, this system was disrupted when *-h* merged with a preceding vocalic element. An imbalance then arose, for stem vowels followed by either *-s* or *-m* now contrasted with lengthened stem vowels rather than with a suffix. When modifying elements after this time were aligned with nouns ending in *-ā* or other lengthened vocalic elements, they too selected that ending. That is to say, adjectival and demonstrative elements came to be marked for congruence.

The forms in *-ā* were in time associated with nouns referring to females. Brugmann proposed that the development was purely by chance, that a noun like Greek *gunê* "woman" came to be regarded as characteristic of the set, leading to the assumption that the set designated feminine nouns. Others have related the development to pastoral culture, where the principal members of a collective, such as cattle, would be female. Whatever the reason, or combination of reasons, the congruence relationship became closely associated with male and female sex, and then with inanimate items in neuter gender as opposed to animates, whether feminine or masculine. As noted above, however, the congruence system never was completely one of sex.

Congruence was highly important when the Indo-European languages shifted from OV to VO structure, as all those attested later did, at least initially. Such shifts take place over a long period. Moreover, not all characteristics are changed at the same time. English, for example, still places most adjectival modifiers before nouns, in contrast with a stricter VO language like French or Spanish that places them after nouns. In the ambivalent stages of Latin, Greek and Sanskrit, some means to relate modifiers with their heads would have been highly important. Gender then came to be firmly installed. It was weakened as a category only after VO order was fully in place, so that congruent relationships are clear without morphological signals but primarily through word order.

7.5 PROBLEMS IN THE TREATMENT OF CASE

We have already noted problems in dealing with cases in the early dialects. The adverbial or concrete cases in the plural of Vedic Sanskrit indicate through their sandhi that the forms are late. Moreover, the use of *-bh-* in these forms may be accounted for as development of the suffix maintained in early Greek as *-phi*. In Greek it is treated as a postposition rather than as a case ending. Since the postposition indicates a variety of functions, it is scarcely hazardous to assume that the case system was expanded in Sanskrit on the basis of the cognate particle; further that the set of case endings in the plural and dual was late. Additional evidence for their late development is provided by the contrasting ending in Germanic and Slavic, where *-mis* is found rather than *-bhis*. Clearly, the plural forms were introduced in individual dialects or groups of dialects rather than in Proto-Indo-European.

Moreover, even in the singular the ablative has no common marker. As illustrated in the set of endings traditionally assumed, it often applies the same ending as does the genitive. In Greek as well as other dialects there is no evidence for it at all; the genitive takes some of the functions it fulfills in other dialects, such as indicating the standard in comparison of inequality. More problems might be mentioned. Pursuing these in the well-known dialects, we do not find it difficult to propose an earlier system with only the grammatical cases – nominative and accusative, and the adjectival case, the genitive. The remaining cases were added to these when selected postpositions came to be affixed to noun stems. Expansion of the noun declension through addition of postpositions was continued in Lithuanian (Senn 1966: 92). That expansion provides further evidence for the assumption of such a development in the earlier system.

As observed above, Hittite supports the assumption of late development of the case system by having virtually the same endings in the plural as in the singular. Endings supposed to be characteristic of the plural, such as *-om/-ōm* in the genitive are also attached to singular nouns in Hittite (Gamkrelidze and Ivanov 1984).

We may speculate on the sources of the endings including the postpositions, though hardly with assurance that we can identify them; the assumption that the nominative *-s* developed from postposing the topicalizer *so* must remain only a hypothesis. Nor is that aim our primary concern here. We seek to indicate the procedures applied to arrive at conclusions on the inflectional system and its method of development rather than to discuss individual elements. As in the treatment of number and gender, the evidence in the late dialects is to be taken from irregularities. The conclusions derived from analysis of them are supported by the situation in Anatolian.

In conclusion, we may state that the evidence in the Anatolian languages supported by that in dialects like Germanic and Greek indicates that even for a late stage of Proto-Indo-European we cannot assume the set of inflections for eight cases in the singular and plural, let alone the additional forms in the dual, that have been traditionally posited on the basis of Sanskrit. The large set of inflections in Indo-Iranian, Italic and Armenian are increasingly ascribed to special developments of the dialect area to which they belong, while the earlier peripheral languages from which

Germanic, Anatolian and Celtic arose did not participate in that development. Accordingly, we reconstruct for the proto-language a system in the process of development, with an earlier set of nouns marked for semantic categories and subsequently a shift to a case system. As we have already remarked and will point out further in chapter 10, the syntactic system that we reconstruct supports these conclusions.

7.6 ADJECTIVES

The class of adjectives in Indo-European differs from that of nouns by admitting all genders; but adjectives take stem suffixes like those of nouns. Accordingly, they may be *i*-stems, *u*-stems, *n*-stems, thematic stems and so on; the thematic class, in which the masculine and neuter follow the inflection of *o*-stems and the feminine that of *ā*-stems, comes to predominate.

As is clear from some of the subclasses, the inflectional patterning corresponds to that of nouns with the same stem. A full set of forms through three genders is found only in the thematic stems even in Latin, which has strongly regularized its paradigmatic system. Adjectives of the Latin third declension have two genders, neuter and combined masculine/feminine; the distinction applies in the nominative, accusative and vocative, while the rest of the case forms exhibit the same endings. Further, Latin also has adjectives in which all genders have the same ending, except for the neuter accusative and vocative, which maintain the form of the nominative. These adjectives are based on consonant stems. Even without taking evidence from other dialects, we may state that adjective inflection was late, developing at the same time as that of nouns.

7.6.1 Comparison of adjectives

Adjectives in the dialects also are distinguished by a further characteristic: comparison; it is generally classified with inflection though it is essentially a derivational process.

As in modern English, with forms like *good*, *better*, *best*, comparison involves three forms, the positive, the comparative and the superlative. This patterning is found throughout the Indo-European branches. Since it is so widespread, it has traditionally been reconstructed for the proto-language.

Yet there are problems with the assumption that Proto-Indo-European included inflection to indicate comparison. The problems are found in the lexicon, in the morphology and in syntax. As a lexical problem, the common adjectives exhibit suppletion, rather than regular comparison. It is well known that the most frequent vocabulary is most apt to maintain archaisms. From comparative forms like the English cited above, or their Latin equivalents, *bonus*, *melior*, *optimus*, we can conclude that comparison was introduced after adjectives were a separate class, and that the common adjectives maintained an older system in which distinct lexical items were used to express "comparison." Greek has still different sets for the adjective meaning "good", *agathós*. Citing only the superlative we may note three of the sets for comparison: *áristos* "best (most virtuous)," *béltistos* "best (strongest)," *krátistos* "best (most powerful)." From evidence like that cited here, we assume that morphological indication of comparison was introduced only in the late proto-language.

The conclusion finds support in Sanskrit; suffixes used to indicate comparison are suffixed to other word-classes, such as nouns, e.g. *vīrátara* "more manly," *mātṛ́tama* "most motherly," and so on. An example is *Rigveda* 8.24.15: *nahy àṅgá purá caná jajñé vīrátaras tvát* "a hero stronger than you has not been born." The suffixation of "comparative" affixes to such nouns, and also to adpositions, indicates their general use in derivation at an early period rather than as a special inflection for adjectives.

Even more cogent evidence for late development of comparison may be derived from the variety of affixes found in the dialects. The two most frequent sets of affixes for the comparative and the superlative are *-yes-* : *-isto-* and *-tara-* : *-tama-*. In the standard handbooks, one of these, generally the first, is assumed to be the set used in the proto-language. The assumption is maintained even after Hittite came to be known. Hittite has no affixed form to express comparison; rather, comparison was expressed as in OV languages by placing the standard before the adjective. The standard is generally inflected in the dative, but the ablative is also found, as in the *Rigveda* passage cited above.

Such a pattern is also used in the older texts of other dialects. It is maintained as late as the early Germanic texts, where especially in poetry many examples are attested, as in Old English; for example, *Elene* 565: *Heo wæron stearce,   stane heardran* "They were steadfast,   harder than stone." It is remarkable that linguists have not recognized the basis of this construction, nor used their knowledge of languages to account for it. Friedrich (1960: 127) in his treatment of comparison in Hittite cites Semitic as parallel in indicating comparison through "syntactic means." Turkish would be a far better parallel, as would other OV languages. Many grammars of Indo-European languages do not even cite the residues that might allow students to understand the Indo-European pattern. Rather, their presentation of comparison is a relic of the period when Classical Sanskrit and Greek served as pattern for reconstructing the proto-language, so that the VO construction is erroneously assumed for it.

As these references indicate, the evidence on late development of comparison that we determine through residues is once again supported by the situation in Hittite. There can be little doubt concerning the method of expressing comparison in the proto-language; (see also 9.5.1, 9.6.1); nor on the basis of the changed pattern in the dialects. Development of affixal means is in keeping with the shift to VO structure, in which comparison is expressed as in English. The variety of expression in the dialects indicates the period in which that development took place. Lexical, morphological and syntactic evidence in this way provides solid support for assuming introduction of the attested patterns in the early dialects, as well as for the pattern used in the proto-language.

7.7 PRONOUNS

The pronouns provide further evidence for gradual development of nominal declension. The personal pronouns for "I" and "we" have no common root; similarly, those for "thou" and "you." Moreover, the first-person pronouns differ in root between the nominative and the accusative, which displays the stem of the remaining cases. We may conclude that a paradigm developed as case inflection was introduced for nouns.

7.7.1 The personal pronouns and reflexives

The enclitic form of the singular, **me*, and of the plural, **n(e)s*, provided the root for oblique cases of the first-person pronoun like the dative singular, **mey*, **moy*, **meghy* and the dative plural **nsmey*. At an earlier stage we may therefore assume for deictic pronouns a form for the nominative, and enclitic forms for the remaining uses. Even the first-person form for the nominative of the proto-language cannot be reliably reconstructed, for the dialects vary between evidence for **eg(h)om* and **egó*; both may have suffixes attached to an earlier **egʰ*.

To this day in many of the dialects the personal pronouns display the shift of stem between the nominative and the accusative that we find in the first person of the earliest languages, e.g. Sanskrit *ahám* : *mãm* / *mā* "I : me," *vayám* : *asmãn*, enclitic *nas* "we : us." A similar shift is found with some of the most common nouns, in the so-called *r/n* stems, e.g. Hittite *watar*, gen. *wetenas*. In contrast with the maintenance of the early shift in stem for the first-person pronouns, the shift in stem of such heteroclitic nouns was subsequently regularized, in some branches through choice of one or the other stem, e.g. Norwegian *vatn* as opposed to English *water*. But the early twofold situation is clear; even the most common demonstrative has the same shift, Sanskrit nom. *sás*, acc. *tám* "this." Such a heteroclitic paradigm is so characteristic of Indo-European that doubters about the inclusion of Hittite in the family were finally convinced when its forms for "water" were pointed out to them.

The differences of the oblique case forms in the various branches support the view that the inflection of personal pronouns was fully developed only in the late proto-language and the dialects. To illustrate the problems we may cite the Hittite forms for "I, me" in comparison with those in Latin: nom. *ug*; acc. and also dat. and loc. *amug*; gen. *amel*; abl. *amedats* – Latin: *egó* acc. and abl. *mē*; gen. *meī* dat. *mihi*. The differences between these sets, and also those in other dialects, illustrate the difficulty involved in proposing a set of inflected forms for the pronoun in the proto-language (see, for example, Brugmann 1904a: 407–13).

The third-person pronouns that are found in the various branches are based on demonstratives. They vary so much from dialect to dialect that accounts of their forms must be left to the grammars of these.

The reflexive arose in the dialects as the middle lost its force. The root *sew- is the basis for many of the forms, especially of the reflexive adjective, e.g. Sanskrit svás, Greek heós, Latin suus. But the late formation of the reflexives may be illustrated by the difference between dialects as late as the Germanic. In English, forms, like herself are based on -self, in German, on the other hand, sich has been created on the pattern of mich "me," dich "thee" to express the dative and the accusative in both the singular and plural. Pursuing the development of expressions to indicate reflexive force when the middle was lost is highly interesting, but outside the scope of this presentation.

7.7.2 Demonstratives and other pronouns

The other pronouns, demonstratives, relatives and interrogatives, are based on anaphoric elements of the proto-language. For demonstratives, the element *so was widely used, as in Sanskrit sa, Greek ho, Gothic sa. Though found as demonstrative with no further ending in the nominative, it came to add the typical nominative ending -s. Further, like the first-person pronoun its oblique forms were made with a different stem, *to-. Endings in the oblique-case forms of these and other anaphoric elements used as demonstratives are much like those of the nouns, suggesting that their inflection was developed in the same stage of the proto-language as that of the nouns.

Similarly, for the relative pronoun a marker indicating focus was equipped with endings as the languages came to be VO in structure. In Hittite and the other early dialects, even in Latin as late as the second century BC, such a marker in a preposed clause indicates "relative" relationship. As example we may cite *Rigveda* 3.48.2:

yáj jáyathās   tád áhar pīyúṣam apibo
what you-were-born that day milk   you-drank
"the day on which you were born you drank milk"

The pronoun that was introduced was based on PIE *yo- in Sanskrit and Greek, on *kʷo- and *to- in the other dialects, as illustrated by English "the man whom/that we saw." As with the development of reflexive pronouns, that of the relatives is highly interesting in each of the dialects but must be left to the grammars of these.

For interrogative meaning forms of PIE *kʷo- were developed in the various dialects, e.g. Sanskrit kás, Greek tís, Latin quis, Gothic hʷas and so on. The differences between these and further forms that might be cited suggest that an anaphoric interrogative was found in the proto-language, and equipped with endings in the several dialects.

An account of the pronouns throughout the family involves some of the greatest difficulties in its comparative grammar. But the general situation is clear. Deictic and anaphoric elements were used in the proto-language. They came to be treated like nouns and, when modifiers, like adjectives. In the course of time they adopted inflections of these two classes. As weakly accented words in many of their uses, they underwent changes that were often specific to them. Individual forms may then be highly difficult to account for. But the system that we find in the early languages must not be assumed for Proto-Indo-European. That must be reconstructed on the basis of its syntactic structure as well as the morphological residues, as noted above. The presentations found in the standard handbooks provide at best only formal elements of the earlier pronouns. They and their roles in syntax will be discussed below.

7.8 THE NUMERALS

Most of the lexical items for numerals remain opaque. Brugmann states frankly that the source of the numerals from 2 to 10 is obscure (1904a: 363). Like others, he relates the cardinal for 1, PIE *oy-no-s*, as in Latin *oinos*, *ūnus*, Old Irish *oen*, Gothic *ains* and so on, with the demonstrative root *ey-* "this." He goes on to say that the numeral has its origin in a demonstrative element used when pointing out objects with one's hand; but for the remaining numerals he has no suggestions.

The problem is complicated by the use of different roots for the ordinals "first, second." Of these, only the two lowest can be accounted for. The source for "first" is a root *per-H-*, as represented in Sanskrit *pūrv-yás*, Greek *prôtas* and so on, from a meaning "foremost." Latin *secundus* "second < the following one" also has a deictic origin; besides it Latin uses *alter*, Lithuanian *añtras*, both also reflecting a meaning that suggests pointing to objects in series. The roots of these differ from that of the cardinals, where PIE *dwō^w* is reconstructed for "two." with reflexes Sanskrit *duvaú*, Greek *duô*, Latin *duo* and so on.

Faced with such difficulties, the handbooks have only been able to list the various forms. We will see in 11.7.3 that Schmandt-Besserat's ingenious interpretation of archaeological evidence provides the means to explain the basis of the lexical items, and to sketch the course of development of the numerals. Yet the sources for many of the lower numerals have not yet been determined, and may remain obscure; some may have been borrowed from languages for which we lack evidence on the lexical items for the numerals.

7.9 CONCLUSIONS ON THE EARLIER NOMINAL SYSTEM

The standard handbooks present a symmetrical system of nominal inflection, and point out irregularities. Attempts were made to account for some of these irregularities before the end of the nineteenth century, as by Schmidt (1889) and Jacobi (1897); but lacking corroborative data, the hypotheses they proposed were not given wide credence. When Hittite material became available, however, new information was at hand to re-examine the reconstructed paradigms and the hypotheses proposed to clarify the irregularities. As a result, the presentations in the handbooks could no longer be maintained.

The additional data from the Anatolian languages confirmed earlier proposals, such as Brugmann's, that the threefold gender distinction must be accounted for as a late development. Similarly, Schmidt's equation of the nominative/accusative neuter plural and the feminine nominative singular endings in *-a* supported inferences that inflection for case and number was late. The nominal system in early Proto-Indo-European must then have consisted of a small set of forms. This set was later expanded in the dual and plural, yielding the forms for the three categories, case, number and gender, that are attested in the dialects. Other inflection was also introduced, as for comparison of adjectives.

Reconstruction of a small set of nominal forms at an early stage finds support in the assumption of Pre-Indo-European as an active language, for active languages are poor in nominal inflection. Subsequent chapters will accordingly supplement the conclusions presented here on the development of the nominal system of inflection from a small set of forms to those found in the dialects.

8 Morphology 2: the verbal system

8.1 THE EARLY PRESENTATION OF THE SYSTEM

The verbal system was the earliest segment of Indo-European grammar to be capably described. Applying insights based on ancient Indian grammar, Bopp compared the Greek and Latin verb with that of Sanskrit, concluding essentially that Sanskrit had maintained the verbal system of the parent language. The results of this conclusion are still obvious in standard treatments of the proto-language. Szemerényi, for example, presents a view of its verbal system that is a composite of the Greek verb, with its many forms related to a base expressed in an infinitive. Accordingly, he assigned to Sanskrit three voices – active, middle, passive – each with seven tenses – present, imperfect, aorist, perfect, pluperfect, future, conditional, as well as other forms (1970 [1989]: 244).

Closer attention to the actual Sanskrit verb forms would be more advantageous. As Whitney and other grammarians describe the Sanskrit language, the verb has no one general system, in contrast with Greek and Latin (1896: 200–403). Rather, it is based on roots. These may be inflected in four systems: present, perfect, aorist, future, as well as in secondary conjugations and nominal forms; but a root is not necessarily inflected in all possible systems, as examples given below of two roots similar in form may demonstrate, *duh* and *tud*. The forms based on individual roots are given in the valuable companion work to Whitney's *Sanskrit Grammar*: *The Roots, Verb-forms, and Primary Derivatives of the Sanskrit Language* (1885). Whitney listed only forms he found in the texts, adding in brackets those that the ancient Indian grammarians posit, which he views sceptically. His lists are doubly important because he indicates the period of the texts in which a given form is attested; these references are omitted here because of the additional exposition they would require.

As is clear from the forms of *duh* "milk, extract" that are given below, the present system and the aorist system, include different formation classes: the present ten, the aorist seven. From a historical standpoint the

Sources for this chapter: Bopp (1816); Delbrück (1897: 1–439); Brugmann (1904a: 480–610); Watkins (1969); Klimov (1983); Gamkrelidze and Ivanov (1984); Szemerényi (1970 [1989]: 244–370).

161

classes of the Indian grammarians can be reduced; we have noted in the discussion of phonology that present classes 5, 7 and 9 derive from one earlier class with nasal infix; see 6.4.2.5. The differences yielding separate classes in Sanskrit result from phonological changes that modified the original forms in accordance with elements following the *-n-*.

Attempts have been made to determine the semantic value of the various classes, but for the most part these have not arrived at clear results; as in any long-established derivational class, the original meaning is often obscured by effects in the development of the language. Among important observations on the Sanskrit set of forms, however, is the analysis of the Indian grammarians that the passive in early Sanskrit is a subset of the present. It makes up the accented *yá*-class; although it takes only middle endings, it is comparable in other respects to the other nine classes of the present system. Accordingly, the position of the passive in early Sanskrit is totally different from that of the passive in later Indo-European languages, including Latin and Classical Greek. It is not a distinct voice form.

The Sanskrit verb includes only two voices, active and middle. In this way it resembles the verb of the Homeric poems, in which the middle often maintains its Indo-European force while infrequently expressing passive meaning. The passive voice was developed in later Greek as parallel to the active; by the time of New Testament Greek the middle had virtually been lost.

Because Whitney only cites attested forms, except for the forms of the grammarians that he includes in square brackets as possibly uncertain, the category of the examples listed varies from set to set, as in the three present classes in which the root *duh* is represented. The root *tud* on the other hand is found in only one present class. Moreover, the specific forms that have been found, and are given below (such as the first, which is the 3rd sg. pres. ind. *dógdhi*), will not be identified since our interest here concerns the overall pattern of the verb in early Sanskrit and Proto-Indo-European. As is evident from the examples, a perfect is made from each of these roots; but they differ in their exploitation of possibilities in the aorist system much as they do in the present system.

	duh "milk, extract"	*tud* "push, thrust"
Present	2. dógdhi 4. duhyati 6. duhet	tudáti 7. tundate (?)
Perfect	dudóha	tutóda
Aorist	[1. ádohi] 3. adūduhat 4. adugdha 7. ádukṣat	[atūtudat]

Future   1. dhokṣyate
                2. dogdhā

In addition to the four systems illustrated above, the Sanskrit verb includes five derivative, or secondary conjugations as Whitney calls them (1896: 360–91): intensive, desiderative, causative, denominative; and as fifth Whitney includes the passive, because it has several distinctive forms in addition to its present inflection. Each of the roots exemplified here happens to have forms in four secondary conjugations. These in turn may be inflected in any of the four systems presented above, though typically the secondary conjugations are not as rich in such forms as are the inflections based on roots like *duh*.

Passive	duhyáte	tudyate
Intensive	[doduh-]	totudyate
Desiderative	dudhukṣati	[tututsa-]
Causative	doháyati	todayati

Finally, we may note the nominal forms – participles, infinitives and gerunds. Of these only the infinitive for *duh* is attested. This situation may serve to indicate the peripheral position of the infinitive in the Sanskrit verb system as opposed to its position in the later dialects of the west. In Hittite as well, the infinitive occupies a different position from that of the later dialects, though specialists disagree in their evaluation of it (Friedrich 1960: 142–4).

Infinitive   dogdhum

The form of the infinitive in Sanskrit has a different suffix from that of the infinitive in Greek (*ein*), or in Latin (vowel + *re*), or in Germanic (**onom > an > en > 0*). The different suffixes indicate that the infinitive was added after the time of the proto-language.

Before examining the derivational morphology of the Indo-European verb we may observe that the inflectional system as found in early Sanskrit resembles that of OV languages. The affixes, including those for person, are loosely attached to the root or base. A set of forms made from a given root is supplemented by secondary conjugations, much like the verbal system in Japanese. The forms found with any root cannot be predicted. And the forms that occur do not make up a conjugation, as do those in Latin and Classical Greek. By contrast, the roots, derivational affixes and inflectional affixes must be viewed as elements with which actual forms are produced; selections from them may be made but not in accordance with a fixed system.

In conclusion, we may state that the traditional presentation of the verb in Proto-Indo-European has relied heavily on verbal forms found in early Sanskrit, although the freedom of formation from roots that is found in Sanskrit has not been adequately observed.

The discovery of Hittite raised many questions about the assumption of a Sanskrit-like system for the proto-language. The questions arose because the Hittite verb has many fewer categories and many fewer forms, resembling the verb of Germanic much more closely than that of Sanskrit or Greek. After comparing the Hittite verb system with that of the other dialects, Szemerényi proposes a tentative Indo-European system of two voices: active and middle; four moods: indicative, subjunctive, optative, imperative; three to six tenses: present, aorist, perfect and possibly as well future, imperfect, pluperfect (1970 [1989]: 245). As we note below, Hittite provides no evidence for positing a subjunctive and an optative mood. Its tense system also fails to support some of the tenses listed by Szemerényi. After examining patterns of derivation, we will deal at length with the Proto-Indo-European verbal system.

8.2 DERIVATION

The presentation of the verb in Brugmann's short grammar exhibits many excellent insights (1904a: 480–610); these are treated more fully in the last two volumes of the *Grundriss*, but we refer here primarily to Brugmann's more compact presentation. In both the shorter work and the *Grundriss* he has profited greatly from Delbrück's treatment. Brugmann's 1904 work also includes useful tables, so that it is very much worth consulting.

Brugmann examines the verb by the forms found; thereupon he determines the interrelationships among these, with specific reference to the advantage of formal classification. He also points out that we classify the Greek and Latin verb through meaning categories, such as present indicative, present subjunctive and so on. Moreover, he notes that if we deal with the forms, the verb in the proto-language differs in many respects from that of these branches. With these insights, he may well have identified characteristics that would have disclosed the earlier system, if he had known the situation in Hittite. As it is, his presentation is more accurate than those based on meaning which include six or seven tenses among the categories; but some later Indo-Europeanists criticize Brugmann's conclusions, on the grounds that they show too little attention to inflections, presumably those of Latin and Greek.

8.2.1 Non-finite forms of the verb

Brugmann's first subclassification is between finite and nonfinite forms. The nonfinite in turn he subclassifies into nomina agentis and nomina actionis. The nomina agentis are identified as participles in the dialects; Brugmann considers them fully developed in the proto-language, for as the participles in -(*e*)*nt*- illustrate, they are found in many of its branches. The nomina actionis are verbal nouns, that may be viewed as precursors of the infinitives. The infinitives Brugmann posits as independent developments in the individual dialects; for they have different endings in many of them, as we have just noted above.

Brugmann's assumption of verbal nouns rather than infinitives for the proto-language is corroborated by Hittite; as Friedrich points out, its so-called infinitive is a verbal noun, as may be illustrated by its use. Among examples Friedrich cites is the following: . . . *uwatar iyanun* "inspection I-made" = "I conducted an inspection . . ." (1960: 142). Such examples demonstrate clearly the difference between infinitives in Greek, Latin among other later languages and the precursor nouns in Anatolian. The problem also alerts us to difficulties caused by using linguistic terms for different categories in different languages. We must remember that specific forms have their meaning only through opposition to other forms within their own language whatever the established terminology.

The absence of infinitives is another characteristic of OV languages; for as complements to finite verbs infinitives can only be interpreted when the principal verb is known. Their function in sentences can be determined only after the finite verb has occurred. Verbal nouns, on the other hand, have a specific meaning, much like that of nouns, so that they can readily be utilized when they are preverbal. Brugmann's observation on the basis of the forms is in accordance with the OV structure of Proto-Indo-European; but findings of typology were not yet available to support it. And, as we have noted earlier, his aims were strictly systematic rather than explanatory. Accordingly, his statement about the dialect development of infinitives was treated as an isolated fact rather than as a characteristic of a specific kind of verb system and language.

8.2.2 Finite forms of the verb

Turning to the finite forms, Brugmann makes much of the various types of reduplication in the Indo-European verbal system. The details are available in his and other handbooks.

Of great interest for understanding the verbal system in its development is Brugmann's discussion of the augment (1904a: 484–6). He identifies it accurately as a temporal adverb, comparable with other adverbs found in conjunction with verbs. After the availability of Hittite there is little question that its use in Indo-Iranian, Greek and Armenian is an innovation in the dialect continuum that these three branches constituted for some time. Efforts to ascribe the augment to the proto-language as a verbal marker must be rejected.

Proper identification of the augment as an adverb clarifies the so-called injunctives – a set of forms that lack the augment but have the secondary endings characteristic of those found with the augment in Indo-Iranian and Greek. These forms in the earliest texts are simply residues from the earlier period when the endings alone indicate nonpresent, noncontinuous meaning. The "synchronic investigation of their function" in an admirable study of their use in Vedic Sanskrit by Hoffmann amply supports this conclusion (1967).

Brugmann thereupon deals with the tenses, as he labels them (1904a: 486–7). Rather than the array given by Szemerényi, he identifies two: the present–aorist and the perfect. As we will see in 10.2.2, 10.3.2 and 10.5, he accurately determined the essence of the finite verb system of the proto-language before it was reconstructed to be like that of Sanskrit, Greek and Latin. It remained then to identify the subclassifications of these two sets, that is the endings for person and number, those of the tenses and the moods, as well as the uses of the stems. We note these below. But first we may mention two further important observations in his presentation.

Brugmann states clearly that the proto-language did not include a pass-ive (*ibid*. 492). The absence of a passive is another characteristic of an OV language. The function of the passive as found in the later Indo-European as well as in many other languages (while the label is idiosyncratically applied in some, like Japanese) is to topicalize the action of the verb; the underlying subject, or the agent of the action, then is downplayed. In OV languages, which do not provide special status for subjects, such a form is unnecessary; the so-called Japanese passive had potential and honorific meanings before the recent impact on the Japanese language by western languages, especially English, which broadened the use of the passive forms. The passive in its normal sense is prominent in VSO and also in SVO languages. Historical examination of Greek indicates the increasing occurrence and use of the passive, after its SVO structure was thoroughly established.

Brugmann also pointed out that indication of transitive or intransitive meaning is a function of roots, citing *$d\bar{o}$*- "give" and *es*- "be." The importance of this observation became clear when the structure of an earlier stage of the proto-language was determined to be that of active languages, for in active languages a comparable distinction between verbs signifying activity as opposed to state is central, as we will note in 10.3.2.

Brugmann's analysis of the verb in the proto-language accordingly con-tains many important insights. These could be fully understood only after the situation of the verb as found in the Anatolian languages became known. The brilliant work of Soviet typologists, as represented by Klimov (1977, 1983), clarified the structure of active languages and its relevance for Proto-Indo-European. The position is accurately presented by Gamkrelidze and Ivanov in their treatment of the verb.

8.2.3 The derivational affixes

After clarifying the uses of the endings, and the status of roots, Brugmann deals with derivational affixes. Details on these could be presented exten-sively; treatment of them occupies much of his section on the verb (1904a: 494–551). We note only a few of the many suffixes, to illustrate the development of the verb both by Brugmann's analysis and in accordance with current views.

For understanding the derivational history of the verb, we may relate the conclusions of Benveniste that take into account a century and a half of attention to word formation in Indo-European (1935) with the verb system in specific dialects. Simple roots of CvC structure, like *sed-* "sit" make up the fourth and fifth classes of strong verbs in Germanic. Reflexes of roots ending in a resonant, e.g. *$g^w em$-*, are assigned to the fourth class, e.g. Gothic *qiman*, cf. Latin *veniō*, Greek *baínō* "come"; those ending in an obstruent are assigned to the fifth, e.g. Gothic *sitan*, cf. Latin *sedeō* "sit." As these examples indicate, the treatment of reflexes in the dialects is quite independent of the situation in the proto-language. The seven classes of strong verbs in Germanic, like the four conjugations in Latin, are subsequent developments in these dialects. Nonetheless we may determine the earlier situation by comparing the divergent dialect systems for common features.

Roots that are extended by consonants, Benveniste's base I, such as PIE *ley-k^w-*, cf. Greek *leip-*, Gothic *$leih^w an$* "leave," have been assigned to the first three classes of strong verbs in Germanic. The simple roots in these three classes have vowel nuclei ending in a resonant: the first class, as illustrated by *$leih^w an$*, in *-y-*; the second in *-w-*, e.g. Gothic *tiuhan*, cf. Latin *dūcere* "lead"; the third in one of the remaining resonants, e.g. Gothic *wairþan* "become," cf. Latin *vertere* "turn." As these examples illustrate, verbs in the first five classes of Germanic are formed from simple roots or from base I of the proto-language.

Examples of maintenance of the other bases presented by Benveniste may also be cited. Base II is exemplified by *dr-ep-*, as in Greek *drépō* "break off" in contrast with the simple root *der-* as found in Sanskrit *dárṣi* "split," Greek *dérō* "flay." An example of base II with an additional consonant is found in Lettish *drugt* "diminish," extended from the root *der*, with the suffix *-ew-* followed by *-g-*. An example of base II with nasal infix is Sanskrit *riṇákti* "let go," which is cognate with Gothic *$leih^w an$* etc. cited above. These examples of suffixed roots could be supplemented with many others to illustrate the use of roots and bases in verbal systems.

8.2.4 Selected suffixes added to the verbal bases

To illustrate the development of the verb in the several dialects we may examine a few of the more widely attested suffixes.

8.2.4.1 Extensions in -yo-

Reflexes of PIE *-yo-* are found in many branches (Brugmann 1904: 523–37). In Sanskrit some verbs so derived make up present class 4; an example is *lúbhyati* "is lustful" from PIE *$lewb^h$-*, as in Old Latin *lubet*, Classical

Latin *libet* "is pleasant, dear." Sanskrit verbs of class 4 tend to be intransitive, indicating a state or condition; in this way they are comparable to the Sanskrit passives, which have accented *-yó-*.

The suffix comes to be extended widely, as in production of denominatives; for example, Sanskrit *rajasyáti* "it becomes dust" based on *rájas-* "dust" and Gothic *riqizein* "is darkened" based on *riqiz* "darkness" are derived from PIE **reg^wos-* "dust." Many verbs of Germanic weak class I are derived in this way. The suffix then has become a means to derive verbs from nouns as well as from verbal bases.

The *-yo-* suffix is also expanded to *-éyo-*, which then is applied to many roots in deflected grade; as examples, Greek *potéomai*, Sanskrit *patáyati* "fly about, flitter" are based on the root **pet-* as in Greek *pétomai* "fly." In many such forms the suffix indicates an iterative or frequentative meaning; but especially in Indic, Germanic and Slavic it contributes a causative meaning, as in Sanskrit *sādáyati*, Gothic *satjiþ* "causes to sit, sets." This formation is characteristic of the secondary inflection in Sanskrit labeled causative that we have already noted.

In Germanic the forms of most verbs with *yo*-suffix are included in the first weak conjugation. Examples were important in determining that the Indo-European accent was maintained in Germanic. The reflex of PIE **wert-* "turn" is found, for example, both in the reflex of the simple root, as in Gothic *wairþan* "become" and in the causative, e.g. *frawardeiþ* "cause to turn, destroy, kill"; the causative shows *o*-grade of the root before the *-éyo-* suffix. If the base ends in a fricative, that becomes voiced in accordance with Verner's law, as in *frawardjan*. The suffixed form then comes to be separated even more from the base. For a more extensive discussion of the development of such verbs, Delbrück's second volume in the first edition of the *Grundriss* may be consulted (1897: 27–40, 109–19).

Besides illustrating changes in the verbal system of the dialects, the employment of the *yo*-suffix in the various branches provides an example how such markers may come to be widely used with specific meanings that have little to do with the application of the suffix in earlier periods.

8.2.4.2 Extensions in *-sko-*

Another suffix so extended, though not as widely, is PIE *-sko-*. It is added to simple roots, such as PIE **gam-* "go," as in Sanskrit *gáchati* "arrives" and Greek *báske* "go." In these verbs it indicates terminative action.

The suffix is found with roots in Latin that imply beginning of an action or inchoative meaning, e.g. *crēscō* "grow," *adolescō* "become old." In Latin this meaning became highly prominent, as in *calēscō* "become warm," *coalēscō* "coalesce," and many other verbs. Moreover, the meaning has been maintained in English, as in such verbs as *convalesce*, and in further derivatives, such as nouns and adjectives like *convalescence*, *convalescent*, *luminescent* and so on. While these examples have little to do with the parent language, they illustrate how affixes or virtually any material of language may be used to fill a function that requires some marker.

It may also be noted that such applications are in keeping with the structure of the language in question. As an SVO language with OV residues, English applies suffixation as a process of derivation. In this way it maintains processes inaugurated in Proto-Indo-European, by which root determinatives and suffixes are used for expressing nominal and verbal functions. However, for most of the extended items we cannot determine the start of the formation, nor even relate that to the original force of the suffix (see Brugmann 1904a: 296–7, 518–19, 537–41).

8.2.4.3 Extensions in -s-

An element with widespread use is the determinative -s-. It is attested with several roots and bases; beside the simple root *ʔew-, as in Lithuanian *aunù* put on shoes/foot coverings," Armenian *aganim* "put on," Latin *indu-ō* "put on," and the form with accented affix, ʔw-es-, as in Sanskrit *váste* "gets dressed," Greek perfect *heîmai* "got dressed," Gothic *wasjiþ* "puts on," Hittite *was-* "put on." The unextended form may also be found in Hittite *unu-* "arrange, adorn," which itself was extended to *unuwai-* in later Hittite.

As another example, the extended root *kl-ew-, as in Greek *ékluon* "he heard," Latin *clueō*, Old Church Slavic *sluti* "be named; be famous," is extended with -s- in Sanskrit *śróṣati* "hears, obeys," Old High German *hlosēn* "listen to," Tocharian A *klyoṣ-*, B *klyauṣ-* "hear."

As with other such suffixes, the meaning of the -s- in the late proto-language is difficult to determine precisely. It may have indicated completion, or terminative meaning. Like the -sko- suffix it seems then to have become specialized for a specific derivational use. Finally it became a marker for aspect and tense distinctions.

The terminative force apparently led to its use for both the aorist and the future after these categories had become established. The basic function of the aorist is to indicate a single action, implying further that the action has been, or is to be, accomplished. The future also often implies that an action will be accomplished. The shift of meaning then was carried out in accordance with the shift in categories of the verbal system.

8.2.4.4 Further extensions used as tense markers, and hypotheses on their origin

By a similar development the -k- of the Greek perfect, the -w- of the Latin perfect, the -d- of the Germanic preterite, and other such markers in the dialects were applied to mark selected verbal categories on bases that did not have available the ablaut distinctions to distinguish perfect/preterite from present. In accordance with the colorful terminology introduced by the linguists in the Romantic period, such bases are called "weak"; by this label they are contrasted with the "strong" roots and bases that were able to carry out internal modifications indicating the present versus the perfect/preterite distinction.

All the branches needed such marking in the period when ablaut was no longer in force, except for the infrequent borrowed verbs that fit the ablaut pattern. Latin *scrībere* "write" is one such example; borrowed into Germanic it was fitted into the pattern of the first strong class, yielding reflexes preserved in literary English – *shrive, shrove, shriven* – and in German – *schreiben, schrieb, geschrieben* "write".

Yet texts do not date from the time when the markers were introduced for nonpresent tenses of weak verbs. Nonetheless, in view of the structure of the early dialects at that time, the spread of a given marker to roots and bases that lacked ablaut distinctions is the most likely explanation for the weak preterite and perfect tenses.

The assumption that such weak tense forms were made by adding auxiliary verbs to bases is a relic of prelinguistic speculation: for example, the proposed explanation by which forms of the Proto-Indo-European root **dhē* "place, put" were suffixed to bases of weak verbs (bases that have never been satisfactorily identified by proponents of the explanation) is still maintained by some scholars today. If we assume that there was some kind of a nominal base, as of the paradigmatic first weak-class verb, Gothic *nasjan* "save," it is difficult to understand how a meaning "I place saving" could have served as a preterite tense form meaning "I saved." In the same way, the affixed *s* of the aorist and future was held to be a reflex of the root PIE **es* "be." Here again the proponents pay little attention to meaning. The meaning conveyed by the verb "to be" after a verbal noun would be totally different from that of the aorist or the future. As another argument against development of the preterites and perfects from compound forms, the conclusions of Delbrück and Brugmann demonstrate that the verbal systems of late Proto-Indo-European and of the early dialects were expanded through affixation of determinatives and suffixes. Compound tenses, as in Latin and the Romance languages, and also other late dialects, were introduced when the structure of these languages differed considerably from the structure of the proto-language and the early dialects.

8.2.4.5 Extension of the -n- infix

The *-n-* affix is unique in the proto-language. As we have noted, it was infixed into base 2. The clearest indications of both its form and its function are found in Vedic Sanskrit. We have already examined the three present classes – 5, 7, 9 – and the basis of their formal differences, in 6.4.2.5. Earlier treatments, as by Brugmann (1904a: 509–17) as well as the Indian grammarians, were unable to account for that basis because they were unaware of the laryngeals. Yet once again we applaud Brugmann's linguistic insights in arguing against introduction of a word, e.g. *ne* > *-n-*, to mark the three classes. We assume instead that the *-n-* is an affix on roots, such as **yew-*, to which further suffixes were added, such as *-eg-*; with zero grade of the root, the sequence resulted in **yw-n-eg-*, of which a reflex is Sanskrit *yunákti* "yokes." The internal suffix *-n-* then came to be treated as an infix.

While disclaiming any possibility of determining the "true proto-meaning of the *n*-element," Brugmann did propose its general function (1904a: 510–11, 518). This he stated to be the same for all three present types. He identifies it as terminative, giving examples from Greek as well as Sanskrit, e.g. *yunákti* "he hitches up." Delbrück had earlier identified this function, in an extensive treatment of the *n*-formations (1897: 40–59).

Delbrück's conclusion may be supplemented by evidence in Hittite. There the *-nin-* infix is used to indicate factitive meaning, as in *harnink-* "destroy" vs *hark-* "disintegrate, perish." Moreover, Hittite has developed *-nu-* as a causative affix, as in *arnu-* "bring to" from *ar-* "arrive at," *warnu-* "ignite," vs *war-* "burn." Hittite then provides chronological evidence for the development and spread of the *-n-* affix. In spite of the age in which Hittite is attested, it had already extended the affix to produce further distinctive inflections.

Such a development is apparent for another suffix of the proto-language, **-sk-*. In Hittite it has an iterative value, as in *dask-* "take again and again" versus **da-* "take." Hittite provides even further information on the use of affixes in the early dialect period. It adds the *-sk-* suffix as well as another to bases that are already suffixed, as in *harninkisk-* "he repeatedly destroyed" (Friedrich 1960: 73–6). The oldest dialect attested then supports the view that suffixes were selected to specify the meaning of a verb, and that the derivational system of the verb, and then also the inflectional, were expanded in this way.

In additional contrast with its introduction as an infix, *-n-* plus a vowel, came to be widely used as a suffix in the dialects. The present class of *nu-* verbs, as illustrated with the verb *zeúgnumi* "harness," is prominent in Greek. In Greek the infix as illustrated by its cognate in Sanskrit, *yunakti* – a seventh-class verb derived from the extended form, Proto-Indo-European **yw-eg* – was extracted and shifted after the base. Another such extended *n*-suffix in Greek is *-anō*, as in *lambánō* "receive." These Delbrück identifies as late formations (1897: 57–9), pointing out that some of them lack the terminative function. Greek in this way illustrates how affixes developed away from their earlier form as well as their earlier function.

Germanic provides another notable example of an *-n-* suffix with a meaning that differs from the terminative, in the *-na(n)* verbs of Gothic and North Germanic – the fourth weak class. These, like the *-scō* verbs in Latin, often have an inchoative meaning, e.g. Gothic *fullnands* from **full-nan* "become full." In an extensive study, Suzuki has identified detransitivization or decrease of transitivity as the general meaning of the *-nan* suffix in Gothic (1989: 122).

8.2.4.6 Conclusions on the development of verbal affixes

The principles of derivational morphology in late Proto-Indo-European may be summed up by reviewing the history of the determinative *n*. Initially an infix that came to indicate a specific meaning, it was extracted as an affix and thereupon its meaning was modified, as well as the formal principles that governed its early use. Such modifications in both form and meaning provide insights into the changes in the verb system from the proto-language to the dialects.

It is also noteworthy that many of the early affixes were characterized in the handbooks as terminative. From this characterization we may assume that many Indo-European roots, also in their extended forms, had a continuous meaning – or imperfective force. To indicate action with a goal in mind, some kind of affix was necessary. When such an affix was applied, it assumed one or more specific additional meanings, some of which became central to the suffixed forms as the verb systems in the various branches were developed.

Moreover, inflectional and further derivational suffixes were appended to the inherited roots, bases and extended forms, for the purpose of specifying a given verbal category. These categories, person, number, tense/aspect, mood and voice or diathesis, came to be marked formally in the early dialects.

8.3 PERSON

The category of person was marked for the verb in Indo-European already in the earliest period we can reconstruct. In this way the proto-language differs from languages like Chinese and Japanese that do not indicate person. Internal analysis of the endings suggests, however, that there may not have been distinct markers for number as well as person at an early period; the plural and dual person endings are apparently constructed on the basis of the singular markers. It is not our aim here to account for all the endings, or even to provide them, but rather to characterize the system in its development. Szemerényi gives an admirably full, though concise, presentation of the personal endings that can be consulted for additional information on the topics in this section and the next section on number (1970 [1989]: 247–69).

8.3.1 The initial endings

Two sets of person markers must be distinguished. The oldest person markers identified for the first set, those of the present, aorist and future systems in Sanskrit, are maintained in the so-called injunctive forms. These are most clearly attested in Vedic. There the endings may be added directly to roots in normal grade, as to *dā* "give," for which the following injunctive forms are attested in the *Rigveda*: *dām*, *dās*, *dāt*, illustrating the simplest form of the first-, second- and third-person markers. (The second- and third-person forms are also attested in the *Rigveda* with accent, which is assigned on the basis of their role in the clause and is accordingly not of immediate interest here.)

These forms provide the basic meaning of the verb, "I, you, he give/s." In Hoffmann's term, the meaning is "memorative" (1967). The injunctive forms are residues of an earlier period in which meanings of tense and aspect were conveyed by inherent value of the root or by particles rather than by ablaut or suffixes of the type discussed in the previous section. In the *Rigveda*, with tense now a major category, the injunctive forms may be translated as past- or present-tense forms; the ambivalence indicates their lack of fit in the contemporary system. As archaic forms they are also important for understanding the "person" category through their preservation of the early pattern.

When tense came to be a category of the verb system, a further suffix, *-i*, was appended to the person markers. In the earliest Sanskrit and Greek texts, we find a contrast between endings with this suffix and endings without it. The extended endings arc applied in the present. The older unextended endings, by contrast, are applied in the aorist and the imperfect. The distinction is also found in Hittite, where the endings are *-mi*, *-si*, *-ti* : *-un*, *-s*, *-t*. Because classical grammarians considered the present "primary" and the imperfect "secondary", in grammars the endings with final *-i* are labeled primary, even though they are more recent than the so-called secondary endings.

We may illustrate the distribution with forms of the root PIE **dō-* "give" in Sanskrit and Greek. Even though it is reduplicated in the present, we choose this root because the endings are not modified in Sanskrit like those of roots ending in an obstruent, in which the endings are somewhat obscured, as illustrated later with selected athematic roots. The Greek endings have undergone some changes, but these are relatively minor and do not modify the inherited system. Moreover, in these dialects and Armenian, the augment is applied in the imperfect.

	Present		*Imperfect*	
	Sanskrit	*Greek*	*Sanskrit*	*Greek*
1 sg.	dádāmi	dídōmi	ádadhām	edídoun
2 sg.	dádāsi	dídōs	ádadhās	edídous
3 sg.	dádāti	dídōsi	ádadhāt	edídou

We may conclude that the category of person was indicated in the proto-language initially by the endings *-m*, *-s*, *-t* attested in the early dialects.

8.3.2 The perfect endings

In addition to these endings, a second set is found in the perfect, as we may illustrate with forms of PIE *woyd-* ("know"), the *o*-grade of *weyd-* "see." These endings correspond to those of the *hi-* conjugation in Hittite; accordingly, we add below the three forms of the Hittite root *sak-* "know," though the endings have been remodeled on the basis of the endings in *-mi*.

	Sanskrit	Greek	Hittite	PIE	PreIE
1 sg.	véda	oîda	sak-hi	-ha	-h
2 sg.	véttha	oîstha	sak-ti	-tha	-th
3 sg.	véda	oîde	sak(k)-i	-e	-0

At an earlier stage these three endings were *-ha* < *-he*, *-tha* < *-the*, *-e*. (The *h* here indicates the Proto-Indo-European laryngeal in contrast with its use in Hittite for a velar fricative.) The *-e* in the three endings is an addition in Proto-Indo-European, comparable to the *-i* in the set of endings discussed above. In Pre-Indo-European, the third person singular would have had a zero ending.

These two sets of endings undergo further modifications as the verb system is modified. Such modifications will become apparent as we note the treatment of number and additional categories.

8.4 NUMBER

To illustrate the development of marking for number in the verb we may list the plural endings of verbs in some of the languages attested earliest. Among the plural endings the third person provides the best evidence for secondary development; it is clearly an expanded form of the third person singular and because of its similarity in the early dialects may be assumed for the late proto-language. The differences among dialects in endings for the first and second plural indicate, on the other hand, that each of the first and second person plural forms was independently developed in the dialects.

	Vedic	Greek	Old Latin	Hittite
1	mas(i)	men/mes	mus	weni
2	tha(na)	te	tis	teni
3	nti	nti	nt	ntsi

(For interpretation of these forms we may note that in Hittite *t* became the affricate *ts* before *i*; and *m* became *w* after high back vowels – that form of the ending was then extended throughout the conjugation.)

The secondary development of expression of the plural category in the verb may be supported by examining the plural forms of endings in the perfect of those dialects that developed it, and of the *-hi* conjugation in Hittite.

1	má	men	mus	weni
2	á	te	stis	teni
3	úr	āsi	ērunt	ntsi

Hittite uses the same endings as those developed to indicate plural number in the *mi*-conjugation. The other dialects exhibit somewhat different extensions of the singular endings; but these are based on the endings in the *mi*-conjugation rather than on those of the perfect, supporting the view that there were no plural endings in the equivalent conjugation of the proto-language. The -*r* endings are attested in a number of branches. We will discuss their origin in 10.5.5; but it is clear from the other dialects that they had nothing to do originally with the "perfect" endings.

When the conjugational system of the verb was further expanded in the dialects, the endings listed above were additionally modified. We will deal with some of the modifications in 10.5.1–3, But the general principle for indicating person and number should be clear from the forms given. The person categories were the earliest expressed, and the number category was not introduced until later; the separate person categories used different devices in the plural.

Efforts have been expended to identify the origin of the affixes. The first person singular *m* is intriguingly similar to the stem used for oblique forms of the personal pronoun: *me*. We have no way of knowing whether this proposed origin is valid. Unfortunately, the second singular ending -*s* does not support such an origin; the characteristic consonant of the second person singular pronoun is *t*, which is equivalent to the third person singular marker. The actual source of the endings then eludes explanation.

8.4.1 Formal effects on introduction of thematic inflection

We have already noted that a major modification of inflection in the late proto-language came through suffixation of *e/o*, which is so extensive that the suffix is simply known as the thematic vowel. The appeal of the thematic inflection may be illustrated by noting the three singular forms of athematic presents in Sanskrit class 2.

	duh "milk"	*lih* "lick"	*dviṣ* "hate"
1	dóhmi	léhmi	dvéṣmi
2	dhókṣi	lékṣi	dvékṣi
3	dógdhi	léḍhi	dvéṣṭi

When these roots were inflected by the thematic inflection, the Sanskrit sixth class as opposed to the second illustrated above, the forms were highly regular. The first three forms of *lih* in the sixth class are *lihāmi*, *lihasi*, *lihati*. This is the pattern of inflection that was adopted and spread in all the branches. In Greek, for example, the three forms of the cognate of Sanskrit *lih* are thematic: *leíkhō*, *leíkheis*, *leíkhei*, as they are in Latin:

lingō, *lingis*, *lingit*. In thematic inflection the bases may vary from dialect to dialect, as illustrated with the root for "lick"; but the endings do not modify them further. The forms eventually come to be even simpler, as in German *lecken*, English *lick*, and other Indo-European languages of today.

While hesitant to propose broad generalizations about language, I have often suggested that when languages are extended to a large number of non-native speakers, the complexities are simplified. Among examples are the morphological complexities of athematic inflection, as illustrated above. We know that the Indo-European languages were extended to many new speakers. It is also clear that the complexities in all the languages were simplified, as by the spread of thematic inflection on nouns and verbs, but we cannot demonstrate the validity of these generalizations or of this hypothesis concerning the reason for the change from inflections that involve many phonological complexities to a system that includes few of them.

It is, on the other hand, obvious that such complexities provide little difficulty for infants acquiring languages. We can cite extraordinary difficulties that have been maintained in languages, such as the broken plurals of Arabic nouns. We can, on the other hand, also point to the simplifications in pidgins and creoles, which by definition are languages used by speakers of various linguistic backgrounds. However, linguistics has not yet had the resources to conduct the social investigations that have been possible for other sciences; until it does, the explanation proposed here for the changes that led to simplification in Indo-European morphological structure remains hypothetical.

8.5 TENSE/ASPECT

Languages of accusative or ergative structure include some device for distinguishing between a verbal meaning that is ongoing and one that has been completed. The distinction may be made by reference to the time of the action; in a sentence like *She saw the parade*, the form of the verb indicates that the act of seeing was in the past. It also indicates that the action has been completed. In contrast with application to time, the reference can also be made to completion or lack of completion of the action. If a verb system is constructed on such a basis, it is referred to as an aspect system. If it is constructed on the basis of reference to time, it is referred to as a tense system.

8.5.1 Complexities of tense and aspect systems in use with verbs indicating a given "manner of action"

English and the other languages of western Europe as well as many others have tense systems; the Slavic languages and Biblical Hebrew among many other languages have aspect systems. In equating many sentences, the two types of systems can readily be interrelated. Completed aspect is often equivalent to past tense, and incompleted aspect to present tense. Verb forms generally have a range of functions, however, as do language categories; accordingly, we cannot simply equate given categories of tense and aspect systems, nor can we expect the system of any language to apply only either tense or aspect. We may note the reason for some of the difficulties in distinguishing between aspectual and tense forms or systems.

The base forms of many verbs have meanings that may indicate primarily a single action or a continuous action: for example, the English verb *look* implies a single action in contrast with the continuous activity implied by *see*. We can use each in the same sentence construction, as in *look here* as well as *see here* (which have differing implications, but these do not concern us here); but other formal parallels are impossible. We can say *She looked out of the window* but not *She saw out of the window*. It is also possible to say *She is looking out of the window* but not *She is seeing out of the window*. Native speakers of English have acquired the difference in usage, even though they may not be able to account for it. In general, we may distinguish between the meanings of the two verbs by stating that *look* implies a unitary action while *see* implies a continuous action. That is to say, the inherent meanings of each verb include implications comparable to the aspect distinctions conveyed by inflections in many languages. To distinguish between inflectional modifications of meaning for aspect and comparable inherent meanings of verbs, the phrase "manner of action" (German *Aktionsart*) is used in parallel with the term "aspect." The meaning of verbs like English *look* and *find* may be said to include a punctual or perfective "manner of action" in contrast with verbs like *see* and *know*, whose meaning includes continuous or imperfective "manner of action."

While tense systems are by no means simple, the treatment of aspect systems provides one of the greatest difficulties for linguists, as treatises on aspect in Russian or other languages with aspectual systems may demonstrate. Determining the uses of verb forms in languages of the past provides even greater difficulties, as disagreements among Indo-Europeanists demonstrate. There is little disagreement on the meaning of the imperfect (continuous) tense in Greek as opposed to the aorist (punctual); but the Greek system clearly differs from that of the proto-language. Many Indo-Europeanists ascribe to the proto-language an aspectual system, but Szemerényi vigorously disagrees (1970 [1989]: 332–41). We cannot therefore provide a description of the Indo-European system that represents a consensus. The following account indicates the difficulties, while proposing that in the earlier stage of the language the verb system was aspectual.

8.5.2 The early verb system; the injunctive

As we have noted above, the early Vedic texts include residues of an earlier verb system that are called injunctives. Characteristic of injunctives is use of the so-called secondary endings with meanings that may be comparable to those of the present-tense forms rather than imperfect or aorist forms. However, as examination of their occurrences may indicate, the meaning cannot be interpreted simply; the hymns in which injunctives are found often have mythical meanings that permit various interpretations. The first stanza of the Strophic hymn, *Rigveda* 4.17, may provide an illustration (injunctives are indicated in italics).

tvám mahā́m̐ indra   túbhyaṁ ha   kṣā́   ánu kṣatrám maṁhánā
you   great   oh-Indra to-you   ptc. earth ptc. power   readily
manyata dyáuḥ
grants   heaven
"You are great, oh Indra; to you the earth, the heaven, readily *grants* the rule over [them]."
tváṁ vṛtráṁ śávasā   jaghanvā́n   *sṛjáh*   síndhū́m̐r
you   Vritra   with-might having-slain   you-release rivers
áhinā   jagrasānán
by-serpent   devoured
"Having slain Vritra with power, you *release* the rivers devoured by the serpent."

The interpretation given here is that of Hoffmann (1967: 178–9). That interpretation is in keeping with his general conclusion that the injunctive has a "memorative" meaning; but he also concedes that both of the injunctives in this stanza could be interpreted as indicating a past action. An interpretation as nonpast rests on the assumption that a vatic utterance might be made in a kind of unreal situation. If, on the other hand, the hymn is interpreted as portraying a real situation, both injunctives would clearly have to be translated in this stanza with a past-tense form. Many additional injunctives might be cited to illustrate the problems of interpretation. As stated above, my chief concern is to indicate the difficulties involved. The basic problem results from the situation that injunctives are residues of an earlier verb system; as residues they are extraneous to the system and cannot therefore be interpreted as we normally do forms in texts, that is, by contrasting them with other possible forms in the language of the period. If we do insist that we interpret them in keeping with a straightforward analysis of the text, objections may be made that the texts in which they are found cannot be interpreted straightforwardly.

We may note that while he is concerned largely with form, Watkins attributes the conjunct of the Old Irish verb to forms with secondary endings comparable with those of the injunctive. However, he states that the injunctive is only an Indo-Iranian category, not an Indo-European, while ascribing the forms to Indo-European times (1969: 45–6). His views differ considerably from those presented here.

The Homeric poems include many verb forms without augment that in later Greek require the augment. These may be equated with the injunctives in Sanskrit. They are found largely in narrative. Commentators have often compared them with "historic present" forms in other languages; these are typically used to convey intensity. The comparison is quite wrong because, as Homeric grammarians state, "the Augment is chiefly omitted where the context shows that past time is meant" (Monro 1891: 62). As Delbrück and earlier scholars point out, the Greek forms without augment must be related to the injunctives in Vedic and Avestan, and were based on earlier forms in the parent language (1897: 352–7).

Hittite, unfortunately, fails to provide material that would permit us to determine whether the late proto-language had a tense or an aspect system. Preterite forms in Hittite may have present meaning, but probably for textual reasons: for example, when royal decrees are introduced, the preterite may be in keeping with epistolary style, as in Cicero's letters, or may reflect the influence of Akkadian, as in LUGAL GAL *Tabarna memista* "The great king Tabarna has spoken = speaks" (Friedrich 1969: 139). We must therefore reconstruct the earlier system from other dialects.

8.5.3 Early expression of aspect

Different root and base structures clearly indicate aspectual differences. In normal grade they express continuous action, while in zero grade they express punctual action. Contrasts are readily available in Greek as in *éleipon* "I was leaving" vs. *élipon* "I left." As reflexes of the ablaut changes, both forms reflect the situation in the parent language. Their formal characteristics also indicate the stage of the proto-language to which we may ascribe the difference. If, indeed, they are inherited without change (except for addition of the augment), they must be reflexes of the system at the time of ablaut brought about by stress accent; accordingly, at that stage the verb system was inflected for aspect. That stage may continue an earlier situation that marked aspect distinctions by other means, as through use of particles; but the aspectual distinction between continuous and punctual action, as illustrated in these forms, must be assumed for early Proto-Indo-European, because of the evidence in Greek and in many other branches.

Further information on the very early verb system may be obtained from other sources. We may recall that three prominent verbal affixes which Delbrück and Brugmann among others ascribe to the proto-language, those in -*n*-, in -*sk*-, and in -*s*- convey a "terminative" force. The choice of descriptor is deliberate; "perfective" might have been used, but choice of it would imply that the system was comparable to that of Slavic or Biblical Hebrew among other languages. What is of interest to us is that terminative affixes were favored to express a characteristic meaning of the verbal system at this stage in contrast with non-terminative bases.

A similar contrast of meanings is found in the early athematic roots (Delbrück 1897: 65–9). Some indicate continuous action, e.g. *ed- "eat," as in *Rigveda* 10.146.3: *agnír jámbhais tigitaír atti* "Agni eats with sharp teeth"; compare also *es- "to exist," *bhā- "to shine," *vā- "to blow," etc. Others have punctual meaning (1897: 71–4); considering this the meaning of most roots, Delbrück lists examples like *duh- "milk," *sū- "generate, give birth to," *vid- "find" and so on.

While maintained lexically in some verbs, as we noted for English *look* and *see*, contrast of meaning through lexical means came to be replaced grammatically by the use of contrasting ablaut grades in many roots and bases; if these were accented and had normal grade, they indicated continuous action, but if they were unaccented and had zero grade, they expressed punctual action. This situation is widely represented in Greek and Sanskrit.

The system must have led to difficulties of interpretation: for example, so-called aorist forms of *bhū- "become" in the *Rigveda* often have resultative meaning, and accordingly are equivalent to present-tense forms of the verb "be" (Hoffmann 1967: 214–16). An example is VIII.93.7 *sá vŕṣā vṛṣabhó* **bhuvat** "he (Indra) is the virile bull." Hoffmann ingeniously attempts to account for such uses, as of this injunctive which might have been expected to mean "he has become"; but they must have been difficult for later interpreters of such passages as they are for us.

8.5.4 Introduction of markers for tense

Whatever the process of development of injunctives and the aspect system, a device was instituted to indicate present meaning: a final suffix -*i*. As Thurneysen pointed out in a brief and brilliant article (1885: 172ff.), this suffix was added to forms like "1st singular *dveism, 2nd *dveiss, 3rd *dveist."

Indicating time, the suffix marks the introduction of a tense system. It is attested in Avestan as well as Vedic and Greek, in Hittite, Old Church Slavic and Lithuanian, as well as in Italic and Germanic, though in these dialects the former presence of the -*i* has to be reconstructed on the basis of modifications left on its loss. Like any innovation, marking for tense was only slowly adopted for the entire verb system. In Homeric Greek the present indicative is distinguished from the imperfect for tense; but the aorist indicative is distinguished from each of these categories through indication of punctual aspect – which often corresponds to past-tense meaning. By the time of Biblical Greek, the system had developed to one marking tense; any attested aorists, as well as perfects, are equivalent in meaning to imperfects.

We may also recall that the three central dialects adopted a further device to mark tense, the so-called augment. As we have indicated for

Homeric Greek, 4.5.2, this marker, a prefixed adverb *e*, was only slowly generalized; but it solidified the tense system as opposed to the earlier aspect system. Other dialects used different devices to mark past tense, notably the suffixes mentioned above: *d* for Germanic, *w* for Latin, *k* for Greek, and so on.

8.5.5 Further developments in the tense-aspect system

The endings discussed above underwent further changes. When in the late proto-language the thematic vowel was widely extended on verbs as well as nouns, it gave rise to a new ending in the first singular, *-ō*, as in Greek *phérō*, Latin *ferō*, and so on, which gradually replaced the athematic ending. Changes whose precise origin is unclear are also found in other endings. These were not accompanied by fundamental changes in meaning; they then are minor modifications.

We will return to discussion of other endings below in 10.5.2, as to the restriction in the singular of the perfect endings. As the endings as well as the ablaut form of the base indicate, the perfect is a reflex of a totally different subsystem from that which adds the endings in *-m*, *-s*, *-t*.

As we have noted, the development of that portion of the verb system expressing tense : aspect (time : manner of action) is highly complex. When we examine dialects in subsequent periods we find systems that express these categories variously. Latin, Celtic and Germanic, as well as late Sanskrit and Biblical Greek, have developed tense systems; Old Armenian, Albanian, Baltic and Slavic, on the other hand, have largely maintained expression for aspect; but the subsequent dialects do not have purely aspectual or purely tense systems, as may be illustrated by the English progressive expressing imperfective force, as in: *They were running past the house* beside the perfective force of *They ran past the house*. Similar examples indicating expressions for aspect as well as tense might be given for other dialects. We may assume a similar situation for the stages of the proto-language, though in early periods expression for aspect was more fundamental than that for tense.

8.6 MOOD

The standard handbooks reconstruct the subjunctive and optative moods as well as the indicative and the imperative for the proto-language. Not all of these have been found in every dialect. The question of their presence in the proto-language became especially acute when Hittite was found to have only the indicative and the imperative. The other moods may then have been developed in dialect continua of the various branches, from affixes comparable to those that were selected to mark preterites and perfects, like the -**w*- for Latin, the -**dh*- for Germanic and so on. We will examine them further below.

8.6.1 The indicative

We may assume that in general the forms discussed above were used for expressions indicating certainty by speakers; for in the modal systems of the dialects they are reflected in the indicative mood. Besides these forms, however, we must assume for the late proto-language others that indicated commands, wishes and possibly also statements of uncertainty. Of these the forms for commands, that is, the imperative, are probably the oldest.

8.6.2 The imperative (Brugmann 1904a: 557–9)

The most general mood in the various branches is the imperative, and accordingly it must be ascribed to the proto-language. Applied for command to a single person, in its simplest form it is equal to the root or base, as in Latin *ei*, *ī* "go"; subsequently in most verbs the singular is marked with the thematic vowel, as in *age* "lead."

Endings for second person plural forms, typically *-te*, were taken from other categories. The ending for the second person singular also came to be modified. Moreover, third- and even first-person forms were incorporated into a so-called imperative mood; for details see Szemerényi (1970 [1989]: 263–6), who, however, does not discuss the first person singular imperative forms. Where found, these are taken over from subjunctives, and might more properly be called hortatives.

The expansion and subsequent history of the imperative mood is a concern for the various branches. For the parent language we assume only a second person singular, and at a late stage also a second person plural.

8.6.3 The optative (Brugmann 1904a: 554–7)

The optative is made from athematic verbs with the suffix *-yē-* in the singular, and *-ī-* in the plural, as may be illustrated with forms of the root "be": Sanskrit *syām*, *syās*, *syāt*; Old Latin *siem*, *siēs*, *siet*, *sīmus*, *sītis*, *sient*. From the two variants we may conclude that at an earlier stage the affix was *-ye²-*; in the singular the laryngeal contacted with the suffix vowel, lengthening it as illustrated by the Sanskrit forms; in the plural the suffix vowel was lost, so that the laryngeal contracted with the vocalic form of the resonant *y*. The optative affix is followed by secondary endings.

Added to thematic verbs, the suffix was reduced to *-y-*, so that the characteristic form is *-oi-*, as in Greek *phéroimi*, *phérois*, *phéroi*, *phéroimen* "I, you, he, we wish to bear," etc. The endings then were often remodeled, as the first person singular form here illustrates.

As a distinct mood the optative is attested in contrast with the subjunctive as well as the indicative mood only in early Sanskrit and Greek. In other dialects, such as Germanic, it formed a contrast with the indicative.

At the time of the early dialects the optative was used to indicate a hope or a desire; its meaning corresponds to that of the base accompanied by "wish." Such uses are often found in subordinate clauses. When conjunctions were introduced to mark subordination, the optative like the subjunctive came to be regulated syntactically rather than to indicate a semantic meaning. By the time of New Testament Greek, it no longer was used with the principal verb of the clause, and thereupon was completely lost.

8.6.4 The subjunctive (Brugmann 1904a: 551–4)

The subjunctive was indicated by suffixes corresponding to the thematic vowel. Accordingly, on athematic bases its forms correspond to thematic indicatives, e.g. Sanskrit subj. *ásat(i)* "will be" vs. ind. *ásti* "is"; on thematic bases the forms have a long vowel suffix, e.g. Sanskrit *bhárāt(i)* vs. *bhárati*. While the endings may be primary, as suggested here in parentheses, they are more likely to be secondary.

Their basic meaning indicates requisition, that is, a stronger form of desire than the optative. They are comparable in meaning to both imperatives and optatives, indicating a weaker form of request than the imperative but one somewhat stronger than the optative. It is scarcely remarkable that the three moods with their comparable meanings are attested in only a few dialects.

We may note further that, as tense came to be indicated in the verbal system, subjunctive forms – or forms comparable to subjunctives – provided the forms for some future tenses; for example, the Latin future *erit* "he will be" is a reflex of the form reconstructed as the short-vowel subjunctive PIE *éset(i)*.

While the moods were part of the verbal system in Greek and Sanskrit, when they were retained in the other dialects the subjunctive and optative were reduced to one category indicating lack of certainty in contrast with the indicative. The process of reduction, as well as the subsequent forms, are problems for each of the branches. The markers are not highly distinctive, especially for the subjunctive. Where found in verbal systems, they presumably replaced earlier means of indicating modal meanings through particles. Their position in the late period of the proto-language requires further attention.

8.7 VOICE, OR DIATHESIS

Voice or diathesis, refers to a verbal category in which the action is presented as contrasting with normal, or active, expression. In English and many other languages there are two contrasting voices, active (in which the subject performs some action that generally affects another person or object) and passive (in which the subject is presented as undergoing some action). We have noted that this contrast did not exist in the proto-language, but instead a contrast between action affecting another person or object and action affecting oneself. This voice expressing action referring to the subject is known as the middle. (The term has its origin in grammar of Classical Greek, which included three voices. Grammarians labeled the voice expressing action by the subject with a term corresponding to "active," and the voice expressing action undergone by the subject with a term corresponding to "passive." The remaining voice seemed to have characteristics somewhat between the two others, and accordingly was given the name "middle.")

The middle has three primary uses: (1) indication of an action that affects the subject, usually beneficially, e.g "rejoice" Sanskrit *bhuṅkté*, "become warm," Greek *théromai*. (2) reflexive, as in *Rigveda* 1.134.3: *vāyúr yuṅkte róhitā ráthe* "Vayu hitches the tawny horses to *his* wagon." (The only indication that the wagon is Vayu's is given through use of the middle rather than the active verb. We may note that the Greek middle *théromai*, cited after (1) above, also means "I warm myself.") (3) Reciprocal, e.g. Sanskrit *spárdhate* "quarrel with one another." These uses are also found in Hittite, as in *unuttat* "she adorned herself" (Friedrich 1960: 135–6). The middle is therefore a category comparable to verb forms in verb-final languages that express reflexive and reciprocal meanings.

The middle is indicated by means of special endings, of which the primary in the present indicative are: first person *-ai*, second *-soi*, third *-toi* (see Szemerényi 1970 [1989]: 253–6). These endings were supplemented to provide a complete paradigm; some of them were then remodeled.

As we will note in 9.9, reflexivization and also reciprocal relationship are indicated in VO languages by means of separate words, usually pronouns. When the Indo-European languages increasingly adopted VO structure, such words were developed to express these categories. For the first and second person German uses personal pronouns; for the third, as we have indicated, it developed a new pronoun, *sich*, rhyming with *mich* "me, (myself)" and *dich* "thee, (thyself)." English adopted a different device, using the noun "self" preceded by a pronominal adjective. These examples may illustrate the recency of development of the VO reflexivization pattern; other branches have introduced different devices for it. When such devices were introduced into any of the dialects, the middle was nonessential. If maintained, it was modified in meaning to a passive, as, for example, in *I was warmed, she was adorned*. As may be determined from grammars of the various dialects, different types of passives were formed, many with compound expressions like those of English and German.

8.8 POSSIBLE PARALLELS TO THE EARLY VERB SYSTEM

The Proto-Indo-European verb system may be best understood in its development by comparison of its early stage with forms in an OV language like Quechua. Quechua is pedagogically helpful because it is agglutinative. Accordingly, the suffixes do not express multiple categories as do many in Proto-Indo-European and the dialects. Moreover, as we have suggested, the late Proto-Indo-European system is the result of numerous extensions, so that it represents a succession of patterns. The comparison is then by no means one to one; but the similar construction of verbal forms may be illuminating.

The Quechua form for "they are only teaching each other" is *yača-či-na-ku-tla-sa-nku*. In this form the first element is the base "learn." This is followed by the causative suffix, modifying the meaning from "learn" to "teach". We may recall that causation is expressed in Indo-European verbs by suffixes that directly follow the root.

The element *na* indicates reciprocal relationship, and *ku* reflexive relationship; these suffixes then are comparable to Indo-European middle suffixes. The next two affixes indicate delimitative and continuative meaning, which are not marked with affixes in Indo-European. Finally, *nku* indicates third person plural.

If the form were in the past, the affix *rqa* would be placed before the person marker. In location it is comparable to the -*s*- of the aorist, or the -*k*- of the Greek perfect, and so on. The sequence of affixes is then comparable to that in Indo-European, with affixes closest to the root modifying its meaning, followed by affixes to indicate voice, tense/aspect, person and number. As in Proto-Indo-European, suffixation may consist of only one element, as in the second singular imperative: *puñu-y* "sleep!". (For further information, see Bills *et al.* 1969: esp. 335).

In Indo-European the affixes modifying root meaning are referred to as derivational. They may be followed by person affixes; but if tense or mood is indicated, suffixes to indicate these precede the person affixes. In many respects the Indo-European verb is simple through not indicating a large number of qualifiers. On the other hand, through the merging of suffixes for tense, mood, voice and even person and number, the forms are far less transparent than are those of agglutinative languages like Turkish, Japanese or Quechua. Whether or not this complexity was the reason for restructuring the verb, the later dialects have greatly modified the early system.

8.9 THE DEVELOPMENT TO AN ANALYTIC SYSTEM

A major shift in the language with a massive effect on the morphological system resulted from use of analytic devices rather than inflections. Already in the early dialects compound tenses rather than forms with verbal inflection were being introduced. Further, instead of indicating subordinate relationship of clauses through use of moods, conjunctions were introduced. These devices came to be increasingly prominent, leading to less importance for morphological marking.

The shift accompanied a shift in arrangement from OV to VO order. All the early dialects except for the Anatolian provide evidence for the shift.

Classical Sanskrit, for example, resembles Classical Greek and Latin in arrangement of its clauses. The Indo-European languages of Europe come to be increasingly VO in structure. The Celtic languages in the north develop further to VSO structure. By contrast the Indo-European languages of India revert towards OV arrangement, probably as a result of their social relationships with speakers of the Dravidian languages which are rigidly OV in structure. These developments are problems for specialists in the individual dialects.

In dealing with the syntax of the proto-language, on the other hand, we are faced with residual constructions that can only be solved by reconstructing its earlier stages. As one example we may cite the use of expressions consisting of the dative and the verb "be" in the absence of a verb for "have." As a further example we may cite the defective forms of the perfect. After examination of the syntax of the proto-language we will be in a position to deal with such questions. Recent typological study has provided avenues for their solution.

9 The syntax of Proto-Indo-European

9.1 SYNTACTIC VIEWS OF THE HANDBOOKS

In reviewing the syntactic treatments of the handbooks it is difficult to forget Hirt's poignant expression: "One assembles a series of facts but doesn't know what to do with them" (1931–4: III: vi). Many syntactic treatments were produced in the nineteenth century and the early decades of the twentieth century for the Indo-European dialects. Speyer treated in separate volumes the syntax of Vedic and of Classical Sanskrit. For the syntax of Greek we may limit ourselves at this point to citing Schwyzer's grammar (1939–50), which was based on four earlier editions, the fourth by Brugmann. Similarly, Szantyr's syntax of Latin (1965) has numerous predecessors; and capable, if not as extensive, treatments of the syntax of other dialects, as well as many monographs and articles on selected syntactic problems, might be cited. Further, after numerous earlier publications Delbrück provided a synthesis for the proto-language in his three-volume contribution to the *Grundriss* (1893–1900).

Theoretical works also were published, and widely discussed, such as John Ries's *Was ist Syntax?*. Jacob Wackernagel contributed a remarkable set of essays called *Vorlesungen über Syntax* (1926–8), to be sure chiefly about the classical languages. Wilhelm Havers published a treatise on explanatory syntax, *Handbuch der erklärenden Syntax* (1931). And the major theoretical work, Paul's *Prinzipien* (1920), dealt at length with syntax. An extensive chapter of the book treats the "basic circumstances of syntax" (*ibid.* 121–50). Subsequent chapters discuss specific matters, such as ellipsis (*Sparsamkeit*) (*ibid.* 313–24), a topic that attracted considerable attention under the rubric "gapping" in early generative grammar. Moreover, Jespersen published a monograph on formalized syntactic analysis (1937). His formal analyses are extensive, including, for example, an italicized *O* for the indirect object besides the three symbols S(ubject), V(erb), O(bject) among numerous others.

It is quite false then to assert that the study of syntax and theoretical

Sources for this chapter: Delbrück, (1871–88; 1893–1900); Hirt (1921–37, VI–VII; 1931–4); Brugmann (1925); Wackernagel (1926–8); Greenberg (1963); Havers (1931); Lehmann (1974).

attention to it was neglected in the nineteenth century and first part of the twentieth. Yet in spite of this massive attention, Hirt prefaced his final books on syntax with his startling complaint. To understand the situation it is useful to examine the general aims of previous treatments, and then to suggest remedies for the shortcomings.

9.1.1 Presentation of syntax in the early handbooks

To understand the grounds for Hirt's complaint, we may examine briefly the syntactic portion of one of the major grammars of a classical language, Raphael Kühner's *Ausführliche Grammatik der griechischen Sprache*, produced in a third edition of 1904 by Bernhard Gerth, which was based on an initial edition of 1834. Its 606 pages begin with a long section on the infinitive and the participle (1904, II.2: 1–113). This is followed by a chapter on the adverb (*ibid*. 113–223). The next section deals with the syntax of the complex sentence, taking up most of the rest of the volume (*ibid*. 224–557), and is followed by three shorter chapters on less common features of word and sentence arrangement (*ibid*. 559–606). The pages are indeed full of facts, supported by quotations; but, in dealing with the complex sentence, the authors treat the constructions by lexical and morphological elements, beginning with the conjunction *te* "and," going on with the conjunction *kaí* "and," and then other conjunctions. That is to say, the treatment is comparable to one on morphology: forms, here in a large section of the volume directed at description of sentences, are identified, and the patterns in which they are found are described. Hirt is justified in stating that such an approach cannot lead to syntactic explanation. The so-called syntax is an annotated list.

What we require instead is a presentation of the syntactic system, and the structures on which it is based. We expect for syntax what Bopp set out to do for morphology in 1816, in accordance with the ideals of Friedrich Schlegel, who in 1806 set as goal determination of the innermost structure of language. We need to describe the syntactic system as Bopp did the morphological, and then we must determine the principles of its structure.

Linguists were not without ideas on determining and presenting syntactic patterns. Hermann Paul in his *Prinzipien der Sprachgeschichte* of 1880 (5th and definitive edition, 1920) identified the devices of syntax, as did Jespersen and others in subsequent works. The devices were examined by Leonard Bloomfield under four rubrics (1933): order or arrangement; selection; intonation; sandhi. We may describe with the help of these devices the pattern of any sentence, such as the first of *Rigveda* 7.71:

```
ápa  svásur uṣáso  nág  jihīte
ptc   f abl sg f abl sg f n sg 3 sg pres mid
away sister  dawn   night departs
```
"Night departs from her sister dawn."

In arrangement, the verb is final, preceded by the subject and earlier by an adverbial phrase. In selection we may limit ourselves to *nág*; it is "selected" from the class of nouns, its nominative singular form in turn from the nominal paradigm. With regard to intonation, the lack of high pitch on the final verb informs us that the sentence ends in falling pitch. With regard to sandhi, the modified final elements *-so*, *-g* rather than *-sas*, *-k* indicate that words of the sentence are pronounced in phrases. We could cite further characteristics to indicate that the sentence is a structured unit.

We can also determine the hierarchy among the characteristics. If the verb were not placed in final position, but rather in initial, it would have a high-pitch accent. Order therefore occupies a more important position in the set of characteristics than does intonation. Similarly, the *-o* of the word for dawn is determined by its order before the following *n-*. Also, while order cannot be said to regulate selection, as of the feminine noun for night, it provides the basic interpretation of the sentence; if the middle form of the verb had not been selected, the verb might well have been placed initially, as is the verb of the following sentence. Order is accordingly the principal device among the four. As we will see later in some detail, it provides the basic principle for the structuring of sentences and their components.

Even from this brief discussion, we may conclude that fuller understanding of syntax, comparable to the understanding that had been achieved of phonology and morphology, would have permitted Hirt to propose an explanation of syntactic structure. As noted earlier, the way to such understanding was gained only after Greenberg's essay of 1963.

9.2 MOVES TOWARDS AN EXPLANATORY SYNTAX

While our means of explaining syntactic constructions are recent, we must also state that earlier linguists provided important contributions for the understanding of the syntactic patterning of the proto-language. We may examine some of these in the publications of Delbrück.

Among his many important contributions, Delbrück published a set of five monographs from 1871 to 1888 under the title "Syntactic investigations." The first two deal with the use of forms: that of 1871 with the use of the subjunctive and optative in Sanskrit and in Greek; that of 1876 with the Sanskrit tenses. The third examines the order of words in one of the oldest Indic prose works, the *Śatapathabrāhmaṇa* (1878). The conclusions are highly interesting, and represent views that are in accord with recent statements on discourse and sentence structure (1878: 76–8).

As his first conclusion, Delbrück proposes a "law of "occasional" word placement." By this "law" a word that is emphasized is either placed at the beginning of a sentence or brought nearer that position. He concludes further that this movement rule implies that the beginning of the sentence is more strongly stressed, possibly also with higher pitch, than is the rest of the sentence. The law has two corollaries: by one, enclitics are drawn, "as by a magnet," towards the initial word; by the other, the verb is unaccented when it stands in its normal place. Finally, for Sanskrit of the time, the sentence begins with stronger stress, and possibly higher pitch, which dropped off at the end. These observations merit commentary. It may be noted that Delbrück's first corollary is a statement of Wackernagel's law, proposed a decade and a half later (1892). The second adumbrates the intonation pattern of the early Vedic sentence. Moreover, the conclusion is achieved from a point of view that is credited to the Prague structuralists at the beginning of this century, and to the discourse specialists of today.

The second major conclusion deals with syntactic structure rather than discourse patterning. Delbrück determines a specific order for sentences. By his finding, the subject stands initially, the verb finally and the object is placed immediately before the verb. Moreover, adjectives are placed before nouns. "Prepositions" are placed after nouns. Delbrück discusses this conclusion at length in an effort to overcome the notion that word order was free. It is not necessary to repeat his argumentation, though it is important to recall how deeply the notion was held that word order of the old languages, including Latin and Greek, is free; the notion is not yet dispelled today. Yet of even greater note for our purposes is his statement that the verb-final order observed in early Sanskrit prose is also found in the other Indo-European languages. That is to say, more than a hundred years ago Delbrück proposed OV order for the early dialects of Indo-European and the parent language as well.

In addition, Delbrück casually tosses off statements of astounding prescience. Discussing the accentuation of the verb in subordinate clauses but not in principal clauses, he accounts for this situation on the grounds that the majority of subordinate clauses precede the principal clause. That is to say, he identified another characteristic of OV language structure.

Finally, he discusses the validity of his conclusions. In the course of this discussion he notes that the word order of the Vedas is like that of his text. Moreover, he alludes to an observation of Wackernagel's (1877: 457ff.) that the Greek verbs "be" *eimí* and "say" *phēmí* are treated similarly in accent. In his final paragraph he states firmly that since Latin and Lithuanian show the same principles of word order, and also the other dialects, with the possible exception of Celtic, these same "laws" must have been present in the Proto-Indo-European period (1878: 78). In view of the recent demonstration that the earliest Celtic, as attested on the Iberian peninsula, is also verb final, Delbrück's qualifier "possible" was well chosen.

As a final comment on Delbrück's short monograph of 1878, we may note that his observations were accurate, as well as his conclusion that the proto-language was OV in structure. What he did not do is relate the several observations with one other. Today we would, and in this way we also consider that the use of postpositions in Vedic and in the proto-language, as well as placement of adjectives before nouns, is to be expected of OV structure. That is to say, Delbrück's facts are correct; but neither he, nor his contemporaries and successors including Hirt, dealt with syntax structurally as they did with phonology and morphology.

9.2.1 Further conclusions on the basis of Greek

In his fourth syntactic monograph Delbrück examined the syntactic devices of Greek (1879). His conclusions corroborate those of his earlier study of Vedic prose, though he finds Greek more complex, partly because its texts are later. In further support of his conclusions he cites the monograph of Henri Weil of 1844 which examined "the order of words in the ancient languages compared to the modern languages" as well as an essay by Bergaigne. However, the monograph of 1879 may have its chief interest in his conclusions on word-order changes in Greek.

Maintaining still that the adjective stood before nouns in the early language, Delbrück is concerned with the effect of adjective placement after the noun. The noun then by his view is "isolated"; the reason is often its strong accent. He finds the same situation for genitives. And for both, in time, the effect of isolation is weakened on grounds he seeks to determine. Prepositions, by contrast, come to be placed before nouns, in a general departure from their early order. These changes, as suggested above, he relates to accentual phenomena. Also in examining the verb, his account of the interrelationships with accent (as limited to placement in Greek on one of the last three syllables) comes to be too complex for restatement in the space available here.

Of greatest interest is his conclusion that the principles of word order change, much as do features in the phonological and morphological systems; and he continues to insist that there are laws of word order. He also attempts to combat an apparently dominant position (not only in his day) that logic determines the order of words, not linguistic principles comparable to those that are applicable in morphology and phonology. We note once again, however, that for him the principles are individual, not interrelated. While pointing to this shortcoming, a result no doubt of lack of attention to other language types, we give him great credit for recognizing accurately the rules of word order in the early dialects and in the proto-language.

The fifth monograph in the series provides in its 634 pages an excellent account of Vedic syntax (1888). In it a great deal more attention is given to the device of selection than in the monograph published a decade earlier, although order and intonation are not neglected. We might well comment on some of its conclusions, especially those regarding relative clauses. We will return to these later, after providing a brief sketch of syntactic structure, as related to the basic order of the clause, whether OV like Proto-Indo-European or VO like most of the current Indo-European languages and many others.

To gain perspective on the problems, as well as to examine the last large-scale treatment of Indo-European syntax, we may first examine Hirt's views and discussion in the last two volumes of his large grammar, Syntax I of 1934 and Syntax II of 1937.

9.3 HIRT ON THE SYNTAX OF THE PROTO-LANGUAGE

After making the statement given at the beginning of this essay, which is from his grammar of Proto-Germanic published from 1931 to 1934, Hirt devoted his last two years to Indo-European syntax. In his admirably lucid manner, he states his point of view, and then moves to a well-organized treatment. The clarity of his presentation allows precise understanding of his views and those of many Indo-Europeanists, as well as the possibility of pointing out their shortcomings.

After a brief treatment of the bibliography, in which he lists eighteen monographs and articles of Delbrück's, which he says were "crowned" by his syntax of 1893–1900, Hirt states his position. Criticizing Delbrück for relying too heavily on Sanskrit, he states as forcefully as possible: "My point of view is as follows. In Indo-European the verb developed from the noun." Further, inflection is a relatively late development. Indicating that he does not aim primarily to present new facts, he states that he wants to explain the facts by treating the prehistoric period. He supports this procedure by recalling his contributions to an understanding of the accent, which resulted from a similar approach (1931–4 III: 5).

He then considers the question of Ries's well-known book: "What is syntax?" In accordance with his own pragmatic approach he dismisses the controversies, and states that in dealing with syntax one must treat the material that has not been treated in phonology and morphology. Turning to the further controversies concerning definition of the sentence, he states most frankly: "I don't know what a sentence is, don't even want to know." He goes on to say that "we Indo-Europeans speak in a specific way, and call that a sentence, i.e. a combination of subject and predicate." But he adds that there are also other things: interjections, shouts, vocatives, and we cannot call these sentences. We call them utterances. And we have to investigate them as well as sentences (*ibid.* 7).

He then summarizes the "means of syntax." These are "sentence accent," word order and inflection (*ibid.* 9–11). The "means" he identifies are comparable to the devices that are now standard; for a reconstructed language we can understand Hirt's reluctance to deal in detail with the devices, now widely assumed: sandhi and intonation, which presumably are incorporated in his first "means." The second of his means, also referred to as arrangement, we have noted to be central. The third has been subsequently treated under the term "selection." While the means, or devices of syntax as he lists them are comparable to those of subsequent theoreticians, his further treatment of syntax is surprising.

His first volume Hirt devotes entirely to the "individual parts of speech," and their subcategorization, labeling this the first section on syntax. Beginning with the noun, he treats number and gender, thereupon case (*ibid*. 17–134), concluding with a chapter on "adverbs, adjectives, pronouns," including numerals (*ibid*. 134–77). The remainder of his first volume on syntax deals with the verb (*ibid*. 177–292). In keeping with his view that the verb developed from the noun, he first discusses the infinitives and participles. It may be clear from this brief sketch that the volume deals with the uses of the forms and their categories, that is to say, with functions of selection classes. Moreover, the approach is much like that of Kühner, as sketched in the first section above.

The second volume, labeled the second section, includes a brief chapter on "utterances" followed by a longer chapter on the "simple sentence" (1921–37 VII: 1–48). The chapter on the simple sentence devotes a great deal of attention to minor types, such as subject sentences, impersonals and verbless sentences. Only on pages 33–4 does Hirt discuss "the simple declarative sentence," and there his chief concern is use of the moods in such sentences – largely the indicative but also the optative. In a sense then the most important segment of syntax barely receives attention.

The third section of the two volumes on syntax deals with "the compound sentence" (*ibid*. 48–268). Its first chapter discusses "expansion of the sentence constituents," as by adjectives with nouns (*ibid*. 48–122). The second chapter deals with subordinate clauses (*ibid*. 122–212). After a short additional chapter on placement of principal clauses in conjunction with one another (*ibid*. 212–26), he treats word order (*ibid*. 226–68). Several remarks on the conclusions in this last chapter may be illuminating for views on syntax among Indo-Europeanists at the time, and among many subsequent specialists on the language family. In advance of those remarks we may note that Hirt provides an additional list of references at the beginning of his chapter on word order, repeating his reference to some of Delbrück's works; it might also be noteworthy that his first reference is to the work of Weil, who demonstrated in 1844 that word order in early Latin is OV.

In a brief paragraph on the comparative (*ibid*. 251), Hirt states flatly that originally it was placed after the standard. He then gives examples in support of his conclusion from Greek, Latin, Germanic and Sanskrit, such as Latin *luce clarior* "brighter than light < light-from brighter"; but he devotes half of the section to use of the ablative with Sanskrit *anyás* and the words for "other" in Greek and Latin. He does not comment on the order of the elements in the comparative construction. Nor does he attempt to account for the early expression of the syntactic pattern: "comparison of inequality," even though Small had published two monographs on the topic in the readily accessible series of the Linguistic Society of America. Instead, Hirt treats the topic by itself, much as though one were commenting on a morphological or a lexical item. No attempt is made to suggest why the order was modified in the later dialects, or why it was observed in the proto-language.

In a further section of almost a page and a half on the "position of the verb" (*ibid*. 252–3), Hirt devotes the first paragraph to a rejection of Delbrück's "views on the position of the verb," based as they were on Sanskrit and a view held at the time with regard to Latin. He goes on to reject Delbrück's distinction between "regular" and "occasional" word order. And then he also rejects Delbrück's assumption that verbs standing initially were strongly accented. Instead, he concludes on the basis of his "wide reading" that there are three possible positions of the verb, as illustrated in the Latin sentences: "*Romulus Romam condidit, R(omulus) condidit Romam* und *condidit R(omulus) Romam*" "Romulus founded Rome." Thereupon he makes the statement that *initial position* was the "*oldest type*," emphasizing his view typographically as suggested here. He concludes the section by stating that the verb could either precede the subject or object or follow them.

In view of Hirt's procedures in dealing with the simple sentence and with constructions like the comparative, it is scarcely surprising that he despaired of providing an explanatory syntax. It is, however, even more surprising, almost unbelievable, that he gives no attention to relative age of texts. Weil's treatment of Latin word order, the first monograph Hirt cites at the beginning of the chapter, drew its conclusions from analysis of early Latin texts; and it can hardly have escaped Hirt's attention that the comparative constructions he himself cited were from early Sanskrit, early Greek, and early Germanic texts. One can scarcely believe that a scholar who was thoroughly steeped in the early languages, especially in Greek, failed to make a distinction between the syntax of the earliest texts and those of later times.

It is equally surprising that many Indo-Europeanists today fail to take the chronology of texts into account. The syntax of Old English texts differs from that of current English, and these two stages are scarcely a thousand years apart. As one example to illustrate the importance of taking chronology into account, we can scarcely conceive of a poet today using a comparative with preceding standard, e.g. *sun brighter* meaning "brighter than the sun," as did Old English poets with the phrase *sunnan beorhtra*. Ample handbooks exist that provide information on the difference between Vedic syntax and Classical Sanskrit syntax, between the syntax of Homer and that of the Classical Greek period, and similarly of "Early Latin" and Classical Latin, to say nothing of Old English and New English. Yet there are still Indo-Europeanists today, whom one hesitates to stigmatize by citing their statements, who refuse to deal with syntax as Indo-Europeanists have long done with phonology and morphology.

In view of Hirt's explicit rejection of Delbrück's differentiation between "occasional" word order – which today would be treated under discourse – and "regular" word order, it may be useful to note briefly the segment following his disastrous conclusions on the position of the verb. This segment treats "initial position" of the verb (1921–37 VII: 253–8). Here he cites a heterogeneous array of examples, including Tolstoy's popular stories, Serbian folk-tales and Indic literary texts, finally noting that the imperative is generally initial. In view of Hirt's other contributions, one is reluctant to cite material from the section, such as his statement that we actually find initial position of the verb in all Indo-European languages, so that it is strange that it has not been recognized to be "a natural position." As a more general observation with reference to theoretical bases, we may note that whenever linguists use Madison Avenue qualifiers like "natural" one must be on one's guard.

Further, in a discussion on theoretical bases of the field, it is important to indicate Hirt's unfortunate treatment of syntax and its persistence among Indo-Europeanists to today. Examples are taken from texts of all types, as illustrated by the reference to folk-tales assembled by the nineteenth century author Tolstoy and to the highly sophisticated literary texts of Classical Sanskrit. As in our treatment of phonology and morphology, we deal primarily with the oldest texts; if Hittite provides examples of the laryngeals, it probably is also an excellent source for determining the early syntax. Moreover, we find archaic patterns in residues, as we have just noted of the comparative construction. Other archaic patterns in syntax need to be identified and investigated.

Fortunately, many syntactic studies have now been carried out that provide the possibility of dealing with syntax as capably as earlier Indo-Europeanists have dealt with phonology and morphology. We can then make use of the data available in the numerous descriptive studies that Hirt and others cite, and of the data in the reliable grammars, proceeding from their statements on the various constructions to an explanatory treatment. To state the Indo-European data succinctly, we may first sketch the general framework for syntactic structures that is now available as the phonological framework has been for many decades.

9.4 MOVES TOWARD A FRAMEWORK FOR SYNTACTIC STRUCTURES

In Schlegel's words of almost two centuries ago, language has an innermost structure. Others use terms like "underlying." For example, the "object" governed by a specific set of verbs in Classical Greek is inflected in the genitive case, after other verbs in the dative, after others still in the accusative; but from the point of view of underlying syntactic structure the pattern of the basic clause is S(ubject) V(erb) O(bject). Disregarding the morphological case, and regardless of the label, we aim to determine the basic structure of the sentence in Greek, and also in the other early dialects, as well as in Proto-Indo-European.

We have noted that some Indo-Europeanists did not choose to do so.

Brugmann, for example, considered the data of his time adequate only for a "systematic" presentation. To evaluate his approach, we may cite the three aims in dealing with language, as stated by the eminent linguist, William Dwight Whitney: "to assemble, arrange and explain the whole body of linguistic phenomena" (1892: 6). For "arrange," subsequent linguists use "describe." By Whitney's terms, Brugmann assembled and arranged the phenomena for a grammar of the proto-language. He did not set out to explain them.

In view of the importance of Brugmann's posthumously published work on the simple sentence in Proto-Indo-European, we may examine his procedures. The book includes many excellent features, such as his repeated insistence that the sentence is the fundamental unit of language, the inclusion of single-word utterances among sentences and the authoritative generalizations supported by copious data. Like Hirt's volumes on syntax, however, it does not provide a statement on the structure of the sentence in the proto-language, nor on that of characteristic elements of the sentence, like adpositional constructions.

After preliminary remarks Brugmann deals with single-unit sentences (1925: 10–41), thereupon with "subject and predicate" (*ibid*. 42–83), then with "groups in the sentence" (*ibid*. 84–147), congruence (*ibid*. 148–86) and finally with a topic that had concerned him earlier, the various sentence formations in accordance with basic psychological functions (*ibid*. 187–229). These extend from exclamation, wish, request and threat to imagined reality and so on. That is to say, Brugmann arranges sentence patterns by their meaning and by the mental processes underlying speech. His syntactic study then is not restricted to treatment of external form; but he does not relate the patterns with one another: for example, he does not interrelate the finding that most early Vedic clauses are verb final, that they contain postpositions rather than prepositions, that their comparative structures have the standard before the adjective, and so on. Syntax for him is adequately accounted for if the structures are related to their psychological or mental functions.

9.4.1 Obstacles to an explanatory syntax in Indo-European studies

When we proceed to an explanatory presentation of syntax we are faced with several prescientific attitudes among linguists today. One is the assumption that an ideal structure must be treated in linguistic study, whether an ideal sentence on a psychological basis or on a social basis. Such an attitude has long been dispelled in the physical and biological sciences. Rather than an ideal atom of oxygen, or an ideal brain cell, or other ideal entities and structures, specialists in these fields aim at generalizations based on data. The several "kinds" of oxygen are identified by observation. Thereupon by statistical methods the principal isotope is identified and others as well. Yet many linguists still insist on dealing with an ideal NP, VP or the like. By contrast, when working appropriately in any scientific field, whether chemistry, biology, linguistics or other, scientists determine classes and their members, identifying when possible one member as most characteristic of the class. They deal similarly with processes.

A second prescientific position held by many linguists requires complete regularity in a process and complete agreement among elements of a set or class: for example, if one proposes that relative clauses precede their heads in an OV language, and the converse in a VO language, instances to the contrary are cited to support the charge by such linguists that the procedure is faulty. By a queer twist of reason, such scholars may then label the procedure of identifying the most characteristic structure as introducing a "Procrustean bed" into the field. It somehow escapes their attention that any unit proposed in language, whether a sound, a phoneme, a morpheme, a syntactic construction, etc., is the result of established procedures for identifying preponderant elements or patterns. Rejecting linguistic generalizations, they continue to deal happily with "words," assuming that these are solid representatives of reality in language.

9.5 BASES FOR AN EXPLANATORY SYNTAX

To achieve explanation in syntax, we must identify the characteristic syntactic entities and the bases for their formation. Further, we identify their interrelationships. The procedure is comparable to identifying phonological entities, e.g. /t/ or /n/ or /e/, and then noting the interrelationships among them. Just as we lack the space to discuss the theoretical bases for identifying phonological or morphological identities, we only identify the syntactic patterns and their interrelationships, referring to other treatises for support of those maintained here (see e.g. Lehmann 1978).

In accordance with the long-established recognition of the sentence as the basic unit of language we adopt as the fundamental entity of syntax the sentence, generally labeled S, though to distinguish it from the label for subject I have also used the Greek form of the letter, Σ.

The fundamental components of sentences that are not single words are *S*ubject, *O*bject, *V*erb. These may be arranged in six different orders. Of the several thousand languages investigated among the approximately 6,500 that have been identified, somewhat under 50 per cent have as basic order SOV, somewhat over 40 per cent SVO, somewhat under 10 per cent VSO; fractional numbers have one of the other possible orders. We note further that the components of SVO and VSO types are highly comparable; further, that an overt subject is not required in many utterances, especially in SOV languages. Accordingly, we posit two major types of language: OV and VO. Illustrations of patterns in the two types may be found in handbooks (e.g. Lehmann 1978b: 16–18, and sections of the essays included in the book).

As a fundamental principle, the units OV and VO are generally maintained in clauses without major insertions. That is to say, if objects (or nouns) are modified, the modification is placed before the O of OV languages and after the O of VO languages: for example, relative constructions precede nouns in OV languages like Japanese, Turkish and Hittite, but follow them in VO languages like Arabic, Spanish and English. The principle also holds for verbs, so that inflectional affixes or auxiliary elements in OV languages are placed after the V, as in Japanese and Turkish, and in VO languages before the V, as are inflections in Arabic and auxiliaries in English.

Each of the two major types has its own rules for further patterning. We note some of these briefly.

9.5.1 Parallelism among government constructions

In the use of adpositions, OV languages have postpositions; VO languages have prepositions: for example, Japanese *Nihon kara* corresponds to English *from Japan*.

In OV languages, comparatives of inequality place the standard before the adjective; in VO languages, it is placed after the adjective: for example, in Sinhalese the sentence: "The dog is bigger than the cat" reads *Balla* (dog) *baləḷətə* (cat-from) *vaḍā* (more). We may note that these three constructions – the sentence, the nominal with adposition, the comparison of inequality – all involve government. A general syntactic rule may then be proposed on consistency of government constructions in language. Either the governing element follows the element it governs or it precedes, regardless of whether the government construction is the sentence, an adpositional construction or whatever.

There are further government constructions but these may be labeled minor. Among them are titles. In OV languages "titles" are placed after the name; **Professor** Field is equivalent to Japanese *Tanaka Sensei*. The title may be considered as equivalent to an adjective in the comparative construction, and the name as standard. Similarly, given names are comparable to adjectives or titles: *John Field* is equivalent to *Tanaka Taroo*. Moreover, additive numerals observe the same order with regard to the "standard," which in the following examples is ten: *thirteen* in Japanese is *juusan* "ten-three." All such patterns are important for interpreting language material, even if only fragmentary texts are available.

The sociolinguistic situation of the texts, as well as borrowings, must always be taken into consideration: for example, the Tocharian texts are translations of Buddhist documents, and the language has been heavily influenced by a language of agglutinative structure. Tocharian texts must be examined with this information in mind. Similar consideration of the social circumstances in which texts have been produced must always be noted before such texts are employed for linguistic analyses.

9.5.2 Parallelism among modifier constructions

Each of the major constituents of the sentence may be modified. Since the O element is generally filled by nouns, we deal with its modifiers by referring to nouns. In keeping with the general principle, as we have noted, relative clauses precede nouns in OV languages, follow them in VO. Genitive constructions and adjective constructions are viewed as reduced forms of relative clauses. Accordingly, they typically observe the same order as do relative clauses; genitives as well as adjectives follow the nouns they modify in VO languages like Arabic, precede them in OV languages like Japanese and Turkish.

It is important to remember that syntactic change takes place slowly; we may then find languages that have relative constructions after their nouns, but adjectives before them, as in English. Such problems may be clarified if texts are available over a long period; the textual tradition of English, scarcely more than a thousand years, provides evidence that during this period genitives shifted from a position before nouns to a position after them. Today most genitival constructions are made with *of* phrases in contrast with preceding genitive forms of nouns in Old English. Even earlier, before the time of origin of most of our Old English texts, the position of relative clauses had been shifted from the position preceding nouns to after them. "Irregular" patterning of constructions of this type is highly important for determining the direction of change in a language.

Verbal modifiers may be expressed variously, through intonation, through affixes, or through words. Among the central modifiers are interrogative markers. When expressed segmentally rather than through intonation, an interrogative marker follows the V in OV languages, precedes it in VO languages: for example, in Japanese *Do you understand* is expressed by *wakarimasu ka*. The English auxiliary *do*, when placed initially as in such sentences, has become little more than an interrogative marker.

Further, sentence negation is similarly placed, though typically closer to the V. *Don't you understand* is expressed by Japanese *Wakarimasen ka*. Negative signals in clauses typically stand between the interrogative marker and the verbal root.

Verbs may have many additional modifiers; see 8.8. These typically observe a relative order with regard to one another, much like sentence negation and interrogation markers. Those indicating causative meaning, as well as others comparable to derivational markers, stand close to the root of the principal verb. Expressions of tense and aspect generally follow such markers; then modal expressions are indicated; and, if they are indicated on verbs, expressions for reflexive or reciprocal meaning follow.

When examining the syntactic structures of any language, we identify the means of indicating such modifiers. We then determine their relationship with regard to these generalizations.

9.5.3 Further syntactic constructions and processes

Typological investigation of syntax involves further structures, such as procedures of coordination, of subordination, placement of adverbial clauses (causal, result, concessive, etc.), complementation (object clauses, infinitives, verbal nouns, etc.). It also requires attention to processes like pronominalization, anaphora, passivization, clefting and so on. The treatment of these constructions according to the basic syntactic pattern, whether VO or OV, must be left to presentations elsewhere. We may note, however, that object clauses, as they are often identified in traditional handbooks, or complements, are comparable to objects. They then occupy the position of the O in OV and VO languages. That position results in characteristically different manners of expression. VO languages typically use conjunctions, such as *that*, to introduce complements. OV languages, by contrast, may use nouns, such as *situation*, *fact* in reduced meaning. The basis of the difference is clear. It would make little point to place a conjunction at the end of a preposed object clause, somewhat before the verb is expressed. On the other hand, it would also be pointless to introduce an object clause in VO languages like English with a noun indicating a situation. Languages of both types have now been adequately studied so that accurate information on the structure of each is available.

The information that has been assembled on these patterns and their arrangement has made possible an explanatory syntax, as we will note with examples below.

9.6 PROCEDURES FOR DETERMINING THE SYNTACTIC STRUCTURE OF A LANGUAGE

In dealing with any language we need to take into account that it, like all social conventions, is open to constant change. The change may be in accordance with internal patterning, or it may be the result of external influence. Each of these kinds of change is labeled by awkward terms: internal-patterning change by the term "drift," externally influenced change by the term "borrowing."

All change requires an extended period of time for acceptance in the language; syntactic change may require a longer period to be carried out than does phonological or morphological change: for example, the voicing of intervocalic American English /t/, as in *butter*, has been under way from the nineteenth century; it has affected all intervocalic /t/s before unstressed vowels, and when these are followed by /l m r/ as in *pretty*, *bottle*, *bottom*, *butter*, though not those followed by /n/ as in *button*. The syntactic change of preposed genitives to postposed genitives, as in Old English *godcundre lāre word* to New English *words of divine doctrine*, has been going on for a millennium; 10 per cent of genitive constructions still precede their heads in current English, largely when the genitive is of an animate noun, as in *Cædmon's words*.

Because languages are constantly undergoing change, and because such change, especially at the syntactic level, requires a long period, virtually all languages include patterns that do not accord with the patterning expected in languages of their type. For example, English, unlike French and Spanish, still maintains OV order for adjectives; in French, on the other hand, that order holds only for very common adjectives, much as morphological "irregularities" are maintained in common lexical items, as of English *mouse* : *mice*. The pertinent syntactic change may have been inaugurated later in the Germanic than in the Romance languages, or other influences may have affected the process of change. Solutions to such problems must be left to specialists in the languages concerned.

9.6.1 Conclusions based on typological patterns

Observations concerning key typological patterning are of great value in historical linguistics. By judicious use of such patterns we can determine earlier stages of the syntax: for example, from the position of adjectives alone we could propose that at one time English was an OV language. A few pages of virtually any Old English text provide full support for the conclusion.

Another observation must be kept in mind on the use of our information concerning typological structures. In discourse, especially literary discourse, the normal patterns are often replaced by abnormal patterns, some of them archaic: for example, in relatively recent English poetry the noun for air in motion may be pronounced to rhyme with *kind*, as in Shakespeare's *Blow, blow thou winter wind*. Rules of syntax are similarly "broken," as in Longfellow's *This is the forest **primeval***. Such departures from normal usage are referred to as *marked*, by a term adopted from Prague Circle linguists. The term was introduced in referring to phonological items that have an additional "mark" that might be lost in certain contexts, such as the mark of voice in final voiced stops of German, where the nominative form of *Bades* "of the bath" is *Bad* [baːt], homophonous with the past-tense form *bat* "requested." Linguists give special attention to items that are marked; as the example of German *Bad-* indicates, marked elements are likely to be replaced by unmarked counterparts. Employing such information, whether or not intuitively, literary figures use "marking" to achieve special effects.

Since much of our early material is poetic, we may have great difficulty determining its basic syntactic type, especially when we make use of the patterns that are readily modified, such as sentence order, order of adjectives and genitives, position of verbal modifiers. We then seek patterns that poets do not modify. One example is the type of adposition; except in archaic expressions, speakers of OV languages would not use prepositions, and speakers of VO languages would not use postpositions.

Another useful pattern, when available, is that for comparison of inequality. As noted above, a poet would simply not modify a pattern like those listed by Hirt (1921–37 VII: 251): Greek *mélitos glukíōn* "sweeter than honey < honey-from sweeter"; Old Icelandic *sōlu fegra* "more beautiful than the sun < sun-from more-beautiful," Sanskrit *yo mártyasya mánaso jávīyān* "he who is faster than human thought < who human-of thought-of faster." When we find such comparatives, we can conclude without doubt that the language at the time of the poet, or at the time his tradition was established, was OV in type. Since we find comparative constructions like these in more than three widely separated branches of the Indo-European family, we can conclude without possibility of contradiction that the proto-language was OV in structure.

These observations about language in use may also be of help in evaluating conclusions proposed by scholars who in sedulous zeal count out all sentence patterns for position of the verb, or for location of adjectives with regard to nouns, or of genitives, and on the basis of their enumerations propose that a language is of a given type, often VO. One mourns at the wasted energy.

A further observation might be made about constructions that may not follow the typical pattern. They may be highly useful in providing information about the relative chronology or native position of the expression under consideration or of other similar expressions. For example, Classical Greek *héneka* "because of" is the only "preposition" that stands after its noun; when we know its etymology, we can account for that position. It is a noun phrase consisting of the neuter numeral for 1 and an old neuter noun meaning "cause."

To provide a modern example of irregular order we may note the title *attorney general*; it is a frozen expression that has remained unchanged in its order from the time that many governmental expressions were borrowed into English from French. Even such expressions need to be treated with care; currently, at least in some states, the person who occupies the position is often referred to as General. The frozen expression may be reinterpreted in accordance with the current structure of the language and modified accordingly.

In short, to deal with any linguistic material, whether of the present or the past, one must apply the principles that were known in former days as philological and were considered an essential element of education rather than the evanescent theories that now are the mark of many in humanistic activities. Every form, every word, every sentence, every text must be interpreted in its context, as Meillet has pointed out so lucidly in the last chapter of his unsurpassed treatise on linguistic method (1925:103–16). The validity of any linguistic generalization depends entirely on precision in the treatment of material of language and in application of methods used in its analysis.

Applying such care, we examine texts of the past with the aim of explaining their syntax and the syntax of their time. Using this procedure with texts of the various branches, we go on to apply the comparative method to determine the syntax of the proto-language. We therefore reconstruct that syntax by means of the same principles that we apply in reconstructing the phonology and the morphology of Proto-Indo-European.

9.7 THE SYNTACTIC STRUCTURE OF PROTO-INDO-EUROPEAN

A large number of examples have been given in this chapter and previous chapters that demonstrate the OV structure of the proto-language. Among these are examples from Hittite, from Vedic Sanskrit, from Greek and also from other languages, such as the Germanic inscription on the horn found at Gallehus (see p. 60). More could be cited; many are given in *Proto-Indo-European Syntax* and other subsequent treatments of Indo-European grammar (Lehmann 1974; Gamkrelidze and Ivanov 1984; Stepanov 1989). And virtually any early text in any of the languages, including even branches attested in very late times, like Lithuanian, supports the classification of the language as OV. We limit ourselves then to a few examples.

A frequently cited sentence from the *Śatapathabrāhmaṇa* may be taken as a paradigm of an Indo-European sentence:

víśaḥ   kṣatríyāya balím   haranti
m nom pl   m dat sg   m acc sg 3 pl pers ind
villagers   to-prince   tax   (they-)pay
"The villagers pay taxes to the prince."

Further examples may be given from the first clause of the initial lines of the two major Greek epics:

mênin   áeide   (*Iliad*)
f acc sg 2 sg imper
wrath   sing
"Sing of the wrath"
ándra   moi énnepe   (*Odyssey*)
m acc sg dat 2 sg imper
man   me tell
"Tell me of a man"

The OV order demonstrated in such examples is evident in other government constructions. Examples of OV comparatives have been cited in 9.6.1. When we examine the texts of the dialects for postpositions rather than prepositions we find evidence as late as Old English. In his careful study that lists the pertinent passages with reference to the texts, Fritz Wende investigated some time ago "postposed prepositions in Anglo-Saxon" (1915: Palaestra LXX). He found that normally prepositions precede their objects, as in *to him*; but he also noted 275 occurrences of the pattern *him . . . to com*, 148 of the pattern *com . . . him . . . to* and 59 of the pattern *him . . . com . . . to*, where *him* represents personal pronouns and *to* any postposition. When we compare the predominant use of postpositions in Hittite, and their frequent use in early Greek as well as other early texts, we are left with little question about OV patterning of adpositions in the parent language.

Relative constructions of the OV type are commonly attested in Vedic Sanskrit, as Delbrück pointed out (1871: 33–4). As an example we may cite *Rigveda* 1.85.12:

yā́   vaḥ   śárma   śaśamānáya sánti tridhā́tūni dāśúṣe
which to-you shelters for-striver   are   threefold to-worshipper
yachatā́dhi
extend-towards
"Extend the threefold shelters to the worshipper, which you have for the striver."

Similar preposing of relative constructions is typical in Hittite (see Justus 1976). Such preposing is also found in Greek and early Latin, although in later texts the relative clause is placed after its antecedent. In keeping with the early position of the relative modifying clause, other types of nominal modifiers, that is genitives and adjectives, generally stand before nouns in the early texts.

Moreover, as objects precede verbs so object clauses are placed before the verbs that govern them in Hittite, as in the following example (Justus 1980):

nu kas-   kuit memai n- at zik sakti
ptc this-one what says   ptc it you know
"You will know what this one says." (*ibid*. 196).

Similarly subordinate clauses precede principal clauses, as we may illustrate with an example from one of the ancient Latin laws:

Si   intestato moritur, cui   suus   heres   nec escit,
conj adv   3 sg pers dat   m nom sg m nom sg ptc 3 sg pers
if   intestate dies   to-him own   heir   not is
adgnatus proximus familiam   habeto
m nom sg m nom sg f acc sg   3 sg imper
agnate   nearest   household shall-have
"If someone dies without a will, and does not have an heir in his family, the nearest agnate male shall have the household."

Further examples of early OV patterning have been cited in Lehmann

(1974). Others may also be found in the grammars of the early dialects, such as that of Friedrich for Hittite and Speyer for Vedic Sanskrit. They provide overwhelming evidence of OV structure for the proto-language.

9.8 THE PATTERN OF DRIFT IN THE EARLY DIALECTS

When change takes place in a language, it is guided by the structure in which the items are found. With its analytic structure English has created further verb patterns by use of auxiliaries, not through suffixes. In contrast with causatives made with the Indo-European affix *-éyo-*, Germanic *-ja-*, as in Gothic *nasjan*, causative constructions are made with verb phrases such as "cause to go," etc. The verb constructions introduced into English follow the same pattern, i.e. "is going, does go." By contrast, in the early dialects, new verb constructions were made with affixes, such as *-k-* in Greek, *-v-* in Latin, *-d-* in Germanic and so on. And at an earlier time, further verb constructions were made by adapting ablaut variants of roots. Similar situations might be cited for phonology and for syntax. As a result, when languages change, the result seems to be guided in a given direction. The process is widely referred to with Sapir's term "drift."

All of the Indo-European dialects change in accordance with the same pattern. As illustrated above, in inflectional morphology verb forms are created by means of affixes. Others are produced by means of compound expressions, as in the perfect forms of the Latin passive, e.g. *amātus sum* "I have been loved" as opposed to *amāvī* "I have loved." These are clearly later than the suffixed verb forms, as is evident in dialects attested earlier than is Latin: for example, Sanskrit has created a periphrastic future with an agent noun accompanied by forms of the verb "be," as in *dātásmi* "I will give"; and the periphrastic forms of the Romance and Germanic languages are well known. When we examine the verbal forms of the various dialects, we can describe their drift as movement from inflected forms through suffixed forms to periphrastic forms.

The general pattern of change in the verb is therefore from synthetic to analytic structure. A similar pattern is found in the noun phrase. If, for example, we examine the expression of definiteness, we find in Germanic, Baltic and Slavic an indication through inflection of adjectives. The so-called weak inflection in these branches signals a definite nominal expression. In the course of time special words were introduced in the Germanic languages for this purpose, definite and indefinite articles. They had been introduced earlier in Greek. The earlier pattern for expressing definiteness is unknown; but in the dialects for which we have evidence, the development is comparable to that in verbs: from suffixation to analytic expression.

Proceeding to examination of a syntactic pattern we may note that of complementation. In Hittite, as in an OV language, complements precede their governing verb. Residues of that construction are also found in other early dialects; but subsequently complements follow their governing verb, as we would expect in VO structure. It is significant that the complementizers and also the complement constructions vary from dialect to dialect. In Indic, complementizers were made with forms of *ya-*. In Greek the general complementizer is *hóti*.

In Germanic the complementizer varies from dialect to dialect, for example, from *at* and *þat* in Old Icelandic to Old English *þæt* and to *dhazs* or *hweo* in early Old High German. In addition, infinitives are widely used, also in the accusative-with-infinitive construction. Examples of the two constructions may be given from the *Anglo-Saxon Chronicle*:

> þa budon hie hiera mægum þæt hie gesunde from eodon
> "then they offered to their kinsmen that they might go away unharmed"
> Se cing het hi feohtan agien Pihtas.
> "The king commanded them to fight against the Picts."

The choice of complement varied with the matrix verb, and also from text to text in specific dialects, as illustrated in the set of articles "on complementation in the early Germanic Languages" in the *Journal of the Linguistic Association of the Southwest* I: 3–4 (1976). The variation of construction within Germanic, on the one hand, and among the various Indo-European dialects demonstrates that a new pattern was being introduced. However, in accordance with the increasing VO structure, the complements are parallel from dialect to dialect – either made up of clauses introduced by a complementizer or of one of the newly developed infinitives in the dialect in question.

Accordingly, syntactic change, like morphological change, observes a common drift throughout the Indo-European family. Subsequent influences may have disrupted the development, or modified it, as in Indic, with some dialects heavily influenced by Dravidian. Yet the process continues, as in English, with the introduction of a further complement construction made with the gerund in *-ing*.

9.9 SELECTED REPLACEMENT OF OV PATTERNS THAT ILLUSTRATE THE SHIFT TO VO STRUCTURE

A characteristic verb form of OV languages, and possibly limited to them, expresses reflexivization through suffixes. The form, or a comparable form, may also express reciprocal meaning. These are primary functions of the middle in the proto-language and the early dialects. In addition, the middle indicated that the action of the verb was applicable to the subject of the sentence. On shifting to VO structure, such a suffixed form would conflict with the structure of the language.

The middle was then lost in the dialects, and its meanings came to be expressed in accordance with their structure. A typical pattern of expression was created through use of reflexive and reciprocal pronouns.

These differ from language to language, even within branches, as illustrated by the use of personal pronouns for the first two persons in German as opposed to forms with -*self* in English. The predominant pattern in the Indo-European dialects is like that of German.

Reflexive adjectives, on the other hand, were developed on the basis of various lexical items. One of the interesting devices is the use of adjectives meaning "dear, beloved." While the meaning is parallel, the item itself differs, as may be illustrated by Sanskrit *priyás*, Greek *phílos*, Old High German *suāsat*. In the course of time these were replaced, as patterning among elements indicating reflexive use came to rest on similar elements. Typically the genitive of the reflexive was substituted, as in English *my*, *your*, *his*, *her*. The general process is in accordance with the drift discussed above; but the new pattern of expression cannot be described as a reflex of the early manner of expression. Instead, a category in the language was remolded in accordance with the possibilities of that structure of that language. We therefore cannot reconstruct the Indo-European expression of the reflexive, nor of the reciprocal, from the modern languages. The changes in expressing these categories illustrate how in the course of time the earlier grammatical structure of a language may be irrecoverable.

Postposed placement of adpositions has been less completely lost. As noted in 9.2, Delbrück assumed only postpositions for early Vedic; Hittite supports the conclusion that adpositions were postposed in the proto-language. We find occasional examples in the later dialects, such as Greek *oíkade* "homeward" and the *Beowulf* line *Scedelandum in* "in Scandinavia." By the time of modern English we find only frozen adverbial expressions, like *herein*, *hereafter*. Moreover, these are restricted to the written language, largely in legal contexts; if used in conversation they are considered stilted. Yet, because we know that adverbs often maintain older patterning, we regard these as residues. Using them, we may tentatively propose that the earlier structure was OV.

The position of the genitive in English provides evidence supporting this assumption. When the possessor is animate, the genitive commonly precedes its head, as in *George's home* rather than *the home of George*. According to a study by Fries, the OV preposed position gave way to the postposed position in a period of approximately a thousand years (1940). Assuming that we had no earlier English texts, we might on the basis of the current situation suggest that of Old English; but our suggestion would be more cogent if we had further such residues.

Indo-European linguistics is fortunate in having early texts in several dialects. These permit us to reconstruct the syntax of the proto-language with assurance. They also provide guidelines for syntactic reconstruction of other language families, and of Pre-Indo-European. Wider application of such reconstruction will provide improved guidelines for interpretation of residues and aberrant constructions.

10 The syntax of Pre-Indo-European

10.1 THEORETICAL PROCEDURES

Almost 200 years of attention to Indo-European linguistics has resulted in capable handbooks that treat the various components of grammar and also the lexicon. These handbooks have been guided by theoretical views that were established at various periods, and applied by subsequent linguists, often with little further consideration. As indicated repeatedly, the basic theoretical tool in Indo-European linguistics, as in all historical linguistics, is the comparative method. With it Indo-Europeanists have achieved notable results, including impressive reconstruction of the proto-language and some explanation of its patterning. The earlier chapters have examined the results, with special attention to the theoretical views under which they were achieved.

10.1.1 The importance of identifying the type of a language

As we will see in this chapter, the results of comparison may be unimpressive unless they are interpreted with regard to the structure of the language to which they are ascribed. For example, almost a century ago Uhlenbeck reconstructed an Indo-European case system consisting of an agent and a patient rather than a nominative and an accusative (1901); but since he proposed no further support for the revised case system, his proposal is routinely referred to while its conclusions are disregarded. We may cite other examples, such as Benveniste's attempt to account for the lack of a verb "have" in the proto-language; see 9.5.7. Unless any proposed reconstruction or explanation, or even a lexical item, accords with other characteristics of the stage of the language for which it is assumed, the reconstruction or explanation carries little weight. As a minimum we must characterize Proto-Indo-European or any language stage as accusative, ergative, or active, and account for our proposals and hypotheses with reference to the identified type.

Sources for this chapter: Klimov (1977, 1983); Gamkrelidze and Ivanov (1984); Stepanov (1989); Lehmann (1958, 1989).

10.1.2 The need to treat a language with reference to the society maintaining it

For the three remaining chapters we will deal with evidence that leads to fuller explanation of the proto-language, in part by examining it in relation to the society that spoke it. The evidence is not as extensive nor as cohesive as that available for reconstructing the late phase of the proto-language. Our earliest recorded texts, those in the Anatolian sub-branch and in Mycenaean Greek, are transmitted in writing systems that are poorly designed for Indo-European languages with their many closed syllables. Moreover, the texts are restricted in content – those in the Anatolian languages largely dealing with political and religious matters, those in Mycenaean Greek with data for taxation. Nonetheless they provide crucial evidence for conclusions about earlier stages of the proto-language that for clarity we refer to as Pre-Indo-European.

10.1.3 The uses of residues

In accordance with long-established procedures in historical linguistics we make use of residues in the sub-branches. As we have pointed out above, the shift in base of the first-person pronoun from *I* to *me* in current English, with parallels in other Indo-European languages, is a long-maintained residue from Pre-Indo-European. Although such retentions are of great interest, the residues of chief importance are found in texts of the early period; but we seek out residues throughout all the texts of the sub-branches, and use them to supplement the conclusions achieved through use of the comparative method and the method of internal reconstruction.

10.1.4 Reconstruction carried out "systematically" or by current linguistic principles

When we reconstruct Pre-Indo-European, it is important to recall the basic procedure of Brugmann, by which he disavowed historical treatment of the proto-language, and instead decided to present it systematically. We have decribed his procedure and summarized the results in 3.1. The publications of Brugmann are of great value in providing reliable data, even though he could not take into consideration the data as yet undiscovered in the Anatolian branch, nor the data of Tocharian and Mycenaean Greek. However, continuation of a "systematic" approach in interpreting those data, without indication or possibly even recognition of Brugmann's aims by subsequent scholars, leads to compilations of facts, not a grammar or a dictionary. Lexical items that are reconstructed may simply be schematic, not to speak of phrases and grammatical constructions. In dealing with any language, whether attested or reconstructed, it is essential, as Bopp already recognized, to determine the system. Without such an approach, there is no possibility of achieving knowledge of what Schlegel called the innermost structure of the language, whether of Proto- or of Pre-Indo-European.

In moving to carry out that aim, we make special use of two sets of data. One set consists of elements that are not in accord with the system proposed for the late proto-language. The other set consists of conclusions determined by study of all languages that are available, that is, the so-called universals.

10.1.5 Identification of aberrant elements in the early dialects

The usefulness of examining discordant elements was sharpened by knowledge of the Anatolian languages, especially Hittite. Problems that were recognized earlier, such as the tantalizing similarities between the perfect tense and the middle voice, were illuminated by the reflexes in Anatolian, which are structured differently from those in the other dialects. The Anatolian data in this way provided a key to their solution. That solution is supported by the results of typological study that has informed us of languages considerably different in type from accusative or ergative languages.

Before we proceed towards an explanatory grammar of the proto-language with reference to its earlier stages, we first sketch briefly elements of the grammar of Hittite that have been especially important for understanding the structure of those earlier stages. These are not the OV characteristics, like preposed relative constructions or postpositions or OV comparative constructions. Those constructions to be sure are important in confirming the OV system of Proto-Indo-European as determined a century ago by Delbrück; but Hittite texts provide additional data that permit us to reconstruct earlier stages, that is, Pre-Indo-European. The conclusions drawn from these data are in turn supported by residues in the other dialects.

10.2 ELEMENTS OF HITTITE GRAMMAR THAT ASSIST US IN DETERMINING THE SYSTEM OF PRE-INDO-EUROPEAN

Three sets of data in Hittite grammar are important for determining the earlier system. One is the sparse inflection of nominal elements. The plural of nouns is very poorly developed. Three of the oblique cases in the plural, the genitive, dative and locative, have the same ending *-as*; this ending is also found in the genitive singular. The two other cases attested in the plural, the ablative and instrumental, have the same endings as do the singular forms. In short, the only case forms that differ in the singular and the plural are the nominative and the accusative. The second fact of importance is the presence of the *hi*-inflection of the verb comparable to the *mi*-inflection. The third is the use of particles instead of verbal inflections to indicate modality and the like.

10.2.1 Defective nominal inflection in Hittite

Under a systematic approach in Indo-European studies, the defective inflectional system of the Hittite noun was accounted for either by assuming the language to be creolized or an early form in the development from a monosyllabic to an inflectional type of language; both are explanations of last resort.

As we note in section 10.3, languages of active type have little nominal inflection, especially in the plural. Identification of Pre-Indo-European as an active language permits us to account for the pattern of nominal inflection in Hittite. Other evidence supports that assumption. We find very few instances of the plural oblique case forms in the *Rigveda*.

10.2.2 The two Hittite conjugations of the verb, *-mi* and *-hi*

In contrast with the languages attested later, among them Greek and Latin, Hittite has two conjugations of the verb, known by their first person singular as given in the heading here. In each there is an active and a medio(-passive) voice. Each voice has a present and a preterite tense, and an imperative mood, with forms for three persons in singular and plural. In order to be fully explicit about the system, and its differences from the set of forms proposed for the proto-language by Szemerényi among others, we point out that there are no verbal forms for moods besides the imperative; further, that the imperative, like the present and preterite, is inflected for three persons in the singular but only two in the plural. There are also nominal forms of the verb, but these do not concern us here.

10.2.2.1 The limited number of distinctive forms in the hi-conjugation

The *hi*-conjugation is inflected like the *mi*-conjugation in all but the three forms of the present indicative. The other endings of the two conjugations are not without their interest; but they have no direct pertinence for our discussion. While the three present singular endings of the *mi*-conjugation are exactly those of the comparable Sanskrit and Greek conjugation (*mi*, *si*, *zi* – with affricated *t* before *i*), these endings in the *hi*-conjugation are *-hi* (*-ahhi*), *-ti*, *-i*. There is little question that the *hi*-endings are equivalent to the endings of the perfect in Sanskrit and Greek. Interpreting them with the help of the laryngeal theory, we may reconstruct them as *-he*, *-the*, *-e*, and at an earlier stage *-h*, *-th*, -0. It is also noteworthy that the third person plural endings in the preterite are *-er*.

10.2.2.2 Similarities between the hi-conjugation and the medio-passive

Moreover, the three singular endings of the medio-passive closely resemble those of the *hi*-conjugation. For both conjugations the endings in the indicative singular present are *-hahari*, *-tati*, *-tari*, in the preterite *-(ha)hat*, *-tat*, *-tat* with variants, such as an additional *i* in the preterite (see Friedrich 1960: 77ff.). The middle endings are clearly remodeled, and extended with the suffixes *-ri* and *-t(i)*. Accordingly the markers *-h-* in the first singular and *-t-* in the second are comparable to those of the *hi*-inflection; and the characteristic marker of the second is extended to the third person.

Indo-Europeanists have long been concerned about the similarities between the perfect and the middle, as we note in greater detail below. Both indicate state or the result of action, rather than action. The similarities between the two sets of endings in Hittite as well as the additional syllables in the longer forms suggest that they have the same earlier source and that those of the middle were differentiated from the endings retained for the perfect.

10.2.2.3 Hittite characteristics comparable to those of active languages

The basic insights leading to an explanation of these three sets of data have come from an understanding of active languages. In them the essential distinction between forms of the verb consists of a contrast between verbs associated with animate (active) meaning and those associated with inanimate (stative) meaning. When we examine the roots that inflect in accordance with either conjugation in Hittite, we find a similar contrast. Among roots inflecting by the *mi*-conjugation are *ep-* "seize," *wek-* "request," *kuen-* "strike," *kuer-* "cut," *sanh-* "look for"; among roots inflecting by the *hi*-conjugation are *ak-* "die," *sak-* "know," *pahs-* "protect." Hittite is no longer an active language, and accordingly there most likely was a redistribution of roots, as of *pahs-*. But the array of meanings of roots in either conjugation is still remarkably similar to the distribution among active and stative verbs in active languages.

10.2.3 The use of particles for modal purposes

A remarkable feature of Hittite is frequent use of particles. Study of these has been directed largely at their position, both in the clause and in regard to each other. Generally standing at the beginning of clauses, they are found in sequences like the following: *mahhan-ma-mu-kan* "when-however-me-to," *kinun-ma-wa-tu-za* "now-however-quotative-you-self" (see Friedrich 1960: 147–69). Cited without the remainder of the sentence they may seem awkward. They indicate the basic structure of sentences and their relation to other sentences in a text. In this way they fill the role of inflections in accusative and ergative languages, especially verbal inflections for moods.

Leaving additional discussion of particles aside for the time being, we may cite one illustration of their modal use. The sentence involves use of *man* indicating a contrary-to-fact situation: *man-kan mān ANA ¹Attarsiya hwiswetenn-a kastita-man akten* "even if you had escaped at Attarsiya with your lives, you would nonetheless have died of hunger" (Friedrich 1960: 166). The verbal forms *hwisweten* and *akten* are "indicative"; modal modification is indicated by the particles *man* in conjunction with *mān*. In the dialects attested later, the modal meaning would have been signaled at least in part by modal forms of the verb.

As we note below, the use of particles is a major characteristic of active languages. Each of the early languages, notably Homeric Greek and also Vedic Sanskrit, makes frequent use of particles. In none, however, do particles fill as many functions as in Hittite. In the other dialects the development of modal inflections in the verb has provided means for expressing modal meanings, with resultant loss of particles.

10.3 CHARACTERISTICS OF ACTIVE LANGUAGES

As a principal characteristic of active languages, congruence plays a much larger role than it does in accusative and ergative languages. In these, government is prominent; sentences, as well as verbal and adpositional constructions in them, are bound together through government constructions. That is to say, transitivity is a central feature of accusative and ergative languages. In active languages, by contrast, the binding element of sentences is brought about by agreement between types of lexical elements. We may review their characteristics in somewhat more detail than we have above.

10.3.1 The lexicon

The structure of the lexicon is central in active languages. Both nouns and verbs fall into one of two sets: active or inactive. Nouns are distinguished as animate or inanimate, verbs as representing action or state. Examples of the animate (active) are nouns indicating persons and animals, such as "human, horse, cow"; by contrast, nouns indicating things, for example, "earth, stick, stone," belong to the inactive (stative) class. Verbs of the active class indicate action, often with voluntative force, such as "lead, put, throw," while verbs of the inactive (stative) class denote states or involuntary actions, such as "know, shine, think."

The lexicon then may contain two items for objects that can be viewed as active or inactive, and also for activities that can be viewed as states as well as actions. Typical examples of such objects are "fire" and "water." Speakers may regard fire as a vibrant process and water as moving, or treat them as states. Similarly, items like "lie, stand" may refer to the process of lying down or standing up, or to states resulting from such a process. In view of the basic principle of agreement or congruence, active nouns are associated in sentences with active verbs, and inactive nouns with inactive verbs.

10.3.2 Characteristics of verb systems in active languages

The principal inflection to indicate relationships in sentences is found in the verb system. Separate conjugations are found for active as opposed to stative verbs. Because action is associated especially with animate nouns, inflection for the active conjugation is more extensive than that for the stative conjugation; the stative conjugation may even be defective in such categories as the plural. Affective verbs fall into a distinct third class; they correspond to impersonal verbs in the later dialects that express meanings like "it is painful, it is a matter of shame, it is cold."

In keeping with the prominence given to consideration of action or state, verbs are inflected for aspect rather than tense. Moreover, since transitivity is not a central force, there is no place for a passive; because objects lack a role in active languages, the passive is not essential for thematizing them. Verb systems, on the other hand, have inflections for centrifugal and centripetal force; centrifugal meaning corresponds to that of the Indo-European active, centripetal to the middle. And since individuals are not viewed as possessing objects, active languages lack a verb for "have." Instead, items corresponding to those viewed as possessed in accusative languages are portrayed as in location near the individual.

10.3.3 Characteristics of the pronominal system

As another characteristic in keeping with the concentration on activity or state, active languages distinguish between inclusive and exclusive pronouns for the first person plural. Inclusive pronouns depict relationships that involve shared activity on the part of the person or persons addressed. On the other hand, since exclusive pronouns report a situation that does not involve the persons addressed, they typically report a state of affairs or the result of previous actions. In this way the pronominal system corresponds to the structure of active languages.

10.3.4 Characteristics of the nominal system

Active nouns, typically referring to animate beings, are likely to be found in constructions indicating agents for verbs of action, as well as in constructions indicating the items affected by such action. Inactive nouns, on the other hand, are more likely to represent affected items, whether as the result of actions or as patients with inactive verbs. Active nouns then have two inflected forms, one signaling the role of agent in an action, the other indicating an item affected by an action or the participant in a state.

Moreover, since nominal inflection is designed largely to indicate agreement between nouns and verbs, indication of place or time through inflection is absent in active languages. That is to say, there are few oblique forms or none. A genitive/possessive case form as well is not essential. Relationships like "possession" are associated with animate nouns; the thing possessed is indicated by means of expressions indicating contiguity.

Finally, forms for the plural are weakly developed. Nouns, however, have affixes to designate a collective or mass noun.

10.3.5 Consequences of the earlier active structure

The earlier active structure of Pre-Indo-European then accounts for the characteristics listed above that have remained without explanation. Among them are problems in the verbal system, such as the lack of evidence for reconstructing a verb meaning "have." Moreover, the poor inflection of stative verbs provides an explanation for the defective inflection of the Indo-European perfect – which indicates a state. It also allows us to account for the small number of characteristic forms in the Hittite *hi*-conjugation.

Similarly, in the nominal inflection we may understand why there are no separate forms for the neuter (inactive) nominative and accusative in the proto-language and the early dialects, and why the neuter nominative–accusative has the same form as the masculine accusative. In the uses of these forms the noun indicates an item affected by an action or a state. If such nouns referred to an inanimate item, they became neuters in Proto-Indo-European. If, on the other hand, they indicated animate items, the ending characteristic of inanimates (neuters) in the nominative and accusative was used to mark them when they were used as patients, that is, as accusatives.

We now examine in greater detail patterns in the Indo-European languages that we may clarify as residues of active structure. The patterns were identified by earlier Indo-Europeanists, but remained without explanation because the characteristics of active structure were unknown.

10.4 CHARACTERISTICS OF PROTO-INDO-EUROPEAN SYNTAX AND THE LEXICON IDENTIFIED, THOUGH NOT ACCOUNTED FOR, BY EARLIER INDO-EUROPEANISTS

In the presentations of syntax by Delbrück, Brugmann and Meillet, items are identified that do not agree with the patterning of the proto-language as based primarily on Sanskrit, Greek and Latin. These can now be accounted for as residues of the earlier active structure.

10.4.1 Autonomy of the word in the sentence

In characterizing the syntax of Proto-Indo-European, Meillet stated that "the word is autonomous and suffices of itself to indicate its sense and its role in discourse" (1937: 356). His statement implies that the verb does not govern the object in a sentence; rather, the relationship is determined from the specific meaning of each form. Somewhat earlier he defined the nominative as indicating the topic of the sentence, adding only in quotation marks that it designates the subject (*ibid.* 342). That is to say, sentences in the proto-language were not bound together by means of government constructions, but simply by the relationships between the inherent meanings of the components and their inflections in a sentence. The characterization applies to the structure of sentences in active languages.

10.4.2 An earlier gender system of animacy or inanimacy

When we compare Meillet's description of gender in the proto-language, we find further similarity to the patterning of active languages. Positing two genders, animate and inanimate, he goes on to state that

> to comprehend the value of the "animate" and "inanimate" genders, it is necessary to assume different views from those for modern languages. In Indo-European, everything that moves, everything that acts may be considered "animate." It may even happen that a given notion accords with two nouns, one "animate," the other "inanimate" (*ibid.* 339–40).

As examples he gives the two competing forms for "fire" and "water." For fire "as an object" and "in neuter gender" he lists Greek *pûr*, Umbrian *pir*, Armenian *hur*, Old High German *fiur*; for fire "as an active being" and "in animate (masculine) gender" he cites Sanskrit *agníḥ*, Old Slavic *ognĭ*, Latin *ignis*, adding that in Vedic *agníḥ* is a "divine personality" (340). The description is in total accordance with the treatment of nouns in an active language. As we have stated above, in such languages items like fire are often represented by two lexical items, one in active or animate inflection, the other in inactive or inanimate.

While Meillet described the proto-language in this way, his explanation for its structure differs from ours. Noting that other nouns are classified as animate or inanimate, he ascribes the alignment to a semi-civilized mentality. Support for that conclusion in his eyes comes from animate gender for visible biological entities like the word for "foot," e.g. Greek *poús*, Latin *pēs*, and for "hand," while nouns indicating interior organs are classed as inanimate, such as the word for "liver," Sanskrit *yákrt*, Greek *hêpar*, Latin *iecur*. In addition, nouns indicating trees are animate, while those of the fruits are inanimate. And he cites other nouns indicating active forces that are of animate gender, such as the "religious formula," Vedic *mántraḥ*, and the wind. Remarkably, the alignment is comparable to that in active languages, for in them exterior parts of the body are treated as animate while interior organs as treated as inanimate. Meillet's analysis of the nominal system then must be aligned with linguistic structure, not with the state of civilization or mentality of the speakers.

10.4.3 Lack of transitivity in given verbs

Although transitivity is an important feature of the Indo-European verbal system it may be lacking in frequently occurring verbs. Homeric *bállō*, for example, can mean either "throw" or "hit." Moreover, Greek *ékhō* is used in the sense "have" or "be," as in *eû ékhei* "things are going well" and *lógos ékhei* "the story goes," in contrast with the many transitive uses of the verb. In contrast, Delbrück discusses at some length the use of the accusative with "verbs of being" (1893: 370–2). His predecessor, Curtius, had accepted use of the accusative with reflexes of the Proto-Indo-European root *es-* "be" in Greek, a view Delbrück rejected; but he admits use of the accusative with reflexes of *bhew-*, as in the early Sanskrit clause *sá idám bhaviṣyati* "he will achieve it, he will have good luck." We account for both the twofold uses of verbs in transitive and intransitive constructions and the use of transparently intransitive verbs like "be" with accusatives as residues of Pre-Indo-European.

It is instructive to see that when preverbs are compounded with verbs, either the basic verb or the compound may be used as transitive, the other as intransitive: for example, as Wackernagel has observed, Latin *regō* "rule, direct" is transitive, while *surgō* "be directed upward, arise" is intransitive; similarly, *petō* "request" is transitive as opposed to intransitive *suppetō* "be at hand, suffice" (1926–8 II: 177–92). Another example, Latin *plōrāre* "cry out, weep" as opposed to the transitive *explōrāre* "examine, determine," illustrates that the basic verb may be intransitive as well as transitive. We may conclude that before shift of active structure to accusative structure, a basic verb might be in either category; but when the distinction between transitives and intransitives was introduced, a basic verb came to be either transitive or intransitive. Compounds were then selected to express the other force.

10.4.4 Approach illustrated by the examples above

The data presented here were selected by design from Indo-Europeanists who are highly respected for their control of the material and for their accurate presentation of it. Because we are concerned with the theoretical bases of the field, we point out again that their approach was descriptive, or in the term of Brugmann, systematic. Yet, while presenting the material, they considered that cited here to be out of keeping with the proto-language as they viewed it. When an explanation is attempted, like Meillet's, the aberrant patterns are ascribed to a different, primitive mentality. In our view linguistic problems should be accounted for through linguistic explanations. Since the examples accord with the structure of active languages, we explain them as residues of an earlier stage of the proto-language with such structure. In this way the theoretical basis is explanatory, providing solutions to problems through linguistic means that were unknown to our predecessors.

10.5 THE PRE-INDO-EUROPEAN VERB SYSTEM

In an impressive monograph on "The Hittite medio-passive and its Indo-European bases," Neu examined in great detail this Hittite category, comparing its position in the Hittite verbal system with that in "early Indo-European." His study led him to reconstruct the Indo-European verbal system differently from the system proposed by Brugmann and his successors (1968: 154–60). While I present his data, I interpret them as indicated in the subheadings.

10.5.1 Pre-Indo-European Active and Stative

Neu assumes an early Indo-European verb system of two categories that he labels, with an explanatory phrase here put in parentheses, as *Aktivum* ("form of action") and *Perfektum* ("form of state"). We may reinterpret this system as that of an active language, with inflections for active and stative verbs.

The endings that he proposes in the singular of these two forms are as follows (1968: 154):

	Aktivum	*Perfektum*
1	**m*	**ho*
2	**s*	**tho*
3	**t*	**o*

It is clear that the endings for the active inflection (Aktivum) are those of the injunctive; these have been generally accepted as the original endings in the later -*mi* inflection. The endings in the stative (Perfektum) are reconstructed by Neu on the basis of Hittite forms. If we do not propose final -*o*, its endings are those that have been reconstructed as precursors of the Indo-European perfect.

Neu does not reconstruct a middle for this stage of the proto-language. In his view that category was introduced later, as a development from the Perfektum (stative).

10.5.2 Development of the Indo-European perfect and the Hittite *hi*-conjugation from the stative

The Indo-European perfect also developed from the Perfektum (stative). In this way Neu accounts for the relationships between the perfect and the middle that have long been noted.

In further changes, final *i* was added to the endings. Interpreting these as indicating tense, Neu takes the new forms as precursors of the Proto-Indo-European present active, with endings in *-mi*, *-si*, *-ti*, while the original endings marked the preterite. I might note that by my interpretation the *i* indicated "declarative" meaning (1974: 99), so that the contrast between the two sets of endings at this point was one of aspect rather than tense.

Assuming a comparable differentiation between the Perfektum present and preterite, Neu proposes that the present in this Hittite conjugation was marked by the endings **ha*, **tha*, **a*. To these the *-i* was added, providing initially **hai*, **thai*, **ai*; the **ai* then was changed to *i* of many of our Hittite texts, especially those of the later period. This is the source of the Hittite *hi*-conjugation. The preterite in the *hi*-conjugation Neu derives from the forms in final *o*. This conjugation then developed in parallel to the *mi*-conjugation, maintaining the unaffixed forms for the preterite but marking the present with a final suffix.

10.5.3 Development of the middle from the stative

While the forms of the perfektum with final *i* were associated with the forms in *mi*, to maintain a parallel inflection, by Neu's view the unextended forms in **ha*, **tha*, **a* were maintained in stative meaning. These were suffixed with *-r-* as well as *-i*, to yield the Hittite and Luwian endings in *hari*, *thari*, *ari*. In this way the middle developed in the Anatolian languages. In the other dialects the endings of the Perfektum were modified by those of the Aktivum, yielding the endings *(m)ai*, *sai*, *tai*. The Perfektum was then the origin for both the middle and the perfect.

Many details of Neu's ingenious account of the development of the middle inflection, with relation to the Indo-European perfect and the Hittite *hi*-inflection, have been omitted here. Our prime concern has been to illustrate how a purely analytic interpretation of the forms in Hittite and the other dialects led him to the assumption of a verbal system that would be found in active languages.

10.5.4 Additional views of Neu's

Neu also accounts for the development of the passive from the middle, so that it was not a distinct category in Pre- or Proto-Indo-European. The imperative, as generally assumed, made use of the simple stem in the second person singular. It, the active and the stative, constituted the basic verbal paradigm of Pre-Indo-European. While we value Neu's monograph highly because of its presentation and interpretation of the Hittite data, some of its conclusions suffer from a lingering assumption of the view of Proto-Indo-European as based primarily on Sanskrit and Greek. As we have suggested, the earlier system was totally different, not even accusative in structure. As an active language, Pre-Indo-European very likely lacked inflection for categories that Neu posits, such as plurals, especially in the stative (Perfektum). Reconstruction of the plurals provides considerable difficulty for him, in great part because of the varying forms in dialects, especially Greek, Sanskrit and Hittite. When we assume that those forms were created in the individual dialects, the reason for the difference becomes clear; lacking in Proto-Indo-European, they were constructed independently in the dialects. This conclusion, resulting from application of the comparative method, is supported by the patterning in active languages. Active language structure also provides guidance for interpreting other elements in the verbal system.

10.5.5 Impersonals

Impersonal verbs with a variety of markers are found in the various Indo-European dialects. Examining them at some length, I have concluded that the situation in Italic and Celtic is closest to that of the proto-language. In these dialects, impersonals are preserved with ending in -*r*.

The forms have been described capably by Zimmer (1890). His basic conclusion may be summarized and illustrated in a paraphrased version that maintains his translations with English versions (1890: 244):

> *curritur* "man läuft = one runs," *itur* "man geht = one goes" are then not really third singular passives but remodeled *currur, iur* of the same meanings. It is extremely important to note that the older form is maintained in Umbrian *nosve ier ehe esu poplu* "if one does not go out of this folk." These third singular "passives" of intransitive verbs (*curritur, itur*) like the third singular passive of the Old Irish substantive verb *bethir* "one is," were formed on the basis of the present tense.

That is to say, in investigating the *r*-forms in these dialects, Zimmer recognizes them as presents as well as impersonals.

Active languages include a small class of such impersonals. They clearly do not fit in the structure of accusative languages. In most of the Indo-European dialects they have accordingly been remodeled. Even in Latin many are maintained as simple presents, e.g. *miseret, paenitet, piget, pudet, taedet* "it makes one pitiful, repentant, disgusted, ashamed, bored." Similarly in other dialects, such as Germanic, for example, Gothic *mik huggreiþ* "I am hungry < it hungers me." Since they were out of keeping with the verb systems of these dialects, they were fitted into the most likely place in those systems.

Although the source of the forms in -*r* remained opaque to earlier scholars, some of their observations are of great interest. Among these is Hirt's recognition of their relationship with neuter nouns in -*r*. He finds correspondence between Latin *itur* "es wird gegangen = travel takes place" and *iter* "way." He also compares the *r*-ending of other nouns, such as Greek *húdōr* "water" (1939: 81–2). The point is of some interest since Gamkrelidze and Ivanov contrast Hittite *watar* as the inactive form and *wetenant-* as active (1984: 174, 303). The -*nt*- suffix has been maintained in the widespread participial forms of the various dialects, while the -*r* was adopted to mark the third person plural of inactive verbs as opposed to -*nt* in the third person plural active (*ibid*. 304–5). It is also pertinent to recall that the Hittite medio-passive extended syllable -*ri* is "obviously identical with the r that marks the medio-passive." (Sturtevant 1951: 146). Its application only in the present indicative corresponds to the limited range found for affixes in the stative conjugation of active languages. This characteristic of such languages also permits us to account for its primary use in the third person plural. In the active period of Pre-Indo-European that form did not exist. When the verbal inflection was extended, the *r* provided a ready marker that could be applied in the third plural, as well as more widely in other dialects such as Tocharian.

But the ending was not applied only in the plural. As Sturtevant indicates, the Oscan "perfect, subjunctive 3 sg. *sakrafír*," which Buck translates "let there be consecration of," maintains "impersonal usage" (1951: 146; Buck 1904: 178. The basis for its use is now clear, as well as the source of morphological markers for middle and perfect. The "impersonal meaning" that according to Buck, "prevails . . . in the Oscan–Umbrian forms in -*r*" continues the use of the -*r* to mark impersonal verbs. Following Zimmer's analysis, we may account for it as the marker for a subclass of inactive verbs that is characteristic in active language structure. Its function has long been recognized, but the explanation has not been adopted in the absence of an understanding of the type of language in which it is a regular feature.

10.5.6 Forms for "have"

The treatment of the verb "have" has special interest in examination of the theoretical approaches pursued in Indo-European studies. The eminent linguist Benveniste devoted an essay to its situation in language (1966: 113–34, translated in 1971: 163–79). His views repay some attention, since he identifies "have" as a verb of state; but he simply takes recourse in generalities for an explanation, as if the situation were somehow "natural," to use an adjective often applied in recent times as support for specific conclusions about language.

Benveniste follows Meillet in asserting that "to have" is a late acquisition "among the Indo-European languages" (1971: 169). No other conclusion could be drawn from the evidence. One merely has to examine the forms to conclude that no etymon can be reconstructed for Proto-Indo-European (Buck 1949: 740–1). As Buck states, the notion is "regularly expressed by phrases"; even these differ, from Indo-Iranian use of "be" with the genitive, Latvian with the dative and the well-known Latin construction with the dative, as well as Celtic. Dialects that have introduced verbs comparable to transitives have adapted a variety of bases: Greek *ékhō* was taken from a base meaning "hold, possess"; Latin *habēre* from a base meaning "take, seize." For Germanic the base is disputed; the form, as in Gothic *haban*, is related by some scholars with Latin *capere* "seize, take," by others with Latin *habēre*, or even a merger of the two. We may well recognize this diversity of forms, but we must also account for the situation.

Noting that "have" is expressed most frequently by "to be-to," Benveniste states that "everything becomes clear when one recognizes *avoir* for what it is, a verb of state" (1971: 171). He finds his solution "verified by a parallel from the other end of the world in an Amerindian language. In Tunica (Louisiana) there is a class of verbs called static"; they have the "peculiarity of not being able to be inflected with pronominal prefixes and of requiring prefixes of "inalienable" possession." Belonging to the class are verbs meaning "to be ashamed, angry, excited, happy," etc., as well as physical state, mental state and state of possession. In this way he considers the Indo-European situation solved.

But, as we have noted elsewhere, his solution is inadequate. It is based on a general view of language that might be proposed by logicians. We give Benveniste every credit for his careful analysis and description; further, for his knowledge of linguistic scholarship, including grammars of the Amerindian languages. It is also remarkable that he compared Tunica, for it is an active–stative language. Benveniste's analysis of impersonals as classes of stative verbs is then quite accurate; but he unfortunately did not recognize active languages as members of a specific type. And failing that, he could not propose that Pre-Indo-European was an active language.

That understanding permits us to explain the absence of a verb for "have" in Pre- and Proto-Indo-European. It also illustrates the importance of treating languages as structures of specific types. Because the active language type has now been determined, as well as many of the characteristics of active languages, we can account for the problems treated here that had remained unsolved in the verb system.

We may emphasize once again the difference between describing the data of a language or of a language family and explaining them. Further, we emphasize the importance of explaining data on general linguistic grounds. On the basis of his superb control of the field, Benveniste recognized the essential facts; but, since he dealt with language as a phenomenon with a general or universal structure, the key to an explanation eluded him. The key has been provided by the knowledge gained from fieldwork with a large number of languages, and from careful analysis of their structures.

10.6 THE PRONOMINAL SYSTEM

Careful formal analysis has led scholars to account for complexities in the forms for first- and second-person pronouns. Like the first person singular, the first person plural pronoun employs different bases in the oblique forms, as still in English *we : us*, German *wir : uns*. The roots are reconstructed as *we-* and *me-*, with the *m > n* before following *s* in the oblique forms. In this way the personal pronouns are comparable to noun inflections like the *r/n* stems, in which the oblique forms have a different base from those of the nominative/accusative. We account for the difference in the discussion of nouns below (10.7).

10.6.1 Inclusive and exclusive pronouns

As a further complexity of the pronominal system, *we-* is found in the second person plural, as in Latin *vōs*, Slavic *vy*, Sanskrit *vas-*, and Gothic *iz-wis* "you." Prokosch interprets the situation by suggesting as explanation "two types of the plural . . . of the 1st pers., the inclusive and the exclusive" (1939: 282).

Prokosch supports his explanation by referring to the existence of such forms in Australian, Austronesian, Dravidian, North American Indian and Caucasian languages. Such information assures us that the pattern is credible; but it provides no reason for its existence in Pre-Indo-European. When, however, we know that inclusive and exclusive pronouns for the first person plural are characteristically found in active languages, we have an explanation for the forms; they are residues of the earlier pronominal system. Since other characteristics demonstrate that Pre-Indo-European was an active language, we are assured of this explanation in contrast with the tentativeness expressed by Prokosch. Just as we credit Benveniste for his insights, we acknowledge Prokosch's careful analysis and description of the forms. Through our understanding of active languages, the "two types" recognized by Prokosch and found as residues in early dialects now can be accounted for as residues of the earlier inflection for inclusive and exclusive pronouns.

10.7 THE NOMINAL SYSTEM

As we have noted earlier, many linguists have assumed that Proto-Indo-European an an early stage had an inflectional system for nouns that was far simpler than that reconstructed on the basis of Sanskrit, Greek and other dialects. Moreover, by some proposals the nominal system posited had a semantic rather than a syntactic basis. Uhlenbeck's proposal of an

Aktivus (agent) with -*s*-ending and a Passivus (patient) with -*m* may be the most striking. Instead of eight cases, he assumed these two forms for animate nouns, but only the patient for inanimates. Besides basing his assumption on formal characteristics in the dialects, like the use of the same form for nominative and accusative neuter, Uhlenbeck supported it by referring to languages that have such a system, citing Eskimo, Dakota and Basque. It is notable that Dakota has active structure.

Moreover, Meillet, as discussed in 10.4.2, assumed two genders rather than three in the proto-language. Like Uhlenbeck's proposal, Meillet's was based on analysis of forms. Since Johannes Schmidt had showed that the ending -*a* indicated a collective (1889), pointing out further that nouns ending in -*a* like Latin *nauta* could be masculine in a predominantly feminine declension, Meillet concluded that the earlier system distinguished only animate and inanimate nouns. Hittite provided additional information, in lacking forms for the feminine. Even the proposed distinction between animate (genus commune) and inanimate (genus neutrum) is weakly marked in Hittite, indicated only through lack of a distinctive nominative for inanimate nouns. In an active language, inanimate nouns would have functioned as subjects only with inactive verbs so that the frequency of a "patient" in the "nominative" would have been small. In this way Meillet's conclusions provide further support for an earlier active system, though such a system does not distinguish two genders; rather, it, and Pre-Indo-European as well, had two classes of nouns, an active/ animate and a stative/inanimate, in accordance with the structure of active languages.

Besides its evidence that gender was only weakly distinguished, Hittite provided grounds for assuming that inflection for number is late. The oblique case forms in Hittite, as discussed above, are comparable to the singular. The nominative and accusative plural for animate nouns have only the additional suffix -*s*. Further, as Gamkrelidze and Ivanov demonstrate, the -*n* considered a characteristic ending for the genitive plural is also found for the singular in Anatolian (1984: 267–71). Moreover, even in early Vedic texts there is evidence that plural forms were not sharply distinguished from singulars. As a result of the evidence briefly sketched here, and presented in greater detail in Lehmann (1974: 190–203), we conclude that Pre-Indo-European had very few inflectional markers for nouns. In this way it agrees with the structure of active languages.

10.7.1 The nominal endings in Pre-Indo-European

As I indicated in 1958, the system of nominal endings consisted of four markers. The ending -*s* indicated an animate noun functioning as agent or actor; -*m* a noun functioning as patient or target, often an inanimate; -*h* a collective; and zero ending implied no marking for syntactic function, only the lexical meaning that would be further characterized by a particle or by intonation. This system has been supported by the observations of Gamkrelidze and Ivanov, who view the earlier language as active (1984: 271–81). We may note further that active languages commonly include a form for the collective.

While the forms in *-s* correspond to the later nominative, and the forms in *-m* to the accusative and to the nominative of inanimate nouns used with stative verbs, the system did not include a precursor of the genitive. The lack of a genitive is characteristic of active languages. Since relationships are indicated by agreement, expression for the government relationship indicated by genitives is not in keeping with such a system. Survivals of such a system are attested in Hittite, and in the older Vedic texts. As long ago as 1960 Friedrich pointed out that forms ending in *-s*, ostensibly genitives, indicate individuals (123): for example, *wastulas* "sinner" is apparently the genitive of *wastul* "sin." Such forms of abstract and inanimate nouns are interpreted by him as genitives with the meaning "(he of) . . ."; they may more properly be taken as nouns with the ending indicating animate individuals. This use of *-s* may then be interpreted as a precursor of one of the Indo-European endings for the genitive case.

10.7.2 Development of the nominal inflection in late Proto-Indo-European

The nominal declension with eight cases, three genders and three numbers developed in a late stage of Pre-Indo-European, though not with fixed forms for all possible categories. It is clear from Hittite, and from Vedic, that forms for some oblique cases were not standardized until the time of the dialects: for example, the diverse forms of the genitive singular do not permit an etymon to be reconstructed for the proto-language apart from the form mentioned in the preceding paragraphs. And in Vedic sandhi the oblique-case forms in the dual and plural are treated as phrases consisting of a noun base and an ending; see 7.5.

The Vedic situation indicates how the case system expanded. Affixes of various origins came to be associated with nouns in specific functions. One that indicated location, *-bh-*, was expanded with additional affixes. A transitional situation is found in Greek, where the reflex of the form *-bh-* followed by *-i* remained as an enclitic in early Greek; there *-phi* is suffixed to singular and plural forms of nouns, where it corresponds to the instrumental, ablative and locative of other dialects as well as to the genitive and dative. In short, *-phi* may mark any oblique-case meaning. Additional affixes led to the Sanskrit case endings: instrumental plural *-bhis*, dative/ablative plural *-bhyas*, instrumental/dative/ablative dual *-bhyām*. Various origins have been proposed for the additional affixes, as well as the other case endings, but, in the absence of texts at the time of their formation, the hypotheses have remained vague. As Brugmann put it, "what we know about the origin of the Proto-Indo-European case endings is naturally little, however much has been written about the topic" (1897–1916, 2.2: 118). The extent of publication about the topic by the early years of the twentieth century may be examined in the *Grundriss*.

Of interest in treating theoretical bases is the approach of Indo-Europeanists who reconstruct Proto-Indo-European as a composite of Sanskrit and Greek. They confidently posit eight cases for the proto-language, and assign specific functions to each. By their view the situation in the dialects often represents losses of case forms: for example, such scholars assume that Greek *-phi* is a reflex of a Proto-Indo-European instrumental that was not maintained in the case system of Greek; even Brugmann tentatively adopts this position (1897–1916, 2.2: 120). The Sanskrit sandhi rules provide strong evidence against it.

Especially after the availability of Hittite texts, it is far more likely that the case system was gradually expanded rather than reduced in the late proto-language. Some cases, for example the ablative, never became members of the declensional system of specific dialects. Forms parallel to Latin ablatives are the bases of adverbs in Germanic, e.g. Gothic *galeiko* "similarly." By our point of view the Proto-Indo-European affix *-ōd/-ēd* or *-ōt/-ēt* came to have a narrowed meaning in Latin with the meanings "from, apart from, than"; but in Germanic it remained a particle with less specific meaning. This view is supported by the presence of a special form for the ablative only with thematic stems (Brugmann 1897–1916, 2.2: 163). The thematic declension is late, varying in endings like the genitive from dialect group to dialect group; and only in this formation was a distinctive ablative created in Latin.

We may conclude that the Pre-Indo-European set of forms for nouns came to be associated with syntactic values when the language was shifting to accusative structure, e.g. *-s* for the nominative, *-m* for the accusative. Other affixes came to be fixed for specific syntactic values as well as retaining semantic values: for example, in Latin the forms ending in *-ō(d)/-ē(d)* came to be used to indicate the standard in comparative constructions and also the place of origin of an action. Forms with *-bhi-* affixes came to indicate locational relationships, and were incorporated in the nominal inflections of some dialects; others incorporated comparable endings in *-m-*. In this way a meager nominal system as found in active languages developed into the moderately large declensional system of nouns in Proto-Indo-European, and also the early dialects, which exhibit different sets of cases.

10.7.3 Adjectival forms

The position of adjectives in Proto-Indo-European was accurately described by Whitney: "The division-line between substantive and adjective, always an uncertain one in early Indo-European language, is even more wavering in Sanskrit than elsewhere" (1896: 111). While scarcely distinguished in the proto-language, in the dialects two morphological characteristics come to identify adjectives: (1) they may be affixed for comparative and superlative degrees; (2) they may be inflected in the three genders.

In early Sanskrit, nouns also may be affixed with the comparative and superlative markers, e.g. *vīrátara, vīrátama* "more man(ly), most man(ly)." The several affixes for indicating comparison from dialect to dialect, as well as the absence of affixation for comparison in Hittite, demonstrate the late development of the comparative and superlative. The time of origin of the two categories may be linked to those of the dual and plural number. When affixes for comparison were affixed primarily to adjectives, one basis for distinguishing them from nouns was installed.

While thematic adjectives have inflection for three genders, adjectives in other declensions do not. Eventually the thematic pattern came to include all adjectives. Yet as late as Classical Latin, adjectives with a consonantal stem are inflected without differentiation for gender except in the accusative masculine/feminine, and in the nominative/accusative plural, e.g. *vetus* "old" and the present participles as a class. Moreover, in Hittite some lexical items are used alternatively as adjective or as noun, e.g. *kurur* "inimical; enmity," *taksul* "friendly, peacefully; pact, peace." These reflect the earlier lack of distinction between adjectives and nouns.

In the absence of a distinct class for adjectives, Pre-Indo-European demonstrates characteristics of an active language. As noted here, a separate class of adjectives developed only in late Proto-Indo-European, with clear marking for the three genders initially in the thematic inflection. Assumption of such late development permits us to account for the forms in Germanic, where some endings of the strong declension are based on noun inflections, others on pronoun inflections. The weak declension of adjectives is based on the *n*-stem inflection in Germanic; in Baltic and Slavic it has a postposed pronominal element. These innovations point to the late development of adjectives as a separate class. Similarly, the different markers for comparison among the dialects, and within some dialects, support the conclusion that adjectives as a distinct class are largely dialectal. The late development of adjectives then provides further support for the view that Pre-Indo-European was an active language.

10.8 PARTICLES

The third major class of lexical items besides verbs and nouns in active languages consists of particles. When we examine the handbooks, we find that they list a great many. Brugmann, for example, lists thirty-seven sets that he labels prepositions (postpositions) for the proto-language, some like *per* with several subsets (1897–1916, 2.2: 792–918). Delbrück also includes large lists in his several works, using the label "preposition" in the volume of the *Grundriss* devoted to nouns (1893: 643–74), and "particle" in the volume on verbs (1897: 497–540). Brugmann also discusses sentence particles in his treatment of verbs (1897–1916, 2.3: 969–1009). Among these are negative particles, which Delbrück distinguishes as a separate group from the group that conveys emphasis.

As the labels suggest, both Brugmann and Delbrück viewed these items as earlier forms of the function words in the dialects; both also recognize that "prepositions" stood after the nouns they governed in the proto-language. Moreover, they both deal with the relationships between the "prepositions" and verbs, which resulted in the compound verbs of the dialects. As this introductory sketch indicates, particles have been treated largely in accordance with their position in the later dialects, that is, basically as individual and independent lexical elements with comparable functions to those found for their reflexes in the dialects.

Determining their roles or sets of roles in Pre-Indo-European is still in its beginnings; but we can obtain leads from the situation in Hittite, where particles are prominent. Here many of them are clitics, generally appended to an initial particle. Besides preserving something of the earlier uses, the Hittite particles illuminate residues of the patterning as maintained in early Greek.

10.8.1 Particles indicating adverbial relationships

When we examine the use of a set of Hittite particles, for example *kan*, we find them associated with relationships expressed by the oblique cases in Proto-Indo-European and the dialects. Found in the sequence introducing sentences, *kan* is used with noun forms inflected in the locative, as in the following (Friedrich 1960: 121):

> nu- smas-kan peruni parhanzi
> ptc you (to) rock-to they chase
> "They will chase you to the rock."

Initial sequences like that here serve to indicate the structure of the sentence. Yet their elements, like *kan* in this sentence, may be pleonastic, as here with -*ni*. In other sequences they alone may indicate the local relationship, as in the following clause from the Hittite laws, I.28:

> na- an- si- kan tuhsanta
> ptc prn prn ptc they-separate
> "they will separate her from him."

Although *an* is accusative of the clitic personal pronoun and *si* dative, the locational relationship is indicated only by the particle *kan*. Since inflection for oblique cases is late, we may assume that particles like *kan* were the sole markers of the adverbial relationships in Pre-Indo-European that subsequently were expressed by the oblique case forms.

Otten and Soucek have discussed at some length the use of particles in an Old Hittite text (1969: 80–7). They find that the particles in this text are used with certain verbs or in specific constructions to indicate a locational modification, as in the clause where *kalulupi* is in the dative–locative case:

man-kan kalulupi-smi kanki
if   (on) finger-her   he-hangs
"If he hangs it on her finger, . . ."

They then point out that the later language has developed different devices for the expression of location, for example preverbs; syntactic relationships may also convey the locational meaning adequately, so that in time the particles lost their former meaning (*ibid*. 80).

The pattern in the later language may be illustrated by examples in Vedic and early Greek: for instance, *kam* in *Rigveda* 7.33.3 is scarcely more than a filler:

evén nú kaṁ síndhum ebhis   tatāra
ptc ptc ptc river   with-them he-crossed
"Indeed he crossed the river with them."

This lack of a specific meaning in Vedic supports the view that such particles gradually lost their function as the case system developed.

10.8.2 Particles expressing modality

In much the same way as nominal particles, those used with verbs fill roles that inflections fill in the later dialects. The particle *man*, which expresses potentiality, provides excellent examples, as in the following clause (Friedrich 1960: 140):

man-war-as- mu ᴸᵁMUTI-IA kisari
ptc ptc he me spouse   he-becomes
"He could become my spouse."

Hittite has no inflection for moods. Besides its use to express potentiality, the particle *man* serves to indicate uncertainty, and also an unreal condition, when used with the conjunction *mān*, as in the sentence cited in 10.2.3 above.

Yet some particles have survived in other dialects for use in conjunction with modal forms. These uses may be examined in the handbooks. Here we note only Greek *án*, as with the optative in *Odyssey* 1: 301:

pôs àn Odusêos lathoímēn
how ptc O.   I-could-forget
"How could I forget Odysseus?"

As Smyth and Messing indicate, this particle is enclitic and difficult to define compactly. "No separate word can be used to translate *án* by itself; its force varies as it modifies the meaning of the moods" (1956: 399; see

398–412 for details). In the line cited here it scarcely does more than support the contrary to fact implication of the optative verb. Since in earlier Greek more modal particles were so used, e.g. *ken*, *ke* (Munro 1891: 331–5), we may assume a gradual shift from use of verbal particles in Pre-Indo-European to modal forms of verbs, and subsequently to verb phrases constructed with modal auxiliaries.

We may propose then a second major use of particles in Pre-Indo-European: they serve to modify the meaning of verbs in the direction of potentiality, uncertainty and other modal modifications.

10.8.3 Particles used for conjoining

The early dialects express coordination with reflexes of Proto-Indo-European *k^we: Sanskrit *ca*, Greek *te*, Latin *que* "and". Hittite uses *a*, *ya* in this way, with parallels in the other Anatolian dialects. Disjunctive coordination is expressed by Proto-Indo-European *we*, *wē*: Sanskrit *vā*, Greek *we* as in *ē-we* > *ē*, Latin *ve*. All of these particles are clitics.

In the later dialects the clitic conjunctions come to be replaced with full words, for example *et* "and" in Classical Latin. Full words have also been introduced to indicate other conjoining relationships, such as the adversative Greek *allá* "but," causal *gár* "for," inferential *ára*, *nūn* "now." The pattern of development of conjunctions then is like that of the other particles.

10.8.4 Particles in pronominal use

The Hittite examples given above illustrate the use of clitic particles for personal pronouns, as in the sequence *na-an-si-kan*. In the same way, clitic forms of the first and second person personal pronouns are used in the early dialects. The occurrences are virtually too frequent in texts to require further examples; for example, the second word in the *Odyssey* is the clitic *moi* "to me." In statements we may see something of the colloquial usage, as in Agamemnon's of Iliad 1.106:

> ou pṓ   poté moi tò kréguon eîpas
> not at-all ever me the good   you-said
> "Never have you told me anything advantageous"

Here, as typical, the enclitic personal pronoun comes after conjunctional and adverbial particles (Munro 1891: 336). In this respect the order of the particles is similar to that of Hittite.

Clitics are also found for indefinite pronouns, again after adverbial particles, as in *Iliad* 5.516:

> metállēsán ge mèn oú ti
> they-ask   ptc ptc not anything
> "Yet they did not ask him anything."

Since examples are well provided in the handbooks, we leave further reference to consultation of them.

10.8.5 Particle strings in early Greek

To illustrate the abundant use of particles in the proto-language, and its continuation into the early dialects, we may cite an example, *Iliad* 4.160–1:

eí per gár te kaì autík'   Olúmpios ouk etélessen,
if ptc ptc ptc ptc temporarily O.   not he-fulfill
ék te kaì opsè teleî
ptc ptc ptc late he-will-fulfill
"Zeus may not impose the penalty at the moment, but he exacts it eventually."

As Deniston has pointed out, "in Homeric Greek particles of emphasis (*ge*, *dé*, *ê*, *mén*), and certain other particles, such as *ára* and "Epic" *te*, are heaped on in almost reckless profusion, and with but little definiteness of application" (1954: lxv).

We may interpret his characterization as representing a stage in the gradual shift away from use of particles for specific functions that have been allotted to case endings, verb inflections, and adverbial expressions. As Deniston goes on to say, "the language . . . [then tends] towards an exacter delimitation of the functions of particles." We assume that particles did have exact functions in Pre-Indo-European. When, however, inflections came to express some of these functions, the particles were maintained for some time, often with meaning overlapping that of the inflections. Coming to be redundant semantically, eventually they were either lost or sharpened in function, as when combined as preverbs with verbs, as was *ek* with the verb *teléō* of line 4.161 of *Iliad* above in Classical Greek. When maintained separately, they were treated as individual words with a specific accent.

10.8.6 Particles in active languages

The examples and discussion above indicate the range of use of particles in the early dialects, and accordingly in the proto-language. As we have noted, particles make up one of the three major classes of elements in active languages. In order to gain perspective on the Indo-European situation we may briefly compare the uses of particles in Indo-European with their uses in a characteristic active language.

In an article on Navaho, Hoijer noted that particles serve in it for pronouns, numerals, modifiers, conjunctions and postpositions (1951). They are not inflected; but they may take clitics. The examples above illustrate all of these functions for Indo-European, except for the numerals.

Yet examination of these below suggests that the numerals might also have been particles in the early proto-language.

In spite of many treatments of particles in handbooks and monographs, they, their arrangements in sets, the strings in sentences, as well as their uses require much further study. As is clear from the references, the earlier handbooks treat them as comparable to the grammatical classes of the later dialects, whether as pronouns, prepositions, conjunctions, adverbs or whatever. Through investigating their position at the stage in which they formed a central class, we will achieve more complete understanding of the Proto- and Pre-Indo-European items that have been reconstructed as particles.

10.9 THE STATUS OF PRE-INDO-EUROPEAN STUDIES

As the data provided above indicate, Pre-Indo-European, as determined by analysis of the results of reconstruction which are supplemented by residues in the dialects, includes many features of active languages. Since our interest lies in theoretical bases, we have merely sketched the general features of the lexicon and the grammar of the language at this early stage. Many details remain to be pursued, of which we note a few.

10.9.1 Reflexes of stative verbs

Indo-Europeanists have identified verbs that are inflected only in the middle. Delbrück provides extensive lists (1897: 417–25). It is instructive to compare these with the verbs that are stative in active languages. Among the Greek verbs he cites, some indicate a situation, such as "sit, lie"; Others indicate a characteristic or quality, such as "redden, become warm, be angry"; Others indicate functions that may not be regarded as voluntary, such as "laugh, fart, vomit." It would be useful to examine the verbs that have been identified for uses of their cognates in all the dialects, not merely Greek, Sanskrit and Avestan as is done in this section of Delbrück's work.

Similar study might be carried out for the verbs that inflect according to the Hittite *hi*-conjugation. Here as well we find meanings that correspond to those of stative verbs in active languages, such as "die, reach." Others indicate human functions, such as "see, know."

Among the interests in examining these two sets of verbs is investigation of the extent of time during which a specific dialect maintained active language characteristics.

10.9.2 Extended verbal roots

Extensive examination has been made of affixes to Indo-European roots, as by Persson (1912), accompanied by attempts to determine their meaning. Those attempts have been successful for only some of the affixes. There is general agreement on the early intransitive sense conveyed by the affixes that yielded the Greek aorists in *-ēn* and *-thēn* (Delbrück 1897: 437–8). Benveniste's interpretation of the meaning of the *-dh*-suffix has also been well received (1935). If studies were now undertaken from the perspective of active languages, the kinds of functions of verbal affixes found in them might provide leads for identifying the uses of further such affixes in the proto-language.

In connection with study of the suffixes, Delbrück examines a few that have an identifiable position and meaning in the early dialects: *-yo-*, *-n-*, *-sko-* (1897: 27–61). It is a characteristic of verbs in active languages to have extensive sets of forms made with affixes; moreover, in Hittite and other dialects, such as Germanic, the system of verbal inflection is meager. We may suggest that the affixed roots attested in the early dialects are reflexes of an extensive verbal system relying heavily on derivational affixes rather than inflectional endings. Additional scrutiny may show that some of affixes retained their earlier meanings in the dialects. By comparing the rich sets of derivational forms in active languages, those meanings might be reconstructed.

On the basis of these and similar studies a grammar of Pre-Indo-European might be produced. Supplementing the formal reconstructions of early stages, as in Lehmann (1952, 1989), these would fulfill one of the aims of historical study in providing a picture over a longer period of time during which Proto-Indo-European developed. It would also provide improved means for relating other language families. Moreover, the greater understanding of language that has been achieved since Brugmann's day has provided the means to proceed beyond a "systematic" presentation of Proto-Indo-European and also beyond a historical presentation that leads only as far back as the proto-language. With improved knowledge of active languages, we can extend our presentation of the early period of the Indo-European language family to its greater clarification and also for providing a basis from which we may explore the linguistic situation of the fifth millennium and earlier.

11 The lexicon

11.1 ASSEMBLING THE DATA

Concern with the structure of Proto-Indo-European and the early dialects has always seemed more attractive to linguists than attention to the lexicon; but the difficult work of assembling the data was begun early in the course of Indo-European studies. August Pott (1802–87) is the acknowledged pioneer in the effort. In his *Etymologische Forschungen auf dem Gebiete der indogermanischen Sprachen* (1833–6) he set out to determine the words that could be identified for the early period of the family. His work must be credited as well for directing attention to phonology, which led to greater accuracy in representing forms. However, even the enlarged second edition (10 vols, 1859–76) suffers from the persistent notion that etymology, according to its early meaning, seeks out the true (Greek *étumos*) meaning of words.

Pott's work was superseded by the *Wörterbuch der indogermanischen Grundsprache in ihrem Bestande vor der Völkertrennung* (1868) of August Fick (1833–1916). It was planned as a dictionary of Proto-Indo-European and the early dialects. While not extensive in its treatment of the stock of roots nor of the bibliography, the fourth edition (1890) is still useful, especially for the volumes on individual subgroups. These include dictionaries of the proto-language, of the Aryan and the Western European subgroups, as well as separate volumes on the lexicon of the period of Celtic unity by Stokes and Bezzenberger (1894; see Fick 1890) and that of the Germanic by Torp (1909; see Fick 1890). Meillet refers to it in his bibliographical section (1937: 490–1), with criticisms, however, on deficiencies in phonology.

Fick's dictionary of the proto-language was superseded in turn by the *Vergleichendes Wörterbuch der indogermanischen Sprachen* of Alois Walde, edited by Julius Pokorny (1927–32), which is now the standard lexical handbook. While, as Meillet notes (1937: 491), it inevitably includes errors of detail and incomplete coverage, it is also "rich in facts." Pokorny's subsequent rearrangement by the Latin alphabet rather than by

Sources for this chapter: Whitney (1885), Persson (1912), Walde and Pokorny (1927–32), Buck (1949), Pokorny, (1959–69, 1989), Watkins (1985).

the devanagari order, though briefer, is somewhat more convenient to use (1959–69). In his upgraded version Pokorny decided against revising the phonological system in accordance with the laryngeal theory. Our current dictionaries are therefore presented with obsolete phonology. Watkins's more compact *American Heritage Dictionary of Indo-European Roots* (1985) includes representation for laryngeals, but its limitation by English reflexes and its production for a general audience led to reduced coverage and to exclusion of bibliographical references.

For etymological purposes today we must consult dictionaries of the individual branches, that of Mayrhofer for Indic (1956–80, now under revision), of Chantraine for Greek (1968–80), of Lehmann for Gothic (1986a, with copious bibliography) and even earlier dictionaries like that of Walde and Hofmann for Latin (1938–56) as well as others. Until there is a replacement for Walde and Pokorny and the subsequent Pokorny, these dictionaries must serve as repositories of the lexical data, to be interpreted in accordance with subsequent phonological advances.

In contrast with repositories arranged by form, Carl Darling Buck set out to produce a dictionary arranged by meaning. His *Dictionary of Selected Synonyms in the Principal Indo-European Languages* (1949) is highly useful in exploring the lexicon for its representation of Indo-European culture. Somewhat like *Roget's Thesaurus*, it treats the vocabulary under selected headings for twenty-two sections that Buck called chapters; they and parts within them may be read like well-planned essays. The chapters range from topics like "the physical world in its larger aspects" through "animals," "dwellings, house, furniture," "time," "mind, thought," "law," concluding with the chapter on "religion and superstition." Lacking attention to Anatolian, Buck's dictionary has a valuable supplement in Tischler's compact dictionary of Hittite (1982), which is especially welcome in view of the period of the texts.

Segments of the lexicon arranged by meaning categories have been similarly examined, as Specht did with nouns to provide a "mirror of Indo-European culture" (1944: 1). His groupings center on (1) nature, (2) the animal world, (3) the plant world, (4) the parts of the body, (5) the family and household, and (6) terminology for wagonry (1944: 9–103). In many respects the procedure is similar to that of Jacob Grimm in his *Geschichte der deutschen Sprache* (1848); concerned with the social arrangements and culture of speakers of the early Germanic languages, Grimm supplemented the data of texts with inferences based on the vocabulary. The procedure is also applied by Benveniste in his *Indo-European Language and Society* (1973). The large second volume of Gamkrelidze and Ivanov (1984) examines the basic vocabulary in even greater detail, with the further aim of determining the homeland of the speakers.

This sketch of representative publications may illustrate that investigation of the lexical stock by meaning as well as form has been energetically pursued, followed by statements on implications that may be derived from its study. The validity of the collections and even to a greater degree of the conclusions based on their examination depends heavily on procedures applied in such study. Lexical items may be reconstructed on the basis of inadequate evidence, with unfortunate results, especially if the item is further employed for cultural inferences.

We have already noted (3.8) the example of Sanskrit *rā́j-*, long taken to be a Sanskrit word inherited from the proto-language with the meaning "king." Before Scharfe showed definitively that it is a ghost word in this meaning, massive conclusions were based on it, as that Indo-European society included political units with kings. Such conclusions are now totally discredited.

The position of other terms as well may be disputed: for example, Greek *pélekus*, Sanskrit *paraśú-* has been assumed to be a borrowing into one subgroup of dialects from Akkadian *pilaqqu* "ceremonial axe"; Gamkrelidze and Ivanov, on the other hand, take it to be possibly an Indo-European word (1984: 716, 739). Decisive evidence in favor of one of these interpretations may be unavailable; but, as Scharfe's finding illustrates, that evidence may not yet have been detected, and may be uncovered by careful philological study.

The example of a reconstructed word for "king" illustrates that generally accepted results may have been based on premature conclusions. Authoritative reconstructions require precise formal analysis and credible semantic interpretation, each tested by examination of all available evidence. As we note below, the so-called roots assumed by Pokorny's as well as other handbooks were proposed on the basis of subtracting affixes and endings, and vary greatly in their forms. The lexicon that we must produce needs to be based on application of formal and semantic procedures that have been determined in the course of Indo-European linguistic study. The procedures that are decisive in resolving different interpretations and proposing improved reconstructions must be noted, both for evaluating the elements reconstructed for the Indo-European lexicon and for improved solutions where evidence is available.

11.2 DEVELOPMENT OF AN ANALYTIC APPROACH FOR DETERMINING THE INDO-EUROPEAN LEXICON

Knowledge of the Indic treatment of the Sanskrit lexicon alerted Indo-Europeanists to the importance of analysing words for their basic components: roots, affixes and endings. In Indic linguistic study the affixes and endings were treated in the grammar; the identified roots and lexical items were listed separately. Following the pattern of the Sanskrit linguists, Whitney published the list in the unsurpassed supplement to his *Sanskrit grammar: The Roots, Verb-Forms and Primary Derivatives of the Sanskrit Language* (1885). As the title of the supplement indicates, roots are not only presented for their inflectional categories, but also for so-called secondary conjugations and derived forms. The secondary conjugations are characterized by specific suffixes or reduplication, accompanied by inflectional endings. Other suffixes characterize the derivatives, which are nominal. Moreover, the forms are labeled for the texts in which they are attested. The supplement then provides the basic information for determining the elements of the Sanskrit lexicon at various stages, and may be used as an important guide for reconstructing the lexicon of the protolanguage. It is well to recall that the principles observed by Indian grammarians in determining roots differ from those of western Indo-Europeanists as given in definitive form by Benveniste (1935).

11.2.1 Determination of lexical structure

We may survey briefly the forms made from the Sanskrit root *bhṛ* "bear" < PIE **bher-* to illustrate the make-up of the lexicon. Three different present classes are found in the *Rigveda*, the second-class athematic *bhárti*, the first-class *bhárati*, and the third-class, reduplicated athematic *bibhárti*, also recorded with accented reduplication (*bíbharti*) in other vedas and early prose texts. Attempts have been made to determine meanings for the various classes, as between the punctual "bring" and the continuous "bear, carry," which are found for **bher-* (Joachim 1978: 116–17). Except for the *n*-infix classes (Sanskrit 5, 7, 9), however, with factitive implication, any distinction determined between their meaning and formal characteristics is general and tentative. Moreover, even in early texts, such as the *Rigveda*, most forms of roots are generally inflected in one present class. Eventually the thematic inflection is most widely adopted.

Besides the three present classes, forms from the root *bhṛ* are made in the three other systems. Forms of the perfect, of three classes of aorists and two classes of futures are attested, as well as the nominal forms associated with verbal inflection. Among the nominal forms is the infinitive (more properly called a verbal noun) *bhártum* with inflected forms as well as the perfect participle *bhṛtá* and other participial forms.

In addition, forms of secondary conjugations – the passive, the intensive, the desiderative and the causative – are attested for the root. These secondary conjugations may be further inflected through the four systems, though for the root *bhṛ* only forms in the present system are attested for these secondary conjugations. The derivatives consist of nominal forms with various meanings, for example, *bhára* "acquisition; song of praise," etc., *bhárana* "burden," *bharatá* "one to be borne > cared for," and so on.

When we compare the forms made from the Sanskrit roots *duh* and *tud* as given in 8.1, as well as those from other roots, it is clear that early Sanskrit did not have conjugations like those of Latin or dialects attested later, such as Germanic. Three classes of presents are also made from *duh*, but only one of the three made from *bhṛ*; those from *tud* are in still different classes. Such examples indicate that the set of forms derived from any one root, including the secondary conjugations and nominal forms, are unpredictable in early Sanskrit and presumably also in Proto-Indo-European. It would therefore be pointless to posit principal parts for the Vedic and the Proto-Indo-European verb. Roots like *bhṛ* in form and meaning may be inflected in another selection of the ten present classes, or in only one, as well as in different aorist, future and secondary-conjugation forms. For this reason the Sanskrit grammarians and Whitney identify the form classes in the four primary systems, as well as in the secondary conjugations. Moreover, the root is a crucial element of the language, not simply a result of linguistic analysis. Since early Greek is comparable, as are other dialects that provide residual forms, the same assumption must be made for the proto-language.

The assumption does not imply that all roots were free forms in the proto-language. Some have survived as such into the dialects, and accordingly must have been so used in the proto-language. Formerly, every schoolchild learned the Latin set *dic, duc, fer, fac*. From such surviving forms we may assume that any appropriate root might have been used earlier as second person singular imperative. Yet for the purposes of the lexicon it is adequate for us to point out that roots must have been identified as such by speakers of early Sanskrit and Proto-Indo-European. By adding appropriate affixes and endings a large number of forms could be produced from any given root.

11.2.2 The endings

Of the three constituents, the endings were most readily determined by the early Indo-Europeanists. Relatively few, and consistent in shape, as in the personal affixes *mi, si, ti*, they were easily identified.

Interrelations among them, also chronologically, were determined only later. While it is now generally agreed that the *mi, si, ti* endings themselves were extended by an *-i*-suffix from earlier *m, s, t*, we maintain the labels of early Indo-Europeanists; the extended endings were labeled primary because they are found in the present, and the original endings are labeled secondary because they are found in the imperfect and aorist. If identification were by time of origin, the labels should be reversed; but like other inappropriate linguistic labels they are too well installed to be changed.

Conviction that the endings *m, s, t* were extended by a suffix was provided in great part by Hittite, for in it other post-affixes as well may be added to the accepted endings, i.e. *-ri* and *-ti*, as noted in 10.5. Hittite also, with its evidence for laryngeals, clarified the structure of the perfect endings, so that they are now posited as originally *-h* *-th*, *-0*, later affixed with *-e* to become *-he*, *-the*, *-e*, with coloring in the first and second persons singular to *-a*, as in the forms found in Greek *oîda, oîstha, oîde* "know."

Such further analysis, after assumption of laryngeals for the earlier period of the proto-language, has disclosed the endings of the time, in continuation of the procedures that identified the structure of lexical elements in Proto-Indo-European.

11.2.3 The roots

As we have noted, the Sanskrit grammarians determined roots by abstracting endings of forms and possible affixes: for example, a root *bhṛjj* "roast" was posited by them on the basis of the attested form *bhṛjjáti* in accented thematic class 6, which except for location of accent is parallel with *bhárati* of class 1 from the root *bhṛ*. Similarly, they posited a root *bhyas* "fear" on the basis of first-class present forms like *bhyásāt*. These examples may illustrate that roots as determined in Sanskrit lexicography could vary greatly in structure, consisting of only one element like *i* "go" or *ṛ* "go, send", as well as of many elements like the roots cited above.

Indo-Europeanists, by contrast, sought to identify "the laws of root formation," as Schleicher put it (1871: 331). Admitting that these had not yet been determined, Schleicher posited shorter forms, such as **ma* for **ma-t* "increase," but allowed as many as nine different shapes, from single vowel as in **i* to two initial and final consonants, as in **skand* "leap" (*ibid.* 332).

The canonical form of the root that we now assume was proposed by Saussure in his monograph published ten years after the death of Schleicher (1821–68). As noted above, the canonical form is C*e*C. Requiring the assumption of "coefficients" for roots with fewer than two consonants, e.g. **ag-* "lead," the assumption was largely disregarded until the "coefficients," now known as laryngeals, were supported by Hittite evidence. Though represented for some roots in handbooks by Hirt and Meillet among others, the canonical form for all, or virtually all, roots was not definitively accepted until the publication of Benveniste's monograph of 1935.

It may be noted that Kurylowicz's important monograph of the same year allows quite different root patterns: for example, he admits roots such as **teqʷ*, **bheid*, **leik*, calling the first light, the two others heavy (1935: 123). Kurylowicz's analysis has not been maintained. We now assume the canonical shape C*e*C as proposed by Benveniste, as well as the possible extensions identified by him (see 5.1.1 and 6.4.1).

11.2.4 Affixes

While the forms and meanings of roots and endings have been well identified and described, for affixes many problems remain. Schleicher assumed that affixes were based on roots, typically of the structure CV; but that assumption requires many earlier reconstructions which we have no means to substantiate; accordingly, it is no longer held.

A major subclassification has been proposed between single-element affixes, known as determinatives or root-determinatives, and suffixes. In two massive works, Persson provided exhaustive lists, accompanied by words in which they are found (1891, 1912). The meanings of some determinatives have been ascertained, as in Benveniste's exemplary chapter on *-dh-* (1935: 188–210). For many, however, the formations are so early that a basic class meaning cannot be established.

Suffixes provide additional problems. We must recognize a variety of forms, as in the causative *-éyo-* in contrast with *-skelo-*, and others, such as *-ti-*, *-tu-*. For each such suffix the meanings in the proto-language must be found. For some, a relatively central meaning can be determined, as for the causative *-éyo-*. This in turn is associated with *-yo-* suffixes having denominative and other meanings. The *-skelo-* suffix may illustrate the difficulties of determining the early central meaning. Found in Greek, Latin and Iranian with inchoative force, as in Latin *lūcēscō* "grow light," it exhibits the same meaning in some Greek verbs, e.g. *gēráskō* "grow old." But it is also found with other meanings, and with no distinguishable meaning in presents such as Sanskrit *pṛccháti* "request," Sanskrit *gácchati*, Greek *báskō* "come." We assume that specific meanings like the inchoative result from the inclusion of one or more prominent verbs with that meaning, and influence of these on others. As a result, the original force of the suffix may be unrecoverable.

Impressive studies have been carried out that result in identification of specific meanings for some affixes, such as Benveniste's on *-ti-* and *-tu-* (1948). In examining nominal affixes, Brugmann provided extensive descriptions of these two suffixes, with their extensions, e.g. *-eti-*, *-etu-*, (1897–1916, 2.2: 428–40, 440–50), identifying them as abstracts. Moreover, in a separate section on the meaning of nominal stems (*ibid.* 528–644) he states that *ti*-stems were originally nomina actionis (*ibid.* 615, 633). His treatment of nominal suffixes (*ibid.* 120–582) and verbal suffixes (*ibid.*, 2.3.1: 178–390) is in accordance with his systematic procedure; these sections are highly valuable for the listing of the elements, the formations in which they are found, and for Brugmann's identification of their general meaning. Monographs like Benveniste's build on Brugmann's treatment, attempting to provide greater detail.

Although such identification of form and meaning of affixes may be difficult, in view of the period of our data, it is essential if we wish to understand the developments of the proto-language and the early dialects. Patterning their hypotheses about the development of "weak"-tense forms like the Latin perfect signaled by *-w-*, the Germanic preterite signaled by *-d-*, the Greek perfect signaled by *-k-*, and by the *s*-aorists in a number of dialects, linguists from the time of the early eighteenth century have attempted to find the origin of weak tenses in periphrastic formations. As we have noted above, such attempts require scarcely credible nominal elements for the first component, and are carried out in disregard of many phonological problems as well as of semantic explanation.

In view of the morphological principles of late Proto-Indo-European, an origin of such "weak" preterites by suffixation is far more likely. Periphrastic formations, as exemplified in Latin and the Romance languages, in Greek of the koinē period, in Classical Sanskrit and still other dialects, including English with its progressive forms and those made with forms of *do*, belong to a later stage of the language family. At this stage constructions made up of function words and nouns or verbs are introduced and developed: for example, in contrast with the so-called weak adjective inflections made in Germanic with an *-n-* suffix, and in Baltic and Slavic with a *-yo-* suffix, the Germanic dialects at a later period develop a construction made up of demonstratives, e.g. *the*, or of limiting adjectives, e.g. *an* (*one*) to indicate definiteness.

The attempts to account for the development of weak tenses from periphrastic formations disregard the structure of the languages concerned when their constructions and their change are examined. It would be pointless to determine roots for the verbs of English, German, or other contemporary Indo-European languages. From the time of the classical languages it has been found useful to sort out principal parts rather than roots, that is, a selected set of forms characteristic of the total set made for a verb. As we have noted above (11.2.1), it is also pointless to seek principal parts for verbs in Sanskrit, and presumably also in Proto-Indo-European. On the other hand, in view of the structure of early Sanskrit and the proto-language, determination of the roots, as well as the affixes and endings, is essential in achieving an understanding of the language at the time. In pursuing that aim, the Sanskrit grammarians demonstrated excellent insight into the basis for explaining their language as well as providing a model that can be used to account for the proto-language.

11.3 TREATMENT OF THE INDO-EUROPEAN ROOTS

In his treatment of the verb, Schleicher states that a complete list of the proto-language roots ought to be included (1871: 333). Inadequate coverage of the lexicons in the dialects blocked that aim at the time. Subsequent study has provided it, exemplified especially in the dictionaries of Walde and Pokorny (1927–32), Pokorny (1959–69) and Watkins (1985). The roots determined by Pokorny have been listed with further classification of various kinds by Bird (1982). Accordingly, Schleicher's aim has not been disregarded.

But as we have noted, Pokorny's analysis for roots yields a variety of shapes. The nearest verbal root to the root **bher-* "carry" is **bhendh-* "to tie" (1959–69: 127), that is, by Benveniste's analysis a theme/base I, not a root. And the root following the seven **bher-* homophones is **bheredh-* "to cut" (1959: 138), a form that fails to fit Benveniste's patterns. Yet when we examine the reflexes of **bheredh-*, we find them based either on **bherdh-*, as in Sanskrit *bardhaka-* "cutting," or **bhredh-*, as in Old English *bret* "board," etc. Watkins gives the root as **bherdh-* (1985: 7) If re-examined by Benveniste's criteria, the two shapes are identified as reflexes of Benveniste's theme I and theme II; the root then would be posited as **bher-*. Among Pokorny's seven homophonic **bher-* roots (1959–69: 128–38), one is glossed "worked with a sharp tool, cut" (*ibid.* 133–5), with reflexes like Latin *ferō* "bore through," Old Icelandic *barja* "strike"; it scarcely seems unlikely that **bherdh-* is an extension of this root with the *-dh-*-determinative modifying the meaning to that of a result of previous action (see Lehmann 1942: 125–32).

We propose then that, in view of the wide variety of forms that Pokorny lists as roots, achievement of Schleicher's aim would be possible only by further scrutiny of the forms as listed, and thereupon by analysis for the root structures that Benveniste posited. That is to say, in keeping with current approaches in the human sciences, generalizations must be made in terms of a model.

As a further step, the roots should be classified for their meanings, whether active or stative, inasmuch as the root structure must have been in effect at the time of Pre-Indo-European. Residues of the earlier meaning alignments are maintained in roots that are inflected only or primarily in the middle, such as **key-* "lie," **nes-* "approach in a friendly way," **ās-* "sit," as listed by Delbrück (1897 2: 417–25). In the preceding section he lists roots used only in the active, e.g. **ed-* "eat," **dak-* "bite," **dō-* "give" (*ibid.* 416–17).

These examples may indicate that determination of the meanings of roots must be carefully done. For meanings may be modified by association with preverbs, as of **dō-* with *ā́* in middle forms with the meaning "take for oneself"; such modifications of meaning may be extended to the simple root, obscuring the earlier meaning. Moreover, affixes may be added, either to accentuate the force of the root, as when in Greek the factitive suffix *-n-* is added in *dáknō* "bite," or to modify it, as from the reduplicated Sanskrit form *jígāti* "repeatedly put down one's foot in going" as opposed to *gáchati* "go." With such procedures in mind, Schleicher's aim should now be pursued.

In seeking to determine the earlier meaning of roots we may build on Delbrück's lists, such as those of roots found only with middle inflection (*media tantum*) in Homer that later acquired active forms, e.g *théromai* "become warm" from the root **gʷʰer-* "be hot, be warm," *maínomai* "rave" from the root **men-* "think," as well as those in Sanskrit, e.g. *namate* "bow" from the root **nem-*.

We may also make use of Delbrück's generalizations and classes of middles, as in his four groups (1897 2: 419–24): (1) middles that indicate a condition of the subject or a process affecting it, as with the root **key-* "lie"; (2) middles that indicate bodily processes, like those made from *perd-* "break wind"; (3) middles that view motion as a process and not as an action, like those made from **kyew-*, e.g. Sanskrit *cyávate* "move, stir"; (4) middles that indicate emotional processes, such as Sanskrit *módate* "rejoice," as well as a last miscellaneous group.

Summing up the characteristic meaning features of the middle (*ibid.* 424–5), Delbrück finds that as in *bhuṅkté* "enjoys" it indicates a process in which the subject as a whole is involved, while in the active the action is in focus. When we assume that *media tantum* roots are reflexes of those that were stative in Pre-Indo-European, the basis of their inflection in the proto-language is clear. The "total involvement" of the subject results from the stative pattern in which subject and stative verb are equated. By contrast, the meaning expressed by active verbs requires equal attention to object as to subject. Delbrück's conclusion then suggests a starting point for determination of roots by their reflection of stative or active classification in the earlier language. The results can thereupon be scrutinized for nominal use, and for possible support of the classification of roots into stative/inactive/inanimate, on the one hand, and active/animate, on the other.

11.4 THE SIMPLEST LEXICAL ITEMS

The simplest forms in the verbal system are the so-called injunctives. They were admirably characterized as "unaugmented verb-forms" by Avery (1885). We find them attested in the oldest texts; for example, Avery found that the "normal" forms of the Sanskrit root *krand* "cry out" have secondary endings when used as presents in books of the Rigveda other than the late first and tenth (see also Renou 1925: 79). Moreover, the hymns in which injunctives occur are predominantly classed as strophic or archaic; the classification is in part based on their presence, but also on other criteria.

The class meaning of injunctive forms may also reflect that in the earlier verb system, as exemplified by an occurrence of the root *bhṛ* in the third stanza of Hymn 106, Book 9:

vájraṃ ca vṛṣaṇam bharat   sám   apsujít
club   and manly   he-bears firmly water-victor
"And (Indra) the victor over water bears the virile club firmly."

Found in a stanza reporting on Indra's drinking of soma, the line indicates an eternal characteristic of the god. A similar use may be observed for the root *dhā* in the second stanza of Hymn 30, Book 6:

ví sádmāny urviyā́ sukrátur dhāt
ptc dwellings widely powerful places
"(Indra) the powerful one has distributed the dwellings widely."

Here as well the injunctive form indicates an eternal fact; it may be translated with a present perfect to indicate a state resulting from previous action. It is also noteworthy that the Homeric "unaugmented" forms are much more frequent in narratives than in speeches; in view of our knowledge of oral epic as determined by Milman Parry (1971), the narratives would tend to be the earliest and central parts of the epics as handed down among the bards. The occurrences of the forms labeled injunctives in both Sanskrit and Greek texts then indicate their archaic status as well as meaning and form.

They have, however, been misinterpreted. Homeric grammars treat them under rubrics indicating "loss of augment." This interpretation results from the assumption that Sanskrit and Greek are the most archaic languages, and that the augment must be assumed for the proto-language. In view of its application, as to *s*-aorists more commonly than to root aorists in Greek, the augment is clearly a subsequent development, found in the central dialect group consisting of Sanskrit, Greek, Armenian and Phrygian. Its absence in Hittite supports the conclusion that it cannot be assumed for Proto-Indo-European.

The "unaugmented verb forms" then are residues from the earlier verb structure. As such they were not incorporated in the verb structures that had developed for Greek and Sanskrit. The very name "injunctive" fashioned by Brugmann, and also the difficulties in the interpretation of many occurrences, demonstrate their unusual position. In his perceptive article Renou speaks of the "independence" of the injunctive (1925: 66) as well as its "indeterminateness" (*ibid*. 76). He also points to other characteristic features, such as absence of distinction between the voices in injunctive forms (*ibid*. 79).

Hoffmann, by contrast, posits distinction of voice, presumably on the basis of medio-passive aorists (1967: 67). In keeping with his descriptive procedure, he also insists that the injunctive must be interpreted in contrast with the other verbal categories in Vedic Sanskrit (1967: 35). But his view that manner of action (Aktionsart) is incorporated in the lexical meaning indicates that their aspectual meaning derives from the active and stative roots on which they are formed. Nonetheless, assuming that injunctives indicated only "aspect, person and number," aside from the disputed voice distinction, Hoffmann concluded that their basic purpose was to "mention" (*erwähnen*) a verbal action, which leads to his suggestion that it should properly be called a "memorative" (1967: 279). Such a characterization may apply to the use of verbs in active–stative languages. In view of the central position of nouns in languages of this type, the verbs simply "mention" the state or the action they represent. We conclude then that the injunctives and the augmentless Greek forms reflect a verbal structure with a basic contrast between active and stative roots.

By the late Proto-Indo-European period, however, verb forms did not consist simply of root and personal ending, as exemplified by the addition of a final -*i* to the endings *m*, *s*, *t* in the present indicative. In the imperfect and aorist, the augment was added in the central dialects; in the others, such as Italic, Germanic, Baltic and Slavic, the non-present tense forms were signaled by ablaut change or affixes. The first, second and fourth conjugations in Latin, for example, had such distinctive affixes throughout. That is to say, roots by themselves no longer were treated as bases for verbal inflection.

While the injunctives provide a considerable amount of evidence for the earlier use of roots verbally, there is relatively little evidence for the use of roots as nouns. Some are indeed attested, but largely as elements of compounds; but it is difficult to state that these were transmitted from earlier stages or produced on the basis of noun bases in late Proto-Indo-European. Among such examples are Latin *tubi-cen* "trumpeter," with the root of *canō* "sing." Others have a nominative ending, such as Latin *au-spex* "augur < one who observes birds" with the root of Latin *speciō* "inspect." Those attested as single words have such an ending, for example, Latin *vōx*, Sanskrit *vāk* (with final simplification of the consonant cluster) beside Avestan *vāxš* "voice." Many of the so-called root-nouns are actually bases, with reduced vowel, such as Greek *líps* "stream, source" beside the verb *leíbō* "pour." The commonly cited, **rēg-* on the basis of Sanskrit **rāj-*, Latin *rēx* "king" has now been dismissed from the Indo-European lexicon. Yet even such meager attestation of roots used as nouns suggests, as Meillet has pointed out, that they may well have been employed for nominal use in the proto-language (1937: 254–6). When so used, they would have expressed the basic meaning of the root, as the illustrations given here may demonstrate.

Since the root nouns as well as the verbs refer to common actions or items in the early culture, it has been suggested that the earlier language was agglutinative in morphology. As support we may point out that in the injunctive inflection the endings had only one function, as is characteristic of agglutinative languages. The sole function of -*m* was to indicate first person. Indication of plurality was introduced later, by affixing -*es*; similarly for the other endings. The subsequent introduction of the number category is especially evident in the -*h* inflection, as we have noted above. Yet both the verbal and the nominal inflections were so greatly modified that it is difficult to insist on agglutinative structure in the earlier period. The presence of many determinatives, however, supports the assumption that individual suffixes were added to roots in order to bring about specific meanings. These may in part be determined, as we note from the heteroclitic nouns.

11.5 HETEROCLITIC NOUNS

One of the remarkable characteristics of Indo-European is the heteroclitic inflection of nouns in which the affix differs in the oblique cases from that of the nominative/accusative. Like root nouns, the heteroclitic nouns are attested only as residues, certainly in the dialects other than Hitttite.

Petersson in his important study of "heteroclisis" (1921) cites only three that are attested in three of the early dialects, and even there with modifications: Sanskrit nom. *ûdhar*, gen. *ûdhnas*, Greek *oûthar*, *oúthatos*, Latin *über*, *überis* "udder"; Sanskrit *yákr̥t*, *yaknás*, Greek *hêpar*, *hêpatos*, Latin *jecur*, *jecinoris* "liver"; Sanskrit *ásr̥g*, *asnás*, Greek *éar*, *éaros*, Latin *aser* "blood." The Indo-European form for "udder" he reconstructs as **oudh-er*, **ūdh-n-es*; for the other two he posits vocalic *r* contrasting with *n*, as in **ēs-r̥-g*. In addition to these three that can be confidently reconstructed, he proposes many other heteroclitic nouns from residual forms.

If we reconstruct the situation of the *r/n* stems on the basis of our assumptions for Pre-Indo-European, we assume that only the *r*-forms were found at the active stage of the language. The heteroclitic nouns have neuter gender in the early dialects as reflexes of earlier inanimate nouns; in active languages, non-active and internal organs are treated as inanimate. Relationships between such nouns and others in the sentence would have been expressed through the use of particles rather than through oblique case forms.

As inflections developed, oblique case forms were also introduced in the inanimate inflection. I assume that *-n-* was selected for its limiting sense as in the Germanic weak nominal inflection; in contrast with the descriptive force of adjectives in the strong declension, the *n*-stem or weak inflection indicates specific nouns. If we apply the contrast to the heteroclitic inflection in its development, we may assume that when they were used in the nominative/accusative, the *r*-forms imply the substance in general, as in Hittite *watar* as opposed to the genitive *wetenas* "water," similarly, Sanskrit *śákr̥t*, *śaknás* "excrement," Indo-European **kor*, **ker-n-és* "horn," reconstructed by Petersson (1921: 6), and so on. When, however, used in the genitive or the locative, a specific, individual representation of that substance is singled out, e.g. "of the water, on the horn," etc. In this way we may account for the characteristic inflection, partly on the grounds of differing chronological layers, partly on the grounds of distinction in meaning.

The *r/n* inflection is very prominent in Hittite; Meillet ascribed its prominence to the early attestation of the language (1937: 266), but the other Anatolian languages do not attest it (Kronasser 1966: 321–2). Accordingly, we may seek another explanation for its retention and expansion in the language. We propose as reason that Hittite in general maintained more active-stative characteristics than did the other dialects. The characteristics of the verbal system support this conclusion; *hi*-verbs were maintained. The verbal *r*-endings were widely applied. The heteroclitic inflection then is only one of the structures that was kept and even extended in Hittite.

11.6 NOUNS CENTRAL IN THE CULTURE OF THE EARLY SPEAKERS

When we examine the nouns that Specht assembled on the grounds that they might be expected for the period of the proto-language, we find that the bases end in consonants; some also belong to the heteroclitic inflection. By scrutinizing the nouns as he did, he provided convincing evidence that the addition of *e/o* to bases, in the so-called thematic inflection, was a feature of late Proto-Indo-European and the early dialects. Examples have been provided above, as for the root **bher-*, that thematic inflection was extended widely in conjugation; similarly in declension, where we may point to Old English *wæter* "water," which is a neuter *o*-stem, in contrast with the heteroclitic inflection of the proto-language, as reflected in Hittite and Greek. In each of the subgroups the consonantal inflection is gradually replaced by the thematic. And many nouns that were formerly *i*- and *u*-stems have become *yo*- and *wo*-stems in a dialect attested later, the Germanic.

To illustrate the relationship between the nouns assumed for the early culture and consonantal inflection in the proto- and pre-language, we may cite examples from Specht's five semantic groups.

The first group deals with items of nature. Specht's first four items may be illustrated by Sanskrit *s(ú)var*, Latin *sol* "sun," Sanskrit *mås*, Greek *mền* "moon," Sanskrit *star-*, Greek *astḗr* "star," Sanskrit *uşás-* "dawn," all by his term "irregularly" inflected (1944: 9–10); the remaining items in the section are similarly "irregular" in the early dialects (*ibid*. 10–28).

The designations in the animal world are similarly accounted for, although some may be reconstructed as regular in the proto-language (*ibid*. 18–53). Most important of these is the word for horse, which Specht reconstructs as **éḱu̯-os*. But in his recognition that bones of wild horses were found in areas that he considers part of the homeland, he proposes that there must have been an earlier form of the word for the undomesticated horse, and that this may be retained in Balto-Slavic **ašu-* "sharp." The problems surrounding the name may never be resolved. As one of them, scholars have sought a distinctive designation for the domesticated horse as opposed to the wild horse. In my view the Indo-European word was borrowed, possibly even independently in some of the dialects; in this way we account for the unexpected palatalized *k* before *w*, and for the vowel *i* as well as the initial *h* and the double consonant in Greek *híppos*. Because Specht considered the horse to be the "most recent of the domestic animals," the thematic inflection agrees with his views as well as with subsequent archaeological data (*ibid*. 36). Whatever designation was applied earlier to the wild horse may not have been maintained, or it may have been an etymon of the widely adopted **eḱu̯-o-*. The names of the other animals for the most part agree with Specht's criteria for early nouns.

In much the same way, the nouns in Specht's third group, the plant world, are also irregular (*ibid*. 54–73). Among these is the word for "wood," Sanskrit *dắru*, Greek *dóru*, *drûs*, Hittite *taru*. Here too a key word troubles him, the noun for beech, Greek *phāgós*, Latin *fagus*, Gothic *boka*. Yet the problem arises because he places the homeland in northern Germany, and assumes that the word must be reconstructed for the proto-language in spite of its attestation only in western dialects. Since we now reconstruct it only for a subgroup, the problem has been resolved, especially because we also differ with Specht on the location of the homeland. While the names for trees provide numerous difficulties in view of varied forms, the etyma to the extent they can be reconstructed are "irregular" in Specht's sense, and accordingly add to the set of nonthematic nouns at an early stage of the proto-language (see also Friedrich 1970).

For Specht's fourth group, parts of the body (*ibid*. 73–87), we have already cited three archaic examples, the words for udder, liver and blood. Numerous others could be added, among a selection of which we cite examples from only one language: Sanskrit *hṛd* "heart," *pād-* "foot," Greek *kheír* "hand" and so on.

The last group includes kinship terms, which are well known for their archaic inflection, and designations for the household (*ibid*. 87–98). Pointing to the simple form of "house" as maintained in Sanskrit *dámpati-*, Greek *despótēs* "master of the house," to the term for the group of houses, Sanskrit *viś-*, Gothic *weihs* and so on, Specht singles out the earlier forms for these nouns that later became *o*-stems, as in Greek *dómos* and *oîkos*.

Specht's collections, which take due account of earlier scholarship, provide carefully determined and impressive evidence for reconstructing the earlier nominal system of the proto-language. From the inflection of the *r/n* stems as well as "irregular" forms that are attested only in the nominative/accusative, we may conclude that in the active stage of Pre-Indo-European there were only forms for the "agent" and the "patient," to recall Uhlenbeck's terms. In the course of time these were supplemented by additional cases and by adverbial forms, such as those found in Homer with *-phi*; the various subgroups and dialects then developed the inflectional paradigms that we know from the early texts.

11.7 SETS OF LEXICAL ITEMS

The phonology of a language is determined by the interrelationships of its elements; the most significant feature of a phonological entity like Proto-Indo-European *d* is its relationship to the entities generally represented as *t* and *dh*, and also to those represented by *b g g^w* (and by some analyses also *g'*). The same principle applies in morphology and syntax, as exemplified above in examination of the "meaning" of the genitive in a language like Greek, with four other cases in contrast with Sanskrit with seven other cases. Application of the principle to the lexicon strengthens conclusions about individual items as well as about the sets themselves.

Few coherent sets can, however, be determined for the lexicon. The most thoroughly studied set is that of kinship terms. These were assembled and interpreted in the nineteenth century (Delbrück 1889). The interpretations were upgraded and amplified by examination of kinship terms and systems in all accessible languages. Like other systems, that of Proto-Indo-European was then classified in accordance with characteristic patternings. Szemerényi has presented the results admirably, with copious bibliography, while proposing his own views (1977).

The system of kinship terms is presented below. It illustrates once again the advantages gained from dealing with language in accordance with findings based on typological investigations. The significance of the utilization of the same word, Proto-Indo-European *awos*, for (maternal) grandfather and maternal uncle was puzzling when words were simply treated as individual lexical items and the Indo-European system was examined in isolation (Walde and Pokorny 1927–32 I: 20–1; Pokorny 1959–69: 89). When, on the other hand, the lexical pattern is examined with reference to those found in other cultures, and thereupon interpreted by generalizations based on general study of kinship systems, the terms may be accounted for; the lexical set and the cultural patterning of the society using it are then illuminated.

The same principle may be applied to other sets, the terms for social organizations, the numerals, reference to deities and so on; but none of these sets, with the possible exception of the numerals, is as tightly structured as that of kinship terms. We may also examine much looser and larger sets, like the twenty-two that Buck identified in his portrayal of the lexicon (1949). Here we limit ourselves to examining three well-organized sets.

11.7.1 The Indo-European kinship system

The set of terms employed in kinship systems has been studied more extensively than any other in the lexicon. Types of systems have been identified. Items in systems and their semantic features, have been determined. Among features are consanguinity, generation, sex and age. The set in a given language is based on these. Japanese, for example, includes the feature for age, as in having separate terms for older sister and younger sister; English and other Indo-European languages do not. For lexical study then, the basic principles have been explored so that the system in any language can be interpreted with reference to the overall classification of kinship systems (see Lévi-Strauss 1969 for generalizations, and references to more technical treatises; Benveniste 1973: 163–223 for Indo-European).

The Indo-European kinship system has been repeatedly examined, with varying conclusions summarized by Szemerényi as he proposes his own interpretation (1977: 5–95; see also Delbrück 1889, Benveniste 1973:

165–223 and Gamkrelidze and Ivanov 1984: 761–75). Since most of the terms are well known, they will not be listed here; an adequate presentation would duplicate that of Szemerényi in extent. We may note that he treats sixteen possible terms denoting consanguineals, and eleven additional for denoting affinals. The sixteen for consanguineals are father, mother, son, daughter, brother, sister, grandfather, grandmother, grandson, granddaughter, as well as uncle, aunt, nephew, niece, male cousin and female cousin. The eleven denoting affinals include father-in-law, mother-in-law, daughter-in-law, son-in-law as well as husband and wife, widow, and husband's brother, husband's sister, husband's brother's wife, wife's sister's husband. The evidence for specific terms varies, as is indicated in Szemerényi's monograph.

As noted above, the feature of the Indo-European kinship system that has been taken as central for its interpretation is use of the same term for grandfather and uncle, a term that Szemerényi reconstructs as *HauHos; the term was also extended by affixes when used for "uncle" as in early Latin *auonculus* in contrast with *auos* for "grandfather." In application of the results of typological classification, as determined in anthropological study, the Indo-European system has been identified as belonging to the Omaha class largely on grounds of the position of *HauHos.

Szemerényi, however, objects to identification with the Omaha system on the grounds of differences from it (1977: 181); in Indo-European, for example, shifts of other terms like that of sister for daughter are not found. In his explanation of the twofold use for *HauHos he relies on more general principles, such as that formulated by Sol Tax; he then applies these to a patrilineal society like that of the Indo-Europeans which follow the custom of acquiring wives from outside the family. In that society the relationship between father and son tended to be authoritative, while that between nephew and uncle and presumably also grandfather may have been more kindly. Still other reasons may be suggested for assuming a similar bond between such members of an extended family. By the principle formulated by Tax, "persons toward whom EGO behaves in the same manner, he will call by the same term" (1977: 190); hence the twofold use of *HauHos. Szemerényi's argumentation in support of his explanation in contrast with one based on comparison with the Omaha system is impressive. Yet, rather than deciding in favor of one of these explanations, we observe that both seek to clarify the twofold use of *HauHos by examining it by principles resulting from examination of semantic sets as systems.

It is useful to contrast the two efforts with explanations given in the earlier handbooks. Walde and Pokorny examine it as a single lexical item, *HauHos, or in their reconstruction, *au̯o-s (1927–32 I: 20–21). By their explanation it is probably derived from *awo-, a pronominal stem reflected in Old Church Slavonic *ovŭ* "that one," i.e. those outside the immediate family. This explanation may provide an etymology (Szemerényi relates it to Sanskrit *avati* "help, support," 1977: 48); in contrast with reliance on

Tax's principle or the Omaha type it fails, however, to account for the twofold use. That is to say, Walde and Pokorny provide a formal explanation as derived from a pronominal stem; but they do not account for the word within a recognized structure; moreover, in objection to their etymology one might argue that a grandfather would hardly be considered "outside the immediate family."

When, on the other hand, principles have been determined for types of semantic structures, such as kinship systems, and one of those principles illuminates the use of a word like *awos*, the explanation is more credible; it also provides more secure evidence for cultural conclusions. Examination of the study that has been carried out on kinship systems illustrates how elements of the vocabulary of Proto-Indo-European may be clarified, and also how such clarification may advance our information on the culture of the speakers.

11.7.2 The terms for social organization

A further set that is potentially well structured is that for social organization (Gamkrelidze and Ivanov 1984: 741–2). This set has also been thoroughly studied, although as we note below it has greater possibility of variation than does the kinship set; as a result, conclusions may have been drawn that are not supported by the data.

When we examine the words for social groups, two stand out as widely attested, as in Sanskrit *dám-*, Avestan *dam*, possibly Greek *dô* "house," as well as the thematic forms Sanskrit *damá-*, Greek *dómos*, Latin *domus*, Old Church Slavic *domŭ* "house"; Sanskrit *víš-* "dwelling, village," Greek *oîkos* "house," Latin *vīcus* "village," Old Church Slavic *vĭsĭ* "village." In spite of occasional similarity of reference, as of Greek *oîkos* for house, the *delom-* words denote a smaller entity or habitation than do the *weloík-* words. Moreover, the *dómos* words are derived from the root *dem-* "build," suggesting that in origin they referred to a building rather than to a social unit; the source or further relationship of the *weloik-* words is unknown though Szemerényi relates it to Sanskrit *višati* "comes, arrives" (see Lehmann 1986a: 345–6, 399 for further examples and discussion). Evidence is lacking to reconstruct an Indo-European term for a more comprehensive social unit.

The forms of the two words reflect their relative time of origin. Both are attested with consonantal inflection, that is, forms that may be ascribed to an early stage of the proto-language. Yet some forms of each word, as in Greek and Latin, are *o*-stems with *o*-grade of the base, suggesting additional formations during the later period of Proto-Indo-European. Moreover, the *o*-stem attested in Sanskrit *veśas*, Avestan *vaēso* has the meaning "house" in contrast with that of the consonantal stem, as in Avestan *vīsǿm*, Old Persian *viþǿm* "village, clan" as well as "house." Because the later affixed forms of *weik-* refer to a dwelling, as does also

Latin *villa* < **weiks-la-*, the morphological structure by itself suggests an earlier use for a larger community than that of a unit family. The Sanskrit plural *víśas* "people" supports this assumption.

Further support for the assumption that the **we/oik-* words refer to a larger social entity or to a building for such an entity is provided by the Sanskrit term *viś-pátiṣ* "head of a community/house" and the Lithuanian *viẽš-pat(i)s*, which came to be used for the Christian God, Lord. Sanskrit *dám-pati-*, Greek *des-pótēs* < **dem-s-poti-s* "master (of the house)" indicate a lesser status (Gamkrelidze and Ivanov 1984: 742–3).

For higher ranks and larger units we have only negative evidence from the absence of appropriate lexical items. Words for "people, nation" can be reconstucted only for subgroups, that is, at best for late Proto-Indo-European. In the northwest, Old Irish *tuath*, Umbrian *tutas*, Gothic *þiuda*, Lithuanian *tautà* "people" has been fashioned from the root **tew-* "to be strong." Porzig takes this set of words to be late substitutes for the **weik-* words, which he interprets as "tribe, clan," accounting also for Greek *phulē* "tribe, clan" as a late substitute (1954: 151, 200). Like other such words, e.g. *marshal*, originally "keeper of the horses," the words for "people, leader of the people" represent elevation of a grouping or rank as society expands. This raising of status is clear in the term for "leader, chieftain, king" that has been formed in Germanic, as in Gothic *þiudans*. Made with the suffix *-no-*, as in Latin *dominus* "lord," cf. *domus*, *tribūnus* "chieftain", cf. *tribus* "tribe," it is clearly a late formation.

The words cited may be adequate to illustrate the difficulties involved in proposing terms for social groupings and ranks in Proto-Indo-European, especially for larger groups. We have noted amply that there is no basis for reconstructing Proto-Indo-European **rēg-* "king." The more secure terms for social ranks as well as for social groupings suggest organization of the community at the time of the proto-language into small entities.

Many other terms for dwellings, shelters for domestic animals and storehouses have been compiled, as by Schrader (1883, 1906–7, 1917–29), as well as for social ranks. Some of these, like Latin *dominus* and *rex*, are obviously late. Others are hopeful interpretations, such as *triχá-ikes*, an epithet of the Dorians that was formerly assumed to mean "of three clans" but today is taken to mean "of waving plumes." The set for social groups and ranks is then much less structured than that for kinship. As the examples cited here illustrate, it must also be treated with greater circumspection.

11.7.3 The set of numerals

The numerals in a language provide another set that is limited in extent and follows a restricted group of patterns. Treatment of the set has, however, been hampered by the absence of an adequate analysis of numeral sets in language. Greenberg has presented some leads in his "Generalizations about numeral systems" (in Greenberg, Ferguson and Moravcsik 1978 III: 249–95); yet its most significant generalization may be the statement that "a full-fledged study of the syntax of numeral systems . . . would require a full-length study in itself" (*ibid.* 282). Lacking such a study, the interpreters of the Indo-European system have assumed a well-developed set extending as far as 100, and then have proceeded to account for the divergences as subsequent modifications (Brugmann 1897–1916, 2.2: 1–82; Szemerényi 1960 with copious references). While we will examine some characteristics of the Indo-European system, our primary concern is the underlying principle that has guided such interpreters.

Numeral systems in general are constructed around some selected standard, often that of the digits of one hand or both. The Sumerian system is constructed on the set of fingers for one hand; 6 is 5 + 1, 7 is 5 + 2, and so on to ten, which is an independent lexical item, as are the numbers 1–5. The Indo-European system is also based on the digits of one hand (Greek *pénte* "five" = Hittite *pankus* "the whole"), but differs from Sumerian in having independent lexical items for 6, 7, 9, and probably 8 as well, although the suggestion has been made that the word for eight is a dual of the etymon of Avestan *ašti-* "four fingers" that was selected to represent the numeral (Henning 1948: 69).

After 10, differences are found from dialect group to dialect group. Germanic and Baltic represent 11 and 12 as "one left over" and "two left over," Latin and Greek as 1–10, 2–10, but from 13 the Greek form is "three and ten," etc.; moreover, Latin represents 18 and 19 as "two from twenty, one from twenty." More such forms that are restricted to one dialect or one dialect group could be cited.

The numerals from 20 to 100 show further differences. For our purposes these numerals may be adequately represented by giving side by side representations for 20, 40, 60, 80, 100.

Sanskrit	Greek	Latin	Gothic
viṃśatí	eíkosi	vīgintī	twai tigjus
catvāriṃśát	tetterákonta	quadrāgintā	fidwor tigjus
ṣaṣṭí	heksékonta	sexāgintā	saihs tigjus
aśītí	ogdoékonta	octōgintā	ahtautehund
śatá	hekatón	centum	hunda

A glance at any one of these sets indicates clearly the different patterning. Yet in spite of the differences, Szemerényi among others attempts to account for all forms of each numeral as reflexes of the same Proto-Indo-European etymon (1960).

Before proposing an alternative possibility, we may note that the value of the entities was by no means fixed. In Germanic the value of the words for hundred is "120." In Homeric Greek the value of its equivalent in the compound *hekatómbē* may be given as "a large number"; as the handbooks have long pointed out, the term literally means "a sacrifice of a hundred oxen" but in the Homeric poems that quantity is not observed: for example, in *Iliad* 6: 115 the sacrifice of a hecatomb is made with twelve oxen. Proto-Indo-European *kṃtóm*, whatever its origin, may then simply mean a sizeable figure.

In view of the great discrepancy between the lexical items for 20–90, and also for 11–19, it seems far more likely that the numeral system was constructed independently in each dialect group or even dialect. We accept the set to 5, and at a later period to 10, as Proto-Indo-European.

For additional numerals the possibilities of formation are limited, as well as fairly obvious. In the teens an additive procedure is very common, with the word for 10 treated as the standard as in comparative constructions. That is, in OV languages the word for 10 precedes the lower numeral, as in Turkish *on yedi* "ten seven = seventeen," while in VO languages it follows, as in English *seventeen*; and as in any such lexical compound, the pattern is frequently preserved regardless of subsequent syntactic shifts. Similarly, the decades are commonly indicated by means of multiplication, as in "twain (two) times ten" = 20, etc. If each dialect group, or dialect, built its own system of higher numerals rather than inherited it, the problems involved in reconciling the forms would not be so tortuous, as a glance at the discussion in any of the explanatory grammars, such as those of Leumann and Schwyzer may illustrate.

Treatment of the system of the lower numerals has yielded explanations for those to 5. Proto-Indo-European **oinos* has long been explained as based on the root *ʔey-* "this one". I have proposed that the word for two is based on the root **dew-* "further," as in Hittite *tuwa* "distant." Moreover, that the word for three is based on the root **ter-* "even further," as in Sanskrit *tiráḥ* (1990a: 40). We may recall that Greek *énē* "the third day" is in origin "that (day)" (Specht 1944: 16). And if the Hittite *meywes* is a reflex of the Proto-Indo-European word, an additional numeral has been explained (Neu 1987: 176–7); based on the root **mey-* "lessen," the word for 4 would represent the lesser hand of four fingers, in contrast with 5 for the whole hand. The initial system would then have been based on pointing to objects – first as closest at hand, second as farther from the speaker, the third as even farther, while the words for 4 and 5 represent symbolization with four and five fingers.

The most convincing explanation for the words for 6 to 9 is by means of borrowing, or calques, although the word for 9 may be related to the root **new-* as in Latin *novus* "new." As stated above, however, I am chiefly concerned here with the approach applied with the aim of providing interpretations and explanations rather than with furnishing etymologies.

In contrast with the two other sets discussed, the set of numerals to and including 100 is conventionally held to be inherited from Proto-Indo-European. The position requires assumption of extensive remodeling through analogy in order to account for the forms. By contrast, an explanation assuming a set of simple numerals as far as 5, or even 10, in the proto-language, with further development of the numeral system in the individual dialects or dialect groups, as is generally assumed for "thousand," seems far more credible in view of the problems involved in deriving the attested forms from a putative set in the proto-language.

11.8 COMPOUNDS

If the general treatments for the set of numerals are inadequate, principles to account for the incidence of compounds in language are totally lacking. To be sure, in many handbooks and monographs dealing with individual languages, compounds are analysed for their components, and for the arrangement of these, as well as their accentuation when the data are available. Moreover, extensive treatments have been produced for the compounds in Indo-European, as by Brugmann (1897–1916, 2.1: 49–120); but the incidence of compounds in languages has not been related to language types or otherwise explained. It is accordingly difficult to account for the situation that is projected for specific proto-languages.

As a further difficulty, we must distinguish between compounds and phrases. In setting out to do so, Brugmann differentiates compounds from "indissoluble complexes" such as Latin *nudius tertius*. Treating this phrase repeatedly, he explains it as an "incorporated clause" that originally corresponded to "*nunc dies tertius* 'now (is) the third day = day-before-yesterday' " (1897–1916, 2.2: 679). Elsewhere he deals with its phonological structure as well (*ibid.* 1: 501, 2.1: 133). In contrast with such complexes, compounds are entities that are accented, inflected, and otherwise treated like simple words. Brugmann examines in great detail the compounds attested in the early dialects, as have others, describing especially their morphological characteristics and semantic relationships. More recently, explanations have been proposed for the types of compounds found; the productive compounding principles in a language are assumed to be in accordance with its syntactic patterns, as noted in 7.2.2 above.

In this way the differences in type between the earliest compounds that can be reconstructed for the proto-language and those predominant in the late dialects can be accounted for. The types that Risch and others found to be most prominent, synthetics and possessives, were productive at the time when Proto-Indo-European, like Vedic Sanskrit and early Greek, were OV syntactically, and active–stative in structure.

The synthetic compounds, e.g. Sanskrit *vīra-hán*, Greek *andróthnēs* "killing men," Latin *fructifer* "providing fruit," were produced in accordance with the OV clause pattern, with the second element corresponding to a verbal root or base. In the later dialects, compounds resembling this type are made with a nominal element of the verb, e.g. Gothic *arbi-numja* "inheritance-taker = heir," Old Slavic *medv-ĕd-i* "honey-eater = bear." The pattern then has gradually been modified in accordance with the syntactic shift of the language. Similarly, the possessives, while prominent in the early dialects, come to be restricted to words of a specific connotation, as in the often cited English *Bluebeard*. While the loss of productivity for this pattern may be related to the loss of the possibility of expressing "have" by patterns like the Latin *mihi est* construction, the regularization of the position of the accent may also have contributed. In Vedic Sanskrit, possessives had their accent on the first component, as in *ındra-sakhi* "having Indra as friend," while modifying compounds have it on the second, as in *indra-senắ* "Indra's army." When accent came to be placed by phonological rather than morphological principles, a formal basis of distinction between the two types was no longer available. Thereupon the adjectival pattern came to predominate, inasmuch as it was in keeping with the syntactic patterning of the language.

When we attempt to reconstruct the situation of compounding in Pre-Indo-European, we are faced with the problem of accounting for the virtual absence of compounds in Hittite. A few possessive compounds are attested, for example *ta-a-i-ú-ga-as* "two-yoke = a two-year old < having had two yokes." In setting out to account for the small number of compounds, we may recall Renou's observation that nominal compounds are far less frequent and of fewer types in Vedic Sanskrit than in the later language (1953: 231–3). We may propose then that Proto- and Pre-Indo-European had few nominal compounds; but we are unable to account for their relative infrequency. As noted earlier in this section, we would seek an explanation on the basis of general principles concerning the occurrence of compounds in languages that have been determined by study of their incidence by language types or other specific characteristics. Since such principles have not been determined, we are left with the observations provided here as based on the data in the Indo-European languages with earliest records. These observations indicate a gradual shift in type of compounds and of their role in the dialects from the periods of Proto- and Pre-Indo-European.

11.9 CONCLUSIONS DRAWN FROM EXAMINATION OF THE INDO-EUROPEAN VOCABULARY

In our examination of the vocabulary, we have been primarily interested in efforts to determine its bases of formation, which then may be used as a means for sorting out successive strata. As has long been clear, and also demonstrated above, suffixation is the process both for forming derivatives and inflections in the proto-language and in the early dialects. This process provides further evidence for identifying Proto-Indo-European as an OV language. Similarly, when specific formations, like injunctive forms and the *r/n* stems, are examined, they provide additional information for reconstructing an even earlier system.

We have also noted that examination of the words used in daily affairs permits identification of subclassifications in the lexicon. Forms of such everyday words are often inflected in accordance with procedures that have been superseded, as in Proto-Indo-European by the thematic inflection. Examination of the lexicon then assists us in singling out words that may reveal an earlier form of the language and through reconstruction of it insights into the culture and society of the speakers at an earlier time.

Analysis of the lexicon in this way provides one of the three bases for determining that culture, and for further inferences, such as the likely homeland of the speakers. Combined with data provided by archaeological discoveries, and by scrutiny of early texts, the lexicon has been examined for more than a century for evidence it contains to determine the culture of the Indo-European peoples and their early location. In the next chapter we review the principles that have been followed in combining information from these three sources.

12 The community of Indo-European speakers

12.1 SOURCES OF DATA: LANGUAGE, ARCHAEOLOGY, ANTIQUITIES

Treatment of the language and the early dialects should be the primary concern of Indo-European linguistics; but many Indo-Europeanists have also emphasized the importance of dealing with the speakers as well as with their languages. This aim was one of the major points made by Brugmann in his manifesto; he severely criticized Indo-European studies carried out before his time for dealing abstractly with languages rather than with languages in reference to the societies in which they were used. The last sentence in his second paragraph may well be recalled as pertinent for linguists also at other periods: "languages were indeed investigated most eagerly, but the person who speaks, much too little" (1878: iii).

Moreover, Meillet in his Oslo lectures strongly stressed the necessity of observing and describing dialects and languages to see how they function, and under conditions as varied as possible. ". . . What interests the linguist is not the norms but the way in which the language is used" ([1925] 1967: 132–3). He goes on to point out with examples various different language communities and types of language use, and language spread. Among his examples is Algeria, which "is tending . . . to eliminate Berber" in favor of Arabic, but not replacing it with French even though accepting "certain . . . material elements" of European civilization (135). As one of his major principles "language exists only by virtue of society" (104). The selection of Arabic by the dominant society in Algeria presumably illustrates that principle. Comparable selections in the past, as of an Indo-European language, must have similarly been made by the societies in which the language was adopted. For such reasons, two of the outstanding Indo-Europeanists have urged that the society of speakers be investigated as well as their languages.

Earlier as well, scholars dealt with the evidence for determining the activities and social organization of the speakers whose languages were studied. An example that has not lost its importance today is Jacob

Sources for this chapter: Schrader (English translation, 1890); Gimbutas (1970); Renfrew (1987); Mallory (1989); Gamkrelidze and Ivanov (1984).

Grimm's *Geschichte der deutschen Sprache* (1848), which has been cited above for its treatment of various everyday activities as well as the description of the language, to be sure in the Proto-Germanic not the Proto-Indo-European period. The cardinal work on the Indo-Europeans, Otto Schrader's *Sprachvergleichung und Urgeschichte*, first published in 1883, cites Grimm's account of the early Germanic speakers as a model. Published before Brugmann and Delbrück undertook their summary of the linguistic data, Schrader's work on the culture and society of the speakers of Proto-Indo-European was well received, as demonstrated by the publication of three editions, the second of which appeared in an English translation (1890). Under the title *Prehistoric Antiquities of the Aryan Peoples: a Manual of Comparative Philology and the Earliest Cultures*, the work reviews previous scholarship before presenting what might be called an anthropological description of the Indo-Europeans.

Schrader based his account on three sources: evidence from the language, from archaeological findings and from texts supplemented by artifacts like pottery and sculptures. Procedures applied in the archaeology of the time were admittedly primitive; only in this century did archaeologists pay careful attention to strata. Yet some advances had been made; the German emperor, Wilhelm II, is said to have been amused by the deductions based on absence of overt evidence, such as the difference in soil of post-holes that permitted assumption of posts which had rotted and disappeared. However, it was not until Flinders Petrie carefully observed successive strata that determination of the relative chronology of finds became a routine procedure.

Archaeological evidence today is much more detailed than that of Schrader's day; moreover, various procedures like use of carbon-14 tests provide relatively accurate dates. Yet Schrader's generation and that of his predecessors had the advantage of knowing thoroughly the pertinent texts, especially those of historians who wrote in Latin and Greek. Schrader's work cannot then be dismissed; on reading it, one is struck by the data that have remained crucial for identifying the early sites of the speakers, such as the word for "bull, steer" – in his transliteration, Greek *taûros*, Semitic *taura*, or that for "vine, wine," Greek *oînos*, Semitic *wainu* (Schrader 1890: 75; Gamkrelidze and Ivanov 1984: 519–21, 872, 968; 647–8, 881, 968, with somewhat different reconstructions). It may also be instructive to note his recollections of Kuhn's statement in 1845 that "the Indo-Europeans . . . were not merely pastoral, they had already made the transition to agriculture" (1890: 12). While archaeological and linguistic data have been greatly augmented, they have not provided the key to crucial issues, as the recent number of proposed "homelands" may indicate. Moreover, Schrader's book has not been followed by an equally comprehensive work. If read with care, it still provides a useful introduction to many problems, besides including the bibliographical sources in which some characteristics of Indo-European society were illuminated.

In contrast with his supposed reliance on palaeontology resulting presumably in naive views on the Indo-European community, Schrader states flatly that few concrete generalizations are possible, given the information at his time. However, he does not confuse language and race; instead, he dismisses any such notion, stating that the earliest Indo-European peoples in history show "no uniform physical type" (1890: 114). Rather than basing his conclusions on palaeontology, he concludes his section on methods and principles (107–49) with the statement:

> Comparative Philology [= linguistics] of itself is not in a position to reconstruct the primitive culture of the Indo-Europeans, and if we are to secure our advance step by step over this difficult ground, we can only do so on the condition that the three sisters, Linguistic Research, Prehistoric Research, and History, unite in the common work. (149)

A century later we possess vastly increased archaeological information, much earlier linguistic data, especially Anatolian, and some additional "history," as from the Anatolian texts and Linear B inscriptions of Greek. Unfortunately, however, the "three sisters" have by no means been united, in part because of the increasing specialization of each. When they are conjoined, as presumably by Mallory in his "search for the Indo-Europeans" with its subtitle *Language, Archaeology, and Myth* (1989), the extent of material from each, and its reliability, permits improvement over Schrader's work and that of subsequent scholars, if improved methodology is also employed. Since differences in methodology have led to differing views on the early speakers, any conclusions that are presented must be examined with reference to the methodology of the author who advances the views. We may examine briefly some of the issues.

12.2 INTERPRETATION OF THE DATA

Even brief consideration of the uses of Schrader's "three sisters" reveals the handicaps of each. These require attention, as well as their several strengths.

12.2.1 Shortcomings and strengths of linguistic research

Linguistic research carried out on the proto-language is faced with problems resulting from the situation that it must rely entirely on reconstructed material, which is by definition incomplete. Moreover, the reconstructed proto-language is assumed for the end of the fifth millennium; since our earliest Indo-European written text is the edict of Anitta (c. 1750 BC), several millennia elapsed between the time of Proto-Indo-European and its production.

During this period words may have been completely lost, as were possible reflexes of the proto-form of "water" in Latin and other dialects; nor can we assert that we know the word for "hand" in the proto-language, since the concept was subject to taboo, as was the word for "tongue," both of them items in the severely reduced "universal set of words" selected by nostratacists because of their supposed permanence in language. Many further examples could be cited of ways in which words are obscured or lost; the ongoing losses in the lexicon lessen the usefulness of the data that Schrader and other commentators on Indo-European society call on when employing the results provided by the first sister, linguistic research.

Moreover, as recent attention to the glottalic theory indicates, even the apparently most secure elements of the grammar may have been inadequately reconstructed until recently. Whatever one's opinion of the glottalic theory, there is little possibility of rejecting laryngeals for the proto-language; the most conservative scholars now posit at least one. The results of linguistic research must therefore be subjected to constant scrutiny, in the interests of credibility.

Of even greater importance than views on the phonology, morphology or syntax is one's treatment of the dialects, or of subgroups including two or more dialects, when reconstructing the proto-language. The history of reconstructing Proto-Indo-European might be characterized as a continuing effort to liberate it from the heavy hand of Sanskrit. Each move has proceeded slowly, as the long effort required to recognize that an early form of Sanskrit, and accordingly the proto-language, included /e/ because a palatalized form of velars is found before some Sanskrit *a*, as is *c* from **k* in the reduplicated perfect form *cakara*. And many more years were required to rid the consonantal system of aspirated voiceless stops, an achievement of Kurylowicz that was long questioned, even after 1927. Moreover, many Indo-Europeanists still assume that the subgroup including Sanskrit and Greek is closest to the proto-language. The assumption requires extraordinary effort to account for the morphological structure of Hittite, especially because of its similarity with that of Germanic. It also overlooks innovations in Greek and Sanskrit that have not been extended throughout all categories in the early stages of these languages, such as the augment. But the assumption of such a proto-language has not yet been totally abandoned. Linguists who maintain the assumption hold different views on crucial reconstructed words in the lexicon from those who consider many characteristics of Indo-Iranian, Greek and Armenian to be innovations in the central subgroup that they represent. In short, linguistic research has been faced with many problems for which solutions have been offered that depend on the methodology of the linguists concerned as well as on linguistic evidence.

Yet language, in contrast with "prehistoric research" (i.e. archaeology) provides the only certain data for recognizing speakers of Indo-European. If there were any doubts on this score, they might be resolved by the reaction to Hittite when discovered at Boğazköy. Many scholars were sceptical about its classification as an Indo-European language, even after Hrozny published his proofs, as in citing the heteroclitic inflection of *watar*: *wetenas* "water." The authoritative scholar, Kretschmer had prompted the hesitancy by his statement that no further Indo-European language could be expected from Asia Minor (1896: 289ff.). Yet the virtual impossibility of finding heteroclitic nouns with *r* : *n* interchange in a non-Indo-European language, as well as the similarity of the lexical element for water to that in Germanic and other languages, and also other data eventually led scholars to disregard Kretschmer's pronouncement.

Like any scientific activity, linguistic research must be performed with appropriate methodology for credible results. The linguistics carried on within Indo-European studies has been repeatedly renewed, as by the growing understanding of phonetics in the nineteenth century, by the improved morphological procedures under influence of Indian grammarians, and by the fuller understanding of syntax in our generation. Still, impressions arise that the methodology is dated or obsolete; the view is strengthened by supposed revolutions in the field. Yet now that the generative-transformational revolution is being unmasked as increasingly vacuous, reasons for defection astound Indo-Europeanists. A recent handbook cites as a major reason for abandoning the generative approach its inability to deal with clitics, scarcely a novel finding for linguists who had even elementary acquaintance with the classical languages. As a solution it adopts an "orientation [that] resembles in broad outlook the sort of view that underlies descriptive grammars of the last century, where one finds the discussion divided into more or less independent sections called something like 'phonology,' 'flexion,' 'wordbuilding,' and 'syntax' " (Sadock 1991: 5). The highly touted theory that was proclaimed to have illuminated well-documented and long-understood developments like that of modal auxiliaries in English (Lightfoot 1988: 313–19) may then have joined Grotefend's of over a century and a half ago.

We may recall bases for the validity of Indo-European grammar. From the start many of its prominent scholars aimed to determine underlying structure, as noted in 1.1. In carrying out this aim they regarded language as a structure in which all the parts are interrelated. And they gave careful attention to facts, methods and principles, as noted in 2.1. Shortcomings and disagreements are due in part to approaches of lesser scope. But when the central methods were applied on the basis of these procedures, they led to results that are now generally accepted.

12.2.2 Shortcomings and strengths of archaeology

The chief problem faced by archaeological research is its inability to relate with assurance its findings to a given society speaking a specific language unless specimens of that language are discovered with those findings. The handicap is repeatedly stated, so that successive archaeologists struggle for novel ways to express it; according to a recent version, "pots do not equal people" (Mallory 1989: 164).

On the other hand, archaeology provides us with the only secure evidence we have for prehistoric peoples. "Stones may not speak," in Renfrew's variant of the saying, but if images are carved in them, these images provide some information on the carver. Similarly, pots are generally distinctive from one culture, or from one subgroup of a culture, to another. We then are faced with the frequently embarrassing situation that we can identify a culture but not the people that maintained that culture, including its language. A few minutes with any handbook on the cultures of the fifth to third millennia that have been determined for the areas in which Indo-European languages were spoken during the second and first millennia are adequate to indicate the large number of societies that developed distinctive cultures. Relating these cultures with precursors of the speakers of recorded languages is, however, highly difficult.

A central problem facing specialists in linguistic research who cooperate with specialists in archaeological research has to do with the means by which languages are and have been disseminated. There is no question whatsoever that non-Indo-European languages were spoken in the subcontinent before Indic speakers settled there; there is little question that other such languages were spoken throughout virtually the entire subsequent area, including Europe, in which Indo-European languages were introduced; but massive problems remain concerning the introduction of those Indo-European languages.

Formerly, linguists and archaeologists ascribed change of dialects and languages to invasions of new peoples. Even Meillet states that "the Greek dialects result from the fact that there were successive and different thrusts of invaders over the Hellenic domain," while he ascribes the Gallo-Romance dialects to separate political regions, and the expansion of Parisian French to the dominant cultural and political status of Paris ([1929] 1967: 71–2). In attributing the spread of the Indo-European languages, the massive tribal movements of Germanic speakers from the first century before our era to the collapse of the Roman Empire were often taken as model. Little archaeological evidence could be assembled to support the model for the spread of the Indo-European languages and their speakers. In time it became clear that in the fifth millennium tribal groups lacked the means and population to carry out such massive shifts.

More recently, archaeologists have emphasized diffusion in accounting for language and culture change as through the "wave of advance model." By the model, innovations in culture and technology were examined for their advantages, and when so viewed were adopted by neighboring peoples. Some migration is accepted, but not that of large-scale groups such as those around the beginning of our era.

The contrast between the two proposed bases for spread of the Indo-European languages attracted dramatic attention with the publication of

Renfrew's book of 1987. On the assumption that success in spread of languages is directly associated with economic advances provided by agriculture, Renfrew placed the original home within the area that practised and extended agriculture. Moreover, in a subsequent essay he asserted that one of his chief contributions is a replacement of the earlier equation: culture = people = language, by an approach examining relationships between change in material culture, social and demographic change, language change (1990: 21). The replacement may have been an innovation in his field but scarcely in historical linguistics.

The homeland of the Indo-Europeans that he proposed is in the area of the recently excavated site in south-central Turkey known as Çatal hüyük. It is widely accepted that the practice of agriculture spread from the Middle East, presumably through Anatolia, to Europe; but associating the spread of agriculture with extension of the Indo-European languages finds no support in any of the identified linguistic changes. Moreover, we have pointed out above that as early as 1845 Indo-Europeanists held that "the Indo-Europeans . . . had already made the transition to agriculture." The proposed "change in material culture" cannot then be related to the "language change" wherever the homeland may have been. Happily, Renfrew now admits in his review of Mallory (1989c) that the practice of agriculture may have been extended from the Middle East to the southern area of Russia that others have assumed for the homeland of the Indo-European speakers.

As we note further below, when we examine Renfrew's hypothesis and also the discussions following it, he has neglected Schrader's third sister. Any examination of the wall paintings at Çatal hüyük leaves little question that the culture of the Indo-European speakers as indicated in their early texts was totally different from that of the peoples at Çatal hüyük. There is no reflection in any site associated with the Indo-Europeans of "skeletons, often with their skulls painted and decorated . . . buried under the sleeping-platforms in houses" (Mellaart 1978: 15). Similarly, the shrines dedicated to the goddess are totally out of keeping with Indo-European religion (*ibid*. 20, with illustrations).

Of prime importance in examining the discussion on language spread is the attention given to conclusions based on typological investigations. In the special section of the journal *Antiquity* devoted to "archaeology and Indo-European Languages" (62: 563–95) the initial paper is by the Africanist Christopher Ehret. On the basis of observing interrelationships leading to change in language and culture Ehret distinguishes sharply between "language and ethnic shift . . . in small-scale societies" and those in "urban and class societies" (1988: 570). Without excluding the effects of migration, he indicates the readiness of small-scale societies to adopt more advantageous technology and also different languages, often providing no evidence for subsequent archaeological discovery. Accordingly, there is no inherent reason to accept Renfrew's thesis associating the spread of the

Indo-European languages with the adoption of agriculture in Europe. The most significant result of Renfrew's book may be the renewed association between at least some archaeologists and linguists.

It is highly important, however, that each camp be aware of the current state of the other. Renfrew seems to assume that Indo-Europeanists adhere to the family-tree model, and that application of the comparative method requires its assumption. Yet the wave model has long superseded it, based on tenets that are closely comparable with those of models emphasizing diffusion among the archaeologists.

The continuing attention to the problem of the homeland, whether by scholars favoring migration or diffusion, illustrates the importance of including all data, or in Schrader's terms, of calling on the three sisters. Each has its shortcomings, as we will note also of the third sister, history – in Renfrew's terms, of social and demographic matters. Only constant consultation and correlation of the data provided by the three will yield credible results.

12.2.3 Shortcomings and strengths of conclusions based on history

Data taken from texts, including poetic texts, might well be assumed to provide the most reliable information about the speakers of the early languages. Herodotus has given us detailed descriptions about peoples who lived in areas that have been identified as the homeland, and who observed social and material practices that seemed appropriate for the area also in earlier times. Further, the accuracy of much of his account has been dramatically supported by archaeological discoveries, such as the remarkable Scythian treasures. Yet there is a considerable time differential between the period of the proto-language and the texts that have come down to us. The text of Herodotus is about 1,300 years later than that of Anitta, dated 1750 BC. Even if we assume that change was carried out more slowly in a period when communication was limited, we cannot avoid the notion that cultures of the fifth and fourth millennia before our era must have undergone considerable change before the time of our early texts.

Moreover, the early texts deal with very limited topics. Anitta's account simply reports conquests, which are of importance for the history of the Hittite kingdom though dealing with little besides warfare. Some information on material and social culture is indeed included. Anitta speaks of a crown of iron, suggesting greater control over the metal than do the epics of Homer, where a chunk of iron is valued as a prize, not material for fashioning objects. He also refers to his god Sius, who as sun god may be directly equated with Proto-Indo-European *dyēus*, also maintained in Greek *Zeús* and Latin *Jupiter* as well as gods in other dialects. Other Hittite texts provide further information, notably the laws; but later they are gradually overlaid by influences from Mediterranean culture.

The early Greek texts transmitted in Linear B are restricted in a different way. Very short, they give us little but inventories for tax purposes. The Homeric poems, those of Hesiod and other early authors provide some data to reconstruct the life of their characters. When not idealized, as in the account of Odysseus' swineherd Eumaeus, these may well represent daily life of the time; but if presenting situations that might have been actual in Indo-European times, even the early Homeric poems reflect Mediterranean influence on such situations.

Hymns of the *Rigveda* may maintain the oldest language material of any dialect. They and later Vedic hymns, however, present ideas concerning religion, worship and mythology, with scarcely any information on other social activities; the Avestan hymns are comparable. Some highly interesting hymns, as that depicting the plight of the gambler, are among the latest of the *Rigveda*; but since Tacitus reports of the Germanic peoples a love for gambling to the extent of forfeiting one's liberty, we may ascribe fondness for gambling to the proto-speakers. While some hymns may reflect Indo-European conditions in this way, many more are concerned with the conditions of the subcontinent, as in the intense desire and need for rain.

Rather than providing information through accounts of social conditions, our earliest texts must be examined for data conveyed through lexical items, which often permit varied interpretation. When we finally have an account that is compared with an anthropological description of today, Tacitus' *Germania*, more than 4,000 years have elapsed from the time of the proto-language. In addition, the material is tendentious, seeking to illustrate to the effete Romans a more appropriate way of life. Schrader's third sister for these reasons loses much of her promise.

In the early period of Indo-European studies the information from the texts, such as the Homeric poems, semed more significant than it does today; for during that period the proto-language was proposed for the end of the third millennium. In view of the great divergence among the languages of our earliest materials, we can scarcely place the community of speakers of proto-Indo-European later than the early part of the fourth millennium. In contrast with possibilities of our predecessors, we consider this date reasonably accurate, supported by methods of dating that have been introduced in the last half century. Our conviction that we can date the period of the proto-language allows us to speak with much greater assurance about the evidence each of the sisters provides, whatever its inadequacies and shortcomings.

12.3 INFERENCES BASED ON TEXTS

While descriptive materials deal with societies and cultures two or more millennia after the Proto-Indo-European period, scholars have attempted to reconstruct by the comparative method segments of texts that represent characteristic items or practices of culture at the time of the proto-language. These segments may consist of several words, or also of single lexical items that reflect cultural beliefs and practices.

12.3.1 Reconstruction of phrases

The phrase most often re-examined was pointed out by Adalbert Kuhn (1853: 467). It is reflected by the Rigvedic phrase *ákṣiti śrávaḥ* and by Homeric *kléos áphthiton* "imperishable glory." The phrase is notable formally because it includes the archaic cluster reconstructed as Proto-Indo-European *dhgʷh*. Semantically, it corresponds to a notion that is central in a predominant type of verse in cultures of the subgroups as late as the time of Icelandic literature. Further, the Greek phrase is found in a passage in *Iliad* 9: 412, where Achilles is considering his course of action for battle in a discussion with other heroes, Ajax, Phoenix and Odysseus, that is to say, the type of situation that can readily be imagined for the Proto-Indo-European period. The *Rigveda* passages in which the phrase occurs are also archaic. Accordingly, there is good evidence that the phrase may have been inherited from that period. It is rightly treated at great length by Rüdiger Schmitt (1967: esp. 1–2, 61–79).

Yet Schmitt's treatment and that of other scholars is curious. As he points out, the phrase is found three times in the *Rigveda*, in the form *ákṣiti śrávaḥ*. Two of these occurrences are in poems identified as Archaic by E. Vernon Arnold (1905: Appendix IV, 269–88), those in Book 8.103.4b and 9 66.7c; a verse identified as Strophic, that is, the second chronological layer, Book 1.40.4b, repeats the line of Book 8. By contrast, the passage in which the adjective appears in thematic inflection, *Rigveda* 1.9.7bc is identified as Normal, that is, the third chronological layer. On these grounds alone the adjective should be reconstructed with *i*-stem rather than thematic inflection.

Moreover, in the thematic passage the adjective is predicatival. That is to say, there is no evidence in the *Rigveda* for the phrase *śrávas ákṣitam*. Further, it has been clear since Delbrück's syntactic studies of more than a century ago (1878, 1888) that Vedic syntax is OV, that is, descriptive adjectives precede the nouns they modify.

Yet Schmitt, and others, disregard the linguistic evidence and reconstruct for Proto-Indo-European **kléṷos *ńdhgʷhitom*, in accordance with the order found in post-Homeric verse. It is difficult to understand why the phrase should be reconstructed on the basis of its occurrences in late Greek verse rather than on the basis of the clear philological as well as the linguistic evidence of older texts. One can only assume that the scholars who posit the phrase in accordance with late Greek adhere to the obsolete practice of reconstructing for the proto-language any comparable items, with no consideration of chronological layers.

Finally, the presence of the phrase in only Indo-Iranian and Greek leaves doubts about its inheritance from the proto-language, for it is clear that these dialects with Armenian formed a subgroup in which innovations were introduced. While we can assume short poems, like those of the *Rigveda*, for the period of the proto-language, long epics like those labeled Homeric may well be based on non-Indo-European poetic tradition. When attention is given to reconstructions, whether of individual words or phrases, it is hazardous to forget the sociological situation.

The phrase for "imperishable glory" may have been treated here at some length. But in a consideration of principles, those underlying philological treatment of texts cannot be overlooked. We may also point out once again the importance for Indo-European studies of the principles that the early scholars adopted from Cuvier. When any phrase or word is treated for reconstruction, the context, social as well as linguistic, in which it is found must be taken into account for credible results.

12.3.2 Reconstruction of individual words

Since the time of Schleicher the reconstruction of words, not simply roots or bases, has been required as a basis for acceptance of further assumptions about the structure of the language or conclusions on culture. For many words the situation has long been demonstrated. The reconstructed word for the "foot," Proto-Indo-European *$pès$ or *$pós$ is generally accepted, as is that of many other nouns, verbs and particles to be assumed for use in everyday speech; but often such words furnish little information about the early culture. Problems with reconstructing some words, such as that for "hand" or the verb "have," provide indirect information. The inability to reconstruct the proto-language word for "hand" from the words available in the several dialects has been interpreted as indicating that the topic was tabooed, so that neologisms were introduced and maintained; the various words for "have" are accounted for through the view that the earlier language had no word for the meaning, since it was active in structure. While the reconstruction of words that might be expected in every culture is useful for linguistic purposes, our chief interest after a century and a half of attention is reconstruction of words with special significance in Indo-European culture and their connotations.

The most comprehensive such work published before the second volume of Gamkrelidze and Ivanov (1984) is Benveniste's two-volume handbook on "The vocabulary of Indo-European institutions" of 1969. In it Benveniste treats sets under headings like economics and religion. His treatment is rigorous, and his conclusions have been generally well received, if not adopted in their entirety.

Instead of dealing with any of Benveniste's words or sets, I illustrate the procedure with a term explicated by Calvert Watkins (1991), Latin *tarentum* "grave, tomb." Found in a corrupt passage of Varro's *De lingua latina*, the words lead to intricate conclusions about conceptions of the afterlife among the speakers of Proto-Indo-European. The Latin word is derived from the Indo-European root *ter-* "cross over," commonly extended in base I with laryngeal, yielding *ter-h₂-*, as in Vedic *tīrthám* "crossing place, ford." Comparing other formations from the base, as in Hittite, Watkins glosses it "overcome" and proposes that the basis of the meaning for the Latin word was the notion of overcoming death. Further, the *ludi Saeculares* held at the site Tarentum in Rome were celebrated once every century to "assure the long life and orderly succession of the generations" (*ibid*. 143). Watkins supports the conclusion with data from other dialects, such as Greek *néktar* "nectar," a compound consisting of the root *nek-* "death" and the root *ter-*, with the meaning "rescuing after death"; the food of the gods then provides them with immortality.

In this way the lexicon of the proto-language is illuminated, as well as the culture of the speakers. As examination of Watkins's article or of Benveniste's studies (1969) as well as the second volume of Gamkrelidze and Ivanov (1984) will indicate, the process of expanding our information of the lexicon and the society of speakers beyond that achieved at the time of Schrader is slow and laborious. The material provided by the Anatolian group is highly useful in this effort, though even dialects attested only in our era like Old Irish and Germanic contain evidence that remains to be interpreted, among it that in the early recorded popular verse.

As support for any conclusions, it would be helpful to relate those drawn from such lexical analyses with archaeological finds. These in general are late, as we have noted of the Scythian treasures. And those from earlier periods, as in Val Camonica near Milan or in the Scandinavias as at Kivik, cannot be certainly ascribed to Indo-Europeans. For the most part, then, the treatment of words and textual material must rely on evidence in their own sphere.

12.3.3 Assumptions drawn from texts

In view of similarities between texts in various groups, efforts have been made to reconstruct texts. These have been applied largely for verse, as for magic charms. Parallels have long been noted, for example, between Germanic charms and popular verse of the *Atharvaveda*. Rather than reconstructed verse, however, scholars have been primarily concerned with views that may be ascribed to the early poets.

A remarkable conception attested in texts of various branches, from Indo-Iranian to Germanic, distinguishes languages of the gods from those of men. The conception, and expressions of it, have been thoroughly examined, especially by Toporov in an important article (1981; see also Bader 1989 and Campanile 1977). Discussing the topic would require more space than is available here. The point is included in great part to indicate that there are grounds for assuming a sophisticated view of language among the early speakers, as well as carefully structured texts.

On a somewhat different plane we may recall the fable that Schleicher invented in a step that still elicits criticism or even ridicule. Yet, as Toporov indicates (1981: 193), Schleicher's aim was severely restricted. Using a content as vapid as the Dick and Jane stories that made up a mindless part of American education until recently, Schleicher merely wished to point out that syntactic sequences could be reconstructed as readily as lexical sequences. His syntactic reconstruction has been superseded as much as has the lexical reconstruction of his time (see Lehmann and Zgusta 1979). The successive reconstructions illustrate the underlying syntactic principles determined by successive generations of Indo-Europeanists just as the lexical reconstructions illustrate their phonological and morphological principles, around all of which the texts were constructed.

12.4 INFERENCES BASED ON ARCHAEOLOGICAL FINDINGS

While some historical linguists object to the use of models for language, archaeologists rely heavily on them. Models are proposed in the efforts to explain "new culture manifestations" (Mallory 1989: 165). Other models are applied in accounting for the introduction of different languages, whether by migration or diffusion. Models are also used for "exchange systems, prestige chains, peer-polity interaction," etc. (*ibid.*) By such models and by scrutiny of artifacts, especially pottery, archaeologists isolate, label and interpret cultures and cultural practices. In the current concern for the position of the horse in a given culture, a recent anthropological article analyses its effect in a society, drawing largely on observations in Mongolia (Levine 1990).

By these methods archaeologists have succeded in isolating and interpreting many cultures in Eurasia, beginning with the resettlement after the retreat of the glaciers. Since the speakers in these cultures were preliterate, the cultures cannot be identified with language communities. Any proposed identification must then be based on models of cultural traits examined in conjunction with language structures.

12.4.1 Inferences on the spread of the Indo-European speakers

Disregarding archaeological discussion before the possibility of carbon-14 dating and its subsequent upgrading, we can for Indo-European purposes limit ourselves to proposed models and conclusions that have been prominent after the dating process was determined. As noted above, the conclusions have revolved around two models on the spread of languages. The first, now widely identified with Gimbutas, but held by many earlier scholars, assumes invasion of warlike, mounted peoples from southern Russia who imposed their language on the autochthons; by Gimbutas's variant of the view, there were three different invasions that overwhelmed the peaceful, matrilineal autochthons. The second model, now identified with Renfrew, but proposed by earlier scholars as well, assumes gradual extension of the Indo-European languages; by Renfrew's variant of the view, the extension of the languages accompanied expansion of agriculture from the Middle East.

In Mallory's interpretation of Renfrew's position, by holding firmly to a "wave of advance" model, Renfrew virtually condemns himself to associating the spread of the languages with the only "basic and widespread cultural and economic change" that can be identified for Europe after neolithic times (1989a: 177). It is scarcely necessary to add that there is as little evidence to associate Indo-European speakers with the expansion of agriculture as there is to assume successive waves of warlike invaders from southern Russia.

If archaeologists are to contribute to the identification of prehistoric societies of Indo-European speakers and their expansion, they must concentrate on segments of culture that can be correlated with linguistic and historical data. An obvious candidate is the culture surrounding the horse. Early texts and practices, such as the horse sacrifice, indicate its central position in Indo-European society. Most of the dialects have reflexes of its designation, as in cognates of Latin *equus*. Yet, as is well known, attempts to equate the forms of the designation attested in the various dialects result in many phonological problems, for which somewhat desperate solutions have been proposed.

Without reviewing those attempts, I illustrate briefly through a parallel my view that different forms of clearly the same etymon may result from a borrowing that is restructured in individual dialects or dialect groups. The term for "potato" was introduced to Europe in the sixteenth century with the native designation for the sweet potato, *batata*. Reconstructing the original form would provide substantial difficulties for strict application of the comparative method, with variants like Spanish *patata*, Spanish and Portuguese *batata*, Galician *pataka*, Languedoc *patalo*, and even less similar forms in other regions, such as *tapin*, *katin*, *patal* and so on in the Romance area alone. The variants beside *equus* differ far less among one another.

Since it is agreed that the horse is closely aligned with Indo-European society, information on its domestication and use, as for riding, is highly desirable. After painstaking study by Anthony and Brown, that information has now been provided (1991). The earliest teeth showing wear from a bridle have been found at Dereivka, a site south of Kiev on the Dnieper. They have been dated around 4000 BC. The date fits well the period during which the Indo-European dialects began to spread. And the situation furnishes a positive example of coordinating linguistic and archaeological information. If in addition the cheek-pieces shaped like a horsehead are taken into account, we have further evidence for siting the Indo-Europeans in the area required as central to domestication of the horse.

The evidence does not answer all questions. Nor does it provide support for the assumption of the Indo-Europeans through warlike conquests; but it correlates with the morphological evidence provided by the inflection of the word for "horse." It is thematic, as Specht emphasized half a century ago (1944). Accordingly, it would have been introduced, whether by borrowing or from native lexical elements, at the period of the proto-language when it was being separated into dialect groups and dialects. Further, we date this period around 4000 BC.

In view of the central position of linguistic evidence, it may be useful to comment briefly on a topic that is often raised concerning the use of only one word for an item so central in a culture. Other such items, such as the automobile or the airplane, are rarely referred to with these designations but rather with terms like Sentra or Colt, and B-47 or Airbus. With reference to various terms for the horse we may recall with Toporov a passage from the *Śatapatha-Brāhmaṇa* (X.6.4.1) in which a number of words for the horse are recorded (1981: 204).

> háyo bhūtvá deván avahad vājí gandharván árvā ásurān áśvo manuṣyán
> "As haya he bore the gods, as vajin the Gandharvas, as arvan the Asuras, as ashva the people."

Variant terms may well have been introduced in post-Indo-European times, as late as this prose passage in Sanskrit, or even later, as in the various words for "horse" in English. Whether or not the late proto-language included more than one term for horse, the presence of only one term attested throughout the dialects supports assumption of the recency of the borrowing. Like the words *automobile* and *airplane*, the generic term may have been the word initially adopted and then maintained.

In short, the information provided by archaeological work concerning the domestication of the horse, correlates well with the data from the language. Since in addition the archaeological data on the development of wagonry drawn by oxen is also increasingly well documented, its correlation with Specht's conclusions based on the language add assurance to the information determined from both sisters for the use and extension of means of transportation.

12.4.2 Inferences from absence of tokens

As one of the major contributions of recent times to our understanding of the development of civilization, Denise Schmandt-Besserat has identified the early means of carrying on commerce and eventually introducing taxation as well as writing systems through her brilliant work on tokens (*Before Writing*, 1992, with copious bibliography). The time of their introduction has been determined as approximately 8000 BC. Developed with increasing sophistication, as inferred from the increasingly complex tokens found at successive strata, they have been excavated in well-identified sites throughout the Middle East. The locations indicate the extent of trade, and also provide insights into the culture of the societies using them. According to Schmandt-Besserat, they are closely associated with the priestly society well known through data derived from recorded material of Mesopotamia and adjacent areas.

That society is quite different from the society we can project for the early Indo-Europeans. Whether we accept or reject Dumezil's views on the tripartite structure, we can firmly reject any notion that leaders in the Indo-European communities were priest-kings.

It is similarly remarkable that there is absolutely no evidence for tokens in the sites that have been identified as the homeland of the Indo-Europeans, unless we were to accept Renfrew's discredited suggestion of Çatal hüyük; he seemed himself to disavow it in his flippantly titled review of Mallory's book (1989c). No tokens have been discovered in the Balkans, nor in the broad geographical band from southern France to the Urals that has been projected as including a possible site since the days of Brugmann and even earlier.

With all allowance for inferences based on the use of negative evidence, the correlation between the absence of tokens and the data on Indo-European culture that we derive from the languages provides another example of a dual source for our conclusions on the early home, and the subsequent dissemination of the early speakers. As additional archaeological discoveries are made known, this use of information as well as the information provided by very similar linguistic and archaeological evidence promises to illuminate further our understanding of the early Indo-European society.

12.5 INFERENCES FROM HISTORY

We have noted the shortcomings of our early texts in providing information about the culture of the early groups of speakers, as well as the long interval between the production of the texts and the time of the proto-language. In spite of the difficulties resulting from this situation, some accounts by Greek and Roman historians yield a tantalizingly similar picture to that we might well assume for the earlier society. These accounts have been interpreted for their views of daily living, and also for information on religious beliefs.

12.5.1 Inferences from historical accounts about daily living

Herodotus' account of the life of the Scythians in the fourth book of his history seems to provide an accurate picture of life as determined by the topography and resources of southern Russia up to a few centuries ago – according to Schrader, up to one century ago. Correlated also with

Strabo's observations of northern Europe in the third century before our era, of Caesar's of central Europe in the first century before our era, and those of Tacitus at the end of the first century, as well as with observations of the life in unspoiled areas of the Balkans in the nineteenth century, Herodotus' account could readily be projected for peoples in the area two or three millennia earlier.

After a credible description of the Danube in Book 4, section 50, Herodotus identifies the other rivers, noting especially the Dnieper in section 53. Painting an attractive picture of its clear water with large supplies of fish, and the abundant pastures on its shores as well as fertile fields for grain, Herodotus seems to have identified the location that led to the increase of population necessary for the extensive dissemination of the Indo-Europeans. Customs of the Scythians, such as the absence of altars and temples, fit the type of worship. Burial customs, including the raising of a mound, are comparable to that at the end of the *Iliad* and similar to that at the end of the *Beowulf*. And the mobility, by means of horses for the men to ride and wagons for family transportation, can scarcely have differed from that in the fourth millennium, after wagons were introduced.

Details that Herodotus included on special practices we cannot verify. Some of them, such as drinking blood of slain enemies out of skulls, have been luridly repeated; yet comparable tales have been told about poorly known peoples in all continents, so that here one suspects Herodotus of giving way to his fondness for sensational anecdotes. Other details are credible, such as the use of hemp. The earlier form of the word *cannabis* was taken over by Indo-Europeans in Europe, presumably from Thracian, before the completion of the Germanic shift in which *k* was modified to *h*, *b* to *p*, etc. While the word was also introduced into Greek as *kánnabis* as well as to Latin, the utilization of the drug was scarcely central to Scythian culture. The anecdote must have lent an aura of the exotic to his account.

In spite of some credible reports, and verification through the images on materials found especially with burials, current Indo-Europeanists hesitate to depict Indo-European life with the color of such accounts in the nineteenth century. As the second volume of the Gamkrelidze and Ivanov work illustrates, sets of words are interpreted instead for possible leads about customs and practices. The texts of the Greek and Roman historians are generally viewed as based on unreliable hearsay evidence, much of it elaborated to arouse interest, or as by Caesar for self-glorification, and by Tacitus for providing a model of a people with higher ethical standards than those of the Romans of his day.

12.5.2 Inferences from historical accounts about religion and mythology

The most notable exploitation of the texts for inferences about Indo-European culture is that of Georges Dumézil. Recognized by Meillet as a "young French scholar" who had already made contributions to the interpretations of "Indo-European myths" ([1925] 1967: 13–14), Dumézil went on to produce a large number of studies that brought him acclaim comparable to that accorded a small number of recent French intellectuals.

As in the treatment of linguistic and archaeological data, our primary concern is the theoretical basis of Dumézil's conclusions, however his successors in the fields of mythology and religion regard them. Polomé (1982b: 5) lists his "disciples in France" and elsewhere, while Littleton includes also his critics (1982: 153–203). To evaluate the principles applied in research on mythology, it may be helpful to recall the treatment of the topic by earlier scholars, notably Schrader.

After rejecting many of the procedures and conclusions of Jacob Grimm, Adalbert Kuhn, Max Müller and others for their almost exclusive reliance on language as source of myths (stated briefly in one of Müller's aphorisms such as those forwarded from time to time by flamboyant scholars: "mythology is but an old form of language"), Schrader examines the proposed equations of key words, and also the reports on Germanic religion by Caesar and on Persian religion by Herodotus (1890: 406–11, 416–17). By his conclusion "the common basis of the ancient Indo-European religion was a worship of the powers of nature" (*ibid*. 418), but "rites and ceremonies of a religious kind" remain for "inquirers of the future" to determine (*ibid*. 420). Dumézil is clearly the most prominent of these inquirers.

One of Schrader's objections to earlier conclusions had to do with their limitation of inferences to texts in two branches, Greek and Indo-Iranian; even Schrader may have suspected that the similarities between data from these two branches may have been post-Indo-European. Faced with the same limitation, Dumézil hit on a far-reaching principle to broaden the basis for determining the mythology and religion of the Indo-Europeans. By the principle, variously expressed, for the Romans, "mythology, and in fact a very ancient mythology in large part inherited from Indo-European times, while it has been destroyed at the level of theology, has prospered under the form of history" (Dumézil 1970a: 4). That is to say, the texts produced by Roman historians, Laelius, Florus and Livy among others, provide data on mythology from a third branch of the Indo-European family, when we reinterpret the accounts of early Roman history as "a history of origins tracing the significant adventures of men who . . . correspond to . . . gods" (*ibid*.). The principle was extended, as to Celtic and Germanic texts, providing additional grounds for the conclusions from even more branches.

The results are the well-known "triad," "tripartite ideology" and "trifunctional classes": priests, warriors, producers (Polomé 1982b: 7) that are proposed as a "common Indo-European heritage. Polomé, like others no doubt, is puzzled by "the disappearance of the trifunctional system in the elaboration of the theology of the Greeks" and by "the fate of the Indo-European religious heritage in Anatolia" (*ibid*. 12). But he and other disciples continue to elaborate the system, drawing among other sources on such records as Arthurian texts, on Icelandic saga, on folk-tales, on Geoffrey of Monmouth's "tale of Lear" and on an emended word in *Beowulf* (Polomé 1982).

Moreover, the way is again open to further inferences based on the lexicon. Puhvel in his brilliantly written work, *Comparative Mythology*, now finds evidence to equate Vedic *Apā́m Nápāt* and Latin *Neptūnus*, drawing on a remarkable array of Latin texts, while also correcting a historian as well known as Plutarch for "carelessly placing the October Equus on the Ides of December" (1987: 280). Moreover, requiring a twin in explaining the "much more sophisticated anthropogony in Germanic, Indo-Iranian, and Roman sources" (*ibid*. 284), Puhvel posits Roman **Yemos* or **Yemenos*, which then is modified to *geminus* by "cross-attraction," to match *Yamá*; thereupon it is "transformed to *Remus* by alliterative association with Romulus" (*ibid*. 289).

On reading such explanations by the "disciples" of Dumézil, one recalls the concern of Schrader "that the linguistic science of the Comparative Mythologists is no longer coincident with the linguistic science of Comparative Linguists" (1890: 412). Even though Puhvel bewails the earlier "mythological disaster" that identified Greek **Kéntauros* . . . with Sanskrit *Gandharvás* – which Schrader did not – no attention is given in his book to the reasons for which Schrader rejected "the explanation of the Lat. *Neptûnus* by means of the Vedic *apâm napât*" (Puhvel 1987: 13). We may wonder whether the field is again free for application of "a series of philological feats of legerdemain, etc." (Schrader 1890: 412).

Whatever the views held concerning the "new comparative mythology," its procedures represent attempts to draw on texts to support inferences based on linguistic data. Such attempts are highly welcome when rigorously undertaken. In addition, it would be advantageous to have archaeological evidence in further support of any inferences based on the two other sisters. Unfortunately, no archaeological support has been discovered for the tripartite ideology. In the harsh words of the archaeologist Renfrew, without it "the work of the late Georges Dumézil and his followers [is] a dream world" (1990: 18).

12.6 RECOGNITION OF CHRONOLOGICAL SEQUENCES IN THE INDO-EUROPEAN COMMUNITY

Adequate information has been given above to dispel any notion, as by Renfrew (1990: 18–19) or other archaeologists, of linguists' failure to propose "temporal sequences" on the basis of linguistic data through procedures other than the too discredited use of glottochronology. It has also been obvious without their notice that reconstructed forms of prehistoric languages, that is, languages with no attested texts, cannot be dated absolutely, no more than archaeological findings can be identified with language communities without availability of textual data. Hence the importance of involving Schrader's three sisters when we deal with the proto-language and its community of speakers.

It is also true that conclusions drawn from the data available concerning speakers of the proto-language are less reliable than those provided by recorded texts that can be verified by other data concerning a community. But there has been some progress since the days of Schleicher beyond the conclusions proposed about the Indo-European community and its language. Further linguistic and archaeological data carefully scrutinized will lead to additional progress. We may sketch briefly some of the positions that can today be held, details of which may be further explored.

12.6.1 Sequences in social organization

When we examine the social organization of the earliest Greek society that has been depicted in any detail, we find small kingdoms. Odysseus, Nestor, Priam and other Homeric leaders rule over their communities, as one of their heirs is expected to do after their death. There is minimal information about clusters of houses that correspond to villages, somewhat more about households, such as that of Eumaeus (*Odyssey*, Book 14). Accounts of communities in other branches of the Indo-European family, as in the Scandinavias around AD 1000, suggest a similar situation for social groupings at the time of the early dialects.

For the proto-period, it is now well established that we cannot propose a community with a king. The term, Greek *basileús*, whatever its origin, should have suggested as much. Mycenaean Greek provides further evidence that it signifies a lesser rank, by indicating that the earlier form *qasireu* referred only to a minor dignitary. For the other Greek terms translated as "king," *ánaks* and *túrannos*, no Indo-European etymon has been found, though a possible, if dubious, etymology has been suggested for *ánaks* (Gamkrelidze and Ivanov 1984: 752). The finding that the terms are borrowings strongly suggests that even the rank of chieftain over a small group was the highest established in the society in which Greek was used.

For the Indo-European community, and only for a part of it, can we suggest small groupings corresponding to a village, as supported by words based on *weyk-*. Yet the use of *weyk-* for the word *oîkos* "house" in Greek also informs us that the community was not large, possibly even no larger than the extended family as found in Serbia in the nineteenth century. That the family, though of unclear extent, was recognized as a social unit is assured through the extensive presence of forms based on the root *dem-* (see also Gamkrelidze and Ivanov 1984: 741–3).

12.6.2 Sequences in recognition of family relationships

As Delbrück, Szemerényi and others who have examined the terms for family relationships have pointed out, these terms suggest recognition of extensive genealogical relationships extending through several generations and beyond direct kinship; see also Gamkrelidze and Ivanov (1984: 755–75).

But, as Brugmann concluded, and subsequently other leading Indo-Europeanists as well (Szemerényi 1977: 8–10), the terms in the proto-language for father and mother are late. The suffix -(*t*)*er*- that forms the basis of these and many other kinship terms had nothing to do with this meaning category, as Brugmann firmly stated (1897–1916, 2.1: 332). We may conclude that at an earlier period the elaborate system of kinship terms found in late Proto-Indo-European had not yet been constructed. At that time the words for "father" and "mother" were probably *pā* and *mā*. A term for child may have existed beside them, an etymon of *sūnu*-applied to both son and daughter, since gender was not yet a category in the language; the term $d^h ug^h Hter$- is demonstrated by its suffix to be late. Other kinship terms may have existed in the language at the time; philological ingenuity may find evidence to propose them for the early period.

12.6.3 Sequences in the economic system

We may propose sequences in the economic system as well by scrutiny of the set of numerals. As we have noted, the set that can be reconstructed by any kind of principle extends to 5, with a basis in deixis. If the word for 10 is in origin "two hands," *de-kṃt*-, the assumption is only strengthened; see Gamkrelidze and Ivanov (1984: 842–51, especially 850 for *kṃt*- as etymon for English *hand*). As Austerlitz has pointed out (unpublished), a deictic basis is also found in Finnish. The sets of numerals as developed may be linked to a simple barter system among small social units.

In keeping with the effort to reconstruct for the proto-language all comparable terms, the differences in form and meaning among the numerals from 10 to 100 in the various dialects have been explained away, and a well-defined set up to 100 has been proposed for Proto-Indo-European. By this effort the word for 100 is derived from that for 10. Some such set may well have existed in a late form of the proto-language; but it did not extend to all dialects, as is clear from the pattern for the teens in Baltic, which was installed for 11 and 12 in Germanic, nor to the subtractive pattern for 18 and 19 in Latin, which was apparently based on Etruscan. Besides these problems we may recall those for the term for 100 and for the "tys," especially from 60 to 90, which have been discussed above, 11.7.3.

In short, we can reconstruct an earlier set of numerals that is realistic for a society structured around small family groups that had not yet progressed to the extended groups documented in Icelandic sagas and other reports of late Indo-European commmunity life.

The progression from such simple communities to those of the branches can readily be documented, as well as the differences that may be noted by comparing Hittite society with that of the Celtic speakers, or others. It would be useful to have this projection treated more extensively against archaeological findings. Rowlett has made a notable contribution with reference to "kings," published even before Scharfe's dismissal of Indic *rāj-*. While Rowlett calls for "more detailed study," his findings and the findings at sites such as Dereivka at the end of the fifth millennium, provide support for assumptions of a community with small social units at the time of the proto-language. Besides demonstrating with archaeological data that the highest social rank would best be called "chieftain," he concludes that "the reconstructed chiefdoms of PIE must have been at a rather embryonic stage of development with minimal elaborations" (1984: 214). The linguistic evidence that we have cited in section 12.6 is fully in keeping with his conclusion.

12.7 CHRONOLOGICAL SEQUENCES IN MATERIAL ADVANCES OF THE INDO-EUROPEAN COMMUNITY

As noted above, much of the material for Renfrew's placing of the Indo-European community in central Anatolia derives from the notion that

> transition from foraging to farming engenders an increase in food production and population growth, which in turn find the need for the colonization of unfarmed habitats – [providing] a socio-economic explanation for the diffusion of farmers to Europe and for the dispersal of Indo-European languages: a clear advance on previous models.
>
> (Zvelebil and Zvelebil 1988: 575)

The statement might well be valid if previous models, including Schrader's had not already concluded that the Indo-Europeans practised agriculture at the site between the Dnieper and the Danube where "the agricultural language . . . [of] the European branch was developed" (1890: 433). The "home of the Indo-Iranians," by contrast, Schrader placed in "the eastern portion of Iran" (*ibid.* 435), going on to propose the "hypothetical home for the Indo-Europeans on the Middle Volga" (*ibid.* 437). Convincing support for this "home of the Indo-Iranians" has been provided by the study of Flattery and Schwartz (1988) on the soma cult. Anthony (1990) associates their "home" with the Andronovo culture. The home of the European branch also has archaeological support.

Schrader's differentiation between the European and the Indo-Iranian subgroups is based in great part on "the new terminology for the Central European forest" as well as the "agricultural language" mentioned above (1890: 433). That is to say, Schrader proposed a chronological sequence concerning "material cultural change" in the Indo-European community a century ago.

For that "material culture change" there is no need for Renfrew's assumed location in central Anatolia. We now have sufficient evidence for agricultural change in other societies that was brought about by adoption of more favorable practice without an "advance" of peoples (see Lehmann 1990b: 144).

The development of new agricultural terminology was carefully summarized by Schrader, so that here we only list the new items in the European group: "cultivated land, to plough, the plough, harrow, to harrow, sow, seed, mow, sickle, mill, furrow, bed, ear (of grain)" (1890: 283). Schrader proceeds to list the "few instances of agreement in agricultural terminology between the Indo-Iranian languages," among them "sickle, wheat, bean" (284). The two different sets of terms may be explained variously. The Indo-Iranians may have adopted new terms from non-Indo-European speakers as their new location led to different agricultural practices accompanied by different tools. Or, the agriculture on the Volga may not have been highly developed, so that only a general term for grain, maintained in Sanskrit *yávas*, Lithuanian *yavaĩ* "grain," Greek *zeiaí* "spelt," etc. and a few others, as for "bread" were in use (see Gamkrelidze and Ivanov 1984: 655–6 for *yávas*, etc.). Future archaeological investigations may provide an answer regarding the various possibilities.

This reference to information assembled by Schrader's time may be adequate to illustrate the situation regarding "material cultural change" in the early community, without continuing here even to touch on the hundred and more pages of detail presented by him (1890: 240–354; see also 150–239). Such details may be explored by archaeologists, though even now they may be examined with reference to publications on early society, as by Glob for Denmark (esp. 1969).

Glob's fascinating data include detailed information on the diet of the Tollund man, based on "remains of the meal in the alimentary canal [which indicated that he] had lived for between twelve and twenty-four hours after eating his last meal." This meal was a gruel made from a "mixture of cultivated and wild grains [which] was no doubt the normal diet in the Iron Age around the time of Christ. . . . Fish and meat were also eaten. . . . But meat was certainly not the daily diet as it was in the time of the Stone Age hunters" (1969: 33–5; cf. Glob 1971: 36, 50–1 for evidence on diets in earlier periods, including the last interglacial). Glob's data illustrate that we cannot assume a fixed progression of human diet from the chance products of hunting to the gathered cereals of the Tollund man and thereupon to the steaks prized by cultivated westerners in this century and finally to the pallid nutrients recommended today. Maintaining flexibility for recognizing change of dietary habits along with other cultural practices, we may use accounts like Glob's to illuminate our views on daily living in the Indo-European community.

12.8 THE PEOPLES INHABITING AREAS INTO WHICH INDO-EUROPEAN LANGUAGES WERE INTRODUCED

Linguists have long held that the members of the Indo-European community moved into areas of previous habitation. They have based this assumption on the presence of loanwords in the dialects. The extent of these was dramatically demonstrated by Furnée for Greek (1972). He examines more than 5,000 words of non-Indo-European origin in the Greek lexicon.

Many of his words, for example, that for milk, might provide the material for an extensive monograph. Found in Classical Greek as *gála*, *gálaktos*, it has a recognized cognate only in Latin *lac*. Among eminent Indo-Europeanists who have concerned themselves with its etymology are Johannes Schmidt, Wilhelm Schulze, Hirt, Kretschmer, Meillet and Szemerényi. Furnée cites the Hesychius gloss *klágos* : *gála Krētes* as one of his examples of *g* : *k* alternation. Thereupon he ascribes the word to the unidentified language of Linear A (398, also 108, 117–18, 319). In spite of the illustrious set of hopeful interpreters, Chantraine as well does not accept any of the Indo-European etymologies proposed, finding it in addition remarkable that we do not know the Indo-European word for "milk" (1968–80: 206–7) and pointing to the rich bibliography in Frisk. Among Frisk's references is one to Karlgren (1926: 1960ff.), who takes the word as a south Asiatic (Turkish) Wanderwort, as in *raky*, *araky* (today *rakı* "an alcoholic drink"), Old Chinese *lak* "kumiss", Arabic *'araq*, Japanese *sake*, etc. (Frisk 1960–82, I: 284).

These observations on the word for milk have been provided at some length to illustrate the extent of earlier scholarship, which may now be followed up by work in archaeology, as well as to illustrate the broad presentation of interrelationship among prehistoric peoples. And *gála* is only one of the words that might be used for such illustration.

Moreover, the presence of many non-Indo-European words has been one of the disappointments of the Anatolian texts, in depriving us of possible words of Indo-European origin. Other dialects also include many non-Indo-European words, as noted for Germanic by Polomé (1986). As with *gála*, some of these may be identified for their possible origin, providing in this way information on earlier contacts as well as about the societies from which the words are imported.

Yet interpretations of the borrowed terms, as well as the societies from which they have been taken, provide many delicate problems. Speakers of languages differ in their receptivity to borrowed words, as the examples of Icelandic and Japanese indicate. Icelandic speakers reject segments of foreign lexical stock, but readily translate foreign terms into native elements, such as German has done with *Fernsprecher* for telephone, etc., though German speakers today prefer *Telefon*. Japanese speakers, on the other hand delight in borrowings; many Chinese elements were borrowed in two successive periods of the first millennium that provided the *Goon*

(Wu Chinese) and *Kanon* (Han or Mandarin Chinese) of their lexicon today. Massive numbers of western words, especially English, have been borrowed recently; recent dictionaries even list *terefon* as well as the word based on Chinese elements, *denwa* ("lightning/electric speak"). The importation of new cultural terms and vocabulary is well known for the Indo-European groups. The Hittites adopted much of Hurrian religion, the Greeks many Mediterranean deities, especially goddesses, and so on. There was then no reluctance among the speakers of Indo-European languages to borrow cultural practices and material, including linguistic elements.

In dealing with borrowed terms, scholars have attempted to identify new items in the culture, also items that are no longer recognized and accordingly no longer available, as well as long-established items. The new items are often recognizable from the forms of the words representing them; an example is Greek *kupárissos* "cypress," which is identified as a new item in the culture on the grounds of the double *s*, which is also found in other identified borrowings. Similarly, Germanists have long pointed to words with initial *p*, such as Gothic *peikabagms* "palm tree," as clear examples of borrowed words.

Items that are no longer available are generally less noticeable, because words for them may be maintained, in part by transfer of reference to other items. Yet some may be recorded in conservative texts, as is *soma* in early Sanskrit. Soma worship, however, died out in India, leading to the assumption that the plant from which the drug was taken was no longer available after the Indic speakers entered India from Iran. Yet, on the basis of the recorded word and the superseded religious practices recorded in hymns of especially *Rigveda* Book 9, we can sketch an earlier cultural situation.

The long-established items are important to recognize, but interpretation may be problematic. Gamkrelidze and Ivanov, for example, take the etymon of *vine*, *wine* to be native Indo-European, and they rely on it in identifying the homeland of the Indo-Europeans (1984: 868). Others have assumed it to be a borrowing by Indo-European subgroups when they came to be acquainted with Mediterranean culture; for this conclusion they rely on groups like the Germanic speakers, who borrowed the terms from Latin. The interpretation of such items is especially difficult because on change of location speakers may apply familiar terminology to new items; in this way early English settlers applied the term *robin* to the American thrush with a red breast, and later Americans the term *cedar* to a juniper. Unfortunately, many of the key terms used to determine the homeland are like these two. The terms corresponding to English *lox* "salmon" and *beech* were long used to identify the homeland as northern Europe. Elaborating on their use of the word *$g^w ow$*- "cow" by noting that tolerance for milk products among speakers of Indo-European languages suggests a homeland near "several peoples of the northern part of southwest Asia," Gamkrelidze and Ivanov have identified eastern Anatolia as the homeland that they have selected (1984: 869). Such support with biological evidence is indeed welcome, though it permits postulation of a broader sphere for the homeland than eastern Anatolia.

As have others, Gamkrelidze and Ivanov use the procedures further. They examine additional lexical items to propose association between Proto-Indo-European and Proto-Semitic as well as Proto-Kartvelian. Details would require too much space for review here. But the selection of words assumed by Gamkrelidze and Ivanov to have been borrowed from Semitic is greater than that of many other specialists, including as it does such terms as Proto-Indo-European *medhu- "honey" as a borrowing from Proto-Semitic *mtk- "sweet" (1984: 874). In much the same way they examine Proto-Kartvelian, ascribing the shared words there to borrowing into Kartvelian from Proto-Indo-European (1984: 877–80).

Borrowings in this way have played a decisive role in reconstructing the culture of the proto-speakers and in proposing hypotheses on their homeland. Reconstructions that have been differently interpreted, such as the etymon of *lox* and its broader application several millennia ago, suggest caution and greater care in arriving at such inferences (see Diebold 1985). Such inferences are more credible if based on consideration of sets, like kinship terms and the terms for social and economic organization, such as the set of numerals, preferably supported by archaeological evidence. Inferences formed with consideration of typology, such as the wave-of-advance model in archaeology, are also more credible than those based on interpretation of individual finds. But we now demand that all such inferences be supported by evidence from fields corresponding to each of the three sisters recognized by Schrader. Since, however, the linguistic material is more closely associated with a social community than are artifacts or cultural practices, it must be given priority in such identification.

12.9 THE HOMELAND OF THE INDO-EUROPEANS

In spite of the problems involved in proposing a homeland or cradle of the speakers of Proto-Indo-European, an identification is difficult to avoid inasmuch as it indicates the position of the investigator regarding the culture and linguistic characteristics of the proto-language and its speakers. To some degree those characteristics may have been selected in part because of the assumptions held or arrived at in the course of investigation. Without wishing to downgrade earlier scholars, we can hardly avoid noting that patriotic motivation in the nineteenth century swayed views of some Indo-Europeanists on the location of the homeland.

But even they, as well as all subsequent scholars, took as their primary evidence the Indo-European lexicon. Words like the etymon for "bee" were posited for the proto-language, and as a result any area in which bees were not found, like the Asian steppes, were excluded. On the other hand, as we have noted amply, positive decisions were reached on the basis of positing the etymon of words like *wolf, beech* and *lox* for the proto-language, whatever the current view on the validity of the assumptions may be. When conclusions were drawn, they were thereupon tested against archaeological and historical, as well as topographical, criteria.

Archaeologists, on the other hand, may take their primary evidence from their sphere, as Renfrew has done. His procedure has been discussed above, as well as his assumption regarding the location. It, like other assumptions, has been massively reviewed and will continue to be scrutinized, though it is no longer heavily favored.

12.9.1 Principles underlying the choice of eastern Anatolia by Gamkrelidze and Ivanov

Because we are primarily concerned with the principles involved in reaching a position, it may be well to recall that leading Indo-Europeanists have arrived at well-considered views. Among the most impressive is Brugmann's, who reached a decision with wide latitude when he proposed a band from southern France to Iran. Moreover, he accepted the likelihood of dialect divisions at an early period, so that the languages of the family at the time would have been comparable to a dialect continuum as proposed by Diakonov.

The differentiation among dialects was credited by Brugmann to processes that are not different from those observed by sociolinguists and specialists in dialects to the present. Some differences are assumed to have arisen as a result of spontaneous innovations. These as well as other differences were delimited by politically or culturally determined social groups. Other differences arose as a result of contacts with different social groups. Centrifugal and centripetal social forces then operated, much as they have at all times. As a result of the broad area he proposes, Brugmann also assigns great breadth of structures to the the reconstructed language (1897–1916 I: 21–7). Meillet presented similar views (1937).

By Brugmann's view, the reconstructed proto-language is comparable to "the German language during the period extending from the time Christianity was introduced to its speakers to his own time, with all of its dialects taken into consideration" (1897–1916 I: 24 in my paraphrase). Brugmann's description of the proto-language in the *Grundriss* is therefore, by his own statement, comparable to a grammar of German through a period of a thousand and more years with all of its dialectal variants taken into consideration.

Further, it should be noted that, while he may not have applied the terms, Brugmann accepts first of all an expansion by a "wave of advance" model but also acknowledges expansion by migration (*ibid.* 24–5).

We may characterize subsequent consideration of Indo-European problems, including attempts to locate the homeland, as efforts to be more precise about both the language and its location. For this end we propose a succession of stages in an attempt to achieve greater understanding of the language (Lehmann 1989b). Such an effort leads also to more precise analysis of stages of the language for identification of the homeland.

Since the major "compendium" after Brugmann's is that of Gamkrelidze and Ivanov, we may briefly review the linguistic data they have selected in their identification. A part of the data consists of native words. These include terms that for them suggest a geographical region that is mountainous. Moreover, they cite terms for flora and fauna, including monkeys and elephants, that in their view suggest an environment like that of the Mediterranean and southwest Asia area. They also hold that the terminology for herding and agriculture speak against location in central or eastern Europe. Finally, they interpret the presence of terms for wheeled transportation and bronze metallurgy as pointing to southwest Asia (1984: 865–70). The site they fix on then is eastern Anatolia.

Without excluding any of their data, it may be pointed out that much of it could be borrowed, some, like the herding terminology, from a society located at a distance. Other terms are nondistinctive, such as those suggesting a mountainous area; these terms are relative, as might readily be documented from designations for sites of higher elevation in numerous relatively flat areas. Unfortunately for the proposal of Gamkrelidze and Ivanov, there is no evidence for monkeys or even elephants in the area at the time, nor for migration from it. The archaeological data are accordingly unfavorable, while the linguistic data are not decisive.

12.9.2 Principles underlying the views of Alexander Häusler concerning continuity of speakers in Europe

In a series of essays Häusler (1992) strongly emphasizes the absence of any archaeological evidence for shifts in culture in central Europe. The lack of any such evidence leads him to object vigorously to the assumption of Gimbutas and earlier scholars that Indo-European speakers invaded the area, and thanks to their control of the horse as well as martial superiority took over as a superior culture. Häusler finds that the archaeological evidence indicates continuous development of the cultures in central Europe, and no marked influences from outside them. Such continuity leads him also to reject the homeland proposed by Gamkrelidze and Ivanov (Häusler forthcoming). His strong objections to the three successive invasions proposed by Gimbutas are well taken, and increasingly held. His portrayal of continuity in culture for Europe is also highly credible; but unfortunately, he has no proposal for the source of the Indo-European language or languages.

Moreover, it has been pointed out repeatedly that introduction of new peoples, and new languages, may not be distinguishable archaeologically. Mallory, for example, refers to the lack of evidence to substantiate the introduction of Gaelic into Scotland, as well as comparable shifts of language (1989: 166). Häusler's evidence then, while basically negative, cannot support the view that the Indo-European languages were indigenous in Europe. Moreover, he dismisses any prior population, disregarding the many non-Indo-European languages, such as Basque and Pictish, that must be languages surviving the earlier peoples (see Mallory 1989: 181). We may indeed agree with Häusler that there is little, if any, evidence for one, let alone several, shifts in culture. Yet the languages had to have their source somewhere.

For Häusler, in addition, the notion of an Ursprache is obsolete. Yet on the basis of linguistic study we must assume that societies maintained common languages that, like languages today, were open to change. Moreover, we hold that change is gradual, in view of the need of older and younger members of social groups to communicate. Accordingly, we posit proto-languages, and seek to determine their earlier stages, or their pre-language. Specialists in such pre-languages, such as the nostraticists, have not reached agreement on Nostratic, nor even on the proto- and pre-languages on which it must be based; but their dedication to determining human language of ten thousand and more years ago requires assumption of a Proto-Indo-European, and many previous stages.

12.9.3 Principles underlying an assumption of the homeland in southern Russia, with gradual expansion of the Indo-Europeans and their languages

If we accept Brugmann's assumption of a proto-language with many dialects, the spread of the differing subgroups and dialects, as to the east, is much more readily explained. Fortunately, archaeologists are uncovering more and more sites that clarify the expansion of the Iranian languages and thereupon the Indic far to the east. The evidence would require too much space for a summary here. In his careful and extensive article, "The coming of the Aryans to Iran and India," Parpola has combined archaeological with linguistic information to provide a highly credible picture (1988). Given the places in which the various subgroups of Indo-European speakers are located, we can account for the spread of the languages much more readily from southern Russia than from any area of Europe or Anatolia.

Linguistic evidence supports that conclusion. Rather than citing further individual words, we may cite more central structural features. One of these is the gender system. Nichols has pointed out that gender is an areal characteristic in language, that is, it is localized in given sectors of the world's languages (1986: 100). One of those sectors is the Middle East. If we compare the relatively late introduction of gender into Proto-Indo-European, we can account for it through adoption of this areal characteristic. As we have noted, the earlier system in Pre-Indo-European distinguished between animate and inanimate sets of nouns. The threefold gender system replaced this distinction. We may suggest that the gender system was adopted when Indo-European languages were in contact with others in the Middle East. We have assumed such contact from introduction of the wheel and of metallurgy. Accordingly, the structural feature of gender supports the identification of the Middle East, including southern Russia, as homeland (see Lehmann 1990a: 34–6 for elaboration).

More briefly, I recall my suggestion above that the Indo-European numeral system, examined in conjunction with the evidence for the distribution of tokens, excludes the Middle East proper, including Anatolia as homeland (1990a: 38–42). We then are directed towards the northern part of the proposed area, that is, southern Russia.

As a last selection of evidence here I point to the comparison of Indo-European and Uralic tree names as given by Campbell (1990). These refer primarily to coniferous trees, as opposed to the "terminology for the Central European forest" identified already by Schrader (1890: 271–5). Among such trees are oak, beech, lime, hazel and elm. Providing a summary of the names that have been compiled by many devoted specialists in Finno-Ugric, Campbell concludes that "the weight of the aggregate of comparisons . . . supports the conclusion that these two language families have a very old historical connection, one which reflects either a genetic affiliation or Sprachbund affinities, or perhaps both" (1990: 174–5). On the basis of different correspondences in some Finno-Ugric languages, such as the equivalent of initial *p* in Ostyak and Votyak for the proto-form **piška*, in contrast with a *b* in their reflexes of the reconstructed ***paj³* "willow species," the explanation by areal correspondence is more credible. The set of relevant tree names then supports location in southern Russia, even in the neighborhood of the Volga as suggested by Schrader.

12.9.4 Possible reasons for the spread of the Indo-Europeans

In conclusion, we may comment briefly on the reason for the spread of the family, and further for the adoption of its languages. The area identified here as the homeland was clearly fertile. As in other societies that prospered and expanded with the introduction of agriculture, we may assume a large increase in population of the Indo-European community. The technological advances like wheeled vehicles, bronze and rapid transportation after the domestication of the horse, facilitated expansion out of the area. The routes and goals of that expansion must have been obvious to the speakers, based in part on reports, in part on imaginative expectations, like those of nineteenth-century Americans who were drawn by accounts of available land and other prospects of wealth to expand westward.

In attempting to account for their prevailing in use of their own Indo-European languages as well as adoption by autochthons, we have no better explanation than that of Meillet (1928). In his view the essential trait of Indo-European society was a striving for independence and individuality.

Further, the social structure was built on small autonomous groups, with no domineering rulers, such as those in many city-states of the Middle East; the problems of Agamemnon and Odysseus as rulers in the Homeric poems may have been influential in Meillet's adoption of this view. Finally, the society was open to change, as is clearly evident in the sphere of religion, and also technology, as in adopting newly developed forms of transportation. By this view, the social arrangements of the Indo-Europeans were more favorable and accordingly more attractive, than those of other societies in areas where the Indo-Europeans prevailed.

In support of Meillet's model of language adoption, we may point out that receptivity among the Indo-Europeans to the views and customs of others contrasts sharply with the treatment exercised by many Middle Eastern peoples on the peoples they opposed. Moreover, the sophistication of the early texts, notably the Rigvedic hymns and the Homeric poems – both large bodies of materials from the early period – indicates that Indo-European culture was advanced, as demonstrated materially by the elaborate poetic forms and intellectually by complex ideas in their poetry on this life, on life after death and on spiritual interpretations of the universe. The societies maintaining the Indo-European languages then provided many advantages for their speakers, as well as for those who adopted their languages and social arrangements.

These proposed reasons for their success may have been determined in part by the results apparent in subsequent history; but, as Herodotus stated at the beginning of his history, and St Luke of his, a historical account must set forth the "great and marvelous deeds" of past peoples as well as reasons for their achievements, if not with certainty comparable to St Luke's. By our view, the successes of the Indo-European peoples resulted less from military superiority than from their social, material and intellectual attainments.

Notes

1 AIMS

1 The celebrated paragraph through which Jones is credited for stirring interest in comparative Indo-European linguistics is so widely cited that it is reproduced here only for convenience. It is included in the first section of his Third Anniversary Discourse, which was delivered in Calcutta on 2 February 1786. That section deals with the language; the second section treats Indian religion and philosophy; the third, their architecture and sculpture; the fourth, their arts and manufactures. In short, the paragraph credited with so much influence is a very small part of a short section of a lecture of ten pages. The entire lecture is reprinted with introductory comments in Lehmann (1967: 10–20).

> The Sanskrit language, whatever be its antiquity, is of a wonderful structure; more perfect than the Greek, more copious than the Latin, and more exquisitely refined than either, yet bearing to both of them a stronger affinity, both in the roots of verbs and in the forms of grammar, than could possibly have been produced by accident; so strong indeed, that no philo-loger could examine them all three, without believing them to have sprung from some common source, which, perhaps, no longer exists: there is a similar reason, though not quite so forcible, for supposing that both the Gothic and the Celtic, though blended with a very different idiom, had the same origin with the Sanskrit; and the old Persian might be added to the same family, if this were the place for discussing any question concerning the antiquities of Persia.

With his other writings the lectures may be consulted in *The Works of Sir William Jones* (1807). The first two volumes consist of *Memoirs of the Life, Writings and Correspondence of Sir William Jones*, by John Shore, Baron Teignmouth (1751–1834). For information on Jones, including the copious secondary material, see Cannon (1990).

2 Friedrich von Schlegel dealt at much greater length with Sanskrit than did Jones in a treatise he published twenty-two years after Jones gave his lecture: *Über die Sprache und Weisheit der Indier: ein Beitrag zur Begründung der Alterthumskunde* (1806). Yet, like the lecture, Schlegel's treatise deals with the "wisdom" of the ancient Indians as well as with the language. And it has similar aims, as its subtitle indicates: "a contribution for establishing the study of antiquity." These aims were in keeping with the Romantic movement, of which Schlegel was a central member. As he states in the initial pages of his work, he is concerned with "the oldest history of the origin of peoples and their earliest migrations."

289

The treatise consists of four parts, the first on the language, the second on philosophy, the third on historical ideas, and finally translations of Indian poetry; excerpts are given from the Ramayana, the laws of Manu, and the Mahabharata, including sections of the Bhagavadgita. It may be noted that in 1816 Bopp followed Schlegel in the practice of presenting translations.

In the very first sentence Schlegel states firmly that Sanskrit "has a very close relationship" with Latin, Greek, Germanic and Persian, but less assuredly with Armenian, Slavic and Celtic. Since "Slavic" probably included for him the Baltic subgroup, only Albanian of the Indo-European languages known at the time is omitted. This conception of the relationship does not keep commentators from criticizing Schlegel for assuming that Sanskrit was the language from which the others are derived.

The continuity of scholarship as well as Schlegel's own aims may be indicated by his crediting Jones, as the one

> who first brought light into the knowledge of language through the relationship and derivation he demonstrated of Roman, Greek, Germanic and Persian from Indic, and through this into the ancient history of peoples where previously everything had been dark and confused.
>
> (Lehmann 1967: 28)

Schlegel is more explicit in demonstrating the relationship through roots and grammatical structure. In relating roots he permits "absolutely no rules of change or replacement of letters, but rather demands complete equivalence of the word as proof of descent." He does, however, admit equation of differing elements "if the intermediate steps can be proved historically." As examples he points out that Germanic *f* is found in words that have Latin *p*, and *h* in words that have Latin *c* (1806: 6–7). It may be noted that he published these equivalences before Rask and Grimm. Evidence on which to base the relationship of the Indo-European languages was in this way gradually being gathered. It is also clear that his procedure represents an incipient use of the comparative method.

In view of the impact of anatomy on early linguistics, we may cite one more passage from the treatise. Here Schlegel states that

> the decisive point [in establishing linguistic relationships] that will clarify everything is the inner structure of the languages or comparative grammar, which will give us quite new information about the genealogy of languages in a similar way as comparative anatomy has illuminated the higher natural history.
>
> (1806: 28)

While not a linguist, Schlegel contributed to the advance of Indo-European studies by directing attention to benefits that might be gained from adopting methods of more advanced sciences, like comparative anatomy, and also by arousing the interest of others, notably Bopp.

The passages cited here may be examined in their context in Lehmann (1967: 21–8). The treatise as a whole may be consulted in volume I of the admirable series: Amsterdam Studies in the Theory and History of Linguistic Science edited by E. F. K. Koerner and published by Benjamins. The volume contains the text with an introductory essay by Sebastiano Timpanaro (1977), and a translation by Ellen J. Millington (1849) of the first part on the language.

3 Although Schlegel advocated comparative study of language, Franz Bopp (1791–1867) is credited as the father of comparative linguistics. In contrast with Schlegel's generalizations, Bopp published in 1816 a detailed account of Sanskrit morphology, with concentration on the verb. His attention to the verb

was determined by his view that knowledge of it would clarify the relationship of the various dialects to the original language and also lead to an understanding of their gradual shift to a verbal system making use of compound forms rather than inflection (*ibid*. 11).

Bopp then proceeds to give the conjugations in accordance with the presentation in Sanskrit grammars (*ibid*. 12). His first paradigm is that of the present of *ad* "eat," for which he gives the three singular forms as *Atti* instead of *adti*, *Atsi* – *adsi*, *Adai*. He goes on to comment on the sandhi change of the *d* of the root, but does not correct the first-person form. Presentation of the Sanskrit conjugation continues, with references to forms of Greek and Latin, to page 136. Then in a supplement he discusses the Germanic verb, citing forms from Gothic (*ibid*. 137–57). In keeping with his views of language, the markers of compound tenses are based on auxiliaries, the personal endings on pronouns. The remainder of the book consists of translations from Sanskrit (*ibid*. 159–312).

Four years later, during his stay in London, Bopp published a revised version of the part of his book dealing with the verb under the title *Analytical Comparison of the Sanskrit, Greek, Latin, and Teutonic Languages, Shewing the Original Identity of their Grammatical Structure*. This work has been reprinted with a preface by E. F. K. Koerner, as well as with other commentary, as volume 3 of Amsterdam Classics in Linguistics (1974). Now the first set of forms listed is the present tense of "be," with the forms of the singular given as *As mi A si As ti*. Bopp thereupon sets side by side present-tense forms of Sanskrit, Greek, Latin and Gothic (1974: 25). Like the book of 1816, the English version was well received. The two works are justly acclaimed as inaugurating the comparative grammar of the Indo-European languages.

Bopp's major work was his comparative grammar, published in three editions. The title of the last is *Vergleichende Grammatik des Sanskrit, Send, Armenischen, Griechischen, Lateinischen, Litauischen, Altslavischen, Gotischen und Deutschen*, published in three volumes. The first of 1868 includes the preface to the first edition of 1833 and of the second of 1857, and of the third by A. Kuhn. The first volume deals with the writing system and phonology (1–196), with roots (197–244) and formation of the cases (245–553). The second of 1870 deals with adjectives (1–54), numerals (55–101), pronouns (101–242), pronominal adverbs (242–54) and the verb, with a separate section on tenses (255–565). The third of 1871 deals with formation of moods (1–75), derived verbs (76–137) and word formation (138–512), concluding with an index (513–22). See also the comments in 1.1.

The grammar was the standard work in its day, but was rapidly outdated by the findings of the neogrammarians. Schleicher's *Compendium*, discussed below, also included advances over it, but was by no means as comprehensive. Both were totally superseded by Brugmann's *Grundriss*, especially the second edition of 1897–1916.

4 The culmination of several centuries of concern with diverse languages in the effort to arrive at a "universal science of language" is found in *Mithridates, oder allgemeine Sprachenkunde mit dem Vater Unser als Sprachprobe in bey nahe fünfhundert Sprachen und Mundarten*, by Johann Christoph Adelung (1806–17). It was published in three parts consisting of five volumes; the second and third parts, 1809–17, were completed by Johann Severin Vater.

After an introduction, the first part deals with languages of Asia, first the monosyllabic, then the polysyllabic. The second part deals with the languages of Europe. The third part consists of three volumes: the first deals with the languages of Africa and South America, the second consists of supplements to the earlier volumes; the third deals with the languages of Central and North

America. Information is provided on each language, as well as bibliography, and then a grammatical sketch, followed by examples, especially the Lord's Prayer, but also word lists. The work is of considerable interest in providing information on the extent of information available at the time. See the comments in 7.1. A ready source for examining the treatment in it of a language may be found in the statement on Turkish, given in translation in Lehmann (1978a: 27–9).

5 Unlike Bopp and Grimm, August Friedrich Pott is not honored as one of the founders of historical linguistics nor as the originator of important procedures; rather, he is virtually forgotten. Yet he inaugurated etymological studies of the family through his *Etymologische Forschungen auf dem Gebiete der Indo-Germanischen Sprachen* (1833–6). The second expanded edition was published over a period of years in six volumes consisting of ten parts as *Etymologische Forschungen auf dem Gebiete der indo-germanischen Sprachen, unter Berücksichtung ihrer Hauptformen Sanscrit; Zend-Persisch; Griechisch-Lateinisch; Litauisch-Slavisch; Germanisch und Keltisch* (1859–76). In it the entries are arranged by roots, as is the practice in the later etymological dictionaries of the family.

Moreover, in the course of his etymological comparison he contributed to the increasing understanding of Indo-European phonology. He published prolifically, as may be noted from the introductory materials to the edition of his introduction to general linguistics, *Einleitung in die Allgemeine Sprachwissenschaft* (1974).

Among reasons for Pott's virtual oblivion is the vast improvement in understanding Proto-Indo-European phonology shortly after the last volume of his revised etymological dictionary was published; works that superseded it are cited in 11.1. Moreover, Indo-Europeanists achieved an improved perspective on the members of the family, no longer relating closely Greek and Latin. As another reason, much of his publication dealt with theory, which, as has been apparent during the past decades, is rapidly superseded. Yet Pott deserves mention for his considerable contributions in the early period of Indo-European studies, which laid the foundation for the lasting work of the neogrammarians.

6 August Schleicher (1821–68) is chiefly remembered for introducing the family tree to represent the development of the Indo-European family and the relationship among its languages, as well as for introducing the device of reconstructed (starred) forms. He also published copiously during his short lifetime, as may be noted from the list of writings pages lxiv-lxvi of the edition of *Die Sprachen Europas in systematischer Übersicht* (1983).

Schleicher produced one of the major comparative grammars of the Indo-European family in his *Compendium der vergleichenden Grammatik der indogermanischen Sprachen: Kurzer Abriss einer Laut- und Formenlehre der indogermanischen Ursprache, des Altindischen, Alteranischen, Altgriechischen, Altitalischen, Altkeltischen, Altslawischen, Litauischen und Altdeutschen* (1861–2). A second revised edition appeared in 1866; a third was published after his death, edited by two of his students, Johannes Schmidt and August Leskien, 1871, a fourth in 1876. After a brief introduction, containing his family tree (which is frequently reproduced, if with modifications) (1–9), the third edition consists of a phonology (10–328) and a morphology (329–829). In the phonology the vowels are first treated, after those of the proto-language (Ursprache) (10–14) those of the individual branches as given above; thereupon the consonants are presented similarly. The morphology first deals with derivation (329–495) and thereupon with inflection (495–829). Like Bopp's grammar, Schleicher's was totally superseded by Brugmann's *Grundriss*.

The role of Schleicher in general and Indo-European linguistics has been intensively discussed. Koerner, as in the introduction to his edition cited above, credits him with many of the contributions ascribed to the neogrammarians. In this way Koerner attempts to counter their critical evaluation of him, which, according to Koerner, was determined largely by their efforts to establish themselves as major innovators. Whatever the final evaluation may be, Schleicher's publications today are only of interest for the history of linguistics. His work was highly original for the time and based on investigations of contemporary languages, notably of Lithuanian. Among reasons for some of the sharpest criticism is his attempt to reconstruct Indo-European syntax, as represented in the fable he wrote. This has been revised, first by Hirt, then by Lehmann and Ladislav Zgusta, as "Schleicher's Tale after a Century" in *Studies in Diachronic, Synchronic, and Typological Linguistics; Festschrift for Oswald Szemerényi* (1979: 455–66). The revision has not checked criticism of any attempt to reconstruct syntax – which may illustrate Schleicher's originality as well as his understanding of appropriate procedures in historical linguistics.

7 The *Grundriss der vergleichenden Grammatik der indogermanischen Sprachen*, published by Karl Brugmann (1849–1919) and Berthold Delbrück (1842–1922) from 1886 to 1900, with the first two volumes revised by Brugmann and published from 1897 to 1916, represents the culmination of historical Indo-European studies in the nineteenth century. Its subtitle indicates its scope: *Kurzgefasste Darstellung der Geschichte des Altindischen, Altiranischen (Avestischen u. Altpersischen), Altarmenischen, Altgriechischen, Albenischen, Lateinischen, Oskisch-Umbrischen, Altirischen, Gotischen, Althochdeutschen, Litauischen und Altkirchenslavischen*. The five volumes have been reprinted 1906–30 and 1967 by De Gruyter, Berlin, so that they are readily available, if at a price.

The theoretical bases of the work have been discussed in various sections of the text above, especially in 3.1. In spite of the reference to history in the subtitle, Brugmann specifically indicates a "systematic" presentation. The subtitle of the second edition is then more exact: *Vergleichende Laut-, Stammbildungs- und Flexionslehre der indogermanischen Sprachen*. Since the sections of the work have been given in the bibliography, they will not be repeated here. It may be useful, however, to state once again the reliability of the data, without any skewing by theoretical biases.

Even more important to recall is the deep knowledge of the authors, and their broad understanding of language as used by speakers. While the sciences of sociolinguistics and psycholinguistics were not yet established, Brugmann insisted in his manifesto of 1878 on examining language as used by speakers. Moreover, he recognized the necessity of regarding the psychological underpinnings of language.

The admirable views as well as the vast knowledge that underlie the work are clear from the numerous monographs and articles that each of the authors published, the findings of which contribute to the authority of the *Grundriss*. These are unfortunately disregarded by subsequent generalists. Only a few can be included here.

Brugmann's understanding of semantics may be determined from his monograph *Die Ausdrücke für den Begriff der Totalität in den indogermanischen Sprachen* (1894). It is further clear from his monograph of ten years later, *Die Demonstrativpronomina der indogermanischen Sprachen* (1904), as its subtitle may indicate: *Eine bedeutungsgeschichtliche Untersuchung*. We may also note that in his day topics cited as titles of monographs and articles referred to language and specifically to the Indo-European family rather than to states or processes, like deixis. Later linguists who deal with such matters without consulting Brugmann's monograph are guilty of poor scholarship, for in spite of

Brugmann's reference to Indo-European, he also includes information from other languages, as on page 71 of his 1904 monograph from Greenlandic Inuit.

It might be salutary to mention as well his brief statement on the difference between deixis and anaphora as observed ever since the time of Appolonius Dyskolos of the second century AD.

Brugmann's views on the usefulness of considering the role of psychology in the use of language may be clearest in his monograph *Verschiedenheiten der Satzgestaltung nach Maßgabe der seelischen Grundfunktionen in den indogermanischen Sprachen* (1918). His monographs as well as his other publications merit reading and rereading because of his rich knowledge, his deep understanding of language, and his ability to express both.

Delbrück's monographs are similarly meritorious. The third of his "syntaktische Forschungen," *Die altindische Wortfolge aus dem Çatapathabrāhmaṇa dargestellt* (1878), should be read by anyone who comments on the word order of Proto-Indo-European or that of early Sanskrit. The last two, issued by the same publisher, *Die Grundlagen der griechischen Syntax* (1879) and *Altindische Syntax* (1888), are equally important. They form the basis of his three volumes of syntax in the *Grundriss*, which have no equal to this day. It must be noted, of course, that, like Brugmann's publications, they suffer from lack of information about the subsequently discovered Anatolian languages.

Delbrück's monograph on the Indo-European kinship terms, *Die indogermanischen Verwandtschaftsnamen* (1889), is similarly important, though upgraded by Szemerényi's of 1977.

After Brugmann took over the *Grundriss*, Delbrück concentrated on the Germanic languages, in addition to his general work on linguistics, *Einleitung in das Studium der indogermanischen Sprachen* (1919). His later monographs are also important for the study of Indo-European grammar, notably his *Synkretismus: Ein Beitrag zur germanischen Kasuslehre* (1907), which, as its subtitle indicates, deals with nominal inflection in Germanic. His series on Germanic syntax, especially the fourth: *Die Wortstellung in dem älteren westgötischen Landrecht* (1918), provides additional evidence on the OV order of the parent language.

As references in the text above indicate, Delbrück's works remain highly important as sources of data and for their systematic presentation.

8 *Prinzipien der Sprachgeschichte* (1920), by Hermann Paul (1846–1921), was the standard theoretical handbook of linguistics up to its fifth edition, which has often been reprinted. The second, published in 1886, was translated by H. A. Strong under the title *Principles of the History of Language* (1891). Though criticized, as by Bloomfield (1933: 16–17) for its "neglect of descriptive language study" and its "insistence upon "psychological" interpretation," the work is still worth examination. A few sentences from the first page of Strong's translation may indicate that Bloomfield's strictures were a bit unfair:

> Historical Grammar took its rise from the older Descriptive Grammar, and retains even now much from its predecessor. It has maintained, at least in the system of its classification, absolutely the old form. It has merely laid down a series of descriptive grammars parallel to each other. In fact comparison, and not explanation of development, is regarded as in the first instance the proper characteristic of the new Science.

While the translation fills a need, in view of the tightly constructed original, the fifth edition is greatly improved. Two sentences from the final part of the first chapter (1920: 21), may illustrate reasons for Bloomfield's criticisms:

> If one attempts to characterize the so-called inner form of language in the

sense of Humboldt and Steinthal, that is possible only by going back to the origin of the forms of expression and their basic meaning. I would have absolutely no notion how one might reflect successfully about a language without conveying something about its historical development.

It may be clear that Paul's views contrast in different ways with both those of the so-called structuralists and the generativists. His position in conflicting with theirs may be further illustrated by a lengthy footnote to the passage here translated, in which Paul defends himself against a charge that his book is actually a "flaming protest against his thesis" that "linguistic science is equal to the history of language," in short, that it is largely descriptive.

As I have pointed out elsewhere, Paul's position, like that of most nineteenth-century linguists, is comparable to that of current historians of science who distinguish the experimental sciences like chemistry and physics from the historical like biology and geology, and of course linguistics. The nineteenth-century linguists may have directed their primary attention to languages of the past; but, as is clear from Brugmann's "systematic" presentation, they treated these systematically, that is to say, descriptively. A major difference between their treatment of language and that of current linguists results, however, from subsequent improvements in understanding of phonology.

Curiously, in view of Bloomfield's criticisms of Paul's *Prinzipien*, this work may even be regarded as superior to his in the treatment of syntax. A long chapter on "fundamentals of syntax" (1920: 121–50) is followed by others treating syntactic processes that have occupied recent linguists: for example, the many treatments of gapping were pre-empted by his chapter on "Frugality of expression" (*ibid*. 313–24); and the following chapter entitled "Development of word formation and inflection" (*ibid*. 325–51) is similarly noteworthy for anyone concerned with grammaticization. Like any outstanding work, Paul's *Prinzipien* is directed to points of interest at the time; yet linguists concerned with phenomena like grammaticization might be spared instances of naiveté if they consulted the book.

9 The preface to the seventh and final volume of Hermann Hirt's *Indogermanische Grammatik* (1937) "breaks off" in the middle of a discussion regretting neglect of Ferdinand de Saussure (1857–1913). The page begins with the paragraph:

> It has been a great misfortunate for our understanding [of Proto-Indo-European] that the book of de Saussure, *Mémoire sur le système primitif des voyelles dans les langues indo-europ.*, which was published in 1879, did not find appropriate recognition. Even though not everything among its ideas is correct, they nonetheless represent a very important advance in contrast with the views of Osthoff and Brugmann.

Since the page is interrupted after only one sentence of a promising paragraph, we cannot know whether Hirt would have gone on to recognize Kurylowicz's identification of Saussure's coefficients with the Hittite sounds represented by *h*. Unfortunately the set of Hirt's notes published posthumously by Helmut Arntz under the title *Die Hauptprobleme der indogermanischen Sprachwissenschaft* simply summarizes Hirt's earlier statements on vowels and ablaut (1939: 127–58); Arntz may have have been capable of representing Hirt's later views.

Saussure authorized a reprint of the work in 1887, though regretting that he could not introduce "notable modifications." Yet, as has been repeatedly stated, the monograph as published by a student aged 21 is one of the most remarkable works in linguistics. On the one hand, through sheer analysis Saussure proposed the phonological system of the proto-language included consonants that were nowhere attested at the time. On the other hand, it established the method of internal reconstruction. Modifications that he might have introduced in a second edition may well be included among the highly regarded articles that have been brought together in *Recueil des publications scientifiques de Ferdinand de Saussure* (1921).

It is difficult to indicate the impact of the *Mémoire* by a few quotations; but the initial sentence, and a further comment at the end of the first paragraph, may illustrate its powerful scientific, as well as clipped and crisp presentation.

> To study the multiple forms under which what is called Indo-European *a* manifests itself is the immediate aim of this little work. . . . But if, when we have fixed on such a restricted field, the picture of Indo-European vocalism is little by little modified under our eyes . . . it is clear that in fact the system of the vowels as a whole must be selected for our scrutiny.

Throughout the work it is obvious that Saussure maintains a structural viewpoint. Moreover, the conclusions are based on scrupulous examination of forms. Though changed in notation, they correspond in general to many current positions on the phonological structure of Proto-Indo-European.

Among all the attention to Saussure it is a pity that the *Mémoire* has not been translated, with appropriate commentary.

10   While Jacob Grimm (1785–1863) cannot be recognized as an Indo-Europeanist, his numerous works have had an important impact on the field. Like the other significant publications in Germanic linguistics up to 1882, they are given with full bibliographic reference, including a sketch of his life, in the admirable work *Die deutsche Philologie im Grundriss* by Karl von Bahder (1883). Here we note only the *Geschichte der deutschen Sprache* – published in two volumes in Leipzig in 1848, with a fourth edition in 1880 – in part as an illustration of a treatment of language in its social and cultural setting.

The work consists of forty-two chapters. After identification of the chronology and languages in the first, the next six deal with matters of the society and economy, under such topics as "shepherds and farmers, cattle, falconry, agriculture, festivals and months, beliefs – law – customs"; six chapters, beginning with the twelfth, deal with phonology; thereupon twelve present the various subgroups of speakers. After a survey of the preceding presentation, nine chapters treat the grammar. Chapter 40 then returns to cultural practices under the title "Right and left," followed by a chapter on "Milk and meat."

The work is notable for its thorough treatment of the vocabulary, in which the corresponding words in the other Indo-European dialects are cited, so that in spite of its title it is pertinent for Indo-European studies.

11   Otto Schrader's *Sprachvergleichung und Urgeschichte*, the second edition of which was translated as *Prehistoric Antiquities of the Aryan Peoples: a Manual of Comparative Philology and the Earliest Culture*, by Frank B. Jevons (1890), remains the most complete and accessible treatment of the speakers of Proto-Indo-European and their culture. Its content as well as its general views are indicated in chapter 12 of the text.

Subsequent advances have obviously been made, especially through archaeological discoveries and information from new texts, especially in the Anatolian languages and Mycenaean Greek. These have, however, only added details to the general description of the early society and culture. The continuing importance of Schrader's work results from its cautious treatment of the evidence, and its awareness that information from the language is only one of the three sources of information, so that data in the texts and from archaeological activities must always be taken into account. Thus the charges resulting from the shortcomings of palaeontology cannot be directed against the work.

Bringing it up to date would represent an important contribution to Indo-European studies.

While archaeologists point to the advantages that may result from drawing on models, we still face the problem of identifying archaeological finds of preliterate peoples with peoples of whom we have information through language and texts. It may well be that future Indo-Europeanists will be able to trace population movements up to the time a given society produces texts, and accordingly to determine the earlier location and even the home of the Indo-Europeans, through innovations like identification of relative peoples by analysis of mitochrondial DNA. Until they do, Schrader's cautious presentation merits attention.

2 METHODS

1 Note 2 above on Friedrich Schlegel recalls his reference to comparative anatomy as a pattern for linguistics. The outstanding anatomist of the time was Georges Cuvier (1769–1832). In the introduction to his book, *Recherches sur les ossemens fossiles de quadrupèdes* (1812) followed by numerous editions, he includes statements that had a great influence on linguists, and probably determined their views.

Cuvier stated that every organism makes up a complete system. Further, that the parts of it are intimately interrelated, so that if one of them changes its form, other parts introduce corresponding changes. Linguists followed anatomists in viewing language as an organism. As a corollary, language was considered a system; and, as is clear from Grimm's rules on the obstruents, if one element of the system, such as *p*, changes, *t* and *k* show corresponding changes.

Cuvier also proposed that, in view of the system of organisms, the entire structure could be reconstructed if only one bone were found. This tenet of his was not taken up by linguists until Schleicher.

Eventually the view of language as an organism was replaced by other models. Treatment of language as a complete system, however, was not, as we have noted in the theoretical statements of Brugmann and Meillet.

References

Adelung, Johann Christoph (1781) *Deutsche Sprachlehre*, Berlin.
—— (1806–17) *Mithridates, oder allgemeine Sprachenkunde mit dem Vater Unser als Sprachprobe in bey nahe fünfhundert Sprachen und Mundarten*, 3 vols, completed by J. S. Vater, Berlin: Voss.
Adrados, Francisco Rodríguez (1963) *Evolución y estructura del verbo indoeuropea*, Madrid: Instituto Antonio de Nebrija.
—— (1975) *Lingüística indoeuropea*, Madrid: Gredos.
—— (1982) *Die räumliche und zeitliche Differenzierung des Indoeuropäischen im Lichte der Vor- und Frühgeschichte*, Innsbruck: Institut für Sprachwissenschaft der Universität.
—— (1988a) *Nuevos Estudios de Lingüística Indoeuropea*, Madrid: Consejo Superior de Investigaciones Cientificas.
—— (1988b) Review of R. S. P. Beekes, *The Origins of the Indo-European Nominal Inflection,* Innsbruck: Institut für Sprachwissensschaft der Universität, 1985, *Indogermanische Forschungen* 93: 292–4.
Allen, William Sidney (1964) "On one-vowel systems," *Lingua* 13: 111–24.
—— (1973) *Accent and Rhythm*, Cambridge: Cambridge University Press.
Ammerman, Albert J. and J. L. Cavalli-Sforza (1984) *The Neolithic Transition and the Genetics of Populations in Europe*, Princeton: Princeton University Press.
Ananthanarayana, H. S. (1970) "Intonation contours in Vedic: a hypothesis," *Vishveshvaranand Indological Journal* 8: 48–55.
—— (1980) "A note on intonation contours in Vedic," *Indian Linguistics* 41: 51–5.
Anthony, David W. (1990) "Migration in archaeology: the baby and the bathwater," *American Anthropologist* 92: 895–914.
Anthony, David W. and Dorcas R. Brown (1991) "The origins of horseback riding," *Antiquity* 65: 22–38.
Arens, Hans (1969) *Sprachwissenschaft: der Gang ihrer Entwicklung von Antike bis zur Gegenwart*, 2nd edn, Freiburg: Alber.
Arnold, E. Vernon (1905) *Vedic Metre in its Historical Development*, Cambridge: Cambridge University Press.
Aufrecht, Theodor (1877) *Die Hymnen des Rigveda*, 2 vols, 2nd edn, repr. Wiesbaden: Harrassowitz, 1968.
Austerlitz, Robert (1991) "Alternatives in long-range comparison," in Sidney M. Lamb and E. Douglas Mitchell (eds) *Sprung from Some Common Source: Investigations into the Prehistory of Languages*, Stanford: Stanford University Press, 353–64.
—— (1991) "Deixis, personal names, numerals, kinship terms," unpublished paper presented May 1991.
Avery, John (1881) "On relative clauses in the Rigveda," *Proceedings of the*

American Oriental Society 11: 64–6.

—— (1885) "The unaugmented verb-forms of the Rig- and Atharva-Vedas," *Journal of the American Oriental Society* 11: 326–61.

Bader, Françoise (1989) *La Langue des dieux, ou l'hermétisme des poètes indo-européens*, Pisa: Giardini.

von Bahder, Karl (1883) *Die deutsche Philologie im Grundriss*, Paderborn: Schöningh.

Baldi, Philip (1983) *An Introduction to the Indo-European Languages*, Carbondale: Southern Illinois University Press.

—— ed. (1990) *Linguistic Change and Reconstruction Methodology*, Berlin: Mouton de Gruyter.

Bammesberger, Alfred (1984) *Studien zur Laryngaltheorie*, Göttingen: Vandenhoeck & Ruprecht.

—— ed. (1988) *Die Laryngaltheorie und die Rekonstruktion des indogermanischen Laut- und Formensystems*. Heidelberg: Winter.

Bechtel, Friedrich (1892) *Die Hauptprobleme der indogermanischen Lautlehre seit Schleicher*, Göttingen: Vandenhoeck & Ruprecht.

Bednarczuk, Leszek (1971) Indo-European Parataxis, Kraków: Wydawn.

Beekes, Robert S. P. (1969) *The Development of the Proto-Indo-European Laryngeals in Greek*, The Hague: Mouton.

—— (1985) *The Origins of the Indo-European Nominal Inflection*, Innsbruck: Institut für Sprachwissenschaft der Universität.

—— (1988) "Laryngeal developments: a survey," in Alfred Bammesberger (ed.) *Die Laryngaltheorie und die Rekonstruktion des indogermanischen Laut- und Formensystems*, Heidelberg: Winter, 59–105.

Benveniste, Emile (1935) *Origines de la formation des noms en indo-européen*, Paris: Adrien-Maisonneuve.

—— (1937) "Le problème du þ indo-européen," *Bulletin de la société linguistique de Paris* 38: 139–47.

—— (1948) *Noms d'agent et noms d'action en indo-européen*, Paris: Adrien-Maisonneuve.

—— (1962) *Hittite et indo-européen*, Paris: Adrien-Maisonneuve.

—— (1966) *Problèmes de linguistique générale*, Paris: Gallimard.

—— (1969) *Le vocabulaire des institutions indo-européennes*, 2 vols, vol. I: *Economie, parenté, société*, vol. II: *Pouvoir, droit, religion*, Paris: Gallimard.

—— (1971) *Problems in General Linguistics*, trans. by Mary Elizabeth Meek, Coral Gables, FL: University of Miami Press, trans. of 1966.

—— (1973) *Indo-European language and society*, trans. by Elizabeth Palmer, Coral Gables, FL: University of Miami Press. trans. of 1969.

Bergaigne, Abel (1879) "Essai sur la construction grammaticale considérée dans son développement historique, en sanskrit, en grec, en latin, dans les langues romanes et dans les langues germaniques," *Mémoires de la Société de Paris* 3: 1–51, 124–54, 169–86.

Bills, Garland D., C. Bernardo Vallejo and Rudolph C. Troike (1969) *An Introduction to Spoken Bolivian Quechua*, Austin: University of Texas Press.

Bird, N. (1982) *The Distribution of Indo-European Root Morphemes*, Wiesbaden: Harrassowitz.

Birnbaum, Henrik (1975) *Common Slavic*, Cambridge, MA: Slavica.

—— (1977) "Linguistic reconstruction: its potentials and limitations in new perspective," *Journal of Indo-European Studies* 2: 361–83.

—— (1984) "Indo-Europeans between the Baltic and the Black Sea," *Journal of Indo-European Studies* 12: 235–59.

Birnbaum, Henrik and Jaan Puhvel, eds (1966) *Ancient Indo-European Dialects*, Berkeley and Los Angeles: University of California Press.

Birwé, Robert (1956) *Griechisch-arische Sprachbeziehungen im Verbalsystem*, Walldorf-Hessen: Vorndran.

Bloch, Jules (1965) *Indo-Aryan from the Vedas to Modern Times*, English ed, largely revised by the author and trans. by Alfred Master, Paris: Adrien-Maisonneuve.

Bloomfield, Leonard (1933) *Language*, New York: Holt.

Bökönyi, S. (1974) *History of Domestic Mammals in Central and Eastern Europe*, Budapest: Akadémiai Kiadó.

—— (1978) "The earliest waves of domestic horses in East Europe," *Journal of Indo-European Studies* 6: 17–76.

Bomhard, Allan R. (1988) "Recent trends in the reconstruction of the Proto-Indo-European consonant system," *Historische Sprachwissenschaft* 101: 2–25.

Bopp, Franz (1816) *Über das Conjugationssystem der Sanskrit-sprache in Vergleichung mit jenem der griechischen, lateinischen, persischen und germani-schen Sprachen*, ed. K. J. Windischmann, Frankfurt-on-Main: Andreä.

—— (1820) *Analytical Comparison of the Sanskrit, Greek, Latin and Teutonic Languages, Shewing the Original Identity of their Grammatical Structure*, ed. by E. F. K. Koerner, 1974, Amsterdam: Benjamins.

—— (1836) *Vocalismus*, Berlin: Nicolai.

—— (1868–71) *Vergleichende Grammatik des Sanskrit, Send, Griechischen, Lateinischen, Litauischen, Gotischen und Deutschen*, 3 vols. 3rd edn. (1st 1833–52, 2nd 1857–61) Berlin, Dümmler.

—— (1974) *Analytical Comparison of the Sanskrit, Greek, Latin, and Teutonic Languages, Shewing the Original Identity of their Grammatical Structure*, with a preface by E. F. K. Koerner, (Amsterdam Classics in Linguistics, 1.3), Amsterdam: Benjamins.

Borgström, Carl (1949) "Thoughts about IE vowel-gradation", *Norsk Tidsskrift for Sprogvidenskab* 15: 137–87.

Bosch-Gimpera, P. (1961) *Les Indo-européens: problèmes archéologiques*, trans. by Raymond Lautier, Paris: Payot.

von Bradke, Peter (1888) *Beiträge zur Kenntnis der vorhistorischen Entwicklung unseres Sprachstammes*, Giessen: Münchow.

Brandenstein, Wilhelm, ed. (1952) *Studien zur indogermanischen Grundsprache*, Vienna: Gerold.

Braune, Wilhelm and Ernst A. Ebbinghaus, (1981) *Gotische Grammatik*, 19th edn, Tübingen: Niemeyer.

Brønsted, Johannes (1960) *The Vikings*, trans. by Estrid Bannister-Good, Harmondsworth: Penguin.

von Brücke, Ernst W. (1856) *Grundzüge der Physiologie und Systematik der Sprachlaute*, 1st edn (2nd edn 1876), Vienna: Gors.

Brugmann, Karl (1876) "Nasalis sonans in der indogermanischen Grundsprache," *Curtius Studien* 9: 287–330.

—— (1878) Preface to *Morphologische Untersuchungen*, in Winfred P. Lehmann (ed.) *A Reader in Nineteenth-Century Historical Indo-European Linguistics*, Bloomington: Indiana University Press, 1967: 197–209. (See H. Osthoff and Karl Brugmann, *Morphologische Untersuchungen*, 1878–1910.)

—— (1891) "Zur Frage der Entstehung des grammatischen Geschlechtes", *Paul und Braunes Beiträge* (subsequently resolved as *Beiträge zur Geschichte der deutschen Sprache und Literatur*), 15: 523–31.

—— (1894) *Die Ausdrücke für den Begriff der Totalität in den indogermanischen Sprachen*, Leipzig: Edelmann.

—— (1897–1916) *Vergleichende Laut-, Stammbildungs- und Flexionslehre der indogermanischen Sprachen*, 2nd edn. Strasburg: Trübner: 1897. vol. 1: *Einleitung und Lautlehre*, vol. 2: *Lehre von den Wortformen und ihrem*

Gebrauch; vol. 2.1: *Allgemeines, Zusammensetzung, Nominalstämme*; 1911. vol.
2.2: *Nomina*; 1913, vol. 2.3.1: *Verbum finitum*; 1916, vol. 2.3.2: *Verbum finitum*
= *Grundriss der vergleichenden Grammatik der indogermanischen Sprachen*.

—— (1904a) *Kurze vergleichende Grammatik der indogermanischen Sprachen*,
Strasburg: Trübner.

—— (1904b) *Die Demonstrativpronomina der indogermanischen Sprachen: eine
hedeutungsgeschichtliche Untersuchung*, Leipzig: Teubner.

—— (1918) *Verschiedenheiten der Satzgesbaltung nach Maßgabe der scelischen
Grundfunktiones in den indogermanischen Sprachen*, Leipzig: Teubner.

—— (1925) *Die Syntax des einfachen Satzes im Indogermanischen*, Berlin and
Leipzig: de Gruyter.

Brugmann, Karl and Berthold Delbrück (1886–1900) *Grundriss der vergleichende
Grammatik der indogermanischen Sprachen*, 5 vols, vols. 1 and 2 replaced by
Brugmann 1897–1916.

Buck, Carl Darling (1904) *A Grammar of Oscan and Umbrian*, Boston: Ginn.

—— (1933, 1937) *Comparative Grammar of Greek and Latin*, Chicago: University
of Chicago Press.

—— (1949) *A Dictionary of Selected Synonyms in the Principal Indo-European
Languages*, Chicago: University of Chicago Press.

Burrow, Thomas (1973) *The Sanskrit Language*, 3rd edn. London: Faber & Faber.

Campanile, Enrico (1977) *Richerche di Cultura Poetica Indoeuropea*, Pisa:
Giardini.

Campbell, Lyle (1990) "Indo-European and Uralic tree names", *Diachronica* 7:
149–80.

Canedo, José (1937) *Zur Wort- und Satzstellung in der alt- und mittelindischen
Prosa*. Ergänzungsheft zur *Kuhns Zeitschrift* (subsequently resolved as
Zeitschrift für vergleichende Sprachforschurg) 13, Berlin (Göttingen).

Cannon, Garland (1990) *The Life and Mind of Oriental Jones*, Cambridge:
Cambridge University Press.

Cardona, George, Henry M. Hoenigswald and Alfred Senn, eds (1970) *Indo-
European and Indo-Europeans*, Philadelphia: University of Pennsylvania Press.

Carnap, Rudolf (1958) *Introduction to Symbolic Logic and its Applications*, trans.
by William H. Meyer and John Wilkinson from the German of 1954, New York:
Dover.

Carruba, Onofrio (1969) *Die satzeinleitenden Partikeln in den indogermanischen
Sprachen Anatoliens*, Rome: Ateneo.

Chantraine, Pierre (1968–80) *Dictionnaire étymologique de la langue grecque;
histoire des mots*, 2 vols, Paris: Klincksieck.

Couvreur, Walter (1937) *De hettitsche h*, Leuven: Museon.

Cowgill, Warren (1968) "The first person singular medio-passive in Indo-Iranian,"
in J. C. Heesterman *et al.* (eds) *Pratidânam*, The Hague: Mouton, 24–31.

—— (1986) *Indogermanische Grammatik*, vol. I.1.11–71, Einleitung, Heidelberg:
Winter.

Cuny, Albert L. M. (1924) *Etudes prégrammaticales sur le domaine des langues
indo-européennes et chamito-sémitiques*, Paris: Champion.

Curtius, Georg (1868–77) *Studien zur griechischen und lateinischen Grammatik*, 10
vols, Leipzig: Hirzel (repr. 1972).

Cuvier, Georges (1812) *Recherches sur les ossemens fossiles de quadrupèdes*, Paris:
Dufour & d'Ocagne.

Delbrück, Berthold (1871–88) *Syntaktische Forschungen* I–V, Halle: Waisenhaus,
vol. V, *Altindische Syntax* was repr. Darmstadt: Wissenschaftliche Buchgesellschaft (1968).

—— (1878) *Die altindische Wortfolge aus dem Çatapathabrâhmana dargestellt*,
(Syntaktische Forschungen 3), Halle: Waisenhaus.

—— (1879) *Die Grundlagen der griechischen Syntax*, Halle: Waisenhaus.
—— (1888) *Altindische Syntax* (Syntaktische Forschungen 5), Halle: Waisenhaus (repr. 1968).
—— (1889) *Die indogermanischen Verwandtschaftsnamen*, Abhandlungen der phil.-hist.-classe der Königlichen sächsischen Gesellschaft der Wissenschaften 11: 381–606, Leipzig.
—— (1893, 1897, 1900) *Vergleichende Syntax der indogermanischen Sprachen*, 3 vols (vols 3–5 of Brugmann and Delbrück *Grundriss*, 1st edn), Strasburg: Trübner.
—— (1907) *Synkretismus: ein Beitrag zur germanischen Kasuslehre*, Strasburg: Trübner.
—— (1918) *Die Worstellung in dem älteren westgötischen Landrecht*, Leipzig: Teubner.
—— (1919) *Einleitung in das Studium der indogermanischen Sprachen*, 6th edn, Leipzig: Teubner.
Deniston, J. D. (1954) *The Greek Particles*, 2nd edn, Oxford: Clarendon.
Devoto, Dimiter (1961) *Origini Indoeuropee*, Firenze: Sansoni.
Diakonoff, Igor M. (1984) "On the original home of the speakers of Indo-European," trans. Olga Kipnis, ed. Edgar C. Polomé, *Soviet Anthropology and Archaeology* 23.2.
—— (1988) Review of Colin Renfrew, *Archaeology and Language: the Puzzle of Indo-European Origins*, Cambridge: Cambridge University Press, 1987, *Annual of Armenian Linguistics* 9: 79–87.
Diebold, A. Richard, Jr (1985) *The Evolution of Indo-European Nomenclature for Salmonid Fish: The Case of "Huchen"* (HUCHO SPP), Washington, DC: Institute for the Study of Man.
—— (1987) "Linguistic ways to prehistory," in Susan N. Skomal and E. C. Polomé (eds) *Proto-Indo-European: the Archaeology of a Linguistic Problem. Studies in Honor of Marija Gimbutas*, Washington: Institute for the Study of Man.
Dillon, Myles (1948) "Celtic and the other Indo-European languages," *Transactions of the Philological Society* 1947: 15–24.
Djahukian, Gevorg B. (1990) "A variational model of the Indoeuropean consonant system", *Historische Sprachwissenschaft* 103: 1–16.
Dolgopolsky, Aaron B. (1986 [1964]) "A probabilistic hypothesis concerning the oldest relationships among the language families of northern Eurasia," in Vitalij V. Shevoroshkin and Thomas L. Markey (eds and trans.) *Typology Relationship and Time*, Ann Arbor: Karoma.
Dumézil, Georges (1958) *L'Idéologie tripartite des Indo-Européens*, Brussels: Collection Latomus 31.
—— (1970a) *The Destiny of the Warrior*, trans. Alf Hiltebeitel, Chicago: University of Chicago Press.
—— (1970b) *Archaic Roman Religion*, trans. Philip Krapp, Chicago: University of Chicago Press.
Edgerton, Franklin (1934) "Sievers's law and IE weak-grade vocalism," *Language* 10: 236–65.
—— (1943) "The Indo-European semivowels," *Language* 19: 83–124.
Ehret, Christopher (1988) "Language change and the material correlates of language and ethnic shift," *Antiquity* 62: 564–74.
Elizarenkova, T. (1972) Review of K. Hoffmann, *Der Injunktiv im Veda*, Heidelberg: Winter, 1967, *Indo-Iranian Journal* 14: 247–53.
Embleton, Sheila (1991) "Mathematical methods of genetic classification," in Sidney M. Lamb and E. Douglas Mitchell (eds) *Sprung from Some Common Source: Investigations into the Prehistory of Languages*, Stanford: Stanford University Press, 365–88.

Fairbanks, Gordon (1976) "Case inflections in Indo-European," *Journal of Indo-European Studies* 4: 101–31.

Feist, Sigmund (1913) *Kultur, Ausbreitung und Herkunft der Indogermanen*, Berlin: Weidmann.

—— (1924) *Indogermanen und Germanen*, 3d edn, Halle: Niemeyer.

Fick, August (1868) *Wörterbuch der indogermanischen Grundsprache in ihrem Bestande vor der Völkertrennung*, Göttingen: Vandenhoeck & Ruprecht.

—— (1890) *Vergleichendes Wörterbuch der Indogermanischen Sprachen*, 4th edn; 1894, vol. I. *Wortschatz der Grundsprache, des Arischen und der Westeuropäischen Spracheinheit*, vol. II: *Urkeltischer Sprachschatz, von Whitley Stokes*; 1909. vol. III: *Wortschatz der Germanischen Spracheinheit, unter Mitwirkung von Hjalmar Falk gänzlich umgearbeitet von Alf Torp* (1st edn 1868, 2nd 1870, 3rd 1873ff.), Göttingen: Vandenhoeck & Ruprecht.

Fillmore, Charles J. (1968) "The case for case," in Emmon Bach and Robert T. Harms (eds) *Universals in Linguistic Theory*, New York: Holt, Rinehart & Winston, 1–88.

Flattery, David Stophlet and Martin Schwartz (1989) *Haoma and Harmaline: the Botanical Identity of the Indo-Iranian Sacred Hallucinogen "Soma" and its Legacy in Religion, Language, and Middle Eastern Folklore*, Berkeley: University of California Press.

Friedrich, Johannes (1931) "Hethitisch und 'Kleinasiatische' Sprachen," in Albert Debrunner and Ferdinand Sommer (eds) *Die Erforschung der indogermanischen Sprachen* 5.1, Berlin: deGruyter.

—— (1952–4) *Hethitisches Wörterbuch*. Heidelberg: Winter.

—— (1960) *Hethitisches Elementarbuch*, vol. 1. *Kurzgefasste Grammatik*, Heidelberg: Winter.

Friedrich, Paul (1966) "Proto-Indo-European kinship", *Ethnology* 5: 1–36.

—— (1970) *Proto-Indo-European Trees: the arboreal system of a prehistoric people*, Chicago: University of Chicago Press.

—— (1975) *Proto-Indo-European Syntax: the order of meaningful elements*, Journal of Indo-European Studies, monograph 1.

Frisk, Hjalmar (1960–82) *Griechisches etymologisches Wörterbuch*, 3 vols, Heidelberg: Winter.

Fulk, R. D. (1986) *The Origins of Indo-European Quantitative Ablaut*, Innsbruck: Institut für Sprachwissenschaft der Universität.

Furnée, Edzard J. (1972) *Die wichtigsten konsonantischen Erscheinungen des Vorgriechischen*. The Hague: Mouton.

Gamkrelidze, Thomas V. and Vyacheslav V. Ivanov (1984) *Indoevropejskij jazyk i indoevropejcy*. Tbilisi: Tbilisi State University.

Garde, Paul (1976) *Histoire de l'accentuation Slave*, 2 vols, Paris: Institut d'Etudes Slaves.

Gimbutas, Marija (1970) "Proto-Indo-European culture: the Kurgan culture during the fifth, fourth, and third millennia B.C.," in George Cardona, Henry M. Hoenigswald and Alfred Senn (eds) *Indo-European and Indo-Europeans*, Philadelphia: University of Pennsylvania Press.

—— (1974) *The Gods and Goddesses of Old Europe, 7000–3500 B.C.: Myths, Legends, Cult Images*, 2nd edn as *The Goddesses and Gods of Old Europe, 7000–3500 B.C.: Myths, Legends, Cult Images*, London: Thames & Hudson, 1982.

—— (1985) "Primary and secondary homeland of the Indo-Europeans," *Journal of Indo-European Studies* 13: 185–202.

—— ed. (1980–1) "The transformation of European and Anatolian Culture, 4500–2500 B.C. and its legacy," *Journal of Indo-European Studies* 8.1–2, 1–230; 8.3–4, 231–414; 9.1–2, 1–175.

Glob, P. V. (1969) *The Bog People: Iron-Age Man Preserved*, trans. Rupert Bruce-Mitford, London: Faber & Faber.

—— (1971) *Danish Prehistoric Monuments*, trans. Joan Bulman, London: Faber & Faber.

—— (1974) *The Mound People: Danish Bronze-Age Man Preserved*, trans. Joan Bulman, London: Faber & Faber.

Grassmann, Hermann (1863) "Ueber die Aspiraten und ihr gleichzeitiges Vorhandensein im An- und Auslaute der Wurzeln," *Zeitschrift für vergleichende Sprachforschung* 12: 81–138.

—— (1873) *Wörterbuch zum Rig-Veda*. Wiesbaden: Harrassowitz, repr. 1955.

Greenberg, Joseph (1963, 1966) "Some universals of grammar with reference to the order of meaningful elements," in Joseph Greenberg (ed.) *Universals of Language*, Cambridge: MIT, 73–113.

Greenberg, Joseph, Charles A. Ferguson and E. A. Moravcsik, eds (1978) *Universals of Human Language*, 4 vols, Stanford: Stanford University Press.

Grimm, Jacob (1819/1822–37) *Deutsche Grammatik* (repr. and ed. by W. Scherer, G. Roethe. 1870–98), Göttingen: Dietrich; Berlin: Dümmler; Gütersloh: Bertelsmann.

Grimm, Jacob and Wilhelm Grimm, eds (1854–1954) *Deutsches Wörterbuch*, vols. 1–32, Leipzig: Hirzel (reprinted 1984, vol. 33 added, Munich: Deutscher Taschenbuchverlag).

—— (1848) *Geschichte der deutschen Sprache*, (3rd edn 1868), Leipzig: Hirzel.

Grotefend, August (1827) *Grundzüge einer neuen Satztheorie*, Hannover: Hahn.

Güntert, Hermann (1916) *Indogermanische Ablautprobleme: Untersuchungen über Schwa secundum, einen zweiten indogermanischen Murmelvokal*, Strasburg: Trübner.

—— (Festschrift for) (1974) *Antiquitates indogermanicae*, ed. Manfred Mayrhofer, Wolfgang Meid, Bernfried Schlerath and Rüdsger Schmidt, Innsbruck: Institut für Sprachwissenschaft der Universität.

Güterbock, Hans G. and Harry A. Hoffner (1980–) *The Hittite Dictionary of the Oriental Institute of the University of Chicago*, Chicago: Oriental Institute.

Halle, Morris (1962) "Phonology in generative grammar," *Word* 18: 54–72.

Halle, Morris and Paul Kiparsky (1981) Review of *Histoire de l'accentuation slave*, by Paul Garde, 2 vols, Paris: Institute d'Etudes Slaves, 1976, *Language* 57: 150–81.

Haudry, Jean. (1970) "L'Instrumental et la structure de la phrase simple en indo-européen," *Bulletin de Société Linguistique de Paris* 65: 44–84.

—— (1977) *L'Emploi des cas en védique: Introduction à l'étude des cas en indo-européen*, Lyon: L'Hermes.

—— (1979) *L'Indo-Européen*, Paris: Presses Universitaires de France.

—— (1982) *Préhistoire de la flexion nominale indo-européenne*, Lyon: Institut d'études indo-européennes de l'Université. Jean Moulin.

Häusler, Alexander (1983) "Zu den ältesten Streitwagen in Osteuropa," in Peter Snoy (ed.) *Ethnologie und Geschichte: Festschrift für Karl Jettmar*, Wiesbaden: Steiner, 222–33.

—— (1985) "Die Anfänge von Rad und Wagen in der Kulturgeschichte Europas," in *Produktivkräfte und Produktionsverhältnisse*, Berlin: 121–33.

—— (forthcoming) " 'Kurgankultur' und Urgeschichte Griechenlands," paper given at the 6th International Colloquium on Aegean History, Athens, 1988.

—— (1992) "Archäologie und Ursprung der Indogermanen," *Das Altertum* 38: 3–16.

Havers, Wilhelm (1931) *Handbuch der erklärenden Syntax*, Heidelberg: Winter.

—— (1946) *Neuere Literatur zum Sprachtabu*, Vienna: Rohrer.

Hehn, Victor (1911) *Kulturpflanzen und Hausthiere in ihrem Übergang aus Asien nach Griechenland und Italien sowie in das übrige Europa*, ed. Otto Schrader, Berlin: Borntraeger, (repr. 1963; repr. of translation, as *Cultivated plants and domesticated animals in their migration from Asia to Europe*, Amsterdam: Benjamins, 1976).

Henning, W. B. (1848) "Oktō(u)," *Transactions of the Philological Society* 1948: 69.

Hermann, Eduard (1895) "Gab es im Indogermanischen Nebensätze?," *Zeitschrift für vergleichende Sprachwissenschaft* 33: 481–534.

—— (1923) *Berthold Delbrück: Ein Gelehrtenleben aus Deutschlands grosser Zeit*, Jena: Fromann.

—— (1931) *Lautgesetz und Analogie*, Berlin: Weidmann.

Hiersche, Rolf (1964) *Untersuchungen zur Frage der tenues aspiratae im Indogermanischen*, Wiesbaden: Harrassowitz.

Hirt, Hermann (1900) *Der indogermanische Ablaut*, Strasburg: Trübner.

—— (1905–7) *Die Indogermanen, ihre Verbreitung, ihre Urheimat, und ihre Kultur*, 2 vols, Strasburg: Trübner.

—— (1921–37) *Indogermanische Grammatik*, 7 vols, Heidelberg: Winter.

—— (1931–4) *Handbuch des Urgermanischen*, 3 vols, Heidelberg: Winter.

—— (1936) (Festschrift for) *Germanen und Indogermanen: Volkstum, Sprache, Heimat, Kultur*, ed. Helmuth Arntz, 2 vols, Heidelberg: Winter.

—— (1939) *Die Hauptprobleme der indogermanischen Sprachwissenschaft*, ed. Helmuth Arntz, Halle: Niemeyer.

Hodge, Carleton T. (1991) "Indo-European and Afroasiatic," in Sidney M. Lamb and E. Douglas Mitchell (eds) *Sprung from Some Common Source: Investigations into the Prehistory of Language*, Stanford: Stanford University Press, 141–65.

Hoenigswald, Henry M. (1960) *Language Change and Linguistic Reconstruction*, Chicago: University of Chicago Press.

—— (1973) *Studies in Formal Historical Linguistics*, Dordrecht: Reidel.

Hoffmann, Karl (1967) *Der Injunktiv im Veda*, Heidelberg: Winter.

Hoijer, Harry (1951) "Cultural implications of some Navaho linguistic categories," *Language* 27: 111–20.

Holtzmann, Adolf (1844) *Über den Ablaut*, Karlsruhe: Holtzmann.

Hoops, Johannes (1905) *Waldbäume und Kulturpflanzen im germanischen Altertum*, Strasburg: Trübner.

—— ed. (1911–19) *Reallexikon der germanischen Altertumskunde*, 4 vols, Strasburg: Trübner.

Hopper, Paul (1973) "Glottalized and murmured occlusives in Indo-European," *Glossa* 7: 141–66.

Hrozny, Bedrich (1915) "Die Lösung des hethitischen Problems," *Mitteilungen der deutschen Orient-Gesellschaft* 56: 17–50.

—— (1917) *Die Sprache der Hethiter*, Leipzig: Hinrichs.

Hübschmann, Heinrich. (1875) *Über die Stellung des Armenischen im Kreise der indogermanischen Sprachen*, Weimar: n.p.

—— 1897. *Armenische Grammatik*, vol. I: *Armenische Etymologie*, Leipzig. Breitkopf & Härtel (repr. 1962).

Ivanov, Vyacheslav V. (1963) *Chettskij jazyk*, Moscow: Nauka.

Jacobi, Hermann (1897) *Compositum und Nebensatz*, Bonn: Cohen.

Jakobson, Roman (1957) "Typological studies and their contribution to historical comparative linguistics," in *idem* (ed.) *Selected Writings*, The Hague: Mouton, 1962, vol. I, 523–32.

Jankowski, Kurt R. (1972) *The Neogrammarians*, The Hague: Mouton.

Jasanoff, Jay H. (1978) *Stative and Middle in Indo-European*. Innsbruck: Institut für Sprachwissenschaft der Universität.

Jespersen, Jens Otto H. (1922) *Language, its Nature, Development and Origin*, London: Allen & Unwin.
—— (1937) *Analytic Syntax*, Copenhagen: Munksgaard.
—— (n.d.) *Selected Writings of Otto Jespersen*, London: Allen & Unwin.
Joachim, Ulrike (1978) *Mehrfachpräsentien im Ṛgveda*, Frankfurt: Lang.
Joki, Aulis J. (1973) *Uralier und Indogermanen: die älteren Berührungen zwischen den uralischen und indogermanischen Sprachen*, Helsinki: Suomalais-Ugrilainen Seura.
Jones, William (1807) *The Works of Sir William Jones*, 13 vols, London: John Stuckdale.
Justus, Carol (1976) "Relativization and topicalization in Hittite," in Charles N. Li (ed.) *Subject and Topic*, New York: Academic, 215–45.
—— (1980) "Typological symmetries and asymmetries in Hittite and IE complementation," pp. 183–206 in Paolo Ramat (ed.) *Linguistic Reconstruction and Indo-European Syntax*, Amsterdam: Benjamins.
Karlgren, Bernhard (1926) *Deutsche Literatur Beitung* 1926: 1960ff.
Katre, Sumitra M. (1987) *Aṣṭādhyāyī of Pāṇini in Roman Transliteration*, Austin: University of Texas Press.
Kiparsky, Paul (1973) "The inflectional accent in Indo-European," *Language* 49: 794–849.
—— and Morris Halle (1977) "Towards a reconstruction of the Indo-European accent," *Studies in Stress and Accent*, ed. Larry H. Hyman (Southern California occasional papers in linguistics 4), Los Angeles: University of Southern California.
Klein, Jared S. (1978) *The Particle u in the Rigveda: a Synchronic and Diachronic Study*. Göttingen: Vandenhoeck & Ruprecht.
Klimov, Georgij A. (1974) "On the character of languages of active typology," *Linguistics* 131: 11–25. (Also *Vaprosy jazykoznanija* 4 (1972): 3–13.)
—— (1977) *Tipologija Jazykov Aktivnogo Stroja*, Moscow: Nauka.
—— (1983) *Principy kontensivnoj tipologii*, Moscow: Nauka.
—— (1985) "Zu den ältesten indogermanisch-semitisch-kartwelischen Kontakten im Vorderen Asien," in Hermann M. Ölberg and Gernot Schmidt, with the help of Heinz Bothien (eds) *Sprachwissenschaftliche Forschungen. Festschrift für Johann Knobloch*, Innsbruck: Institut für Sprachwissenschaft der Universität, 205–20.
Kluge, Friedrich (1895) *Deutsche Studentensprache*, Strasburg: Trübner.
—— (1911) *Seemannssprache*. Halle: Waisenhaus.
Koerner, Konrad (1981) "The neogrammarian doctrine: breakthrough or extension of the Schleicherian paradigm," *Folia Linguistica Historia* 2: 157–78.
Kortlandt, Frederik (1988), "The laryngeal theory and Slavic accentuation," in Alfred Bammesberger (ed.) *Die Laryngaltheorie*, Heidelberg: Winter, 299–311.
Krahe, Hans (1962) *Indogermanische Sprachwissenschaft*, Berlin: de Gruyter.
Krauss, Michael (1990) "Typology and Change in Alaskan languages," in Winfred P. Lehmann (ed.) *Language Typology 1987*, Amsterdam: Benjamins, 147–56.
Kretschmer, Paul (1896) *Einführung in die Geschichte der griechischen Sprache*, Göttingen: Vandenhoech & Ruprecht.
Kronasser, Heinz (1966) *Etymologie der hethitischen Sprache*; vol. 2. *Ausführliche Indices*, by Erich Neu, Wiesbaden: Harrassowitz, 1987.
Kuhn, Adalbert (1845) *Zur ältesten Geschichte der Indogermanischen Völker*, Programme des Berliner Real-Gymnasiums.
—— (1853) "Über die durch nasale erweiterten verbalstämme," *Kuhns Zeitschrift* 2. 467.
—— (1864) "Indische und Germanische Segenssprüche," *Kuhns Zeitschrift* 13: 49–63; repr. in part in Rüdiger Schmitt (ed.) *Indogermanische Dichtersprache*,

Darmstadt: Wissenschaftliche Buchgesellschaft, 1968, 11–25.

Kühner, Raphael and Friedrich Blass (1966) *Ausführliche Grammatik der griechischen sprache*, I.I (1890), I.2 (1892), II.1 (1898); 2.1 (1904), 3rd edn, Hannover: Hahn (reprinted Darmstadt: Wissenschaftliche Buchgesellschaft, 1966).

Kuiper, Franciscus B. J. (1937) *Die indogermanischen Nasalpräsentia*, Amsterdam: North Holland.

Kuipers, Aert H. (1968) "Unique types and typological universals," in J. C. Heesterman, G. H. Schokker and V. I. Subramoniam (eds) *Pratidânam*, The Hague: Mouton, 68–88.

Kurath, Hans, *et al.* (1939) *Handbook of the Linguistic Geography of New England*, Providence: Brown University.

Kurylowicz, Jerzy (1927) "Schwa indoeuropéen et *h* hittite," in *Symbolae grammaticae in honorem Ioannis Rozwadowski*, vol. I, 95–104, Kraków: Gebethner & Wolff.

—— (1935) *Etudes indoeuropéennes*, Kraków: Gebethner & Wolff.

—— (1964) *The Inflectional Categories of Indo-European*, Heidelberg: Winter.

—— (1968) *Indogermanische Grammatik*, vol. II; *Akzent und Ablaut*, Heidelberg: Winter. (See Cowgill (1986), Mayrhofer (1986), Watkins (1969) for other volumes.)

Kuz'mina, E. E. (1983) "Stages in the development of wheeled transport in central Asia during the Aeneolithic and Bronze Age. (On the problem of the migration of Indo-Iranian Tribes)," *Soviet Studies in History* 22: 96–142.

Lamb, Sidney M. and E. Douglas Mitchell, eds (1991) *Sprung from Some Common Source: Investigations into the Prehistory of Languages*, Stanford: Stanford University Press.

Lehmann, Winfred P. (1942) "The Indo-European *dh*-determinative in Germanic," *Language* 18: 125–32.

—— (1943) "The Indo-European *dh*-determinative as Germanic preterite formant," *Language*: 19: 19–26.

—— (1952) *Proto-Indo-European Phonology*, Austin: University of Texas Press.

—— (1957) "A syntactic reflex of the Indo-European laryngeals," in Ernst Pulgram (ed.) *Studies presented to Joshua Whatmough*, The Hague: Mouton, 145–7.

—— (1958) "On earlier stages of the Indo-European nominal inflection," *Language* 34: 179–202.

—— ed. (1967) *A Reader in Nineteenth-Century Historical Indo-European Linguistics*, Bloomington: Indiana University Press.

—— (1969) "Proto-Indo-European compounds in relation to other Proto-Indo-European syntactic patterns," *Acta Linguistica Hafniensia* 12.1–20.

—— (1974) *Proto-Indo-European Syntax*, Austin: University of Texas Press.

—— (1978) "The great underlying ground-plans," pp. 3–55; "English: a characteristic SVO language," pp. 169–222; "Toward an understanding of the profound unity underlying language," pp. 395–432 in Winfred P. Lehmann (ed.) (1978) *Syntactic Typology*, Austin: University of Texas Press.

—— (1980) "The reconstruction of non-simple sentences in Proto-Indo-European," in Paolo Ramat (ed.) *Linguistic Reconstruction and Indo-European Syntax*, Amsterdam: Benjamins, 113–44.

—— (1982) "The noun in early Proto-Indo-European," in Edgar C. Polomé (ed.) *The Indo-Europeans in the Fourth and Third Millennia*, Ann Arbor: Karoma, 140–55.

—— (1986a) *A Gothic Etymological Dictionary*, Leiden: Brill.

—— (1986b), "Reflexes of PIE d < t'," in Dieter Kastovsky and A. Szwedek (eds) *Linguistics across Historical and Geographical Boundaries*, Berlin: Mouton de Gruyter, 483–9.

—— (1989a) "Problems in Proto-Indo-European grammar: Residues from Pre-Indo-European Active Structure," *General Linguistics* 29: 228–46.

—— (1989b) "Earlier stages of Proto-Indo-European," in Karin Heller, *et al.* (eds) *Indogermanica Europaea, Festschrift für Wolfgang Meid*, (Grazer Linguistische Monographien 4), Graz: Institut für Sprachwissenschaft der Universität Graz.

—— (1990a) "The current thrust of Indo-European Studies," *General Linguistics* 30: 1–52; Russian translation in *Voprosy Jazykoznanija* (1991) 4: 5–30.

—— (1990b) Review of J. P. Mallory, *In Search of the Indo-Europeans: Language, Archaeology and Myth* (London: Thames and Hudson, 1989), *Diachronica* 7.1: 101–16.

—— (1992) *Historical Linguistics: an Introduction.* 3rd edn, London: Routledge.

—— ed. (1991) *Language Typology 1987*, Amsterdam: Benjamins.

Lehmann, Winfred P. and Ladislav Zgusta (1979) "Schleicher's tale after a century," Bela Brogyangi (ed.) in *Studies in Diachronic, Synchronic, and Typological Linguistics, Festschrift for Oswald Szemerényi*, Amsterdam: Benjamins, 455–68.

Leskien, August (1876/1963) *Die Declination im Slavo-litauischen und Germanischen*, repr. Leipzig: Zentral-Antiquariat.

Leumann, Manu, Johann B. Hoffmann, and Anton Szantyr (1963–79) *Lateinische Grammatik*, vol. I: *Lateinische Laut- und Formenlehre*, vol. II: *Lateinische Syntax und Stylistik*, vol. III: *Stellenregister*, Munich: Beck.

Levine, Marsha A. (1990) "Dereivka and Horse Domestication," *Antiquity* 64: 727–40.

Lévi-Strauss, Claude (1969) *The Elementary Structures of Kinship*, Boston, MA: Beacon.

Lightfoot, David W. (1979) *Principles of Diachronic Syntax*, Cambridge: Cambridge University Press.

—— 1988. "Syntactic change," in Frederick J. Newmeyer (ed.) *Linguistics: The Cambridge Survey*, vol. I: *Linguistic Theory: Foundations*, New York: Cambridge University Press, 303–23.

Lindeman, Fredrik Otto (1970) *Einführung in die Laryngaltheorie*, Berlin: de Gruyter.

—— (1987) *Introduction to the Laryngeal Theory*, Oslo: Norwegian University Press.

Littauer, Mary A. and J. H. Crouwel (1979) *Wheeled Vehicles and Ridden Animals in the Ancient Near East*, Leiden: Brill.

Littleton, C. Scott (1982) *The New Comparative Mythology: An Anthropological Assessment of the Theories of Georges Dumézil*, 3rd edn, Berkeley and Los Angeles: University of California Press.

Lubotsky, A. M. (1988) *The System of Nominal Accentuation in Sanskrit and Proto-Indo-European* (Memoirs of the Kern Institute), Leiden: Brill.

Maddieson, Ian (1984) *Patterns of Sounds*, Cambridge: Cambridge University Press.

Mahlow, Georg H. (1879) *Die langen Vocale â ê ô in den europäischen Sprachen*, Berlin: Hermann.

Mallory, J. P. (1989) *In Search of the Indo-Europeans: Language, Archaeology and Myth*, London: Thames & Hudson.

Marstrander, Carl J. S. (1919) *Caractère indo-européen de la langue hittite*, Oslo: Dybwad.

Matisoff, James A. (1990) "On megalocomparison," *Language* 66: 106–20.

Mayrhofer, Manfred (1956–80) *Kurzgefaßtes etymologisches Wörterbuch des Altindischen* I–IV, Heidelberg: Winter.

—— (1986) *Indogermanische Grammatik*, vol. 1–2 *Lautlehre* (Segmentale Phonologie des Indogermanischen), Heidelberg: Winter.

Meid, Wolfgang (1975) "Probleme der räumlichen und zeitlichen Gliederung des Indogermanischen," in Helmut Rix (ed.) *Flexion und Wortbildung*, Wiesbaden:

Reichert.
—— (1984) "Bemerkungen zum indogermanischen Wortschatz des Germanischen," in Jürgen Untermann and Bela Brogyanyi (eds) *Das Germanische und die Rekonstruktion der indogermanischen Grundsprache*, Amsterdam: Benjamins, 91–111.
—— ed. (1987) *Studien zum indogermanischen Wortschatz*. Innsbruck: Institut für Sprachwissenschaft der Universität.
Meillet, Antoine (1908) *Les dialectes indo-européens* (Collection linguistique publiée par la Société de Linguistique I), Paris: Champion.
—— ([1922] 1967) *The Indo-European Dialects*, trans. by Samuel N. Rosenberg, University: University of Alabama Press.
—— ([1925] 1967) *The Comparative Method in Historical Linguistics*, trans. Gordon B. Ford, Jr, Paris: Champion.
—— (1928) "Discussion," in *Actes du premier congrès international de linguistes*, Leiden: Sijthoff, 164–5.
—— (1937) *Introduction a l'étude comparative des langues indo-européennes*, Paris: Hachette. (repr. University: University of Alabama Press, 1964).
Mellaart, James (1978) *The Archaeology of Ancient Turkey*, London: Bodley Head.
Milisauskas, Sarunas (1978) *European Prehistory*, London: Academic.
Möller, Hermann (1879) Review of Kluge, *Beiträge*, with note on laryngeals, *Englische Studien* 3: 157fn.
—— (1906) *Semitisch und Indogermanisch*, Kopenhagen: Hagerup.
Müller, Friedrich Max (1873) *The Hymns of the Rig-Veda*, London.
Munro, D. B. (1891) *A Grammar of the Homeric Dialect*, 2nd edn, Oxford: Clarendon.
Neu, Erich (1968) *Das hethitische Mediopassiv und seine indogermanischen Grundlagen*, Wiesbaden: Harrassowitz.
—— (1974) *Der Anitta-Text*, Wiesbaden: Harrassowitz.
—— (1976) "Zur Rekonstruktion des indogermanischen Verbalsystems," in Anna Mopurgo Davies and Wolfgang Meid (eds) *Studies in Greek, Italic and Indo-European Linguistics, offered to Leonard R. Palmer*, Innsbruck: Institut für Sprachwissenschaft der Universität, 239–54.
—— (1987) "Zum Wortschatz des Hethitischen aus synchroner und diachroner Sicht," in Wolfgang Meid (ed.) *Studien zum indogermanischen Wortschatz*, Innsbruck: Institut für Sprachwissenschaft der Universität, 167–88.
Neu, Erich and Wolfgang Meid, eds (1979) *Hethitisch und Indogermanisch*, Innsbruck: Institut für Sprachwissenschaft der Universität.
Nichols, Johanna (1986) "Head-marking and dependent-marking grammars," *Language* 62: 56–119.
Norman, K. R. (1988) Review of *Archaeology and Language: the Puzzle of Indo-European Origins*, by Colin Renfrew, London: Cape, 1987, *Lingua* 76: 91–9.
Oettinger, Norbert (1987) "Anatolische Wortbildung und indogermanische Chronologie," in Wolfgang Meid (ed.) *Studien zum indogermanischen Wortschatz*, Institut für Sprachwissenschaft der Universität, 189–91.
Osthoff, Hermann (1884) *Zur Geschichte des Perfects im Indogermanischen*. Strasburg: Trübner.
—— (1876) "Zur Frage des Ursprungs der germanischen *n*-Deklination," *Beiträge zur Geschichte der deutschen Sprache und Literatur* 3: 1–89.
—— (1899) *Von Suppletivwesen der indogermanischen Sprachen*. Heidelberg: Winter.
Osthoff, Hermann and Karl Brugmann (1878–1910) *Morphologische Untersuchungen auf dem Gebiete der indogermanischen Sprachen*, 6 vols, Leipzig: Hirzel.

Otten, Heirich and Vladimir Soucek (1969) *Ein althethitisches Ritual für das Königspaar*, Wiesbaden: Harrassowitz.

Palmaitis, Mikolas L. (1979) *Indoevropeyskaja Apofonija i Razvitie deklinatsionnykjh Modelej v diakhronno-tipologicheskom Aspekte*, Tiflis: Tiflis University.

—— (1982) "The New Look of Indo-European declension," *Indogermanische Forschungen* 86: 71–95.

—— (1988) Review of Thomas V. Gamkrelidze and V. V. Ivanov, *Indoevropejskij jazyk i indoevropejcy*, Tbilisi, Tbilisi State University, 1984, *Indogermanische Forschungen* 93: 280–92.

Parpola, Asko (1988) "The Coming of the Aryans to Iran and India and the cultural and ethnic identity of the Dāsas," *Studia Orientalia* 64: 195–302.

Parry, A., ed. (1971) *The Making of Homeric Verse: the Collected Papers of Milman Parry*. Oxford: Clarendon.

Paul, Hermann (1916–21) *Deutsche Grammatik*, 5 vols, Halle: Niemeyer.

—— (1920, 5th edn) *Prinzipien der Sprachgeschichte*. Halle: Niemeyer, repr. since and labeled as further editions. 2nd edn (1886) trans. by H.A. Strong as *Principles of the History of Language*, London: Longmans, Green, 1891.

—— (1988) *Mittelhochdeutsche Grammatik*, 23rd edn, rev. by Siegfried Grosse and Peter Wiehl, Tübingen: Niemeyer.

Pedersen, Holger (1931) *Linguistic Science in the Nineteenth Century*, trans. John W. Spargo, Cambridge, MA: Harvard University Press; reissued as *The Diversity of Language*, Bloomington: Indiana University Press, 1959.

—— (1951) *Die gemeinindoeuropäischen und die vorindoeuropäischen Verschlusslaute*, Copenhagen: Munksgaard.

Persson, Per (1891) *Studien zur Lehre der Wurzelerweiterung und Wurzelvariation*, Uppsala: Berling.

—— (1912) *Beiträge zur indogermanischen Wortforschung*, Leipzig: Harrassowitz.

Petersson, H. P. (1921) *Studien über die indogermanischen Heteroklisie*, Lund: Berling.

Pisani, Vittore (1961) *Glottologia indoeuropea*, Turin: Rosenberg & Sellier.

Pokorny, Julius (1959–69, 1989) *Indogermanisches etymologisches Wörterbuch*, vol. I, II: *Register*, Bern: Francke.

Polomé, Edgar (1965) "The laryngeal theory so far," in Werner Winter (ed.) *Evidence for Laryngeals*, The Hague: Mouton, 9–78.

—— ed. (1982a) *The Indo-Europeans in the Fourth and Third Millennia*, Ann Arbor, MI: Karoma.

—— ed. (1982b) *Homage to Georges Dumézil*, Washington DC: Institute for the Study of Man.

—— (1986) "The non-Indo-European component of the Germanic lexicon," in Annemarie Etter (ed.) *O-o-pe-ro-si: Festschrift für Ernst Risch zum 70. Geburtstag* Berlin: deGruyter, 661–77.

—— (1990) "The Indo-Europeanization of northern Europe: the linguistic evidence," *Journal of Indo-European Studies* 18: 331–8.

Polomé, Edgar and Susan Nacev Skomal, eds (1987) *Proto-Indo-European: the Archaeology of a Linguistic Problem. Studies in Honor of Marija Gimbutas*, Washington: Institute for the Study of Man.

Porzig, Walter (1954) *Die Gliederung des Indogermanischen Sprachgebiets*, Heidelberg: Winter.

Pott, August Friedrich (1833–6) *Etymologische Forschungen auf dem Gebiete der indogermanischen Sprachen*, 6 vols. (2nd edn 1859–76), Lemgo: Meyer.

—— (1977) *Einleitung in die Allgemeine Sprachwissenschaft* (Amsterdam Classics in Linguistics, 10), ed. F. K. Koerner, Amsterdam: Benjamins.

Prokosch, Eduard (1939) *A Comparative Germanic Grammar*, Philadelphia: University of Pennsylvania Press.

Puhvel, Jaan (1960) *Laryngeals and the Indo-European Verb*, Berkeley and Los Angeles: University of California Press.
—— (1984–) *Hittite Etymological Dictionary*. Berlin: Mouton.
—— (1987) *Comparative Mythology*. Baltimore: Johns Hopkins University Press.
Pulleyblank, E. G. (1965) "The Indo-European vowel system and the qualitative ablaut," *Word* 21: 17–48.
von Raumer, Rudolf (1837) *Die Aspiration und die Lautverschiebung*, Leipzig: Brockhaus.
Renfrew, Colin (1987) *Archaeology and Language: the Puzzle of Indo-European Origins*, London: Cape.
—— (1989a) "The origins of Indo-European languages," *Scientific American*, October, 106–14.
—— (1989b) "Models of change in language and archaeology," *Transactions of the Philological Society* 87: 103–55.
—— (1989c) "They ride horses, don't they?," Review of J. P. Mallory, *In Search of the Indo-Europeans: Language, Archaeology and Myth* (London: Thames & Hudson, 1989), *Antiquity* 63: 843–7.
—— (1990) "Archaeology and linguistics: some preliminary issues," in Thomas L. Markey and John A. C. Greppin (eds), *When Worlds Collide: Indo-Europeans and Pre-Indo-Europeans*, Ann Arbor: Karoma, 15–31.
Renou, Louis (1925) "Les formes dites d'injonctif dans le RGVEDA," *Etrennes Benveniste*, Paris, 53–89.
—— (1953) "Observations sur les composés nominaux du Rgveda," *Language* 29: 231–6.
Ries, John (1894) *Was ist Syntax?* Prag. repr. Darmstadt: Wissenschaftliche Buchgesellschaft (1967).
Risch, Ernst (1944) "Griechische Determinativkomposita," *Indogermanische Forschungen* 59: 1–61, 245–94.
Rix, Helmut (1975) *Historische Grammatik des Griechischen*, Darmstadt: Wissenschaftliche Buchgesellschaft.
—— (1988) "The Proto-Indo-European middle: content, forms and origin," *Münchener Studien zur Sprachwissenschaft* 49: 101–19.
Rowlett, Ralph M. (1984) "Archaeological evidence for early Indo-European chieftains," *Journal of Indo-European Studies* 12: 193–223.
Ruhlen, Merritt (1991) "The Amerind phylum and the prehistory of the New World," in Sidney M. Lamb and E. Douglas Mitchell (eds) *Sprung from Some Common Source: Investigations into the Prehistory of Languages*, Stanford: Stanford University Press, 328–52.
Sadock, Jerrold M. (1991) *Autolexical Syntax*, Chicago: University of Chicago Press.
Sandbach, Edmund (1930) *Die indogermanischen schweren Basen und das baltische (litauische) Präteritum*, Heidelberg: Winter.
Sapir, Edward (1921) *Language*, New York: Harcourt, Brace.
—— (1930) *Totality*, Linguistic Society of America, Language Monographs 6, Philadelphia.
—— (1938) "Glottalized continuants in Navaho, Nootka, and Kwakiutl," *Language* 14: 248–74.
—— (1939) "From Sapir's desk," *Language* 15: 178–81.
Saussure, Ferdinand de (1879) *Mémoire sur le système primitif des voyelles dans les langues indo-européennes*, Leipzig: Vieweg.
—— (1921) *Recueil des publications scientifiques de Ferdinand de Saussure*, ed. Charles Bally and Léopold Gautier, Lausanne: Payot.
—— (1916, 1949) *Cours de linguistique générale*, Paris: Payot.
Scharfe, Helmut (1985) "The Vedic word for 'King'," *Journal of the American Oriental Society* 105: 543–8.

Schlegel, Friedrich von (1808) *Über die Sprache und Weisheit der Indier: ein Beitrag zur Begründung der Alterthumskunde*, Heidelberg: Mohr & Zimmer.

—— (1977) *Über die Sprache und Weisheit der Indier: ein Beitrag zur Begründung der Alterthumskunde*, prepared by E. F. K. Koerner (Amsterdam Classics in Linguistics, 1), Amsterdam: Benjamins.

Schleicher, August (1871) *Compendium der vergleichenden Grammatik der indogermanischen Sprachen*, 3rd edn (1st edn 1861, 2nd 1866, 4th 1876), Weimar: Böhlau.

—— (1983) *Die Sprachen Europas in systematischer Übersicht* ed. E. F. K. Koerner (Amsterdam Classics in Linguistics, 4), Amsterdam: Benjamins.

Schlerath, Bernfried (1973) *Die Indogermanen*, Innsbruck: Institut für Sprachwissenschaft der Universität.

—— (1981) "Ist ein Raum/Zeit-Modell für eine rekonstruierte Sprache möglich?" *Zeitschrift für vergleichende Sprachwissenschaft* 95: 175–202.

Schmalstieg, William R. (1980) *Indo-European Linguistics: a New Synthesis*, University Park: Pennsylvania State University Press.

Schmandt-Besserat, Denise (1978) "The earliest precursor of writing," *Scientific American*, June, 50–9.

—— (1982) "The emergence of recording," *American Anthropologist* 84: 871–8.

—— (1984) "Before numerals," *Visible Language* 18: 48–60.

—— (1992) *Before Writing*, Austin: University of Texas Press.

Schmidt, Johannes (1872) *Die Verwandtschaftsverhältnisse der indogermanischen Sprachen*, Weimar: Böhlau.

—— (1889) *Die Pluralbildungen der indogermanischen Neutra*. Weimar: Böhlau.

Schmidt, Karl-Horst (1979) "Reconstructing Active and Ergative Stages of pre-Indo-European," in Frans Plank (ed.) *Ergativity*, New York: Academic, 333–45.

—— (1980) "Zur Typologie des Vorindogermanischen," in Paolo Ramat *et al.* (eds) *Linguistic Reconstruction and Indo-European Syntax*, Amsterdam: Benjamins, 91–112.

—— (1983) *Kaukasische Typologie als Hilfsmittel für die Rekonstruktion des Vorindogermanischen*, Innsbruck: Institut für Sprachwissenschaft der Universität.

Schmidt, *Pater* Wilhelm (1926) *Die Sprachfamilien und Sprachenkreise der Erde*, Heidelberg: Winter.

Schmidt-Brandt, Robert (1973) *Die Entwicklung des indogermanischen Vokalsystems*, 2nd edn, Heidelberg: Groos.

Schmitt, Rüdiger (1967) *Dichtung und Dichtersprache in indogermanischer Zeit*, Wiesbaden: Harrassowitz.

Schrader, Otto (1883) *Sprachvergleichung und Urgeschichte*, 1st edn (2nd edn 1891, 3rd 1906–7), Jena: Costenoble. English translation of the 2nd edn as *Prehistoric Antiquities of the Aryan Peoples: a Manual of Comparative Philology and the Earliest Cultures*, by Frank Byron Jevons, London: Griffin, 1890, repr. Delhi, 1972.

—— (1917–29) *Reallexikon der indogermanischen Altertumskunde*, 2nd edn by Alfons Nehring, 2 vols, Berlin: de Gruyter.

Schrijnen, Josef (1921) *Einführung in das Studium der indogermanischen Sprachwissenschaft*, Heidelberg: Winter.

Schulze, Wilhelm (1885, [1966]) "Indogermanische *āi*-Wurzeln," in Wilhelm Wissmann (ed.) *Kleine Schriften*, Göttingen: Vandenhoeck & Ruprecht, 49–56.

Schwyzer, Eduard (1939–50) *Griechische Grammatik*, 2 vols, Munich: Beck.

Seebold, Elmar (1972) *Das System der Indogermanischen Halbvokale*, Heidelberg: Winter.

Senn, Alfred (1966) *Handbuch der litauischen Sprache. I. Grammatik*, Heidelberg: Winter.

Sherratt, A. and S. Sheratt (1988) "The archaeology of Indo-European, an alternative view," *Antiquity* 62: 584–95.

Shevoroshkin, Vitaly and Alexis Manaster Ramer (1991) "Some recent work on the remote relations of languages," in Sidney M. Lamb and E. Douglas Mitchell (eds) *Sprung from Some Common Source: Investigations into the Prehistory of Languages*, Stanford: Stanford University Press, 178–203.

Shields, Kenneth, Jr (1982) *Indo-European Noun Inflection: A Developmental History*, University Park: The Pennsylvania State University Press.

Sievers, Eduard (1878) "Zur Accent- und Lautlehre der germanischen Sprachen. III. Zum vocalischen Auslautsgesetz," *Paul und Braunes Beiträge* 5: 63–163, esp. 125–31.

—— ed. (1878, [1924]) *Heliand*, Halle: Waisenhaus.

—— ed. (1892) *Tatian*, 2nd edn, Paderborn: Schöningh.

—— (1901) *Grundzüge der Phonetik*, 5th edn, Leipzig: Breitkopf und Härtel.

Skomal, Susan Nacev and Edgar C. Polomé, eds (1987) *Proto-Indo-European: the Archaeology of a Linguistic Problem. Studies in Honor of Marija Gimbutas*, Washington, DC: Institute for the Study of Man.

Small, George William (1923) *The Comparison of Inequality*, Baltimore: Johns Hopkins University Press.

—— (1929) *The Germanic Case of Comparison*, Philadelphia: Linguistic Society of America.

Smyth, Herbert Weir, rev. by Gordon M. Messing (1956) *Greek Grammar*, Cambridge, Mass.: Harvard University Press.

Specht, Franz (1944, [1947]) *Der Ursprung der Indogermanischen Deklination*, Göttingen: Vandenhoeck & Ruprecht.

—— (1952) "Die Herkunft der Griechen und Römer und ihre Sprachen," *Lexis* 3: 69–74.

Steensland, Lars (1973) *Die Distribution der urindogermanischen sogennanten Gutturale*, Uppsala: Almqvist & Wiksell.

Stepanov, Yuri S. (1989) *Indoevropejskoje predlozhenije*, Moscow: Nauka.

Streitberg, Wilhelm (1894) "Die Entstehung der Dehnstufe," *Indogermanische Forschungen* 3: 305–416.

Streitberg, William, Victor Michels and Max Hermann Jellinek (1927–36) *Germanisch: Geschichte der indogermanischen Sprachwissenschaft*, 2.2, Berlin: de Gruyter.

Sturtevant, Edgar H. (1942) *The Indo-Hittite Laryngeals*, Baltimore: Linguistic Society of America.

—— (1951) *Comparative Grammar of the Hittite Language*, 2nd edn, New Haven: Yale University Press.

Suzuki, Seiichi (1989) *The Morphosyntax of Detransitive Suffixes -þ- and -n- in Gothic*, New York: Lang.

Swadesh, Morris (1951) "Diffusional cumulation and archaic residue as historic explanation," *Southwestern Journal of Anthropology* 7: 1–21.

Szantyr, Anton (1965) *Lateinische Syntax und Stylistik*, vol. 2 in *Lateinische Grammatik*, ed. Manu Leumann, Munich: Beck.

Szemerényi, Oswald (1960) *Studies in the Indo-European System of Numerals*, Heidelberg: Winter.

—— (1970) *Einführung in die vergleichende Sprachwissenschaft*, (2nd edn 1980, 3rd 1989), Darmstadt: Wissenschaftliche Buchgesellschaft.

—— (1977) *Studies in the Kinship Terminology of the Indo-European Languages, with special references to Indian, Iranian, Greek and Latin* (Acta Iranica 16) Leiden: Brill.

—— (1985) "Recent developments in Indo-European linguistics," *Transactions of the Philological Society* 1–71.

Thieme, Paul (1958) "The Indo-European Language," *Scientific American*,

October 63–74.

—— "The comparative method for reconstruction in linguistics," in Dell Hymes (ed.) *Language in Culture and Society*, New York: Harper & Row, 585–97.

Thomas, Homer L. (1982) "Archeological evidence for the migrations of the Indo-Europeans," in Edgar C. Polomé (ed.) *The Indo-Europeans in the Fourth and Third Millennia*, Ann Arbor, MI: Karoma, 61–85.

—— (1987) "The Indo-Europeans: some historical and theoretical considerations," in Susan N. Skomal and E. C. Polomé (eds) *Proto-Indo-European: The Archaeology of a Linguistic Problem. Studies in Honor of Marija Gimbutas*, Washington, DC: Institute for the Study of Man, 145–64.

Thurneysen, Rudolf (1885) "Der indogermanische Imperativ," *Zeitschrift für vergleichende Sprachforschung* 27: 172–80.

Tischler, Johann (1982) "Zur Entstehung der -*hi*-Konjugation: Überlegungen an Hand des Flexionsklassenwechsels," in Erich Neu (ed.) *Investigationes Philologicae et Comparativae. Gedenkschrift für Heinz Kronasser*, Wiesbaden: Harrassowitz, 235–49.

Toporov, Vladimir N. (1981). "Die Ursprünge der indoeuropäischen Poetik," *Poetica* 13: 189–251.

Tringham, Ruth (1971) *Hunters, Fishers and Farmers of Eastern Europe 6000–3000 B.C.*, London: Hutchinson.

Trubetzkoy, Nikolay S. (1939) *Grundzüge der Phonologie* (Travaux du Cercle Linguistique de Prague 7), Prague: Cercle Linguistique de Prague; trans. as *Principles of Phonology* by Christiane A. M. Baltaxe, Berkeley and Los Angeles: University of California Press, 1969.

Ucko, Peter J. and G. W. Dimbleby eds (1969) *The Domestication and Exploitation of Plants and Animals*, London: Duckworth.

Uhlenbeck, C. C. (1901) "Agens und Patiens im Kasussystem der Indogermanischen Sprachen," *Indogermanische Forschungen* 12: 170–1.

—— (1916) *Het passieve karakter van het verbum transitivum of van het verbum actionis in talen van Noord-Amerika. Verslagen & Mededeelingen der K. Akad. van Wetenschappen. Afd.: Lett. 5ᵉ Reeks*, Amsterdam: Müller.

Vennemann, Theo (1984) "Hochgermanisch und Niedergermanisch," *Beiträge zur Geschichte der deutschen Sprache und Literatur* 106: 1–45.

—— ed. (1989) *The New Sound of Indo-European: Essays in Phonological Reconstruction*, Berlin: Mouton de Gruyter.

Ventris, Michael and John Chadwick (1973) *Documents in Mycenaean Greek*, 2nd edn, Cambridge: Cambridge University Press.

Verner, Karl (1875) "Eine Ausnahme der ersten Lautverschiebung," *Zeitschrift für vergleichende Sprachforschung* 23: 97–130.

Verpoorten, J.-M. (1977) *L'ordre des mots dans l'Aitereya-brâhmana*, Paris: Les Belles Lettres.

Villar, Francisco Leébana (1971) *Lenguas y pueblas indoeuropeos*, Madrid: Istmo.

—— (1974) *Origen de la flexion nominal indoeuropea*, Madrid: Consejo Superior de Investigaciones Cientificas.

Wackernagel, Jakob (1877) "Der griechische verbal accent," *Zeitschrift für vergleichende Sprachforschung* 23: 457–70.

—— (1892) "Über ein Gesetz der indogermanischen Wortstellung," *Indogermanische Forschungen* 1: 333–436.

—— (1926–8) *Vorlesungen über Syntax*, 2nd edn, Basel: Birkhäuser.

Walde, Alois (1897) "Die Verbindungen zweier Dentale und tönendes *z* im Indogermanischen," *Zeitschrift für vergleichende Sprachforschung* 34: 461–536.

Walde, Alois and J. B. Hofmann (1938–56) *Lateinisches Etymologisches Wörterbuch*, 3rd edn, Heidelberg: Winter.

Walde, Alois and Julius Pokorny (1927–32) *Vergleichendes Wörterbuch der indo-*

germanischen Sprachen, 3 vols, Berlin: de Gruyter.

Watkins, Calvert (1969) *Indogermanische Grammatik* vol. III. *Formenlehre*; 1: *Geschichte der Indogermanischen Verbalflexion*, Heidelberg: Winter.

—— (1985) *The American Heritage Dictionary of Indo-European Roots*, Boston, MA: Houghton Mifflin.

—— (1987) "Linguistic and archaeological light on some Homeric formulas," in Edgar C. Polomé (ed.) *Proto-Indo-European*, Washington: Institute for the Study of Man, 286–98.

—— (1991) "Latin *tarentum Accas*, the *Ludi Saeculares*, and Indo-European eschatology," in Winfred P. Lehmann and Helen-Jo Jakusz Hewitt (eds), *Language Typology 1988: Typological Models in Reconstruction*, Amsterdam: Benjamins, 135–47.

Wedekind, F. (1990) "Glottalization constraints and Ethiopian counter-evidence," *Folia Linguistica* 24: 127–37.

Weil, Henri (1844 [1978]). *The Order of Words in the Ancient Languages Compared with that of the Modern Languages*, ed. Aldo Scaglione, trans. Charles W. Super, Amsterdam: Benjamins.

Wende, Fritz (1915) *Über die nachgestellten Präpositionen im Angelsächsischen*, Berlin: Mayer & Müller.

Whitney, William Dwight (1885) *The Roots, Verb-forms, and Primary Derivatives of the Sanskrit Language*, Leipzig: Breitkopf and Härtel.

—— (1896) *Sanskrit Grammar* (1st edn 1889), Boston, MA: Ginn.

—— (1892) *Language and the Study of Language*, 5th edn, New York: Scribner.

Winteler, J. (1876) *Die Kerenzer Mundart*, Leipzig: Winter.

Winter, Werner, ed. (1965) *Evidence for Laryngeals*. The Hague: Mouton.

—— (1978) "The distribution of short and long vowels in stems of the type Lith. *ėsti*: *vestì* : *mèsti* and OCS *jasti* : *vesti* : *mesti*' in Baltic and Slavic languages," in Jacek Fisiak (ed.) *Recent Developments in Historical Phonology*, The Hague: Mouton, 431–46.

Yener, K. Aslihan, Hadi Özbal, Ergun Kaptan, A. Necip Pehlivan and Martha Goodway (1989) "Kesteli: an early Bronze Age source of tin ore in the Taurus Mountains, Turkey," *Science* 244: 200–3.

Zimmer, Heinrich (1890) "Keltische Studien, 8. Über das italo-keltische passivum und deponens," *Zeitschrift für vergleichende Sprachforschung* 30: 223–92.

Zohary, Daniel and Maria Hopf (1988) *Domestication of Plants in the Old World, the Origin and Spread of Cultivated Plants in West Asia, Europe and the Nile Valley*, Oxford: Clarendon.

Zvelebil, Marek and Kamil V. (1988) "Agricultural transition and Indo-European dispersals," *Antiquity* 62: 574–83.

Index

dialect geography 13–14
diathesis 183–4
dic, duc, fer, fac (Lat) 238
Diebold, A. Richard, Jr 283
discourse patterning 201
Djahukian, Gevorg B. 97–8
*dō- (PIE) 17, 74, 109, 111, 121, 166, 173, 242
dogdhum (Skt) 122
Dolgopolsky, Aaron B., reduced list of words: for glottochronology 37, 43; for mass comparison 43
dolikhós (Gk) 96
dominus (Lat) 252
dōnum (Lat) 111
dôron (Gk) 123
dótos (Gk) 127
drift 200; in the early dialects 205–6
duh (Skt) 122; forms of 161–3, 175
*duh- (PIE) 180
Dumézil, Georges 274–5
Dumezilian conception of IE society 20
*dyéus (PIE) 265

*ed- (PIE) 86, 180, 242
Edgerton, Franklin (1885–1963) 33, 47, 85, 105, 107
edō (Lat) 108
ēdu (Lith) 98
*egʰ(om) (PIE) 157
Ehret, Christopher 264
*ekw-os (PIE) 247
émi, imás (Skt) 30
endings, verbal in PIE 238–9
enê (Gk) 254
English, expression of reflexivization in 184
equus (Lat) 271
ergative languages 41
*es- (PIE) 166, 170, 217
etyma 27

fadar (Goth) 10, 28, 30, 95, 111, 127
fāgus (Lat) 141, 248
family: basis for language classification 4–5; subgrouping of 12; tree 12
fēcī (Lat) 111
ferō (Lat) 96, 110
Fick, August (1833–1916) 11, 234
ficus (Lat) 141
fire 92
Flattery, David S. 279
formalism in linguistics 77
fōtus (Goth) 27, 133
fox : vixen 13
frawardjan (Goth) 168

Friedrich, Johannes 82–3, 156, 165, 171, 184, 205, 225
Fries, Charles 207
fructifer (Lat) 215
Furnée, Edward J. 281

gála (Gk) 281
Gallehus inscription 60
*gam- (PIE) 168
gām (Skt) 59
gámanti (Skt) 96
Gamkrelidze, Thomas V. and Ivanov, Vjacheslav V. 151, 166, 224–5, 235, 269, 282–3; glottalic theory 39, 97; views: on homeland 21, 22, 284–5; on Pre-Indo-European 88
gapping 295
Garde, Paul 119
gender (PIE) 141, 152–3
genealogical/genetic classification 25
generative linguistics 76–7
genétēs (Gk) 134
géranos (Gk) 96
Germanic strong verb classes I–V 167; weak verb class I 168
gharmás (Skt) 96
Gimbutas, views on Indo-European homeland 22, 270, 285
Glob, P.V. 280
glottalic theory 97–100, 112–13
glottalics (PIE) 22, 87
glottochronology 35–7, 44–5
grades (ablaut; stufen) 25, 29–30, 130–1, 133; deflected (=*Abtönung*) 130, 133; lengthened (=*Dehnstufe*) 130, 133; normal (=*Voll-* or *Normal-stufe*) 133; reduced 131–2; zero (=*Nullstufe*) 133
grammar, descriptive 46–7; Sadock's views 47
grammaticization 295
Grassmann, Hermann (1809–77) 9–10, 28, 31–2
Greenberg, Joseph (1915–   ) 39, 81
Grimm, Jacob (1785–1863) 4, 15, 25, 29, 235, 259, 296
Grimm's rules (law) 25–6, 27–8; solutions of 'exceptions' 9–11, 28
Grotefend, August 78, 262
Grundriss (compendium) 48; of Indo-European by Brugmann and Delbrück 48–53; content and arrangement of 50–2; shortcomings of 52–3; systematic approach 49–50
guma (OHG) 102
guna 29
gunê (Gk) 153
*gʷow/gʷōum (PIE) 59, 181